ERRORS IN LINGUISTIC PERFORMANCE
Slips of the Tongue, Ear, Pen, and Hand

ERRORS IN LINGUISTIC PERFORMANCE
Slips of the Tongue, Ear, Pen, and Hand

EDITED BY

Victoria A. Fromkin
Department of Linguistics
University of California, Los Angeles
Los Angeles, California

ACADEMIC PRESS
A Subsidiary of Harcourt Brace Jovanovich, Publishers
New York   London   Toronto   Sydney   San Francisco 1980

ACADEMIC PRESS, INC.
111 Fifth Avenue, New York, New York 10003

United Kingdom Edition published by
ACADEMIC PRESS, INC. (LONDON) LTD.
24/28 Oval Road, London NW1 7DX

Library of Congress Cataloging in Publication Data

International Congress of Linguists, 12th, Univer-
    sity of Vienna, 1977. Working Group on Speech Errors.
    Errors in linguistic performance.

    1. Speech errors—Congresses.   2. Speech percep-
tion—Congresses.   I. Fromkin, Victoria.   II. Title.
P37.5.S67l5   1977   401'.9   79-20764
ISBN 0-12-268980-1

CONTENTS

Contributors   vii
Preface   ix

Introduction   1
    Victoria A. Fromkin

1. What Was the Matter with Dr. Spooner?   13
    John M. Potter

2. How Single Phoneme Error Data Rule Out Two
   Models of Error Generation   35
    Stefanie Shattuck-Hufnagel and Dennis H. Klatt

3. Consonant Features in Speech Errors   47
    Marcel P.R. van den Broecke and
    Louis Goldstein

4. Errors of Stress and Intonation   67
    Anne Cutler

5. Slips of the Tongue in Normal and
   Pathological Speech   81
    Ewa Söderpalm Talo

6. Speaking and Unspeaking: Detection and
   Correction of Phonological and Lexical Errors in
   Spontaneous Speech   87
    Sieb G. Nooteboom

7. Semantic Similarity as a Factor in Whole-Word
   Slips of the Tongue   97
    W.H.N. Hotopf

8. Transformational Errors   111
    David Fay

9. On the Freudian Theory of Speech Errors   123
    Andrew W. Ellis

10. Verification of "Freudian Slips" and Semantic Prearticulatory Editing via Laboratory-Induced Spoonerisms 133
    Michael T. Motley

11. Speech Production: Correction of Semantic and Grammatical Errors during Speech Shadowing 149
    James R. Lackner

12. Correcting of Speech Errors in a Shadowing Task 157
    Anthony Cohen

13. Linguistic Evidence from Slips of the Hand 165
    Don Newkirk, Edward S. Klima, Carlene Canady Pedersen, and Ursula Bellugi

14. On Meringer's Corpus of "Slips of the Ear" 199
    Marianne Celce-Murcia

15. Perceptual Processing: Evidence from Slips of the Ear 213
    Catherine P. Browman

16. A Slip of the Ear: A Snip of the Ear? A Slip of the Year? 231
    Sara Garnes and Zinny S. Bond

17. Bias and Asymmetry in Speech Perception 241
    Louis Goldstein

18. The Limits of Accommodation: Arguments for Independent Processing Levels in Sentence Production 263
    Merrill F. Garrett

19. Toward a Unified Model of Slips of the Tongue 273
    Gary S. Dell and Peter A. Reich

20. Monitoring Systems in the Neurolinguistic Control of Speech Production 287
    John Laver

21. On Eliciting Predictable Speech Errors in the Laboratory 307
    Bernard J. Baars

22. Speech Errors: Restrospect and Prospect 319
    Donald G. MacKay

    Index 333

CONTRIBUTORS

Numbers in parentheses indicate the pages on which authors' contributions begin.

BERNARD J. BAARS (307), Department of Psychology, State University of New York at Stony Brook, Stony Brook, New York 11794

URSULA BELLUGI (165), The Salk Institute for Biological Studies, P.O. Box 85800, La Jolla, California 92138

ZINNY S. BOND (231), Department of Speech and Hearing Science, Ohio University, Athens, Ohio 45701

CATHERINE P. BROWMAN (213), Department of Linguistics, New York University, Washington Square, New York, New York 10003

MARIANNE CELCE-MURCIA (199), Department of English, (TESL), University of California, Los Angeles, Los Angeles, California 90024

ANTHONY COHEN (157), Department of Phonetics, University of Utrecht, Utrecht 2506, The Netherlands

ANNE CUTLER (67), Laboratory of Experimental Psychology, University of Sussex, Brighton BN1 9QG, England

*GARY S. DELL (273), Department of Psychology, University of Toronto, Toronto, Canada, M5S 1A1

ANDREW W. ELLIS (123), Department of Psychology, University of Lancaster, Lancaster, England.

DAVID FAY (111), Department of Psychology, University of Illinois, Chicago Circle, P.O. Box 4348, Chicago, Illinois 60680

VICTORIA A. FROMKIN (1), Department of Linguistics, University of California, Los Angeles, Los Angeles, California 90024

SARA GARNES (231), Department of English, The Ohio State University, Columbus, Ohio 43210

MERRILL F. GARRETT (263), Department of Psychology, Massachusetts Institute of Technology, Cambridge, Massachusetts 02139

**LOUIS GOLDSTEIN (47, 241), Instituut Voor Perceptie Onderzoek, P.O. Box 513, Insulindelaan 2, Eindhoven, The Netherlands

W. H. N. HOTOPF (97), Department of Psychology, London School of Economics, Houghton Street, London, WC2A 2EA, England

*Present address: Department of Psychology, Dartmouth College, Amherst, New Hampshire 03031

**Present address: Department of Linguistics, Yale University, New Haven, Connecticut 06520

DENNIS H. KLATT (35), Research Laboratory of Electronics, Massachusetts Institute of Technology, Cambridge, Massachusetts 02139

EDWARD S. KLIMA (165), Department of Linguistics, University of California, San Diego, La Jolla, California 92093

JAMES R. LACKNER (149), Department of Psychology, Brandeis University, Waltham, Massachusetts 02154

JOHN LAVER (287), Department of Linguistics, University of Edinburgh, Edinburgh, Scotland

DONALD G. MACKAY (319), Department of Psychology, University of California, Los Angeles, Los Angeles, California 90024

MICHAEL T. MOTLEY (133), Department of Communication, The Ohio State University, Columbus, Ohio 43210

DON NEWKIRK (165), The Salk Institute for Biological Studies, P.O. Box 85800, La Jolla, California 92138

SIEB G. NOOTEBOOM (87), Instituut Voor Perceptie Onderzoek, P.O. Box 513, Insulindelaan 2, Eindhoven, The Netherlands, and Department of Linguistics, Leyden University, Leyden, The Netherlands

CARLENE CANADY PEDERSEN (165), The Salk Institute for Biological Studies, P.O. Box 85800, La Jolla, California 92138

JOHN M. POTTER (13), The Medical School, University of Oxford, 43 Woodstock Road, Oxford, England

PETER A. REICH (273), Department of Psychology, University of Toronto, Toronto, Canada, M5S 1A1

*STEFANIE SHATTUCK-HUFNAGEL (35), Department of Psychology, Cornell University, Ithaca, New York 14853

EWA SÖDERPALM TALO (81), Department of Phonetics, University of Lund, Kavlingevagen 20, S-222 40, Lund, Sweden

MARCEL P.R. VAN DEN BROECKE (47), Phonetics Institute, University of Utrecht, Oudenoord 6, Utrecht 2506, The Netherlands

*Present address: Research Laboratory of Electronics, Massachusetts Institute of Technology, Cambridge, Massachusetts 02139

PREFACE

The papers in this volume were among those presented and discussed at a special Working Group on Speech Errors held at the XIIth International Congress of Linguists in Vienna, Austria, in 1977. Linguists, psychologists, neurologists, and aphasiologists from nine countries presented their views and counterviews all with reference to deviant linguistic performance data, showing that the interest in such evidence has grown considerably throughout the world and across many disciplines.

The topics covered also reveal that "speech errors" is obviously too narrow a term; "slips of the ear" or misperceptions are being studied for what they may tell us about speech perception; writing errors or "slips of the pen" can reveal what mechanisms are deeper or more central in language processing as distinct from those which may be peripheral or motor dependent; "slips of the hand," which are produced by deaf users of sign language, provide evidence for universal aspects of language as opposed to those properties that are modality constrained. Other topics concern general models of speech production and perception, the organization of the internal lexicon, the representation of morphemes/words, rules of grammar, units and structures of language, and real-time stages and processes. Freud's hypotheses concerning possible causes underlying "slips" are examined. The richness of the data leading to new understanding explains why linguistic performance errors have come of age and why cross-disciplinary approaches are so insightful.

Only one other collection of papers concerned with these kinds of data has been published (Fromkin, 1973). This earlier volume included 12 previously published papers spanning the period from Freud's 1901 seminal paper to Fromkin's (1971) paper. This volume, however, includes only previously unpublished papers. They draw on the extensive research conducted by the contributors from 1971 to the present.

The Vienna Workshop was a historical first. We who participated learned much from each other. We hope to see many additional meetings of this kind. We are also hopeful that the readers of this volume will gain new insights into language structure, production, and perception.

We are grateful to all those who participated in the workshop and are especially thankful to Dr. W. U. Dressler, president of the congress, who called on me to organize this workshop in commemoration of the Austrian linguist Rudolf Meringer, to whom we dedicate this volume.

I also wish to gratefully acknowledge the financial support provided by USPHS Grant NS 12303 and by a UCLA Academic Senate Research Grant.

INTRODUCTION

Victoria A. Fromkin

Department of Linguistics
University of California
Los Angeles, California

A subject in a word association experiment, on hearing the stimulus "Vienna," might be expected to respond with "waltz" or "Strauss" or "pastry" or "schlag" or "Sacher torte." But if the subjects were contributors to this volume, or among the growing group of linguists, psychologists, aphasiologists, or neurologists engaged in research using errors in linguistic performance as evidence for the construction and testing of hypotheses on language and language behavior, they might rather respond with "Meringer" or "Freud."

In 1895 the first major psycholinguistic analysis of linguistic errors, together with a corpus of over 8000 illustrative errors, was published in Vienna (Meringer and Mayer, 1895; Cutler and Fay, 1978). This was closely followed by the publication of Freud's (1901) now classic psychological treatment of speech errors. The research reported on in this volume, first discussed at the Working Group on Speech Errors held at the Twelfth International Congress of Linguists in Vienna, to a great extent had its origins in that city, and it is therefore fitting that the first meeting of scholars using such evidence should have been held in Vienna. A brief look back to the works of Meringer and Freud might thus be of interest.

As pointed out in a number of papers (Fromkin, 1971, 1973; Cutler and Fay, 1978), Meringer was not the first to become interested in what slips of the tongue and of the ear might reveal about language and language change. Hermann Paul (1880), Georg von der Gabelentz (1891), and Otto Jespersen (1894) working with normal language, and such scholars as Delbruck (1887), among others investigating errors made by brain-damaged patients, were forerunners of Meringer. But Meringer devoted more time and effort in his collection and analysis of such deviances, providing a corpus that has been a rich source of analysis for scholars who came after him. As is pointed out by MacKay in this volume, "We all owe Meringer an indirect debt and many of us owe him a direct debt for providing our first source of carefully collected and catalogued data." Celce-Murcia's chapter continues this tradition

1

by discussing Meringer's "Slips of the Ear," showing that Meringer recognized that the hearer's errors as well as the speaker's can provide important clues in our attempts to understand language. Nooteboom's chapter also uses the Meringer corpus.

We are grateful to Cutler and Fay (1978) for the new edition of *Versprechen und Verlesen* (VuV) (Meringer and Mayer, 1895); the earlier edition was very scarce. This reissue will give more researchers access to this invaluable corpus. In their introduction to VuV, Cutler and Fay (1978) discuss the ways in which Meringer's classification and analysis anticipated current views.

Meringer and the other philologists mentioned above were interested in the linguistic aspects of speech errors; psychologists like Wundt (1900) in Europe, and Bawden (1900), Wells (1906), and Jastrow (1906) in America were interested in these data as "windows into the mind." In this area, Freud's 1901 paper was seminal.

It is interesting that in many ways, the acrimonious disagreements between Meringer and Freud have become a nonissue today among most researchers (for a detailed summary of the historical setting and the debates between Meringer and Freud, see Cutler and Fay, 1978). Few, if any of us, would argue in favor of Freud's extreme position that all speech errors, except perhaps for some of the simplest cases of anticipation and perseveration, could be accounted for by his theory of the unconscious and explained as being caused by repressive mechanisms. But Meringer's equally extreme position, which totally discounted any such causes, cannot be easily supported either.

The chapters by Ellis and Motley deal specifically with Freud's hypothesis. Ellis analyzed the 51 lexical substitution errors from the total of 94 tongue slips listed in Freud's *The Psychopathology of Everyday Life* (1901). He compared these to those discussed in recent papers and found that "the lexical substitution errors which Freud adduces in support of his theory of conflicting intentions do not differ on formal or structural grounds from the errors analyzed by psycholinguists." Thus one need not infer nonlinguistic mechanisms to account for them. Ellis does not, however, discount the possibility of some errors being due to the causes suggested by Freud, but he shows the necessity of other "non-Freudian" mechanisms as well.

Motley provides experimental evidence to support the "Freudian slip" hypothesis. The methods used by Motley to elicit, under controlled conditions, phonological, or word, or phrase "spoonerisms" (reversals) are discussed in some detail in Baar's chapter. Motley shows that the number of errors produced by subjects differ significantly, dependent on the "cognitive set" of the subjects. He further shows that the frequency of errors corresponding to a specific situational cognitive set increased as subjects' anxiety toward that situation increased. These findings are in keeping with Freud's predictions.

Examples of how external conditions (or internal intrusions) can account for some spontaneously produced errors are given in Fromkin (1973). Many of these examples support Baar's notion that errors occur when, prior to articulation, the speaker is presented with a "competing plan." Consider the error given in (1) (T = target utterance; A = actual utterance).

(1)   T: *A student just **completed** an MA exam.*
      A: *A student just **competed** an MA exam.*

One can make a case for the view that the competitive nature of the exam intruded to present a "competing plan." That *complete* and *compete* are phonologically similar may have increased the probability of the occurrence of the error. The chapter by Shattuck-Hufnagel and Klatt discusses the role of phonetic similarity. In their analysis of 1472 single segment substitutions, they find that errors are more likely to occur if the competing segments that are simultaneously available to the utterance processor are phonologically similar.

This might be viewed as at least partial support for the "reality" of independent or semiindependent phonological or phonetic features in the production process. It is thus of interest to know which of the many sets of features that have been proposed by linguists can best account for these data. Van den Broecke and Goldstein (this volume) "evaluated a number of *a priori* feature systems ... in terms of their appropriateness to describe observed speech errors ... and the relation between these feature systems and a ... system that is based more directly on the patterns inherent in errors." Their corpora consisted of two sets of English errors (UCLA and MIT), the Meringer German corpus, and a Dutch corpus collected by Nooteboom (1969). They found that the linguistically devised feature sets were all equally capable of accounting for the speech error data. They also found that these sets were better in describing the errors than they were in describing a random set, showing that all the sets have some basis in production. Furthermore, although they point out that the systematic properties of speech errors "must primarily reflect speech production phenomena," which would lead one to "expect speech errors to display characteristics connected with production, rather than transmission or perception of speech," no evidence was obtained "which points to speech errors as being primarily or exclusively an articulatory phenomenon." The linguistically arrived-at sets then appear to function in linguistic performance, as manifested by speech errors.

It should not then be surprising, given the "reality" of such features, that phonologically similar words should substitute for each other. Assuming, further, the "reality" of semantic properties of words, we would expect semantically similar words also to interchange.

Examples of such semantically and phonologically similar items are also given in Fromkin (1973).

Other examples are

(2)   T: *a verbal **output***
      A: *a verbal **outfit**–output.*
(3)   T: *sufficiently **ambiguous***
      A: *sufficiently **ambitious***
(4)   T: *There are ways to organize **programs**.*
      A: *There are ways to organize **pronouns**.*
(5)   T: *The instructions give no **indication** as to how to do it.*
      A: *The instructions give no **inclination**–indication ....*

(6)   T: *I was thinking it was just a routine **promotion**.*
       A: *I was thinking it was just a routine **proposal**–promotion.*
(7)   T: *I'm **studying** linguistics.*
       A: *I'm **stuttering** linguistics.*
(8)   T: ***readjustment** rules*
       A: ***redundancy** rules*
(9)   T: *Stop with the **tamborine**!*
       A: *Stop with the **trampoline**!*
(10)   T: *You feel like you're playing for your **country***
       A: *You feel like you're playing for your **company**–country.*
(11)   T: *Linguistically significant generalizations are L.S.G.'s.*
       A: *Linguistically significant generalizations are L.S.D.'s–uh–G.'s.*

In the chapters by Baars and Motley, additional evidence is presented to show that both semantic and phonological factors can increase the probability of speech errors.

Semantic errors where there is no obvious phonological similarity do, of course, also occur. Many such errors are highly transparent, requiring no psychoanalytical techniques, as is shown in the following:

(12)   T: *She's marked with a big scarlet A.*
       A: *She's marked with a big scarlet R–uh–A.*
(13)   T: *The **Mafia** moved into **Boston**.*
       A: *The **Mafia** moved into **Italy**–I mean Boston.*
(14)   T: *I'm going to **England** in **May**.*
       A: *I'm going to **April** in May.*
(15)   T: *Are my **tires** touching the curb?*
       A: *Are my **legs**, I mean tires, touching the curb?*
(16)   T: *"Jack" is the **subject** of the sentence.*
       A: *"Jack" is the **president** of the sentence.*

While we do not know the mechanisms by which a prearticulation "competing plan" becomes available, it seems possible that the prespoken *scarlet* triggered *red* which, because it begins with an *r,* competed with the intended *A*. Examples (13) and (14) are somewhat different. They, and many other similar errors, suggest that a semantic property, feature, characteristic (these data do not decide between semantic theories) either persevere as in the case of (13) or are anticipated as in the case of (14). Note that it is not the specific word that is repeated or that preenters, but rather a word in the same or related semantic class. Since we have much evidence to show that phonological elements persevere or are anticipated, these semantic errors may show that similar mechanisms are at work on a different level or at a different stage.

Examples (15) and (16) are semantic substitutions similar to many discussed in the literature and in the Baars, Motley, MacKay, and Ellis chapters mentioned in the preceding paragraphs, as well as in Hotopf's chapter. But the substitution of *legs* for *tires* and *president of the sentence* for *subject of the sentence* do not appear to be semantic substitutions as simple, for example, as the following:

(17)   T: *They're doing some experiments with the four **deaf** children.*
       A: *They're doing some experiments with the four **blind**–deaf children.*
(18)   T: *I better give you a **map**.*
       A: *I better give you a **calendar**.*
(19)   T: *I don't think he's that happy in **Illinois**.*
       A: *I don't think he's that happy in **Hawaii**.*
(20)   T: *He has to pay her **alimony**.*
       A: *He has to pay her **rent**, I mean alimony.*
(21)   T: *You can pull off the sheets and I'll stick them in the **washing machine**.*
       A: *You can pull off the sheets and I'll stick them in the **refrigerator**—(laughs)–washing machine.*

Examples (17) through (21) show that substituted words fall in the same or related classes as the target words. In Hotopf's chapter many such examples are cited, in which the error and target words are in antonymous relations (e.g., *early* for *late*), or are co-hyponyms (e.g., *red* for *black*, or *hour* for *week*), or are related in other similar ways. But one would not ordinarily think of *tires* and *legs* as being members of the same semantic class. The substitution, however, can be *explained* once it was produced. A feature theory of meaning, for example, might posit that the semantic feature matrices of the two words in the lexicon include a feature something like "extremity that permits locomotion." Suppose, then, the speaker were attempting to retrieve *tire* by this particular semantic property and incorrectly selected a different word, *leg,* instead. Or, in keeping with Baar's "competing plans" hypothesis, one might suggest that both words with the targeted meaning feature were primed.

The Dell and Reich (this volume) relational network grammar would account for this type of error in a somewhat different fashion. Their model "explains" the incorrect selection of similar (phonologically similar or semantically similar) units by what they call "spreading activation." They suggest that "just as editing involves spreading between super- and subordinate units, similarity effects result from spreading between coordinate units—or units at the same level" because "the connections between similar units act as pathways for spreading. The more direct the connection and the greater number of connections, the greater tendency for activation to flow from one unit to another." To test their model they simulated a small part of a grammar on a computer and found that they were able to generate errors such as those that occur. The model is of interest, and further simulations may reveal its strengths and possibly also its weaknesses.

Such testing is certainly needed. We also need other experimental means to test the hypotheses generated by our analyses of spontaneously produced errors. It is, however, important to note that different factors may influence the errors produced in a laboratory setting as opposed to those occurring under natural conditions. Differences are already apparent. Baars, Motley, and MacKay (1975) and Baars (this volume) report that when spoonerisms are elicited by their experimental techniques, errors that result in real lexical items (e.g., *barn door* for *darn bore*) occurred significantly more often than errors in which the resulting pair would be a nonsense pair (e.g., *bart doard* for *dart board*). This occurred, however, only when the stimuli pairs were all actual lexical word pairs. Yet an analysis of 1723 errors in the UCLA corpus (anticipations, perseverations, reversals, or substitutions) reveals that 60% of the errors result in nonwords like the following:

(22)   T: *Can I borrow your notes?*
        A: *Can I morrow your dotes?*
(23)   T: *computation*
        A: *ponkutation*
(24)   T: *my better half*
        A: *my hetter baff*
(25)   T: *check the set*
        A: *chet the seck*
(26)   T: *The Golden Fleece award*
        A: *The Folden Gleece award*

Included in this set were errors that resulted in at least one nonword, even if part of the error was an occurring word:

(27)   T: *Don't throw your cigarette down, there's a fire hazard.*
        A: *Don't throw your cigarette down, there's a hire fazard.*
(28)   T: *She's a real bitch.*
        A: *She's a beal rich.*
(29)   T: *leg makeup*
        A: *meg lakeup*
(30)   T: *Who am I to sneeze at a free lunch?*
        A: *Who am I to sneeze at a flee runch?*
(31)   T: *I must leave at five sharp.*
        A: *I lust meave at five sharp.*

Only 40% of the errors resulted in all actual words like examples (32)-(38):

(32)   T: *Did you forget to lock the door?*
        A: *Did you forget to dock the lore?*
(33)   T: *speech production*
        A: *preach seduction*
(34)   T: *Don't make a fool of yourself.*
        A: *Don't fake a mule [mjul] of yourself.*
(35)   T: *He will lead the way.*
        A: *He will lay the weed.*
(36)   T: *When do you leave the house?*
        A: *When do you heave the louse?*

(37)   T: *We're having pot roast for dinner.*
          A: *We're having rot post for dinner.*
(38)   T: *It's not worth two cents.*
          A: *It's not worth sue tense* (or: sou tents [?]).

Word substitutions like those presented in the preceding show the "word" as a structural unit in production. Nooteboom presents other evidence to show how the word serves as a programing unit. He analyzed all the errors in Meringer's corpus that were detected and corrected by the speakers. The great majority of all corrections start at the beginning of a word even if the error occurs later. The remaining occur at the beginning of a root morpheme. The word boundary may not be the boundary of the word in which the error occurs, but the speakers will restart at some word boundary. Nooteboom shows that the words included in the corrections always form a "syntactically coherent phrase." He, like a number of the other contributors shows the necessity of positing phonological, syntactic, and semantic editors, or editing mechanisms.

Thus Nooteboom's analyses support other experimental results that argue for an internal monitor or editor that "checks" the possible output, filtering out, in certain cases, a select set of errors; this "editor" may not be "primed" in the same way or to the same extent in natural conversation situations as in an experimental setting as shown by the 60/40% division reported in the preceding. The fact that any errors occur, and that they do so apparently at each stage in the speech production process, shows that the editor may not always function or may be a lazy servant at best. We have, of course, many examples of editorial "fixing up." Laver's chapter focuses on "the nature of the monitoring systems for the detection and correction of errors in program construction and execution." He presents a complex control system. He is as much interested in the fact that there are, according to him, so few errors as he is in accounting for the kinds of errors that occur. He concludes that this is due to active internal monitoring of covert errors, which prevents them from becoming overt in many cases.

Garrett is, like Laver, concerned with stages in production, and accommodation mechanisms, although he does not attempt to relate these stages to neurolinguistic programing as Laver does. Garrett aims at greater constraints for his model, with fewer feedback loops and stronger limits as to when and where accommodation or editing can occur. He is also concerned with the ordering of the processes that result in overt speech and provides strong support for his claim that "several properties of error distributions seem best accommodated by two levels of syntactic processing, one of which gives rise to errors of word exchange, and the other to errors in which bound morphemes SHIFT their attachment." These "shift errors attach morphemes to stems without regard to any factor other than word boundaries and word form—in particular, without regard to the lexical identity or even the grammatical category of the error site" thus producing such deviant forms as *tooken, putten, point outed,* etc. The one counterexample to Garrett's hypothesis is an error cited by Fromkin (1973), which is restated in (39):

(39)   T: *Rosa always **dated shrinks***. ([*date* + past] [*shrink* + plural])
        A: *Rosa always **date shranks***. ([*date*] [*shrink* + past + plural])

The rule "spelling out" the phonological form of *shrink* + past would then have to occur after the shift, and the shift would have to be of an abstract node rather than a phonologically specified bound morpheme, or one would expect the error to be *Rosa always **date shrinkeds***. Five people heard this particular error, and it was produced as [dejt ʃræŋks] not [dejt ʃrejŋks]. I do not have any other examples that counter Garrett's hypothesis, but the error can't be explained away as a "sound error or some currently unknown exoticism." Yet the Garrett hypothesis is too neat to be tossed out by the presence of one exception (although the error does appear to be a counterexample).

One interesting aspect of speech error data is that no linguistic unit, structure, or grammatical component seems to be immune, and no matter how many editors and monitors may exist, the filter has many holes. Even prosodic aspects of sentences deviate from target (cf. Fromkin, 1974; Gandour, 1977). Gandour (1977) shows that tones or tonal features are anticipated, persevere, or reverse as do segments. Cutler suggests an hypothesis to account for other kinds of prosodic errors, namely, word stress errors. She finds that in almost all such errors there is a "strong tendency for the erroneously chosen stress pattern to be that of a related word" and that these errors can thus be considered to "arise at a fairly early level in the production process, at a point at which words related in the way that, for instance, *psychology* and *psychological* are related, are situated close enough to each other to be confused." Such a view is compatible with a "competing plans" hypothesis, but Cutler also shows that there is "a certain amount of independent evidence which supports the productive formation rather than independent lexicalization of derived words." Fromkin (1974) gives examples like *New Yorkan* for *New Yorker*, *explanatings* for *explanations, motify* for *motivate,* which show that "possible" but nonoccurring words are produced. This suggests that at least at some of the time morphological rules must apply to roots or stems. If only complete words were selected from the lexicon it is hard to account for such errors. If the "competing plans" hypothesis were to account for all errors one would have to posit that the use of a rule competes in these cases with the selection of the correct derived form from the lexicon. There are arguments for the suggestion made by Cutler that the stem and all its derived forms occur in the lexicon. But the rules of morphology must also be stored. It is possible that an error is made if a stem is selected instead of the full word; one would then apply one of the general derivational rules, and at times a selected rule would produce a nonexistent word.

The problem with the competing plans hypothesis is not that it is wrong but that it can be extended to cover any possible case and seems therefore to be too unconstrained. For example, Talo reports on a comparison of phonological errors made by normal speakers and aphasics and shows that the pathological errors contain more simple substitutions than do normal errors. One certainly can suggest that for some unknown reason a competing sound or a competing word was selected. One should, however, in such cases look for other mechanisms at work. It might be that although in the normal errors, as Shattuck-Hufnagel and Klatt have shown, "stronger" or "less marked" sounds do not seem to substitute for "weaker" or "more marked" sounds (that is, their findings show a symmetry of substitutions except in a small class of sounds), for pathology greater asymmetries do occur.

In the preceding we suggested that at least in the case of some morphological errors, we need to posit wrong rule application. This is the question addressed by Fay, in relation to syntactic rules. The Transformational Hypothesis, formulated and discussed by Fay, argues for a model that accounts for errors due to wrong rule application (either failure to use applicable transformational rules, or application of rules that should not apply). This hypothesis was discussed to a lesser extent by Fromkin (1971, 1973). One difficulty with the proposal could arise if it is found that the syntactic theory or specific transformational rules that the analysis assumes are shown to be deficient on internal grounds. For example, Fay discussed an error that he accounts for by showing that there has been an incorrect application of the Particle Movement transformation. What would happen to Fay's argument if there were independent evidence to show that such a rule does not exist in English, or that its particular formulation is incorrect? (Cf. Emonds, 1972). Schachter (1978), working from a daughter-dependency theoretical framework, argues for a nontransformational redundancy relationship between sentences involving verb particles such as those discussed by Fay. Fay's position raises interesting questions, but one would hope that he, and others, would see what consequences, if any, would result from using alternative theories in the seeking of explanations for the syntactic errors that occur.

The chapters mentioned in the preceding are concerned with production errors in speech. Yet, the questions of major concern have not been those relating to articulation or movements of the vocal tract, with speech itself, but rather to "higher-order" units, rules, representation of language and how the linguistic message may be distorted in performance. Thus, the chapter by Newkirk *et al.* is of particular importance. If we find that the same kinds of errors occur in the sign languages of the deaf, we can conclude that we are dealing with language universals, with characteristics of this complex human cognitive system, aspects that go beyond the particular modality utilized. And indeed many such universals are discovered. The research team at the Salk Institute has found that " 'slips of the hand' ... provide equally valuable clues to the organization of sign language for deaf signers" as do slips of the tongue for spoken language. They find that "slips of the hand provide striking evidence for the psychological reality and independence of individual parameters of ASL ... that a sign is organized sublexically, and thus that this language of signs exhibits duality of patterning and arbitrary relationships between meaning and form." This work on the nature of sign language in general, and on "slips of the hand" in particular will make the search for linguistic universals a realizable goal.

A grammar, whether of a spoken language or a sign language, must represent in some way a speaker–hearer's cognitive knowledge. Slips of the tongue and slips of the hand occur when we make use of this grammar. That the speaker, at least at some level, must utilize the grammar in ways that differ from that of the hearer is obvious, and that the grammar itself is distinct from the production and perception process seems, at least to me, to be obvious. A trivial difference may be exemplified by our "mental dictionary"; however, that morphemes or words are stored in our heads, whatever the organization of this internal lexicon is, does not directly relate to how we attempt to retrieve a word in speaking or understanding. We can fail to retrieve a word as shown in tip of the tongue phenomena, and five minutes later "find" it and produce it. It is "in storage" even if we can't get it. We do not yet know, however, how "neutral" the grammar is between speaker and hearer, and whether the process of production and perception utilize at various stages the same units, structures, rules, etc. Research on misperceptions or "slips of the ear" may then provide some information.

Shadowing experiments, like those reported on in the chapters by Cohen, and Lackner, relate to this question in that subjects, in order to shadow acoustic input, are simultaneously listeners and speakers. Such experiments then provide data for both models of production and perception. Cohen, working with Dutch speakers, and Lackner, with English speaking subjects, found that shadowers spontaneously correct errors, whether syntactic or phonological, even when they are told that the speech they would be hearing would contain errors. As pointed out in Lackner's chapter, "the experimental observations support the notion of a symmetry between levels of organization in speech comprehension and speech production because when a subject fails to detect an anomaly while hearing a sentence he also fails to detect it when reproducing it in his shadowing response." Lackner does not conclude, however, that because the organizational units in comprehension and production share similarities that they also have a common neurological substratum. Other studies on misperceptions, based on "slips of the ear" in natural conversations, show dissimilarities as well as similarities.

As mentioned in the preceding, Meringer was also interested in "slips of the ear," although only 47 such errors are included in his two volumes (Meringer and Mayer, 1895; Meringer, 1908). These are analyzed by Celce-Murcia. The 890 misperceptions collected and analyzed by Garnes and Bond show one major difference between these errors and slips of the tongue. They sum up this difference by the statement "A listener attempts to make sense out of what he hears." Obviously speakers also attempt to make sense out of what they say or intend to say, but the result is not always "sensible." Neither, of course, are misperceptions, but if the hearer hears "nonsense," he or she will ask for a repetition or query the speaker. Their findings, those in the shadowing experiments, and Browman's study all show that perception is an active rather than a passive process.

Browman presents a detailed statistical analysis of her corpus of misperceptions. If speech errors (from the production side) are a source of humor, slips of the ear are equally so. Actually, some of them seem so farfetched as to make one wonder how the listener could possibly have made "this kind of sense" out of what he or she heard or misheard. To "hear" *prodigal son* when the speaker said *popping really slow* is more mind-shattering than hearing *carcinoma* for *Barcelona,* although even this incorrect phonologically similar word (same number of syllables, etc.) must have created a very anomolous utterance. Browman shows that there are at least two main sources of misperception errors—acoustic misanalysis and lexical decision errors. She compares her data with tip of the tongue (TOT) data and is able to show how they relate.

Goldstein also is concerned with misperceptions, and approaches his study by looking at the asymmetries in errors made by listeners when asked to identify auditorily presented speech sounds. He compares these findings with the apparent lack of asymmetry in speech production errors and discusses a number of alternate explanations.

One reason why research on linguistic processing using slips of the tongue, ear, and hand may be expanding is that the data are so available. We all make production and perception errors. Some of us seem to make more such errors than others. The most famous of these individuals is the man who fathered the word "spoonerism," the Reverend Dr. William Archibald Spooner, Warden of New College, Oxford, lecturer, tutor, and dean, who was born in 1844 and died at the age of 86 in 1930. Potter's chapter in this volume discusses the man, Spooner, his albinism, and some reasons for his disability which made him more famous than his good deeds. The chapter analyzes his "slips of the pen," showing that Spooner's slips were not normal errors, and were probably due to a motor disability, caused by developmental dyslexia.

While the causes and mechanisms underlying our linguistic performance errors may differ from Spooner's, we all produce slips of the tongue (or hand) and ear (or eye), and those of us trying to understand the nature of language and language use are grateful for this fact.

A certain computer scientist (named John as in "John is easy/eager to please") in discussing some problems regarding computer simulations of language processing once said "I am easy to solve these problems." We are not so easy to solve them, but we are indeed eager to solve them. And we are hopeful that this volume will encourage others to go forth and do likewise.

References

Baars, J., Motley, T., & MacKay, G. 1975. Output editing for lexical status in artificially elicited slips of the tongue. *Journal of Verbal Learning and Verbal Behavior, 14,* 382–391.

Bawden, H. H. 1900. A study of lapses. *Psychological Review: Monograph Supplements, 3,* 1–122.

Cutler, A. & Fay, D. (Eds.). 1978. Introduction. In R. Meringer & C. Mayer, *Versprechen und Verlesen.* Amsterdam: John Benjamins.

Delbrück, B. 1887. Amnestische aphasie. *Sitzungsberichte der Jenaischen Gesellschaft für Medizin und Naturwissenschaft, 10,* 91.

Emonds, J. 1972. Evidence that indirect object movement is a structure preserving rule. *Foundations of Language, 8,* 546–561.

Freud, S. 1966. *Psychopathology of everyday life.* Translated by A. Tyson. London: Benn. (Originally published in 1901.)

Fromkin, V. A. 1971. The non-anomalous nature of anomalous utterances. *Language, 47,* 27–52.

Fromkin, V. A. (Ed.). 1973. *Speech errors as linguistic evidence.* The Hague: Mouton.

Fromkin, V. A. 1974. When does a test test a hypothesis, or, What counts as evidence? Paper delivered at the conference "Testing Linguistic Hypotheses," University of Wisconsin, Milwaukee, May 10–11, 1974.

Fromkin, V. A. 1977. Putting the emPHAsis on the wrong sylLABle. In L. M. Hyman (Ed.), Studies in stress and accent. *Southern California Occasional Papers in Linguistics, 4,* 15–26.

von der Gabelentz, G. 1891. *Die sprachwissenschaft: Ihre aufgaben, methoden, und bisherigen ergebnisse.* Leipzig: T. O. Weigel.

Gandour, J. 1977. Counterfeit tones in the speech of Southern Thai bidialectals. *Lingua, 41,* 125–143.

Jastrow, J. 1906. The lapses of speech. *Popular Science Monthly* (February 1906), 119–126.

Jesperson, O. 1894. *Progress in language with special references to English.* London: S. Sonnenchein.

Meringer, R. & Mayer, C. 1895. *Versprechen und verlesen, eine psychologisch-linguistische studie.* Stuttgart: Göschense Verlagsbuchhandlung.

Meringer, R. 1908. *Aus dem leben der sprache.* Berlin: B. Behr.

Nooteboom, S. G. 1969. The tongue slips into patterns. In A. G. Sciarone, A. J. van Essen, and A. A. van Raad (Eds.), Nomen Society, *Leyden studies in linguistics and phonetics.* The Hague: Mouton. Pp. 114–132.

Paul, H. 1880. *Prinzipien der Sprachgeschichte.* Halle a.d.S.: Niemeyer.

Schachter, P. 1978. Review of *Arguments for a non-transformational grammar* by Richard A. Hudson. *Language, 2,* 348–377.

Wells, F. 1906. *Linguistic lapses.* New York: The Science Press.

Wundt, W. 1900. *Völkerpsychologie. Bd. I: Die Sprache.* Leipzig: Engelmann.

Chapter 1

WHAT WAS THE MATTER WITH DR. SPOONER?[1]

John M. Potter

*The Medical School
University of Oxford
Oxford, England*

Borderlands are fashionable places to visit. The appearance of Dr. Spooner's manuscripts provides an opportunity to reexplore some debatable areas of speech and language: ill-defined frontiers of bordering territories, neurological, psychological, and linguistical; to make a brief tourist excursion into genetics; and, above all, to reconsider the extent of this unusual man's linguistic abnormality.

While neuropsychiatry is being officially eliminated in Britain, it is significant that neuropsychology should be not only alive, well, and respectable, but thoroughly flourishing. Psychology and linguistics, too, have now come together, particularly in the United States, as psycholinguistics after a certain amount of estrangement in the difficult days of Freud and the pure linguist, Bloomfield. Unions of this kind are encouraging to those interested in speech mechanisms and at the same time concerned at the divergence and fragmentation of related disciplines. Fromkin's recent collection of papers, *Speech Errors as Linguistic Evidence* (1973a), expresses the usefulness of the interdisciplinary approach, but the absence of any clinical neurological contribution to that book serves to underline what is perhaps too persisting a separation of clinical neurologists from those now most engaged in the study of speech and language. That Spooner's lapses were not simply uttered, oral eccentricities can be seen from his own handwritten evidence. On the other hand, what he is said to have said is to an indeterminable extent anecdotal.

1. The Man

The Reverend Dr. William Archibald Spooner lived from 1844 until 1930. He was Warden of New College, Oxford from 1903 to 1924, having been a Fellow of the College since 1867 when he was 23; in turn, he had been a lecturer, tutor, and dean. His subjects were ancient history, philosophy, and divinity; but he was a friend of the natural sciences and, though not a feminist, was chairman of the Council of Lady Margaret Hall. He did "good work" for the poor in Oxford and in London, and for the insane at the Warneford Hospital, Oxford. According to his colleague Matheson (1937), "No duty came amiss to him," and to an obituary notice (*The Oxford Magazine,* 1930), "his life was a triumph over physical disability that might have made a weaker man despair." For Sir Frank Benson, the actor (1930: 97), "None took a more kindly vision of the world than he: sympathetic, gentle, understanding, tolerant to indulgence." Arnold Toynbee (1967: 23) records, "He looked like a rabbit, but he was as brave as a lion. He was prepared at any moment to stand up to anybody, however formidable." It is important to be clear at the outset that, by any standards, he was an extremely able man as well as a scholar.

Sir Julian Huxley was a tutor at New College from 1919–1925, and his great range of biological knowledge enabled him to analyze better than others the nature of his Warden's lapses and to separate scanty facts from a superabundance of fiction (see Huxley, 1944: 90).

It is a little surprising that none of the eminent neurologists produced by New College this century appear to have been sufficiently impressed by the peculiarity of their Warden (whom *Punch* once described as "Oxford's great metaphasiarch") to attempt an analysis. Perhaps they saw too little of him. Sir Charles Symonds (personal communication), who went up to New College in 1909, tells me he never heard him utter a spoonerism, though he, Sir Charles, underwent an experience of a type that was as puzzling to him as it seems to have been to others. He had been told "to report forthwith to the Warden." On entering the study he was asked his name and gave it. "Well, what do you want?" asked Spooner. "I told him," relates Sir Charles, "I had been sent for unexpectedly, the reason being unknown to me." He then said, after a pause, "Well, you may go." And that was that.

The late Lord (Russell) Brain recorded in his book *Tea with Walter de la Mare* (1957: 53) an allegation that Spooner had once referred to him as "Brainy Russell," and he also gave a version of a dyspractic episode which has been described elsewhere and will be mentioned later.[2] I have traced nothing written by the neuropsychiatrist, Eric Strauss, who was at New College immediately after the First World War; and Dr. John Aldren Turner did not come up to the college until the year before Spooner's death.

Before presenting Spooner's slips of the pen—an aspect mostly overlooked, though not by Huxley—it is necessary to consider in some detail the several components that went to make up his disability. But first must come Huxley's testimony not only to Spooner's high intellectual quality, but also to his efficiency in the various intricacies of college business. Indeed, he was regarded by another highly qualified observer as having been at least as successful as any of the distinguished heads of Oxford and Cambridge colleges this century, if the many qualities needed for such posts are taken into account. Spooner's general intellectual performance and administrative competence have not therefore been questioned, though he himself was modest about them, even disparaging: "I am, I hope, to some extent an useful kind of drudge, but not a ruler of men." "I fear I must be content to do quite small things." "I rather detest all kinds of Responsibility" (he declined the vice-chancellorship of the university)—and, with reference to his disability, he explained to an American lady who had importuned him at a concert that he was "better known for my defects than for any merits." He would refer also to his "transpositions of thought," and here is a rather sad little passage from his journal dated Christmastide 1896, when he was 52: "We stayed quietly at home—I read a good deal of Butler but did not make much progress with my book[3]—I always find it so hard to screw myself up to write at all—Thoughts do not crowd in on me nor have I a constructive imagination." His journal elsewhere indicates a recurrent concern over his ability as a lecturer and preacher.

Another of his colleagues who commented on this difficulty was Sir Ernest Barker (1953: 45) who wrote, "He was seldom guilty of metaphasis [sic] or the transposition of *sounds;* what he transposed was *ideas.*" Spooner's transposed ideas might be expressed orally, in general actions, or, as we shall see later, in writing. Lashley (1951) believed that motor and perceptual processes had too much in common to depend on wholly different mechanisms, but, whatever the cerebral derangement in Spooner's case, its manifestations were essentially motor. Nowhere have I found firm evidence that his reception was centrally defective though, as I shall show later, his vision—at least its acuity—was very poor indeed.

2. Dysgraphia

Huxley observed, "It is not generally known that he sometimes did the same sort of thing—committing what I call 'paraphrasia' in writing, as well as in speaking," and he gave as an example a letter from Spooner to a pupil of his (Huxley's). Huxley's recall of the letter's contents was, however, incomplete. I have the original from its recipient, Mr. Charles Elton, who points out three errors of writing or thought in its two pages, which are reproduced as Figure 1. It runs: "Dear Mr. Elfood [or possibly Elford—it is not quite clear which, but the name could be a mixture of Elton's and that of a law student, in the room above his, called Welsford and perhaps that of an earlier acquaintance called Elgood], I am afraid I have been very long in writing to congratulate you on your first claſs" [Spooner used the old-fashioned ſ until his death; his punctuation is sparse and there is much economy even in period marks]. Then he asks, "What are you going to do now? Are you going to do some research with your father or what are you going to do?" [Elton's first-class degree was in zoology, and his father was a professor of English literature.] And then he continues, "It will be a great loss not to have Mr. Haldane with us after his term." [Huxley, not J. B. S. Haldane, had been Elton's tutor.]

On other occasions, Spooner would notice his written errors and delete them with, usually, a single line so that the wrong word could still be read, with the cor-

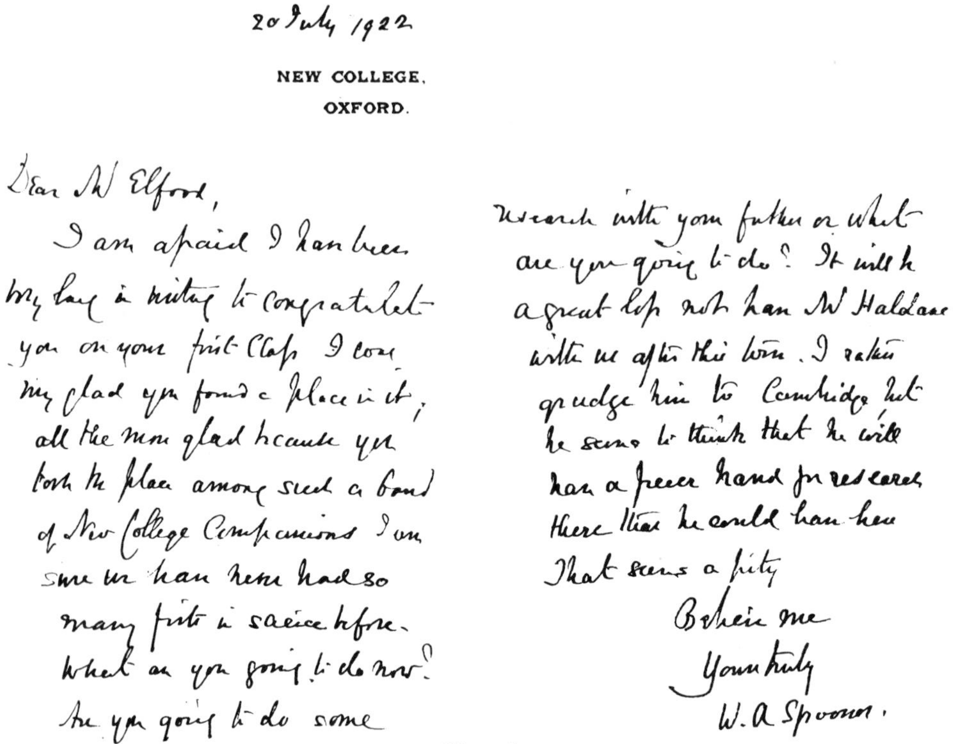

20 July 1922

NEW COLLEGE,
OXFORD.

Dear Mr Elford,

    I am afraid I have been very long in writing to congratulate you on your first Class I was very glad you found a place in it; all the more glad because you took the place among such a band of New College Companions I am sure we have never had so many firsts in science before. What are you going to do now? Are you going to do some research with your father or what are you going to do? It will be a great loss not have Mr Haldane with us after this term. I rather grudge him to Cambridge but he seems to think that he will have a freer hand for research there that he could have here That seems a pity

Believe me
Yours truly
W. A Spooner.

Figure 1

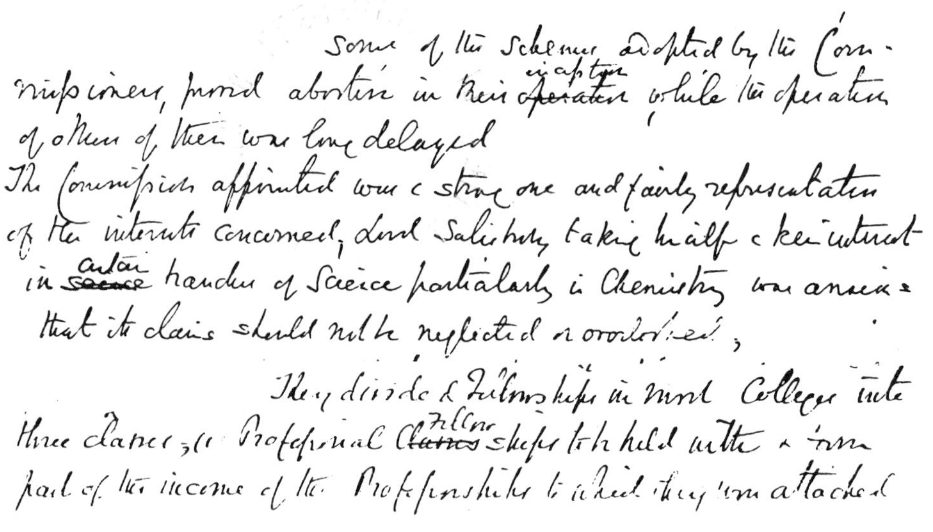

    Some of the schemes adopted by the Commissioners, proved abortive in their ~~operation~~ inception while the operation of others of them was long delayed

The Commission appointed was a strong one and fairly representative of the interests concerned, Lord Salisbury taking himself a keen interest in ~~science~~ certain branches of Science particularly in Chemistry was anxious that its claims should not be neglected or overlooked;

    They divide & Fellowships in most Colleges into three classes, (1 Professional ~~Classes~~ Fellow ships to be held with a sum paid of the income of the Professorships to which they are attached

Figure 2

rect word written above. Figure 2 shows three such examples: two anticipatory
errors and a perseverative one; they occur as a cluster in the space of two pages after
very many quarto pages of writing free from any kind of slip. In the second line, the
word *operation* is crossed out and *inception* substituted. *Operation* is anticipating
operation three words later. And similarly, half way down, *science* for *certain* antic-
ipates *science* also three words later. In the penultimate line *Classes* shows perseveration. At that time Spooner was about 65. Figure 3 illustrates two slips of a different
kind extracted from a letter written in his eighty-second year. The first refers to
examination results, "We seem to have held our heads [*heaps* is deleted] fairly even-
ly with other colleges"; while the lower extract indicates a well-known reason for
disappointing results in examinations: "I think that female charms super added
[something went wrong there] to normal undergraduate allurements are apt to be
overwhelming—[and he starts with *whitless,* changes it to *whirlwind* and finally
amends it to *whirlpool*] a whirlpool difficult to escape." Other dysgraphic errors
will be shown later—there is a great variety of them.

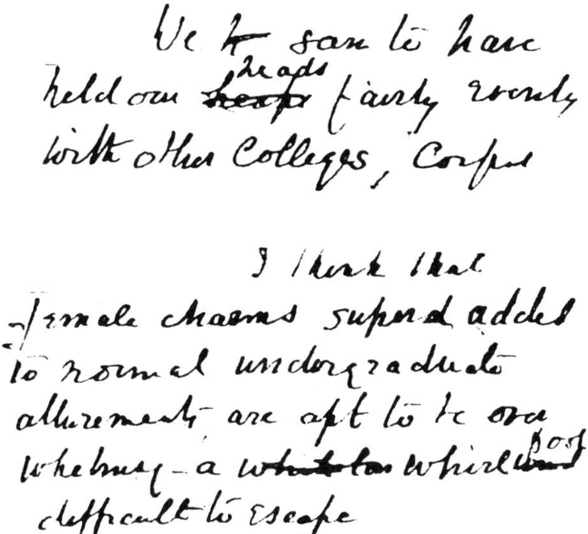

Figure 3

3. Dyspraxia

Huxley (1944) also pointed out that Spooner sometimes made "slips in action"
and described the dyspractic episode that Russell Brain knew about, probably from
Huxley himself who had been his tutor. The Warden once said to a guest (it was
Mrs. J. S. Haldane) whom he had been entertaining upstairs in the Lodgings, "I'll

come and turn on the other lights and see you safely down the stairs" (which were dark and slippery), but he then switched off the only light that was on and led the way down in total darkness until his daughter came to the rescue. Naomi Mitchison (1975:58) gives essentially the same version of this, her mother's strange experience.[4]

A more striking example is that recorded by Toynbee (1967: 23): "Genuine Spoonerisms," he says, "were not confined to transposition of words; they sometimes took the form of *non-sequiturs;* and at least one of them was performed, not in words, but in actions." Spooner had upset a saltcellar at a dinner party. He then poured claret on to the salt, drop by drop—as if he were putting salt on a claret stain. As a good example of dyspraxia this is intelligible enough to neurologists, though one might have a special reason to doubt its authenticity were it not so improbable that such an unlikely episode had been invented. The story came to Toynbee from his mother, but the witness had been her old friend the controversial Miss Eleanor Jourdain, Principal of St. Hugh's College, who, with her predecessor, Miss Moberly, wrote a still much-discussed[5] book, *An Adventure* (1955), about a vision they claimed to have experienced while visiting Versailles together.

Before leaving these dyspractic tendencies, I had better mention—in case it may be thought relevant—that at the age of 52 Spooner took bicycle lessons, "partly from a professional," he tells us; but after two months he records, "I made very slow progress and am doubtful if I shall ever learn." I have not discovered whether he ever did. Incidentally, too, he was on his own admission "unmusical," and not good at keeping accounts. But he had rowed successfully as an undergraduate, and enjoyed riding until he was nearly 80. Unfortunately for this study, hardly anything is known of his childhood.

4. Albinism and Defective Vision

Besides this most unusual propensity for the transposition of expressed ideas, the Warden suffered from another rare but overtly physical anomaly; he was an albino. "Not a full albino with pink eyes," observed Huxley, "but one with very pale blue eyes and white hair just tinged with straw-colour." These are characteristics of the most frequent form of human albinism, in which the enzyme tyrosinase is reduced rather than lacking, so that some pigment can still be produced (Witkop, 1971). Though in this variety the associated defects of vision are normally less severe than in the tyrosinase-negative form, Spooner's vision was nonetheless substantially affected.

The well-known cartoon by "Spy" in *Vanity Fair* (Fromkin, 1973b) shows Spooner in 1898, aged 54 and looking (again I quote someone who knew him) "frail, small and rather bent, like a wraith, an apparition from another world."

His portrait in the hall of New College by Hugh Riviere was painted (Figure 4) about 1913. Spooner, then 69, characteristically has a magnifying glass in his hand. He had not obtained spectacles until he was 47, when, in September 1891, he had

Figure 4. *Portrait of the Reverend Dr. William Archibald Spooner (age 69) by Hugh Riviere. The portrait hangs in the hall of New College.*

consulted Dr. Doyne (whose records unfortunately no longer exist). "On the whole," he says of the spectacles, "a great comfort to me, though I do not like wearing them." Certainly, the size of his writing varies. A year after getting his glasses, it suddenly increases in size half way down one page; and on another, with equal abruptness, it becomes smaller. The writing varies in tidiness, but it is generally neat, even elegant. (Both these pictures and his handwriting suggest right-handedness. I have no other evidence on this point.) In his journal, he refers to lectures illustrated on the blackboard, which "owing to my extremely defective sight, I have always been unable to follow." And he tells us also that, as a schoolboy, "Being short-sighted, I had to apply for a special place to be assigned to me near a window."

I mention this severe visual handicap for two reasons. First, because it should be considered as a factor contributing to his eccentricity. There are stories in which his apparent absent-mindedness in recognizing people, particularly undergraduates, could very well have been due simply to his poor visual acuity. It seems quite possible that he sent for young C. P. Symonds instead of someone else because he had misread a list of names. There were other instances that suggest that this happened. One man, having been told by Spooner that he was to be rusticated, and seeking to know why, was asked his name, which he gave. After a pause, and a closer scrutiny by the Warden of the papers before him, the bewildered man was then congratulated on being awarded an exhibition.

The second point about the vision is the nature of the albino's visual disturbance. The main defects described by ophthalmologists are photophobia, nystagmus, myo-

pia, and astigmatism, and there may be maldevelopment of the fovea. Additionally—
and this does not seem to be generally known—in at least seven mammalian species
the number of decussating fibers in the optic chiasm of albinos is increased at the
expense of the uncrossed ones (Creel *et al.,* 1974); this appears to occur in any individual lacking pigment in the retinal epithelium. In man, only the lateral genicu-
late body, and that of only a single albino individual, has to my knowledge so far
been examined at autopsy (Guillery *et al.,* 1975); but this and the hemispheric
asymmetry of evoked potentials in 14 out of 20 human albinos have suggested to
Creel *et al.* a similar disorganization of the uncrossed optic system in man.

5. An Association of Inborn Errors?

"Scientists know," says *The Periodical* of December 1936, referring to Spooner
and spoonerisms, but giving no reference, "that albinism ... creates a propensity to
mistakes, generally in spelling." I have failed to trace any authority for this statement. Three independent studies—on Negro and San Blas Indian children—in the
past 30 years (Beckham, 1946; Stewart and Keeler, 1965; Manganyi *et al.,* 1974)
have failed to substantiate anecdotal evidence that albinism may be associated with
significant mental retardation. I have not, however, found any investigation specifically of language function in this condition. One may wonder nonetheless what
other physically determinable abnormalities might be found in the human albino
brain were it to be sufficiently and expertly examined. The great neurologist, Hughlings Jackson, seems so often to have been right that we should perhaps note that
his conception of spoonerisms, when he discussed them in 1906 with Kinnier Wilson,
was of the two halves of the brain "not co-operating harmoniously" (Martin, 1975).
As an example of a spoonerism of thought or of idea, Jackson instanced the case of
a flurried man who, when his dentist said, "Open your mouth and I shall put my
finger in," replied, "Oh no, you might bite it."

No clear neuropathological picture has yet emerged for the developmental language disorders: The single autopsy reported by Landau *et al.* (1960) showed gross
brain disorganization hardly appropriate to a purely developmental condition. Indeed, even the clinical picture of developmental aphasia is so variable that Benton
(1960), for example, finds no such thing as a "typical case." It seems to me that a
developmental fault would be the most likely explanation for Spooner's trouble.

6. Genetics

The role of genetic factors in all this seems at present impossibly obscure. I have
no genetical information to offer on Spooner or his family, but there are said to be
more than 70 genes at 40 different loci that affect skin, hair, or eye color in mice
alone (Witkop, 1975). If Chomsky (1968) is correct in his belief that man is geneti-

cally endowed with a highly specific "language faculty," this genetic endowment would presumably be subject to the same processes of variation and mutation seen in ordinary physical features. In this connection, it is interesting that Chomsky should also point to the emptiness of the issue of whether there is a physical basis for mental structures. "The concept 'physical,'" he reminds us, "has been extended step by step to cover everything we understand." Neurologists know well that a clinical condition that is not understood is liable to be labeled "functional"–until an "organic" cause is discovered. For me the functional and the organic components of an individual's neurological problem are essentially one. Rather than this being a matter of "either/or" it is surely one of "both/and" until such a time as knowledge has united them intelligibly. Equally, what is there that our environment can influence in us other than what we are endowed with? And what can it activate apart from what is susceptible to activation? As Broadbent (1971) has said of the naturists and the nurturists, "If pressed, both sides must admit that their antagonism is only a matter of emphasis, since all development requires both an environment and an innate contribution."

Before leaving this particularly speculative and controversial matter, a related phenomenon awaits explanation. A remarkable outcome in a reading experiment of Cohen's (1973) on normal subjects was that "in a number of cases, exact replicas of errors [slips of the tongue] originally observed in spontaneous speech were made, sometimes even several times over" in the tests. Unlike Spooner's (so far as we know), the speech errors of these subjects were exactly reproducible and specific to the individual concerned. Were these propensities inborn, or acquired? Boder (1973) has pointed to the relevance to etiological and genetic studies of three consistent patterns of error that she has found in the reading and spelling of dyslexic children.

7. Oral Spoonerisms

Next, there is the difficult and inescapably anecdotal problem of the oral spoonerisms, and I have purposely left, as the last component of Spooner's disability, these spoken errors, which were alone responsible for the legend. It is impossible to be satisfied about the genuineness of any but a handful of all those that it is said Spooner uttered. Some have doubted whether he ever said any at all; others have believed that he exploited his disability. In Toynbee's (1967) judgment, ". . . most of them are spurious, for, when Dr. Spooner had spontaneously generated a few, many ingenious Oxford minds—well prepared by a long training in the composition of Greek and Latin verse—set to work to improve on nature by art. So the wittier or more elegant the specimen, the less likely it is to be authentic." We might regard this as Toynbee's Law. For my part I was extremely relieved, when starting to prepare this chapter, to discover that the former Warden of New College, Sir William Hayter, had already undertaken the difficult task of spoonerism verification. He was extremely kind and helpful, allowing me to say that for his biography of

Spooner (Hayter, 1977) he had found "at least nine fairly authentic first-hand accounts of oral Spoonerisms of the traditional kind, involving the transposition of letters or syllables between words" and "a still larger number of cases of confusion of thought." Doubt had, however, been cast by Spooner's daughter even on "Kinquering Congs," said to be the earliest and dated by a contemporary to 1879 when Spooner was 35 (*The Periodical,* 1936: 134). The contemporaneous *Oxford English Dictionary* gives the word "spoonerism" as having been in colloquial use in Oxford from about 1885. The relevant (and appropriately titled) section, "Speech-Spring," was published in 1914.

Accounts seem to agree about Spooner's manner of speaking. His voice was high-pitched and, according to Professor Edmund Ford (1975), even "squeaky." It was slow, hesitant before or after words and with many *ers;* but there were also sudden bursts of speed. It was nevertheless distinct and gentle. This form of speech suggests what, I take it, Hockett (1973: 119) would regard as excessive "overt editing," and what Laver (1973: 142) would consider "monitoring"—or perhaps, in common parlance, "choosing one's words with care"—for the sound reason that, though the "internal flow" may have determined what was to be said, there was—in Spooner's case to an excessive degree—always that lurking danger to the uttered performance that lies in wait for us all. This danger is greater when we speak rapidly, particularly when we are fatigued; also, when we are in unfamiliar surroundings or company. Spooner's daughter, Rosemary, never heard him utter a spoonerism, and neither did others. Not everyone, however, always perceives slips of the tongue in other people.

I am conscious of my attempts to borrow from the vocabulary of linguists, and I hope these have been accurate. Much of the difficulty of crossing the frontiers separating linguistics, psychology, neurophysiology, and clinical neurology stems from the profusion of terms used to describe concepts, even similar concepts, of the mechanisms relating thought to language. Moreover, the neurologist Leischner (1969) has given no less than 15 different classifications of the agraphias alone. I do not wish to add to these difficulties.

8. The Written Evidence

I shall now consider in more detail some of the written errors that I have found in Spooner's manuscripts. Unlike the anecdotal evidence for the oral slips, those in his own handwriting cannot be gainsaid, though their significance may be questioned. They are not numerous in relation to the quantity of written material, but they are of such variety that examples of most of the linguists' classified types of error may be found. Moreover, there are more slips from Spooner's pen in his small amount of writing than Freud (1966) himself produced from all his sources to illustrate this aspect of what he so aptly termed *The Psychopathology of Everyday Life.* They occur sporadically, and sometimes in clusters, perhaps when he was fatigued.

Their pattern is not one that has yet been found in "normal" subjects, and there are no actual spoonerisms.

I found 45 lapses in roughly a quarter of a million manuscript words. These include 9 spelling mistakes, but exclude dating errors, which Ernest Jones (1911)— that lucid interpreter of Freud's sometimes obscure views on this subject—pointed out to be so common, and also numerous mistakes in the numbering of pages. How many errors I have overlooked I cannot say; I should guess, many. Jones also noted what he called the "affective blindness" of proofreaders. Certainly, the more I reread the more lapses I found, and Hayter (1977) found others that I had overlooked. This difficulty is well known, and clearly it would be misleading to attach much importance to this attempt at a quantitative estimate.

Spooner's journal is sporadic and, unfortunately, dates back only to 1881 when he was 37; I have found nothing earlier than this in his handwriting. We get no further than the fifth page before we read of Ernest Wilberforce (Bishop "Soapy Sam" Wilberforce's son) preaching in Lambeth Palace. Ernest is, however, spelt *Earnest,* 14 years before Oscar Wilde (1899) did the same thing on purpose. Later, there is an extraordinary error in his account of the funeral of his father-in-law, Harvey Goodwin, Bishop of Carlisle. In the second line of Figure 5 we read, "The ooffin was taken from Bishopsbourne straight to Keswick." *Ooffin* for *coffin* is unmistakable—and inexplicable to me as well as to others more expert in these matters whom I have consulted (though one did offer to discuss it with me sometime at the ooffee table). On the same page, there is also a spelling mistake—*imprssive*—and, in the last line, a perseveration: "divide up the things and break up the things"—the second *things* corrected to *household.*

Five years later, we find mention of another funeral, this time that of Mrs. Goodwin, the Bishop's widow: "We took the coffin [sic!] straight to the church and left it there for the night. On Saturday we buried her in the grace [sic] close by her husband under the tall cross." *Grace* is an agreeable blend between *grave* and *place,* with perhaps a bonus for Freud of religious association.

Another attractive portmanteau word is *emanciated,* which appears in the typescript of a paper Spooner read to a college essay society. The passage reads, "Pattison . . . reviewed the whole situation and emanciated a reasoned scheme." We cannot be certain that it is Spooner's own error; it might be another typist's, but it seems a good word to describe something concerned with emancipation being enunciated. There is a further error in the following paragraph—all the right words are there but they are disordered: "This is the object, he holds, to end to which and which alone all educational endowments should be directed."

Figure 6 shows an extract from one of several passages in his diary where there is reflection and self-examination. It is his fiftieth birthday and, in the third line, he unhappily writes *wife* instead of *life,* and leaves out the word *once* in the next. This is the passage referred to earlier where he says, in the fourth line from the bottom, "I hope I am an useful kind of drudge, but not a ruler of men."

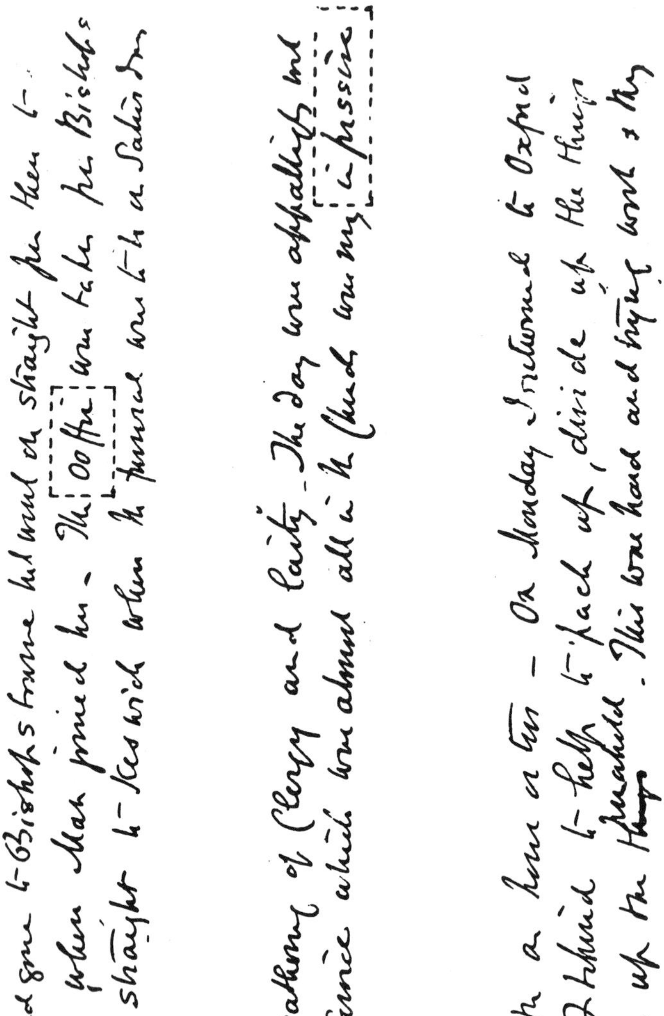

Figure 5

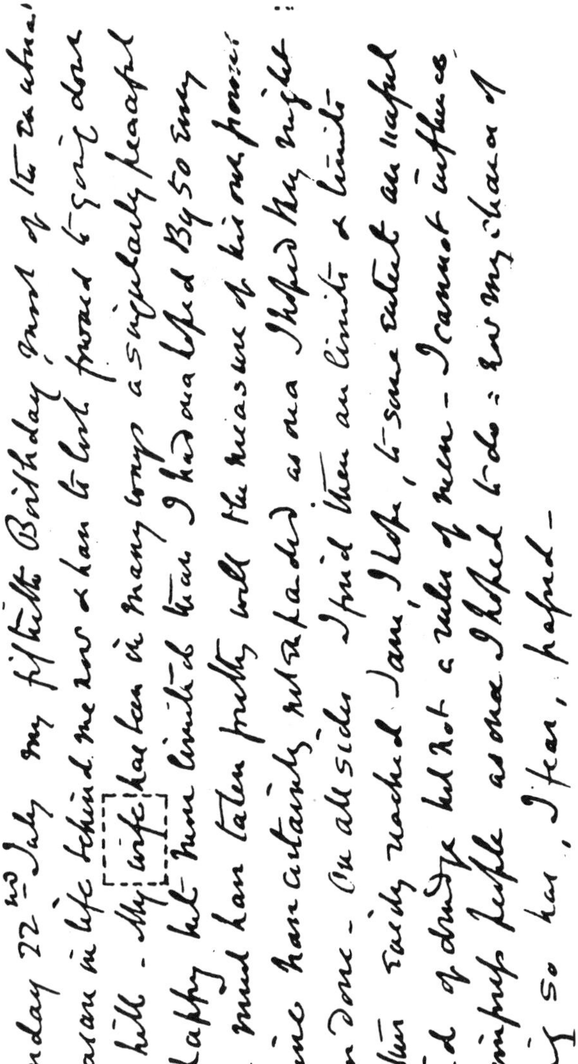

Sunday 22nd July my fiftieth Birthday...

Figure 6

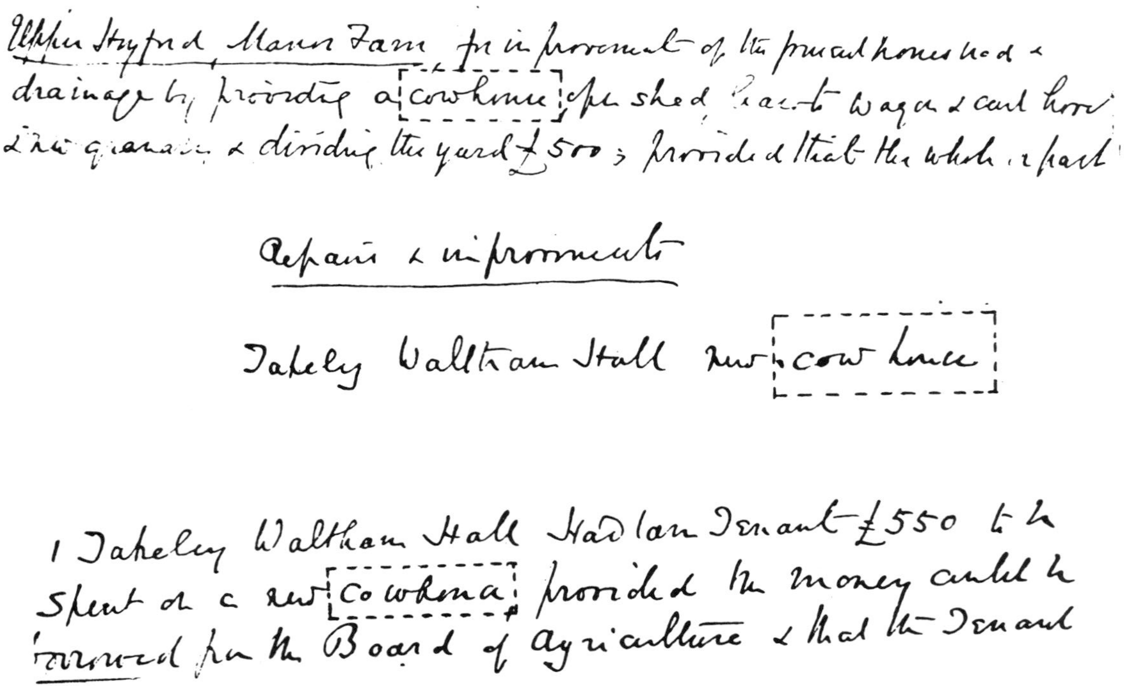

Within Stafford Manor Farm for improvement of the freehold house & drainage by providing a continuing cow shed that & wagon & cart horse & the granaries & dividing the yard £500 ; provided that the whole is freehold

Repair & improvement

Takeley Waltham Hall now cow house

1 Takeley Waltham Hall Hall farm tenant £550 to be spent on a new cow house provided the money could be raised from the Board of Agriculture & that the tenant

Figure 7

There is an odd error in Figure 7. It is taken from Spooner's own records of mundane business relating to his college's agricultural estates. In the lowermost of the three extracts he has failed to separate correctly the two words of *cow house.* Above this are two further versions of the word—or the two words: evidently, he was undecided which it should be.

In Figure 8 he has written, "the old Quire School." Though archaically correct, it is the only example of this quaint form of spelling; elsewhere, he always spells *choir* in the usual way.

Figure 8

Figure 9 reads, "and in 1869 a statute was passed and received the account of the Queen in Council"—instead of "...the assent of the Queen...." Were this spoken, it would be a straightforward phonetic anticipation, the actual sound of *Council* being anticipated. But presumably the same mechanism operates in writing, though no sound is actually uttered—unless Spooner spoke to himself while writing, or heard it in, as it were, the "mind's ear."

Figure 10 shows him perseverating, though with 12 syllables separating one *College* from that following: "To this fact it almost certainly owes the name of New College, being designated The New College in the same way as centuries before the great College [sic] which William the Conqueror so barbarously created had been called The New Forest, because it so greatly exceeded in size and notoriety all the forests by which it had been preceded." Two *New Colleges,* two *forests* and one *New Forest* all in one sentence were too much for him.

The next example appears to have a more evident psychological basis, an association of ideas leading to a substitution that is entirely "external," or out of the general context. This occurred in the typewritten transcript of a letter describing his visit to the Victoria Falls in 1912: "We took a canoe with three black rowers and went up the river above the Falls. There are plenty of rapids and you have to make your way up through them which is quite fun as the Indians [sic] seemed quite skilful at their work." Indians and canoes may be associated in North America, but not ordinarily in Central Africa.

The last two examples are of different kinds of spelling errors. The first (Figure 11), through association, shows *Newnham,* Cambridge being spelt as *Nuneham,* near Oxford, and in the second (Figure 12), *solace* is spelt with two *ls,*[6] and *beguiling* as *beguling.* However, he was at this time 81 years of age.

ī New College and in 106? a statute was passed & received the assent of the Queen in Council erecting the College, of it

Figure 9

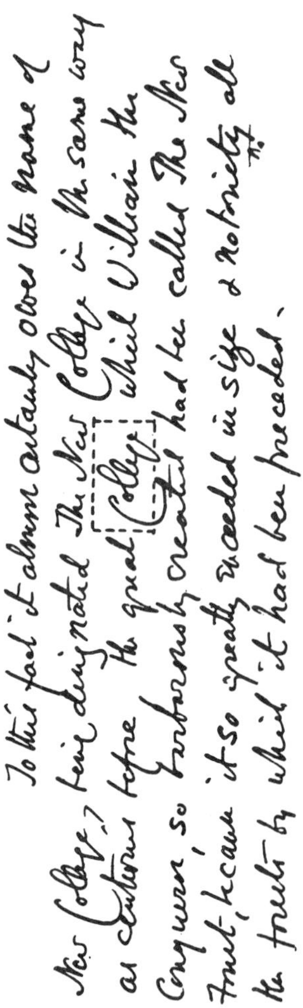

To this fact it almost certainly owes the name of New College, being designated The New College in the same way as Statutes before the great College while William the Conqueror so thoroughly created had ten called The New Fruit, because it so greatly exceeded in size & notoriety all the truth by which it had been preceded.

Figure 10

The Radii Hall at Oxford had been for some years suininces; it had been moved to the immediate neighbourhood of Cambridge, and was rejoined to from a marked success Munchan were by this time going up, but is c left round any

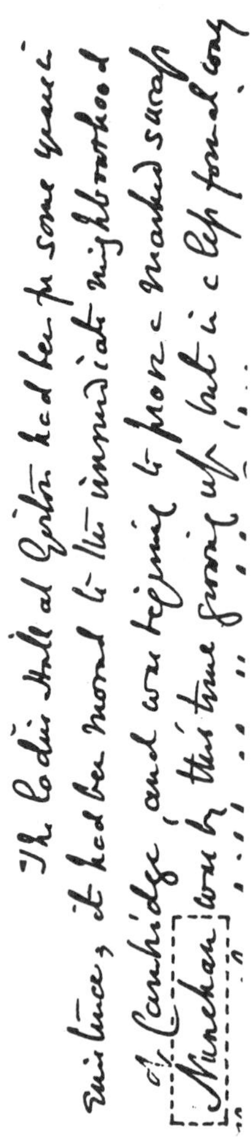

Figure 11

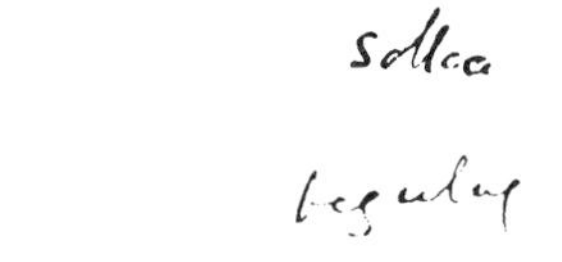

s∂llc∝

leg ul∾f

Figure 12

9. Freud

How much do we need Freud to help us interpret these slips? Not at all, said Lashley (1951) in his classical study "The Problem of Serial Order in Behaviour." "In these contaminations," he observed, "it is as if the aggregate of words were in a state of partial excitation, held in check by the requirements of grammatical structure, but ready to activate the final common path, if the effectiveness of this check is in any way interfered with." And so, he said, "We do not need to accept his [Freud's] theories of censorship and suppression to account for such slips. They are of the same order as those misplacements in typing and represent contaminations of co-existing determining tendencies." (Lashley was referring to his own typing errors, which he had analyzed.) Furthermore, as Fromkin (1973a: 15) has pointed out, it is hard to reconcile the occurrence of nonexistent words with Freud's contentions.

I do not find this sufficient enough an explanation to enable me to do without Freud altogether. He still serves to make many slips intelligible, though at a level of approach complementing the deeper one of Lashley. But I do find it difficult to accept Freud (1966: 61) when, being hardly able to find one slip of the tongue traceable simply and solely to the "contact effect of sounds," he almost invariably discovers a disturbing influence in addition to and from outside the utterance "which," he maintains, "can often be brought to consciousness only by means of searching analysis." It would appear as easy for the initiated to discover Freudian explanations as it is for others to invent spoonerisms—and as much an enjoyable game. I have become aware of many more slips of the tongue since I have been particularly interested in them and "tuned in." There is a psychic contagiousness about them for which Freud had no explanation, but which Fromkin suggests may be apparent rather than real. Indeed, conscious spoonerisms are particularly infectious —and fun: They occur at parties and are facilitated by alcohol, as portrayed in Edmund Wilson's short story, "The Milhollands and Their Damned Soul" (1951: 304) and in Sir John Squire's splendid "Ballade of Soporific Absorption" (1961: 148).[7] Spoonerisms are the relatives of the portmanteau words of Lewis Carroll, of the sayings of Mrs. Malaprop (Sheridan, 1775), and of rhyming slang. All these can be employed imaginatively, even creatively, as Joyce used puns with such brilliance in *Finnegans Wake*.

10. Conclusions

Summarizing the findings, there were only 9 straight spelling errors detected in the 250,000 words. Of the remaining 36 slips only 8 were conventional anticipations "internal" to the sentence, and 5 were perseverations. The remaining 23 errors were a hodgepodge of transpositions, contaminations, and substitutions, some of which appeared to reflect transpositions of thought "external" to what was being written. This distribution of errors appears to be unusual, and it is interesting that there should have been no real spoonerisms.

That concludes my evidence—but evidence of what? "With all these peculiarities," said Huxley (1944), "it was little wonder that the legend grew," and we have noted Toynbee's explanation of how easily this could happen in Oxford which, of all places, would expect a don's linguistic performance to match an assumed high level of linguistic competence. It would not have been much excuse in those days to plead a disability; for this would only have been regarded as "mental," and in the pejorative, pathological sense of the word. Spooner was much wounded by a cruel attack on his physical infirmities that appeared in the *Echo* of 4 May 1892; this press article ridiculed particularly his albinism and short-sightedness. I have seen the piece and conclude that the satirical journal *Private Eye* reads nowadays pretty well in comparison. No wonder he and his family were sensitive. Moreover, reading between the lines of his diary, and from his notes on sermons dealing with sin, I had the strong impression that he may have imagined his disability as some kind of divine punishment for aspects of his character that he himself considered defective.

Apart from the albinism and poor vision, how abnormal in fact was he? My recurrent suspicion that perhaps he was not really abnormal at all has been hard to sustain. Those lapses, to which all of us are occasionally given, seem in Spooner's case to have been altogether too noticeable, numerous, and variable in both time and quality. Those who have studied oral slips in apparently normal people seem to agree with Lashley, who from examination of his own typing errors concluded that anticipations are much the most frequent variety—their incidence, for example, was 78% in a study by Cohen (1973) of 600 spoken slips. Errors of perseveration made up 15% and appeared more related to fatigue; while those of transposition amounted to only 7%. As I have indicated, Spooner's written errors do not reflect this "normal" pattern, nor do the accounts of his spoken ones.

Finally, I should like to make three tentative suggestions. First, that Spooner's form of cerebral malfunction may represent an intermediate state between the slips of the tongue, pen, and action—the lapses, dyspraxias, or absent-mindedness that are Freud's (1966: xi) "parapraxes" (*Fehlleistung*) of everyday life—and the gross dysphasias and dyspraxias of overt disease and damage, often with predictably demonstrable pathological lesions of certain areas of the brain. The everyday lapses are the concern of linguists and psychologists; they are not yet sufficiently approachable by the sort of scientific precision demanded by the physiologist; there is no known pathology, and they are not medical. Thus there is a substantial disciplinary gap between them and the florid dyspraxias of language and action clinically familiar to neurologists and neurosurgeons and, later as their causative lesions, to neuropathologists.

My second tentative suggestion is that a developmental disorder is the most likely explanation of Spooner's striking example of an individual variation. We have no means of knowing whether or not he suffered some self-limiting disease, possibly one acquired during childhood, but this seems less likely as a cause of brain damage so subtle as to be manifested only by such sporadic lapses.

Third, I should like to entertain the possibility that there may be others with Spooner's degree of disability who, not being in his intellectually exposed position, pass unremarked. Their progress at school would not necessarily be retarded, so one would need to seek them out with even more diligence than is required to discover dyslexic children who were, after all, largely unrecognized until comparatively recently. Though now actively sought and increasingly recognized, even the dyslexic child is perhaps not yet entirely understood. Moreover, an organic basis for the condition is not conceded by "nurturists," who appear to believe that environmental influences can somehow act independently of the organ that alone can process them, the genetically developed brain. It seems possible to me that Spooner's trouble might be regarded as an essentially motor member of that family of developmental disorders that has developmental dyslexia as its outstanding example.[8]

Postscript

Spooner and his wife are buried close to the poet Wordsworth in the small and beautiful Lake District village of Grasmere. Above his name on the grave's headstone is the Wykehamist motto, "Manners Makyth Man," and beneath it, "Blessed are the Peacemakers."

Acknowledgments

I am much indebted to the Warden and Fellows of New College for unlimited access to the Spooner documents in their library, and Mrs. Feneley, the Assistant Librarian, spared no trouble to help me. I am most grateful to them, and also to my colleagues Drs. Charles Whitty and Freda Newcombe for criticism.

Notes

1. This chapter is a variant of the abridged version (Potter, 1976) of a presidential address to the neurology section of the Royal Society of Medicine, and is published with the Society's kind permission.

   Linguists will, I hope, tolerate my slender understanding of their subject and its vocabulary.

2. I am grateful to the late Lord Brain's son-in-law, Dr. Leonard Arthur, for this information.
3. The second of Spooner's two major publications was a book on Bishop Joseph Butler [1692–1752] (Spooner, 1901). The first (Spooner, 1891) had been an edition of the Histories of Tacitus.
4. Dr. A. H. T. Robb-Smith points out that the story had appeared also in Mrs. Haldane's own memoirs 14 years earlier (Haldane, 1961: 170).
5. See Iremonger (1975) for a reminder, to all whose open minds are as cavernous as their generous hearts, of the imperfections of our human senses. She is not concerned, as we are here, with what is said to have been said or done; but, rather, with the greater difficulty, or impossibility, of verifying what others are said to have seen and heard, and with "extrasensory perception." Unless neurologists, we seem to bother much less about other peoples' tactile impressions or, unless in certain other circles, about what they have tasted or smelt.
6. Dr. A. E. Mourant, F. R. S., wonders whether this could have been a reference to W. J. Sollas, 1849–1936, the well-known professor of geology in Oxford at that time. "Pure" spelling mistakes are uncommon in Spooner's manuscripts—but see Footnote 8.
7. Again I am indebted to Dr. Robb-Smith who drew my attention to this example, which surely cannot have been bettered. The last line of each verse runs, "But I'm not so think as you drunk I am."
8. Mr. Thomas Braun, Fellow and Tutor in Ancient History of Merton College, Oxford, anticipated this suggestion. In 1968 he was given Spooner's copy of Dindorf's Euripides of 1832–1833, and noted no less than three errors in the titles of the 20 plays that Spooner had himself indexed "in his characteristic, fine and highly literate hand." Dyslexia was much in the news around that time and he guessed at something analogous in Spooner's case.

   I am indebted to Mr. Braun for this note about his specialized evidence of Spooner's disability: "The titles of plays contain 'Troides'—of course unacceptable for 'Troades,' 'Medaea' equally odd for 'Medea,' and 'Icetides,' which one would normally never supply as a latinization of the Greek 'Hiketides'; you would expect the translation 'Supplices.'" (Additionally, I note that Spooner has corrected *Resus* to *Rhesus,* making four errors in 20 titles.)

   However, my colleague, Mr. T. C. W. Stinton, Fellow and Tutor in Classics at Wadham College, finds "scribal errors of a very similar kind" during his study of textual criticism; he mentions their frequency in medieval manuscripts and in papyri, and he refers me to Jackson (1955: 208) for 16 examples of graphical spoonerisms in Greek texts. But among none of Spooner's graphical errors did I find an actual spoonerism.

References

Barker, E. 1953. *Age and youth.* London: Oxford Univ. Press.
Beckham, A. S. 1946. Albinism in Negro children. *Journal of Genetic Psychology, 69,* 199–215.
Benson, F. 1930. *My memoirs.* London: Benn.
Benton, A. L. 1960. Developmental aphasia and brain damage. *Cortex, 1,* 40–52.
Boder, E. 1973. Developmental dyslexia: A diagnostic approach based on three atypical reading spelling patterns. *Developmental Medicine and Child Neurology, 15,* 663–687.
Brain, W. R. 1957. *Tea with Walter de la Mare.* London: Faber and Faber.
Broadbent, D. E. 1971. Cognitive psychology: Introduction. *British Medical Bulletin, 27,* 191–194.
Chomsky, N. 1968. Noam Chomsky and Stuart Hampshire discuss the study of language. *The Listener, 79,* 687–691.
Cohen, A. 1973. Errors of speech and their implication for understanding the strategy of language users. In V. Fromkin (Ed.), *Speech errors as linguistic evidence.* The Hague: Mouton. Pp. 88–92.

Creel, D., Witkop, C. J., Jr., & King, R. A. 1974. Asymmetric visually evoked potentials in human albinos: Evidence for visual system anomalies. *Investigative Ophthalmology, 13,* 430–440.

Ford, E. B. 1975. Personal communication.

Freud, S. 1966. *The psychopathology of everyday life.* Translated by Alan Tyson. Edited by James Strachey. London: Benn.

Fromkin, V. A. (Ed.). 1973a. *Speech errors as linguistic evidence.* The Hague: Mouton.

Fromkin, V. A. 1973b. Slips of the tongue. *Scientific American, 229,* 110–117.

Guillery, R. W., Okoro, A. N., & Witkop, C. J., Jr. 1975. Abnormal visual pathways in the brain of a human albino. *Brain Research, 96,* 373–377.

Haldane, L. K. 1961. *Friends and kindred.* London: Faber and Faber.

Hayter, W. G. 1977. *Spooner, a biography.* London: W. H. Allen.

Hockett, C. F. 1973. Where the tongue slips there slip I. In V. Fromkin (Ed.), *Speech errors as linguistic evidence.* The Hague: Mouton. Pp. 93–119.

Huxley, J. S. 1944. *On living in a revolution.* London: Chatto and Windus.

Iremonger, L. I. 1975. *The ghosts of Versailles. Miss Moberly and Miss Jourdain and their adventure.* London & New York: White Lion Publications.

Jackson, J. 1955. *Marginalia Scaenica.* (Oxford Classical & Philosophical Monographs.) London: Oxford Univ. Press.

Jones, E. 1911. The psychopathology of everyday life. *American Journal of Psychology, 22,* 477–527.

Joyce, J. 1964. *Finnegans Wake,* 3rd ed. London: Faber and Faber.

Landau, W. M., Goldstein, R., & Kleffner, F. R. 1960. Congenital aphasia, a clinico-pathological study. *Neurology, 10,* 915–921.

Lashley, K. S. 1951. The problem of serial order in behaviour. In L. A. Jeffress (Ed.), *Cerebral mechanisms in behaviour.* New York: Wiley. Pp. 112–136.

Laver, J. D. M. 1973. The direction and correction of slips of the tongue. In V. Fromkin (Ed.), *Speech errors as linguistic evidence.* The Hague: Mouton. Pp. 132–142.

Leischner, A. 1969. The Agraphias. In P. J. Vinken & G. W. Bruyn (Eds.), *Handbook of clinical neurology,* vol. 4. Amsterdam: North-Holland Publ. Pp. 141–180.

Manganyi, N. C., Kromberg, J. G. R., & Jenkins, T. 1974. Studies on albinism in the South African Negro. *Journal of Biosocial Science, 6,* 107–112.

Martin, J. P. 1975. Kinnier Wilson's notes of conversations with Hughlings Jackson. *Journal of Neurology, Neurosurgery and Psychiatry, 38,* 313–316.

Matheson, P. E. 1937. Spooner, William Archibald. *The dictionary of national biography,* 1922–1930. London: Oxford Univ. Press. Pp. 800–801.

Mitchison, N. 1975. *All change here.* London: The Bodley Head.

Moberly, C. A. E. & Jourdain, E. F. 1955. *An adventure,* 5th ed. London: Faber and Faber.

The Oxford Magazine. 1930. Dr. W. A. Spooner (obituary notice), *49,* 12–13.

The Periodical. 1936. *21,* 134.

Potter, J. M. 1976. Dr. Spooner and his dysgraphia. *Proceedings of the Royal Society of Medicine, 69,* 639–648.

Sheridan, R. B. 1775. *The rivals.* London: John Wilkie.

Spooner, W. A. (Ed.). 1891. *Cornelii Taciti Historianum Libri qui supersunt (The histories of Tacitus).* London: Macmillan.

Spooner, W. A. 1901. *Bishop Butler.* London: Methuen.

Squire, J. C. 1961. Ballade of soporific absorption. In J. M. Cohen (Ed.), *The Penguin book of comic and curious verse.* London: Penguin Books.

Stewart, H. F., Jr. & Keeler, C. E. 1965. A comparison of the intelligence and personality of Moon-Child albino and control Cuna Indians. *The Journal of Genetic Psychology, 106,* 319–324.

Toynbee, A. J. 1967. *Acquaintances.* London: Oxford Univ. Press.

Wilde, O. 1899. *The importance of being earnest* (first performed 14 February 1895). London: Leonard Smithers.

Wilson, E. 1951. The Milhollands and their damned soul. *Memoirs of Hecate County.* London: Panther. Pp. 278–336.

Witkop, C. J., Jr. 1971. Albinism. In H. Harris & K. Hirschhorn (Eds.), *Advances in human genetics,* vol. 2. New York & London: Plenum.

Witkop, C. J., Jr. 1975. Albinism. *Natural History, 84,* 48–59.

Chapter 2

HOW SINGLE PHONEME ERROR DATA RULE OUT TWO MODELS OF ERROR GENERATION

Stefanie Shattuck-Hufnagel

Dennis H. Klatt

Department of Psychology
Cornell University
Ithaca, New York

Research Laboratory of Electronics
Massachusetts Institute of Technology
Cambridge, Massachusetts

Errors in spontaneous speech often take the form of changes in a small portion of a word:

waple malnut	(maple walnut)
twenty-pive percent	(twenty-five percent)
You can tell Ten	(tell Ken)

In each of these errors, a target segment has been replaced by a single intrusion segment of the same level of description. We will use the neutral term "phonetic segment type" for these error units: Since we do not know how abstractly they are represented at the point when the errors occur, the term is intended to carry no weight in this regard. Although these three examples illustrate three different types of errors (an exchange, an anticipatory substitution, and a perseveratory substitution respectively), they are all instances of the more general category of errors in which one phonetic segment substitutes for another. For a brief summary of the error types included in our discussion, see the section on classification and analysis.

Speech errors have been found to be highly regular, although the precise nature of the observed regularities is a matter of some debate. Since errors are so strongly constrained, they are a useful source of information about the kinds of models that are acceptable descriptions of the psychological process of planning and producing sentences. (For a discussion of this, see Garrett [1975 and 1976], Fromkin [1973], and their many references.) Segmental substitutions like those in the preceding are no exception. For example, there are three major classes of models that could account for the occurrence of these errors, and these three types of theories embody different views of the way in which normal error-free speech is produced. By testing the predictions of these three types of theories against the regular patterns in a large corpus of segmental substitution errors, we can determine which one of them is more nearly right.

The first class of theory includes models in which one segment substitutes for any of the others in a random pattern, with no constraints as to similarity between target and intrusion segments. The second class includes models in which one set of "stronger" segments systematically replaces other "weaker" segments in errors. In models of the third class, a target segment will be replaced by an intrusion segment only if the two are very similarly represented and simultaneously available during the planning process. In this class of models, a pair of segments is equally likely to substitute in either direction, because the error results from their simultaneous availability to the processor rather than from the primacy or "strength" of one of them.

A model of the first class, random substitution without regard to the phonetic nature of target and intrusion segments, would be consistent with the findings of Boomer and Laver (1968). They could discern "no general tendency for interactions to occur between segments sharing one or more articulatory features" in a corpus of 200 errors of all types, and concluded that articulatory similarity was not an important determinant of segmental substitutions. Other investigators, however, have found substantial evidence for distinctive feature similarity between target and intrusion segments in larger corpora of errors. In the corpus we are discussing here the evidence against a random distribution is very strong. (For a brief description of the collection and categorization of this corpus, see the following sections.) The distribution of errors in the cells of the confusion matrix for 24 segments is compared with the expected random distribution, approximated by a Poisson distribution with $\mu = 2.67$ and $N = 1472$, in Figure 1. The difference between the two distributions is significant at the .0001 level.

Moreover, the nonrandom nature of the confusion matrix reflects distinctive feature constraints: See Shattuck-Hufnagel (1975), Shattuck-Hufnagel and Klatt (1975), and Shattuck-Hufnagel and Klatt (1979). The combined weight of these and other studies (especially those by MacKay [1970], Nooteboom [1969], Fromkin [1971 and 1973], and Goldstein [1978]) allows us to reject a model of segmental substitution as a random process, in favor of one in which segments that share distinctive features are more likely to replace each other in errors.

The second type of theory, in which strong segments drive out weak ones, would be consistent with the data reported by Cairns and Williams (1972) for the systematic segmental substitutions elicited in a repetition task from children who had not yet mastered the adult form of English. They suggest that more easily articulated segments often replace more difficult ones in child dialects, and it would be possible to construct a model of adult speech errors based on this principle. Other possible definitions of the "strong" set of segments include frequency of occurrence (more frequent segments might drive out less frequent ones) and markedness (less marked

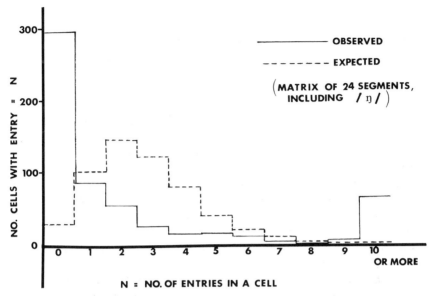

Figure 1: *Comparison of expected and observed distributions.*

segments might replace more marked segments). The definition of the stronger set does not matter for our purposes here. No matter what the dimension, a model of this type makes two predictions:

1A. Across all the errors in which a strong segment appears, it should serve more often as an intrusion, displacing other segments, while a weak segment will serve more often as a target, being displaced by others which are stronger.

2A. Across all the errors in which a given **pair** of segments appears, if one of the segments is stronger it should replace the weaker one more often than vice versa.

The third class of theory, in which simultaneously present planning segments substitute for each other in proportion to their similarity, is illustrated by the model of sentence production described by Shattuck-Hufnagel (1975; and forthcoming). The details of the model need not concern us here. The important thing is that errors occur when two similar segments are simultaneously available to the sentence processor and competing for the same slot in the planned utterance. Simultaneous availability may arise in a number of ways. Both segments may be part of the planned utterance, or one of them may appear in an alternative form of the utterance being considered, or in a strongly associated word (à la Freud); or the speaker may be listening to an utterance, looking at something, or merely thinking about something that contains the competing segment in its verbal form.[1] All that is necessary is that the intrusion segment be available to the processor, and competing for the position of the target segment. In an error, the intrusion segment is selected by the processor for a given slot in place of the target segment.

What predictions does a model of this kind make with regard to the target–intrusion rates for each segment, and for pairs of segments, comparable to predictions 1A and 2A? Since substitution errors occur when two segments /s/ and /s'/ are simultaneously available to the processor, errors of the form (/s/ → /s'/) and (/s'/ → /s/) are equally probable. It will be useful to explore this prediction in more detail, using a hypothetical example.

Suppose that segment /s/ appears in word-initial position in English with a probability of .01, while segment /s'/ appears with a probability of .001. In any reasonable model of the sentence planning process (see Lashley, 1951), planning takes place over some portion of the utterance larger than a single word. Thus the probability that both /s/ and /s'/ will be available to the processor at the same time is some function of (.01 × .001).

However, the simple fact that the two planning segments are both available does not mean that an error will occur. The third factor that determines the probability of a substitution error involving these two segments is the degree of similarity between them. If /s/ and /s'/ are very similar, they will substitute for each other a relatively high proportion of the number of times they are both available, whereas if they are quite dissimilar, they will not substitute for each other very often no matter how many times they are simultaneously available. In other words, the relative frequencies of occurrence of the two segments determines the probability that both will be available to the processor at one time, while the degree of similarity between them determines the likelihood that this simultaneous availability will result in a substitution error.

The notable thing about a model of this type is that the probability is determined in precisely the same way for substitutions of the form (/s/ → /s'/) and (/s'/ → /s/). The two probabilities are the same, and thus the model makes a set of predictions different from 1A and 2A:

1B. Across all the errors in which a given segment appears, it will appear about equally often as a target and as an intrusion.

2B. Across all the errors involving a given **pair** of segments, one direction of substitution will be about as common as the other.

We have tested these predictions against the patterns of substitution in a corpus of 1471 substitution errors, and found that predictions 1B and 2B are better descriptions of our results than are 1A and 2A. Presentation of these data, and further discussion of certain apparent exceptions to the general pattern, occupy the rest of this chapter.

1. Materials

The corpus of errors analyzed here was drawn from the MIT collection of spontaneous speech errors, which has been described elsewhere in detail (see Garrett, 1975; Shattuck-Hufnagel, 1975; and Shattuck-Hufnagel and Klatt, 1975). Briefly, the errors were collected largely from spontaneous conversation among normal adult native speakers of English but occasionally from radio, television, and public occasions such as colloquia, or from speakers who were reading aloud. Errors were written down by the listener as soon as possible after they were heard, usually in ordinary English orthography, although occasionally broad phonetic transcription was necessary to minimize spelling ambiguities. The error was noted with as much of its sentential context as could be recalled verbatim, and with its correction by the speaker if there was one. The advantages and pitfalls of this method of collection have been discussed in Shattuck-Hufnagel (1975) and will not be considered here.

2. Classification and Analysis

The corpus is made up of 1471 errors in which a single phonetic segment type, the target, is replaced by another segment, the intrusion. Other kinds of segmental errors, including consonant cluster errors (CC for CC, C for CC, and CC for C) and vowel errors, are not counted, nor are morpheme, word, and phrase errors that involve a change in more than one phonetic segment type.[2] Thus all the errors considered here can be analyzed as the substitution of one consonantal segment for another. We used 24 segments /ptkbdgfvszʃʒčǰrlwymnŋh/, counting the affricates /č/ and /ǰ/ as single segments and omitting /ts/ and /dz/.

Within these limitations, the corpus includes a wide variety of types of substitution errors, classified as follows:

1. Variations in Source. This category includes errors made in spontaneous speech, while reading aloud and while trying to correct previous errors, as well as errors made in private conversation and on public occasions.

2. Variations in Class of Error. We have classified substitution errors into several different groups, including:

Exchanges	ABCDE → ADCBE	17% of corpus
Substitutions		56% of corpus
Anticipatory	ABCDE → ADCDE	
Perseveratory	ABCDE → ABCBE	
A or P	ABCDA → ABADA	
No apparent source	ABCDE → AXCDE	
Incomplete Errors	ABCDE → ADC...ABCDE	27% of corpus

Note that incomplete errors, if completed, might have taken the form of either an anticipatory substitution (A*D*CDE) **or** an exchange (A*D*CBE); because the speaker corrected himself before completing the error, we cannot be sure which was going to occur.

3. **Variation in Word versus Nonword Form of Error.** Substitutions that form English words and those that do not have been gathered into a single corpus. Preliminary analysis of the two groups of errors revealed no significant differences in distribution. It is not claimed that no interesting differences exist in the pattern of regularities exhibited by each of these different classes and varieties of substitution errors. It is more than likely that such differences exist, but we have lumped all substitution errors together because predictions 1 and 2 for both type A and type B models apply to the general pattern of errors in which each segment appears. We leave more detailed analyses of individual types for a later date when more errors have been collected.

3. Results

The confusion matrix formed by the 1471 substitution errors in our corpus is shown in Figure 2. For purposes of space, the single recorded error involving /ŋ/ has been omitted: it was of the form /m/ → /ŋ/. Error targets are on the vertical axis and intrusions on the horizontal. Thus there are 18 errors in which /t/ → /p/, etc.[3]

3.1. *Prediction 1A versus 1B*

Recall that type A "strong ousts weak" models predict that members of the strong set of segments are more likely to appear as intrusions, whereas those from the weaker set will be more likely to appear as targets. On the other hand, type B models based on the confusion of two simultaneously represented and similar planning segments predict that each segment will serve as a target and as an intrusion about equally often. The sum of the errors in each column in Figure 2 is the number of errors for which that segment was the intrusion, and the sum of errors in each row is the number for which that segment was the target. These sums are shown in Table 1. In Figure 3 we have charted the target and intrusion rates for each segment in our corpus for direct comparison. It is clear that the two curves are very similar, and that prediction 1B, based on simultaneous-availability models, finds considerable support in our data.

To test the hypothesis that the relative frequency with which each segment appears as a target is the same as the frequency with which it intrudes, we performed a χ^2 test on the two distributions. The results support a symmetry model: The identical nature of the two distributions cannot be rejected at the $p = .05$ level.

Figure 2: Confusion matrix, MIT corpus.

Target \ Intrusion	p	t	k	b	d	g	f	v	s	z	ʃ	ʒ	ʧ	ʤ	θ	ð	r	l	w	y	m	n	h
p	×	18	18	6	1	1	31	2	2	1	1	1	3	—	—	1	1	1	1	5	—	1	
t	14	×	18	1	4	—	2	—	22	2	2	1	3	—	3	1	2	3	1	2	1	2	1
k	28	18	×	2	1	11	5	1	8	1	—	1	6	1	2	1	—	1	—	1	1	3	5
b	7	1	1	×	14	9	2	5	—	1	1	1	—	1	1	4	6	3	1	13	2	1	
d	1	10	—	10	×	6	—	6	6	9	1	1	2	1	1	2	2	1	1	2	6	1	
g	1	—	6	10	11	×	1	—	1	1	1	1	1	1	1	1	1	1	1	1	2	2	
f	32	5	4	3	—	—	×	6	14	1	—	1	1	—	3	1	—	3	5	1	—	2	2
v	1	1	2	14	3	2	4	×	2	9	1	1	1	2	1	3	—	—	1	1	3	—	1
s	2	19	2	2	2	1	23	—	×	—	31	1	4	—	18	1	1	2	1	1	2	2	4
z	1	4	1	—	9	—	—	6	4	×	1	5	1	—	1	5	1	1	1	1	—	—	1
ʃ	1	—	1	4	1	1	1	—	1	65	—	×	1	2	—	—	1	1	1	1	1	1	2
ʒ	1	1	1	1	1	1	1	1	1	5	1	×	1	1	1	—	1	1	1	1	1	1	1
ʧ	1	12	9	1	—	1	—	1	12	1	4	1	×	—	—	1	1	1	—	1	1	1	2
ʤ	1	3	1	2	11	—	1	—	2	5	1	—	1	×	1	—	—	2	1	1	1	1	1
θ	1	4	2	1	1	1	4	1	21	1	3	1	1	1	×	1	1	1	1	1	1	1	1
ð	1	—	1	1	—	1	1	3	1	2	1	1	1	1	1	×	1	—	1	1	1	3	1
r	1	1	1	3	1	1	—	—	1	1	1	1	1	1	1	1	×	65	35	4	13	4	2
l	1	6	1	4	3	1	—	—	1	1	—	1	1	1	1	1	72	×	11	13	6	25	1
w	2	1	—	2	1	1	—	2	1	1	1	1	1	—	1	1	29	5	×	1	12	1	2
y	1	1	1	2	1	1	—	1	1	1	1	1	1	1	1	1	5	14	—	×	1	1	1
m	7	3	1	13	3	2	2	5	1	1	1	1	1	3	1	—	3	3	14	—	×	32	1
n	1	5	1	2	10	—	1	1	2	3	—	1	1	—	1	—	—	15	2	2	30	×	—
h	2	1	5	1	1	2	2	1	—	1	1	1	1	1	—	1	—	2	1	1	—	1	×

TABLE 1: *Target and Intrusion Rates for 23 Segments, with and without Normalization for s/š and t/č.*

Segment	Nonnormalized Matrix		Normalized Matrix	
	Target Rate	Intrusion Rate	Target Rate	Intrusion Rate
p	99	88	99	88
t	110	82	101	82
k	73	91	73	91
b	76	68	76	68
d	73	75	73	75
g	37	34	37	34
f	83	83	83	83
v	41	49	41	49
s	163	116	129	116
z	37	40	37	40
š	45	78	45	44
ž	6	7	6	7
č	21	44	21	35
ǰ	26	32	26	32
θ	30	34	30	34
ð	13	10	13	10
r	123	128	123	128
l	123	145	123	145
w	74	57	74	57
y	22	23	22	23
m	90	92	90	92
ŋ	84	78	84	78
h	22	18	22	18

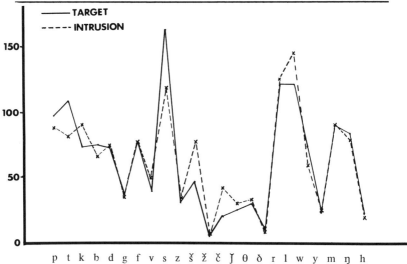

Figure 3: *Comparison of target and intrusion rates for each segment (not normalized for pairs s/š and t/č).*

These results become even stronger if we take into account a phenomenon that involves just a few pairs of segments. Careful inspection of Figure 3 reveals that a substantial part of the small amount of asymmetry between target and intrusion rates is contributed by two segments, /s/ and /š/. The segment /s/ appears considerably more often as a target, whereas /š/ appears more often as an intrusion. In fact, both the asymmetries arise largely from errors involving a confusion between just these two segments: /š/ → /s/ 31 times, whereas /s/ → /š/ 65 times, a difference of 34 errors, which is more than 2% of the entire corpus. What is the cause of this phenomenon?

One possibility is that these 34 errors represent the effect of a "strong ousts weak" mechanism over and above the pervasive symmetry in target-intrusion rates. This is a difficult view to defend, however, since the "stronger" element /š/ is less frequent than /s/ in English, is mastered later during phonological development, etc.

A more reasonable interpretation is that these errors result from the expanded application of the palatalization rule in English that changes alveolar consonants into their strident form in some environments. In support of this possibility, note the asymmetry in Figure 3 for segments /t/ and /č/. Once again, these asymmetries arise largely from an imbalance for one pair of segments: /t/ → /č/ 12 times while /č/ → /t/ only 3 times, a difference of 9 errors.

If we accept the hypothesis that these differences represent an aspect of the planning process that is separable from the normal mechanism for substitution errors, then it is useful to normalize the confusion matrix to remove the effects of this part of the process. Only then will we have a true picture of the operation of segmental substitution. We reasoned that the difference between /s/ → /š/ and /š/ → /s/ errors would not be present without the operation of this extra mechanism, so

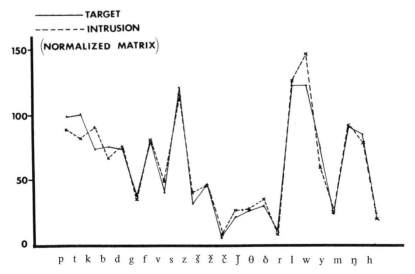

Figure 4: *Comparison of target and intrusion rates for each segment (normalized for pairs s/š and t/č).*

we removed from the matrix those 34 errors as well as the 9 errors representing the difference between /t/ → /č/ and /č/ → /t/. The results of this normalization are shown in Figure 4. The two curves are nearly indistinguishable, and a χ^2 analysis shows that their similarity cannot be rejected at the $p = .2$ level, providing substantial support for prediction 1B.

3.2. *Prediction 2A versus 2B*

Recall that type A models, in which strong segments replace weak ones, predict that for segment pairs including one strong member and one weak member, the strong will replace the weak one more often than vice versa. Type B models based on simultaneous availability predict no such asymmetries for individual pairs of segments. Which description better fits the MIT corpus?

More data are needed before this question can be resolved with certainty, but at least three lines of evidence support prediction 2B. First, the distribution of differences between one direction of substitution and the other for the 253 segment pairs (/ŋ/ is omitted in this analysis) is heavily weighted toward symmetry. The distribution is summarized in Figure 5, which shows that fewer than 10% of the pairs differ by more than 3 errors, while almost 50% substitute exactly the same number of times in both directions.

Second, the symmetrical pairs are not confined to those with a small number of mutual substitutions. For example, /m/ and /n/ substitute for each other 30 times in one direction and 32 in the other. Such symmetry characterizes the majority of pairs with both high and low confusion rates. In other words, it is not the case that the 9% of pairs that differ by four or more errors are the pairs with the largest number of mutual confusions. Some other mechanism appears to be at work.

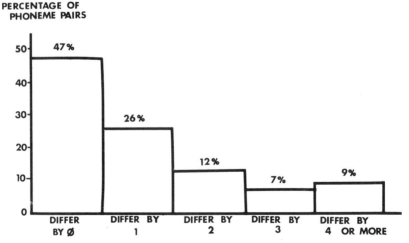

Figure 5: *Difference between one direction of substitution and the other, for each segment pair.*

Third, the asymmetries that exist in the overall target–intrusion curves in Figures 3 and 4 are accounted for by a very small number of individual segment pairs. We are presently investigating the details of these asymmetries. For example, in light of the /s/ – /ʃ/ and /t/ – /ʧ/ discrepancies discussed in the preceding, we are examining the individual contexts in which each of these errors occurred to see if there is reason to predict that the palatalization rule might have been active. In further support of this possibility, we have summarized the overall target–intrusion rates for the four segments /ʃʒʧʤ/ in Table 2, which shows that in general these segments appear more often as intrusions than as targets. If a larger sample of substitution errors reveals that this asymmetry can be attributed largely to pairs of segments for which the palatalization rule is appropriate, our hypothesis will receive further support.

In summary, three conclusions seem warranted. First, the general trend toward symmetry in target–intrusion rates for planning segments at the level discussed here is very strong. This observation supports a production model of type B, in which simultaneously available and similarly represented planning segments are misplaced by the utterance processor. Second, the small number of exceptions to this general pattern can be attributed to asymmetries in just a few related segment pairs. Third, it would be of considerable interest to compare these results with other confusion matrices, both in English and in other languages, to determine whether the apparent exceptions result from the application of a rule or the overlay of a type A mechanism on the basic type B process involved.[4]

TABLE 2: *Asymmetries in Target-Intrusion Rates for /ʃʒʧʤ/*

	/ʃ/	/ʒ/	/ʧ/	/ʤ/	Total
As targets	45	6	21	25	97
As intrusions	78	7	44	32	161

Notes

1. Examples of errors in which the intruding element apparently came from ongoing auditory and visual processing include:

   Where's Diane?   (intent: "Where's Sara?" but speaker was looking at Diane, and Sara was not in sight)

   We need a new refrigerator.   (intent: "We need a new washing machine," but speaker was looking at a refrigerator)

   I'll be so emborrassed   (intent: "embarrassed," but speaker was listening to another speaker saying "pomme pur" in French)

2. The matrix errors make up about 30% of the total error corpus.
3. Exchange errors like *"led retter day"* (red letter day) involve two substitutions, but only the first one was included in our corpus to provide a stronger test of symmetry in direction of substitution. Addition of the second parts of exchange errors could only increase the symmetry, since for every (x → y) error there would then be a (y → x) error to match.
4. For a more complete discussion of the symmetry issue, see Shattuck-Hufnagel and Klatt (1979).

References

Boomer, D. S. & Laver, J. D. M. 1968. Slips of the tongue. *British Journal of Disorders of Communication, 3*, 2–12.

Cairns, H. S. & Williams, F. 1972. An analysis of the substitution errors of a group of English-speaking children. *Journal of Speech and Hearing Research, 15*, 811–820.

Fromkin, V. A. 1971. The non-anomalous nature of anomalous utterances. *Language, 47*, 27–52.

Fromkin, V. A. 1973. Introduction. In V. A. Fromkin (Ed.), *Speech errors as linguistic evidence*. The Hague: Mouton.

Garrett, M. F. 1975. Syntactic processes in sentence production. In R. Wales & E. C. T. Walker (Eds.), *New approaches to language mechanisms*. Amsterdam: North Holland Publ.

Garrett, M. F. 1976. The analysis of sentence production. In G. Bower (Ed.), *The psychology of learning and motivation*, vol. 9, New York: Academic Press.

Goldstein, L. (1978). Categorical features in speech perception and production. Unpublished manuscript.

Lashley, K. S. 1951. The problem of serial order in behavior. In L. A. Jeffress (Ed.), *Cerebral mechanisms in behavior*. New York: Wiley.

MacKay, D. 1970. Spoonerisms: The structure of errors in the serial order of speech. *Neuropsychologia, 8*, 323–350.

Nooteboom, S. G. 1969. The tongue slips into patterns. In A. G. Sciarone, A. J. van Essen, and A. A. van Raad (Eds.), Nomen Society, *Leyden studies in linguistics and phonetics*. The Hague: Mouton. Pp. 114–132.

Shattuck-Hufnagel, S. 1975. Speech errors and sentence production. Unpublished dissertation, MIT, Cambridge, Massachusetts.

Shattuck-Hufnagel, S. 1979. A model of sentence production based on speech error constraints. In W. E. Cooper & E. C. T. Walker (Eds.), *Sentence processing: Psycholinguistic studies in honor of Merrill Garrett*. Cambridge, Massachusetts: MIT Press.

Shattuck-Hufnagel, S. and Klatt, D. 1975. An analysis of 1500 phonetic speech errors, presented at the 90th meeting of the Acoustical Society of America, San Francisco, California, November 1975.

Shattuck-Hufnagel, S. and Klatt, D. 1979. The limited use of distinctive features and markedness in speech production: Evidence from speech error data. *Journal of Verbal Learning and Verbal Behavior, 18*, 41–55.

Chapter 3

CONSONANT FEATURES IN SPEECH ERRORS

Marcel P. R. van den Broecke[1]   Louis Goldstein[2]

Phonetics Institute   *Instituut Voor Perceptie Onderzoek*
University of Utrecht   *Eindhoven, The Netherlands*
Utrecht, The Netherlands

Und mit der Stimmungsinhalt der Seele
verändert sich der Wert des einzelnen Lautes

Meringer (1908)

1. Introduction

Ever since speech errors have been made the object of systematic research, it has been established and reestablished that a great number of regularities occur in such errors on the semantic, syntactic, and phonological level (Meringer & Mayer, 1895; 1908; Cohen, 1966; Nooteboom, 1969; Fromkin, 1971). In this chapter we will deal only with a subset of phonological characteristics of speech errors in English, German, and Dutch. Phonological speech errors can be classified into the following categories:

1. spoonerisms or metatheses   *keep a tape → teep a cape*
2. perseverations   *John gave the boy → John gave the goy*
3. anticipations   *also share → alsho share*
4. elisions   *try and take → tie and take*
5. substitutions   *back home → pack home*

Some of the most notable characteristics exhibited by speech errors as they manifest themselves in the preceding categories are the following:

1. Phonological strings resulting from speech errors will not violate phonotactic constraints characteristic of the language in which the error occurs (Meringer & Mayer, 1895; Cohen, 1966).
2. Anticipations are by far the most common type of errors, reflecting the fact that the part of the utterance that is still in the programing stage is a more powerful cause of speech errors than the part of the utterance that has already been produced.
3. Initial segments in a word and/or syllable are more likely to be affected by speech errors than syllable- or word-final segments, possible because they are more focused on during production.
4. The span over which one segment can influence another as exemplified in a speech error of one of the preceding categories is limited.
5. The pattern of consonant confusions contained in speech errors seems to indicate that segments will be replaced by segments that, from the point of view of phonetic–phonological characteristics, are relatively similar to the segment being replaced.

This last observation has led some researchers (Nooteboom, 1967; Mackay, 1970; Fromkin, 1976) to analyze the relation between the source segments and the replacing segments in terms of features. The results of such analyses indicate that a change of a limited number of features can account for the consonant replacements that may occur in speech errors. Typically, one-feature errors occur more often than two-feature errors, which again occur more often than three-feature errors, etc. in the studies mentioned.

It must be realized, however, that such observations are very much dependent on the particular choice of features used to characterize the segments involved, the amount and type of redundancies contained in the feature system used, which may mean that some feature systems may be more adequate for characterizing speech errors than others. Conversely, it is also possible that the structure of the confusions is such that any of the feature systems used, even if they have not been designed for the purpose of describing speech error regularities as we observe them, is equally adequate or inadequate in explaining them, as is the case in short-term memory confusions of consonants (Wickelgren, 1966). Alternatively, it may also be the case that none of the feature systems established in phonology to describe sound patterns in languages are ideally suited to the purpose of describing speech error regularities and that a new set of features will have to be established for this particular purpose. Such a set, if needed, should preferably be interpretable in well-established phonological–phonetic terms.

It is the purpose of this chapter to evaluate a number of a priori feature systems, designed for other purposes, in terms of their appropriateness to describe observed speech errors, and to evaluate the relation between these feature systems and a feature system that is based more directly on the patterns inherent in errors. Such an a posteriori feature system may be established by discovering the categories that are best suited to characterize speech errors as they occur. It may be hypothesized that since speech errors represent production mistakes, features that are defined in terms of articulation, or rather that have the clearest articulatory correlates, will be more likely to emerge from such an a posteriori analysis than will features that have the clearest correlates at the acoustical or perceptual level. Previous research (van den Broecke, 1976) has shown that it is unlikely that a set of features may be supposed to exist that will be equally powerful in explaining regularities on a linguistic level (i.e., phonological alternations, sound changes, etc.) versus articulatory and acoustic regularities versus regularities in perceptual and production processes. On the contrary, it seems more likely that the relations between these various levels of language description will each require its own feature set, with intricate relationships in terms of redundancies, inherent hierarchies among features, and language-specific, possibly idiosyncratic characteristics that are at present unknown. It should, moreover, be realized that a systematic description of any linguistic behavior in terms of features presupposes transformations between these various levels of language description that are at present unknown, or at least very hard to identify and define (cf. (Ladefoged, 1977). Yet, the structure that has been found to exist in phonological characteristics of speech errors seems to warrant the following attempt to establish speech error features and to explore their relationship to feature sets designed for other purposes that have proved their adequacy within their traditional realm of application.

2. Procedure

2.1. *English: The Data*

Two corpuses of spontaneously occurring speech errors—one that has been collected at the University of California, Los Angeles by Fromkin, consisting at present of a total of some 8000 errors (English 1) and a similar corpus of English (English 2) that was obtained by Shattuck-Hufnagel, Massachusetts Institute of Technology, consisting of 1057 consonant confusions, presented in Shattuck-Hufnagel (1975) in the form of a confusion matrix—were examined to obtain a subset of phonological errors complying with the following restrictions:

1. They should contain single consonant metatheses, anticipations, perseverations, or substitutions.
2. Changes in consonant clusters were regarded as one-phoneme changes, provided the rest of the consonant cluster in which they occurred remained intact.
3. Consonant deletions or insertions were not included in the analysis to avoid complexities arising from ø-phonemes.
4. Changes in which two consonants both changed into a third under the influence of a third consonant or a particular feature in that third consonant were not taken into account.

TABLE 1. Confusion Matrix of One-Consonant Speech Errors: English 1

	p	t	k	b	d	g	m	n	f	v	θ	ð	s	z	ʃ	l	r	w	j	h	tʃ	dʒ
p	26	20	25	12	3		15	1'	23	2	1		4	1		3	2	2		4	3	1
t	22	18	16	7	10	1	2	10	7		3		10	1		12	7	1			3	5
k	18	2	11	7	4	19	1	2	7	1			5		2	1	1	3		5	3	
b	3	6		15	11	15	21	2	7	5	1		2	2	2	2	4	2		1		2
d	9	1	7	12		4	2	7	2	1	1		1	2		10	3			1		9
g	3	5	8	12	4				2	1	1					1	2	1		3		
m				2		2	23	11	4							3	1		5	3		3
n						1	10	27	1					1		2	1		3	4		2
f	25	5	6	7	2	2	4	1		8	1		9		1	1	1	2		1	2	
v		4	1	5	1	1	1	2	11	8		2	1			3	2	1				
θ	1	1		2	1		1	2	3			2	4	1	1	1	1	1		4		2
ð									1		1		10		1			2				
s	4	6	3	2	2		8	11	3	4				1	1	37	42	6	5	1		2
z	3	3	1	5	3	2	4	2	1	5			1		1	3	8	10	3	5		3
ʃ	2	1	1	5	2		4	1	1	1					32	5	2		1	4		5
l	5	1	1	3	2		4	3	7				4	4			4	1		2		1
r	1	1	6	1	3			1		1					2	4		2		2		1
w	2	2	3			2						1	2		2	1						3
j	5	1	5	1	1	3	4			4					4	5	4				1	2
h	5	1	5	1	1	3	4			4					4	5	4				1	2
tʃ	3	3	3										2			1	3	1	1			3
dʒ	1	5		2	9		3	2		1			2		2		3	5	1	1	3	2

5. No context of either the replaced or the replacing consonant was taken into account.
6. One-phoneme spoonerisms were regarded as two substitutions, where both consonants involved functioned once as the source, and once as the target in the count.

The reasons for this series of restrictions are two fold: First, there was the necessity of arriving at a relatively high number of consonant confusions. This high number was needed for reliable subsequent analysis, precluding further subcategorizations; second, if substitutions of more than one consonant or intrusions and deletions were to be included, the complexity of the analysis would increase to a point where it would become unfeasible under the present limitations. This procedure resulted in a confusion matrix containing 1369 consonant confusions (English 1), comparable to the matrix obtained from Shattuck-Hufnagel (English 2) (Tables 1 and 2).

TABLE 2. *Confusion Matrix of One-Consonant Speech Errors: English 2*

	p	t	k	b	d	g	m	n	f	v	θ	ð	s	z	ʃ	l	r	w	j	h	tʃ	dʒ
p		10	16	4			2	2	23	1	1		2					1	1			
t	15		16		5		2	7	3				13	1		2	5				7	2
k	12	16		1		7	2	6	1				2	1						8	4	
b	3		1		9	5	7		4	7			2	1		1	3	3	1			1
d		4				8	6	6	1	1	1		2	5		4					1	4
g		1	10	8	5		1	1	1	2			1	1					1			
m	3		7	1				22	1		1					5	10	12				2
n	1	2	1	1	4	1	24		1				2	2		17	1					
f	25	1	4	4	1	1					3	4	13	1	1	3		3	1	2		
v	1	1		3	3	1	1	1	3		3	1	3			3	2	1				
θ		2							1				6							1		
ð			1		1								1			1						1
s	2	13	3	1	4			2	10	1	7			2	33	2				3	4	2
z				4	1	1	2	3			1											2
ʃ	1	1								1	1		20			1				1	1	
l		3	5	1		3	11	2	2	1			1				36	5	11	2		1
r		2	2	2	5	1										47		21	4	1		1
w			5	1		12	2	3	1							11	26		1	1		1
j								1								11	3					
h			5		1				2				3	1	1		1				1	
tʃ	1	3	4		1								3	2								
dʒ		1		1	7		2	1									2	1				

2.2. German: The Data

In order to obtain some insight into the extent to which findings resulting from the procedure outlined in the preceding section are language-specific, another corpus of speech errors in a different language, namely, Meringer's (1895; 1905) for German, was analyzed in a way identical to that described for English. The confusion matrix, containing 542 confusions, is given in Table 3.

TABLE 3. *Confusion Matrix of One-Consonant Speech Errors: German*

	p	t	k	b	d	g	m	n	ŋ	f	v	s	z	∫	l	r	w	j	h	X	ç	ts
p		2	1	1						3		1					1					
t	6		2	2	5	1	2	1		1		11	2	2	2	3	1			1		6
k	3			7		1	2					2		1		1						2
b	5	1	4		1	15	3			3	2				1	1	1					1
d		2	1	1		2						2	1	1	1	1			1	1		
g	2	4	16					1				1								1	1	1
m	1	1	2					5		2	1	1	2			6	1					
n			1	1			7		1	1		1			14	7	1					1
ŋ								2				1										
f	4			6	1		1				1	6	3	7	1		3			1		1
v	1			1	1							1							1			
s		8	3	3			5	1	5	2			5	2	4					3	1	3
z				1	2	1	2	1	6			11		2	1	2		3				2
∫			1	1					6			1			1							3
l		1	1	2				8	2			1	1	4		47	3	3	3			
r	1							4				7		2	33		2		1	2		
w	1	1	2				5	2		1		1	3	1					1			2
j															2	3						
h		1	2	1		1			1			1		1			4					1
X			1			1				1	4	2										
ç	2	2								1		1		2								
ts	7	1								1			3									

2.3. Dutch: The Data

For the comparative purposes mentioned for German, a confusion matrix for spontaneously occurring speech errors in Dutch was obtained from Nooteboom, Instituut Voor Perceptie Onderzoek, Eindhoven. Some characteristics of this material have been described in Nooteboom (1969). This set of 235 confusions, as given in Table 4, is subject to the same series of restrictions mentioned for the other collections of speech error data.

TABLE 4. *Confusion Matrix of One-Consonant Speech Errors: Dutch*

	replacement															
	p	t	k	b	d	m	n	f	v	s	z	l	r	w	j	h
p		4	8	1		2										
p		4	8	1	2		2	3								
t	5		7	3	1	4				4	1	2	2			
k	5	4								1	2					
b	2				3	2							1			
d	1	7	3				1			1	5	5	1	1	1	1
m	2	1					1		1		1	1	3	1	1	
n		1			1	4				1	1	4	1	2		
f	2	3					1		1							
v	2	1	1		2					1			1			
s	2						1	2	1		6					
z	1	2				1	1	1		1				1	1	1
l		1		1	3		1			1	2		13	5	1	1
r					4					1		19		1		
w			1	2	2	5					2	5				
j						1								1		
h													2			

2.4. A Posteriori Analysis: Procedure

Assuming that the patterns of confusability among consonants in our various speech error matrices are not random, the discernible patterns may lead to some insights with respect to the organization of the speech production system. In particular, we can discover if there are groups of consonants that behave similarly in speech errors. Such similarity within a group may be reflected either in a large number of confusions among the consonants of a group or in similar patterns of confusability with other consonants not in the group. In order to obtain a visual representation of such patterns of similarity inherent in these matrices, we decided to employ the technique of multidimensional scaling.

Nonmetric multidimensional scaling (cf. Shepard, 1974; Carroll and Wish, 1974) assumes that the consonants are points in some n-dimensional spatial configuration, where n is determined empirically, and it attempts to adjust the positions in this space such that the distance between any two points is simply (monotonically) related to the similarity values between the consonants in the original data. In our case, the number of confusions between consonants is not a simple measure of their similarity, since the stimulus objects that may be subject to an error differ radically in terms of their frequency of occurrence. Each stimulus or target is not present an equal number of times, but differs according to its frequency of occurrence in the language. A technique described in Goldstein (1977) was used in order to obtain realistic values for the proportion of times a target was not missed and the result was not a speech error but a correct utterance. To apply this technique, we need to know how often speech errors occur at all in relation to the total number of phonemes uttered in a sample of speech and the frequency of occurrence of each phoneme. Since no reliable estimates exist as to the probability that phonemic speech errors occur in natural language, and since subjective estimates about this probability indicate that it seems to be very much speaker- and occasion-dependent, we chose arbitrary values for this probability, namely, 1/10, 1/1000, 1/50,000, and 1/1,000,000.

Obviously the probability of 1/10 (i.e., that approximately every tenth phoneme will be an error) is much too high, and even 1/1000 seems higher than most observations indicate. As only the rank order of the similarities is relevant to the nonmetric scaling procedure, differences due to the choice of the probability value for making an error were only relevant to the extent that they affected this rank order. It turned out that solutions were stable for probability values of making an error of 1/1000 or less, which means that our method of calculating similarity is robust as long as the probability of making an error at all is low. For a more detailed mathematical treatment of the procedure described here, see Goldstein (1977).

2.5. *A Posteriori Analysis: Results*

Multidimensional scaling was performed on the English 1, English 2, and German data sets. One to six dimensions were analyzed. Inspection of the resulting configurations showed that the two-dimensional solutions were most easily interpretable in phonetic–phonological terms. Goodness of fit of the configurations with the data at various dimensionalities was used to estimate the *true* dimensionality. This measure also showed a tendency for the two-dimensional solutions to be feasible. The two-dimensional configurations obtained are given in Figures 1–3.

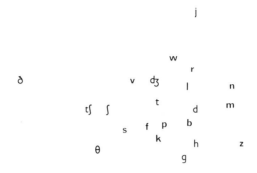

Figure 1: *Two-dimensional configuration: English 1*

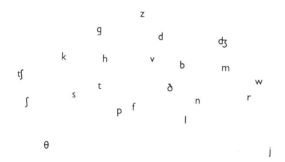

Figure 2: *Two-dimensional configuration: English 2*

Figures 1 and 2 basically show very similar patterns. The configurations for the two English data sets show some quite systematic properties:

1. Voiced versus voiceless consonants form two separate groups, with the possible exception of /d/, for which there is very little data.
2. The nasals and the liquids form two adjacent clusters.
3. The voiced and the voiceless stops form parallel lines with corresponding places of articulation for the cognate pairs.
4. /f, s, tʃ, and ʃ/ group together as voiceless fricatives–affricates.

Figure 3 shows the configuration for German, which exhibits some, but not all the characteristics noted for English: (*a*) No single straight line can be drawn to

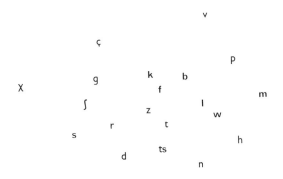

Figure 3: *Two-dimensional configuration: German*

separate the voiced from the voiceless consonants. Yet, the stops are again positioned in systematic voiced–voiceless pairs. For the fricative cognates /s,z/ and /f,v/
the voiced–voiceless distinction is again systematic, but its direction runs opposite
to that of the stops; (*b*) the velars, (bi)labials, and dentoalveolars group together.

On the basis of the properties exhibited by the configurations for English and
German, a speech error feature set (SpE) was devised in which it was attempted as
far as possible to incorporate the cluster formations as noted. The following features
were set up for this purpose: voice, stop, place ([bi]labial, dental, alveolar, palatal,
velar, glottal), nasal. This set was not sufficient to disambiguate all consonants involved in the analysis in terms of feature specifications. Since no further features
could be derived from the configurations, the feature fricative plus approximant
were added to this set for classificatory purposes. This feature set (Table 5) was used
in the subsequent a priori analysis.

TABLE 5. *Speech Error Feature Specifications for English Consonants (SpE)*

	p	t	k	b	d	g	m	n	f	v	θ	ð	s	z	ʃ	l	r	w	j	h	tʃ	dʒ
voi	–	–	–	+	+	+	+	+	–	+	–	+	–	+	–	+	+	+	+	–	–	+
stop	+	+	+	+	+	+	+	+	–	–	–	–	–	–	–	–	–	–	–	–	+	+
place	b	a	v	b	a	v	b	a	b	b	d	d	a	a	p	a	a	v	p	g	p	p
nas	–	–	–	–	–	–	+	+	–	–	–	–	–	–	–	–	–	–	–	–	–	–
fric/ appr.	–	–	–	–	–	–	–	–	+	+	+	+	+	+	+	–	+	+	+	+	+	+

2.6. *A Priori Analysis: Procedure*

In order to assess the appropriateness of various existing feature systems in describing the speech error confusions, the following procedure was used. Fully redundant segment by feature matrices were constructed, using each of the feature systems as described in Jakobson, Fant, and Halle (1952) (JFH), Chomsky and Halle (1968) (ChH), Ladefoged (1975) (Lad), and the speech error feature system that was based on the results of the a posteriori analysis (SpE). The last system should be particularly suitable for describing speech errors since it was derived from speech error data.

A computer program written by Silva, Department of Linguistics, University of California, Los Angeles, was used to establish how many one-feature changes, two-feature changes, etc., were contained in the matrix, and which feature changed how often in which direction in the total set of confusion data. This procedure was followed for each of the data sets with each of the feature systems.

When we compare feature systems with different numbers of features, we may expect differences that are only due to the different number of features, and not to any basic properties of the features contained in each system. All systems classify fewer consonants uniquely than could be achieved if the system contained no redundancies and no restrictions on particular feature combinations with particular values. Since all our feature systems characterize the same set of consonants, the feature systems with a relatively high number of features, namely, ChH and Lad, may be expected to have more intrinsic redundancies and combinatory restrictions than the feature systems with relatively few features, namely, JFH and SpE. Therefore, if we count the number of features that differ between replaced and replacing consonants in speech errors, the ChH and Lad systems may be expected to show more feature switches in absolute terms on the whole, and the dispersion around the number of features that switch most often in value in the speech error corpuses will be larger than will be the case for the JFH and SpE feature systems. If we want to find out which of the four systems best characterizes speech errors in terms of the fewest number of feature switches, we can find out how much less adequately the same feature characterizes random consonant confusions.

In order to generate a random set of consonant confusions, we used the following procedure. If there is no systematic relationship between the replaced and the replacing consonant in a speech error, then the likelihood of a sound replacing any other sound will be a function of its frequency of occurrence. Thus, each cell in a random confusion matrix will contain the product of the probability of occurrence of the replaced and the replacing consonant, multiplied by some arbitrary number, which is the same for all cells of the confusion matrix. Obviously, the matrix will be symmetrical. In order to see in what way each feature system may differ systematically in characterizing speech error consonant confusions rather than random consonant confusions, all four feature systems have been applied to the random data matrix to count how many features switched value how often. The random data matrix is given in Table 6.

TABLE 6. Confusion Matrix for English Random Data.

	p	t	k	b	d	g	m	n	f	v	θ	ð	s	z	ʃ	l	r	w	j	h	tʃ	dʒ
p		27	10	6	12	4	10	25	7	8	2	9	15	8	3	13	26	18	27	10	2	1
t	27		42	28	52	15	45	103	29	32	8	38	66	35	12	57	112	77	116	45	7	1
k	10	42		10	19	5	16	39	11	12	3	14	24	13	4	20	40	28	41	16	3	6
b	6	28	10		12	4	11	26	7	8	2	9	16	8	3	14	27	18	28	11	2	2
d	12	52	19	12		7	20	48	13	14	3	17	29	15	5	25	49	34	51	20	3	2
g	4	15	5	4	7		6	14	4	4	1	5	9	5	2	7	14	80	15	6	1	3
m	10	45	16	11	20	6		41	11	12	3	14	25	13	5	21	42	29	43	17	3	1
n	25	108	39	26	48	14	41		27	30	7	35	60	32	11	51	102	70	105	41	7	2
f	7	29	11	7	13	4	11	27		8	2	9	16	9	3	14	28	19	29	11	2	6
v	8	32	12	8	14	4	12	30	8		2	10	18	10	3	16	31	21	32	12	2	2
θ	2	8	3	2	3	1	3	7	2	2		2	4	2	1	4	7	5	7	3		2
ð	9	38	14	9	17	5	14	35	9	10	2		21	11	4	18	36	25	37	14	2	
s	15	66	24	16	29	9	25	60	16	18	4	21		20	7	32	63	43	65	25	4	2
z	8	35	13	8	15	5	13	32	9	10	2	11	20		4	17	33	23	34	13	2	4
ʃ	3	12	4	3	5	2	5	11	3	3	1	4	7	4		6	11	8	12	5	1	2
l	13	57	20	14	25	7	21	51	14	16	4	18	32	17	6		54	37	55	21	4	1
r	26	112	40	27	49	14	42	102	28	31	7	36	63	33	11	54		73	109	42	7	3
w	18	77	28	18	34	10	29	70	19	21	5	25	43	23	8	37	73		75	29	5	6
j	27	116	41	28	51	15	43	105	29	32	7	37	65	34	12	55	109	75		43	7	4
h	10	45	16	11	20	6	17	41	11	12	3	14	25	13	5	21	42	29	43		3	6
tʃ	2	7	3	2	3	1	3	7	2	2		2	4	2	1	4	7	5	7	3		2
dʒ	1	6	2	2	3	1	2	6	2	2		2	4	2	1	3	6	4	6	2		

2.7. *A Priori Analysis: Results*

If a feature system is to be suitable for describing speech errors, the natural classes that can be formed with it should ideally coincide with relatively high speech error confusability as shown by higher confusion values in the appropriate cells in the confusion matrix. In other words, the largest number of speech errors will be described in an ideal feature system as one-feature changes, and the number of confusions should decrease as the number of feature changes involved in them increases. It must be realized, however, that the notion of an ideal feature system is ambiguous, as a compromise will have to be made between ideal feature systems from the point of view of efficient, nonredundant coding, and from the point of view of being representative of some kind of patterning of linguistic data in other realms.

Whenever the significance of one-feature switches versus more-feature switches is discussed, this point should be remembered because it will provide the proper perspective for evaluating feature systems in terms of number of feature switches. The four feature systems applied to the data show radically different behavior, as shown in Figures 4–8 for the various data sets. It appears that the JFH set is most appropriate for describing all data sets at hand in the sense that the number of consonant confusions in speech errors clearly decreases as the number of JFH feature changes needed to describe them increases. The ChH set shows a peak at two features rather than one in this respect, and the Lad features invariably reach a peak at three features. Both these feature sets may, moreover, reach subsequent, lower peaks at higher feature difference values. As can be seen in Figures 4–8, it turned out that SpE was on the whole equivalent, but not superior, to the JFH set in economically characterizing the number of feature switches.

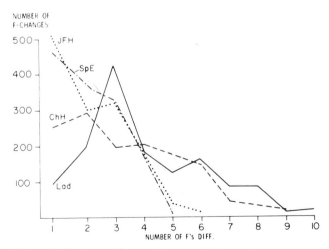

Figure 4: *Number of feature changes in different feature sets on English 1 data.*

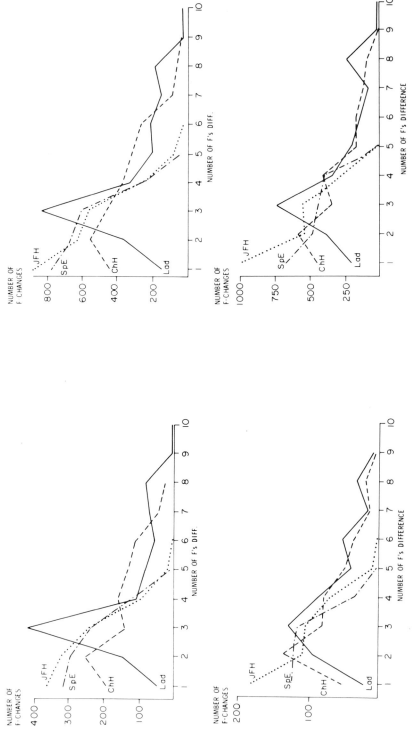

Figures 5–8. Figure 5, top left: *Number of feature changes in different feature sets on English 1 data.* **Figure 6, top right:** *Number of feature changes in different feature sets on English 2 data.* **Figure 7, bottom left:** *Number of feature changes in English 1 and 2 combined.* **Figure 8, bottom right:** *Number of feature changes in different feature sets on Dutch data.*

As observed, these findings should be compared to those obtained on random data. In Figure 9 we observe that all four feature systems have an approximately normal distribution around their mean, with a skew toward fewer feature switches when applied to the random data.

It is evident that all feature systems behave in a different way with respect to random confusions as compared to their behavior with speech error confusions. This means that all feature systems, being more adequate in describing speech errors than in describing the random data set, contain properties that are reflected in speech error confusions. This is confirmed by a quantitative analysis of the data of the following sort. The mean number of feature switches per speech error can be obtained from the following formula:

$$E(x) = \sum_{i=1}^{n} p(x_i) \cdot (x_i)$$

where $p(x_i)$ is the proportion of errors that have x_i number of feature changes.

The number of feature switches per speech error will be a function of the number of features contained in the system with which it is described. This is shown in Table 7 by the increasing value of $E(x)$ when the number of features per system increases. In order to compare feature systems with a different number of features in terms of their effectiveness in describing speech errors, we will have to divide $E(x)$ by the number of features in the system we deal with.

We see that the rank order of the feature sets is the same in the real versus the random data, and that on the basis of the values $E(x_b) - E(x_a)$, i.e., the difference between real and random data, no preference for any feature system can be expressed. All feature systems, however, show an improvement in describing the actual data as compared to their description of the random data in terms of there being invariably fewer feature switches in the speech error data. One of the major

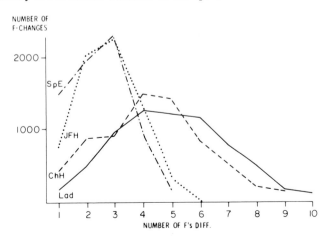

Figure 9: *Number of feature changes in different feature sets on random data.*

TABLE 7. *Feature Switches per Speech Error.*

Feature System	Data Set	$E(x_a)$	$\dfrac{E(x_a)}{n}$	Data Set	$E(x_b)$	$\dfrac{E(x_b)}{n}$	$E(x_b) - E(x_a)$
JFH	English 1 & 2	2.20	.37	random	2.80	.47	.10
SpE	English 1 & 2	2.14	.43	random	2.44	.49	.06
ChH	English 1 & 2	3.47	.39	random	4.31	.48	.09
Lad	English 1 & 2	3.91	.43	random	4.86	.54	.11

differences between the Lad set, on the one hand, and the ChH and JFH sets, on the other, is Ladefoged's abandonment of binarity at the classificatory level (see Ladefoged, 1971) in order to describe phenomena involving adjacent places of articulation for consonants or adjacent heights for vowels in a manner that is more closely related to the physical characteristics of speech than is possible in a binary system. Thus, the Lad feature set allows us to assess whether a change in place of articulation in speech errors tends to go in the direction of adjacent place of articulation. Six different places of articulation are needed to describe all phonemic contrasts occurring in English, German, and Dutch, namely, (bi)labial, dental, alveolar, palatal, velar, and glottal. Hence, any consonantal speech error involves maximally a switch of five places of articulation, and minimally no switch in place of articulation at all. Analysis of the combined English data shows that a switch over two places of articulation, rather than one, occurs most often. Thus, consonant speech errors do not predominantly involve adjacent places of articulation (see Figure 10).

For every feature system it is possible to rank order its features in terms of their susceptibility to its value being altered in speech errors. It can be argued that a low rank on this scale indicates that a feature is relatively stable with regard to speech errors. When we examine which features are most often involved in a switch per feature system in each data set, it turns out that in the Lad and the SpE feature system, place is by far most often affected across all data sets. For the SpE set, the rank order of the features is invariably place-voice-stop-fric+appr-nasal. In the JFH set, the highest ranking features are grave and continuant, the lowest ones vocalic,

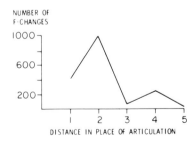

Figure 10: *Distance in place of articulation in Lad's place feature on the combined English data.*

consonantal, and nasal. In the Lad set and the ChH set, there is more variation in the rank orders than in the other two sets. In both sets, as in the JFH, the major class features consonantal and vocalic tend to rank low, as do features that are primarily needed to describe vowels, such as wide and round (Lad) or round and low (ChH). Nasal is one of the few features shared by all feature sets that has a relatively stable, low rank, whereas two other shared features, namely, stop and voice (= JFH tense) have a relatively high ranking across feature systems and data sets.

3. Discussion

When we consider systematic properties of speech errors, it is obvious that such properties must primarily reflect speech production phenomena. Hence, we would expect speech errors to display characteristics connected with production, rather than with transmission or perception of speech. Yet, we have not obtained any evidence that points to speech errors as being primarily or exclusively an articulatory phenomenon. Perhaps this is not surprising provided we regard phonemic speech errors as being in no sense lower level or more superficial in a linguistic description of their origin than, for example, semantic speech errors. When we attempt to evaluate the various feature sets with respect to speech errors, it should be realized that a label applied to a particular feature need not describe its primary characteristic, and need not be the only or optimal way to characterize it. Thus, although stop is an articulatory label, the process it describes can easily be defined in acoustic terms. It is only after examining the consequences of a particular feature value in a particular context in terms of its acoustical and articulatory correlates that we may decide, whatever its name, whether a feature is primarily defined on an acoustic or on an articulatory basis. It is extremely difficult to find out what specific correlates any of the features in any of the systems will have in the domain other than that in which it is defined, i.e., primarily in articulation terms for Lad, ChH, and SpE features, primarily in acoustical terms for JFH. None of the feature systems examined has clear examples of features that can only be defined in one domain, be it articulation, acoustics, or perception. In order to find a clear preference for any of these domains in speech errors, we would need feature systems different from the ones we examined, for example, a purely acoustically oriented one such as is needed to operate a speech synthesizer. In view of the way in which our feature systems are defined, which may involve some features having simpler correlates in one domain than in another, the evidence obtained does not show any strong preference for any domain when describing speech errors. Previous attempts at resolving this issue (Fant, 1962; Delattre, 1967) have indicated that the articulatory, acoustical, and perceptual correlates of most features examined are very complex, with typically no one-to-one relationships in these different domains, but with many-to-many relationships. At present, we can say that feature systems designed without incorporating evidence from speech errors are all capable of showing meaningful structure in phonological speech errors as they occur.

In a way, it is surprising that the systematic properties we found manifest themselves so clearly in view of the severe omissions in our procedure, for example, our
omitting to take into account additional factors influencing the occurrence and
possibly the nature of speech errors, such as similar contexts and stress phenomena,
or any kind of syntactic or semantic information. Inclusion of clusters, insertions,
deletions, and possibly syllabic transpositions would be important if one is to obtain
more insight into the characteristics of phonemic speech errors. The present findings
show that it is feasible to capture properties shared by speech sounds in their behavior in speech errors in terms of feature sets that will also be acoustically and/or
perceptually oriented in spite of the fact that speech errors manifest themselves in
the first place as production phenomena.

Notes

1. Research was supported by a grant from Z.W.O., the Netherlands Organization for the Ad-
   vancement of Pure Research.
2. Research was conducted while the author was at the University of California, Los Angeles
   Phonetics Laboratory, and was supported by a grant from the National Institutes of Health
   (USPHS–NS–12303).

References

van den Broecke, Marcel P. R. 1976. *Hierarchies and rank orders in distinctive features.* Assen:
    van Gorcum.
Carroll, J. D. & Wish, M. 1974. Multidimensional perceptual models and measurement methods.
    In E. C. Carterette & M. P. Friedman (Eds.), *Handbook of perception* (Vol. 2). New York:
    Academic Press. Pp. 391–447.
Chomsky, N. & Halle, M. 1968. *The sound pattern of English.* New York: Harper & Row.
Cohen, A. 1966. Errors of speech and their implication for understanding the strategy of lan-
    guage users. In V. A. Fromkin (Ed.), *Speech errors as linguistic evidence.* The Hague: Mouton,
    1973. Pp. 88–92.
Delattre, P. 1967. Acoustic or articulatory invariance? *Glossal, 1,* 3–25.
Fant, G. 1962. Descriptive analysis of the acoustic aspects of speech. *Logos, 5,* 3–17. Also in
    I. Lehiste (Ed.), *Readings in acoustic phonetics.* Cambridge, Massachusetts: MIT Press. Pp.
    93–108.
Fromkin, V. A. 1971. The non-anomalous nature of anomalous utterances. *Language, 47,* 27–
    52.
Fromkin, V. A. 1976. Computer processing in "tips of the slongue." Paper read at the ASA
    meeting in April 1976, Washington, D.C.
Goldstein, L. 1977. *Three studies in speech perception: Features, relative salience, and bias.*
    WPP 39. Los Angeles: Univ. of California, Los Angeles.
Hood Roberts, A. 1965. *A statistical linguistic analysis of American English.* The Hague:
    Mouton.
Jakobson, R., Fant, G. & Halle, M. 1952. *Preliminaries to speech analysis; the distinctive fea-
    tures and their correlates.* Cambridge, Massachusetts: MIT Press.
Ladefoged, P. 1971. *Preliminaries to linguistic phonetics.* Chicago: Univ. of Chicago Press.

Ladefoged, P. 1975. *A course in phonetics.* New York: Harcourt Brace Jovanovich.

Ladefoged, P. 1977. The abyss between phonetics and phonology. Paper presented at the thirteenth annual meeting of the Chicago Linguistic Society.

Mackay, D. G. 1970. Spoonerisms; the structure of errors in the serial order of speech. In V. A. Fromkin (Ed.), *Speech errors as linguistic evidence.* The Hague: Mouton, 1973. Pp. 164–194.

Meringer, R. & Mayer, C. 1895. *Versprechen und verlesen, eine psychologisch linguistische studie.* Vienna: Verlag.

Meringer, R. 1908. *Aus dem leben der sprache.* Berlin: Verlag.

Nooteboom, S. G. 1967. Spontane fonologische versprekingen. *IPO Annual Progress Report.* Eindhoven: Netherlands.

Nooteboom, S. G. 1969. The tongue slips into patterns. In A. G. Sciarone, A. J. van Essen, and A. A. van Raad (Eds.), Nomen Society, *Leyden studies in linguistics and phonetics.* The Hague: Mouton. Pp. 114–132.

Shattuck-Hufnagel, S. 1975. Speech errors and sentence production. Unpublished doctoral dissertation, Massachusetts Institute of Technology.

Shepard, R. N. 1974. Representation of structure in similarity data: Problems and prospects. *Psychometrika, 30,* 373–421.

Wickelgren, W. A. 1966. Distinctive features and errors in short term memory for English consonants. *Journal of the Acoustical Society of America, 39,* 338–398.

Chapter 4

ERRORS OF STRESS AND INTONATION

Anne Cutler

Laboratory of Experimental Psychology
University of Sussex
Brighton, England

A correctly produced sentence involves the successful imposition of suprasegmental features at several points: the assignment of primary lexical stress to the correct syllable of polysyllabic words, the correct placement of stress within the sentence and within each constituent of it, and the imposition of an intonation contour, the latter determined by a number of factors, linguistic (whether or not the sentence is a yes–no question, for example), paralinguistic (the emotional state of the speaker), and pragmatic (the function of the sentence in context, whether irony is intended, etc.). There appears to be a kind of Murphy's Law of speech errors that states: There is no component or stage in the production of a sentence but an error can occur there; and, indeed, errors arise at each of the above decision points. It will be seen, however, that certain kinds of suprasegmental errors are more detectable than others.

The several suprasegmental components of a sentence are not independent in their effects. The syllable that takes the brunt of the primary sentence stress is that which happens to carry lexical stress in the focused word. Since a primary correlate of assigned stress is pitch movement, the fundamental frequency contour of an utterance is a function not only of the intonation contour assigned but also of the lexical and sentential stress. They must, however, be considered to be independent in production, and the speech error evidence supports this independence. In the following discussion, errors of lexical stress, of higher level stress, and of intonation will be treated separately.

1. Lexical Stress Errors

This is by far the most commonly collected species of suprasegmental error. In a recent paper, appropriately entitled "Putting the EmPHAsis on the Wrong SyLABle" (1976), Fromkin included a large number of examples of misplaced word stress, and the following section draws on her examples (taken both from the 1976 paper and the corpus in Fromkin, 1973) in addition to my own collection of such errors and a number gleaned from the extensive error corpus gathered by David Fay.[1] Examples (1)-(4) are representative of this kind of error:

(1)   *I put things in that abstráct that I can't justify.*
(2)   *The noise sort of énvelopes you—envélops you.*
(3)   *You're in a real advántag—àdvantágeous position.*
(4)   *That was always thought to be véstig—vestígial.*

In (3) and (4) the erroneous stress has been detected and the error corrected before utterance of the word is complete, whereas in (1) and (2) the whole word has been spoken with incorrect stress. On occasion, false stress placement is accompanied by omission or addition of a syllable:

(5)   *In his life there seems to be **ambíguty**.* (T: ambigúity)[2]
(6)   *The theory of psychoánalis* (T: psychoanálysis)
(7)   *computáted* (T: compúted) (from Fromkin, 1976)

The stress shift in (5)-(7) could be held to be a consequence of the error of syllable omission or addition; after all, just such errors occur in contexts where they do not affect stress, as in (8)—uttered by an embarrassed newscaster—or (9):

(8)   *The two orbiting scientists carried out experiments in their **lábatory**—lábo-ratory—oh, I said that word!*
(9)   *Looks like you're doing end-of-the-semester **órganìze**—órganìzing.*

The strong similarity between such errors as those in (1)-(4) and (5)-(7), however, argues for the reverse explanation: that omission or addition of a syllable can be caused by an initial error involving the misplacement of stress. The location of the misplaced stress in these and similar examples appears to be not at all random; it is immediately noticeable in (1)-(7) that the stress placement in each case suggests another existing word, moreover, a word that is closely related to the target word in both form and content, being a different derivative from the same root morpheme. Thus, in (1) *abstract* (N) bears the stress pattern of *abstract* (V), in (2) *envelope* (V) is stressed as *envelope* (N), *ambiguty* as a substitute for *ambiguity* in (5) immediately suggests *ambiguous,* etc. It is extremely unlikely that these correspondences are accidental.

TABLE 1: *Lexical Stress Errors*

I.   Errors with the stress pattern of a morphological relative

A.   No change in number of syllables

abstráct (N)	*hierárchy*
administrátive	*homógĕ–homogéneous*
advántag–àdvantágeous	*homògenéous*
álter . . . native	*idiosyncrá–idiosýncrasies*
altérnately	*imág–imàginátion*
ambíg–ambigúity	*lĭng–línguist*
ánal–análysis	*línguist–lingúistic*
àrith–ărĭthmetic (N)	*Jàp–Jăpán*
articulátory	*methodól–methodológical*
certífication	*orígin*
chromát–chromatógraphy	*pérfectionìst*
conflícts (N)	*persónable*
cón–contéxtual	*phónetic*
còntribúted	*photógraphing* (two separate instances)
deféct (N)	*présent–presénting*
differénces	*prógress* (V)
dígest (V)	*psycholíng–psycholingúistic*
disambiguáting	*psychól–psychológical*
economist	*sarcásm*
economists	*syllabíf–syllábification*
elaboráting	*syntáx* (three separate instances)
énvelopes (V)	*véstig–vestígial*

B.   Number of syllables changed

ambíguty (T: ambigúity)	*óblitory* (T: obligatory)
bicéntial [bajséntɪəl] (T: bicenténnial)	*phenòmenolólogy* (T: phenòmenólogy)
bótnical (T: botánical)	*philósophal* (T: philosóphical)
computáted (T: compúted)	*psychoánalis* (T: psychoanálysis)
fácilty [fǽsəltij] (T: facílity)	*simílárily* (T: similarly)
hóspable (T: hospítable)	*specífity* (T: spècifícity)

II.   Other errors

A.   No change in number of syllables

ádj–adjústed	*commént*
alimóny	*mòbilíty*

B.   Number of syllables changed

polýsabic [pəlísəbɪk] (T: polysyllábic)	*trémenly* [trɛ́mənlij] (T: treméndously)

Table 1 contains my current corpus of word stress errors.[3] Phonetic transcriptions are given only where they are needed to avoid ambiguity (the examples come from speakers of American, British, and Australian English; transcribing the vowels would be both difficult and possibly misleading). Primary word stress is represented in each case by ´, and two other markings are used where necessary: `, representing secondary word stress with unreduced vowel, and ˘, representing an unstressed syllable with a reduced vowel.

In each of the 59 instances in Section I of the table, the reader should have no difficulty in supplying a related word in which the syllable bearing primary word stress is that which carries the misplaced stress in the erroneous utterance (always providing, of course, that the reader is as familiar with the word *chromátograph* as was the speaker in the eleventh example). The six errors of Section II, however, do not seem to have close relations of this kind, and they present potential counterexamples to the analysis to be presented in the following discussion; but they are very few in number in comparison with the errors in Section I, so that a common source for the latter still seems a fair bet. In at least one case in Section II, a different kind of mechanism may have been involved:

(10)   *There's such a thing as level of expectation and level of aspiration and ádj—
       adjústed people . . . .*

The error, in which the initial [æ] is stressed, is almost immediately preceded by a word beginning with a stressed initial [æ], and may therefore simply be a case of perseveration of an initial sound, as in (11):

(11)   *People pounce back and forth . . .* (T: bounce)

Although no such explanation is immediately apparent for the remaining 5 examples of Section II (and there is no context for some of them), Section I will be treated as a homogeneous set for the purposes of the following discussion.

One possible explanation for stress misplacement is that it results from a metathesis of stress markings (for example, ´ with ˘) analogous to the metathesis of other elements. However, the strong tendency for the erroneously chosen stress pattern to be that of a related word speaks against this suggestion; no such principles appear to be at work in the metathesis of features, phonetic segments, or syllables. Nor is there a preference for the primary stress in the error to have moved to the left or right of the target stress; in the 65 errors in Table 1, the stress moves to the left in 32 and to the right in 33 instances. An explanation invoking the supposed preference for initial stress in English can therefore also be discounted.

Another possible explanation for such errors is that they arise at the point at which the motor programs for the articulators are activated, not by selection of the wrong program, as that would result in utterance of the wrong word rather than the right word with the wrong stress pattern, but rather as a blend between adjacent forms, with the overwhelming tendency to semantic relatedness of the blended words being merely an artifact of the internal structure of the motor program list—no other word sounds more like the target. This suggestion would allow explanation of the errors in Table 1, Section II, as blends of adjacent unrelated words, for example, *cómment* with *comménd* to produce *commént*. But the problem with this hypothesis, which assumes an internal organization of the motor program list based on sound (each program's nearest neighbor is that for the word sounding most like it), is that some of the errors do not sound very much like their "distractor" forms at all (for example, [ǽnəlajz]/[ənǽləsɪs]; [ɔ́rədʒɪn]/[ərídʒənəl]). Quite apart from this, length in phonemes, number of syllables, and stress pattern, on which target and distractor almost invariably differ, are three important ways in which words "sound alike" and would almost certainly feature in such an organization.

Instead, the relatedness of target and distractor suggests that lexical stress errors arise at a fairly early level in the production process, at a point at which words related in the way that, for instance, *psychology* and *psychological* are related, are situated close enough to each other to be confused. The data are highly compatible with a model of the mental lexicon in which the rules by which the noun, verb, or adjective derivatives of a particular root are formed are productive in language performance. On this model a cluster such as *psychology, psychological, psychologist*, etc., would have a single complex lexical entry containing a base form and the rules for producing each surface form; a stress error would arise when the syntactic category specification for the intended utterance results in the appropriate word ending being produced, but the stress features assigned to the surface form are those of one of the other members of the lexical entry.[4] Thus the lexical stress error data accord with a model of the mental lexicon involving both morphological decomposition[5] of complex words and conjunct storage of all words derived from a single base.

This suggestion has obvious implications for theories of speech production and comprehension. Evidence from semantically unrelated word substitution errors (malapropisms) suggests that the one mental lexicon serves both the production and comprehension devices, and that its internal organization is comprehension-biased, that is, based on left-to-right phonemic structure (Fay and Cutler, 1977). It was also suggested by Fay and Cutler that the lexicon might be divided into subsections by grammatical category, number of syllables, and stress pattern, since malapropisms are strikingly alike in these three respects as well as in left-to-right phonemic structure. However, the present hypothesis, if correct, would necessarily involve a revision of this picture. The gathering into a single lexical entry of a noun, a verb, and an adjective derived from a single base is incompatible with organization of the lexicon into divisions of syntactic category. Likewise, the presence in one entry of forms with differing stress features precludes the division of the lexicon into sections according to stress pattern. Again, the various members of an entry can have differing numbers of syllables so that organization of the lexicon by syllabic structure could at the most be based, for such complex entries as these, on the number of syllables of the underlying form, whatever that might be.

There exists independent evidence for a division of the lexicon by grammatical category, for which a satisfactory explanation must be found if the present hypothesis is to remain credible. Fay (1975) found that in a lexical decision task, prior knowledge of grammatical category facilitated performance for verbs but not for nouns, and interpreted this as an indication that the lexicon contained separate sections for nouns and for verbs, with the order in which the sections were accessed in the default case (no grammatical category information) being nouns before verbs. His finding can, however, also be accounted for by positing a noun–verb order of scan of separate items within the lexical entry.

On the other hand, a certain amount of independent evidence supports the productive formation rather than independent lexicalization of derived words. First, word formation errors occur that result in a nonexistent form having a correct stem but the wrong affix, even though the affix may be one appropriate to the grammatical category of the target; sometimes such errors involve misplacement of stress, as in (12) and (13), at other times not, as in (14) and (15):

(12)   *a list of donátors* (T: dónors)
(13)   *the deríval of the sentence* (T: derivátion) (from Fromkin, 1976)
(14)   *I read his thesis as it was being writed* (T: written)
(15)   *spécialàting in* (T: spécializing) (from Fromkin, 1976)

Second, some experimental work in comprehension tasks provides support for the morphological decomposition of complex words in lexical access. Taft and Forster (1975; 1976) present evidence that in a lexical decision task prefixed words are analyzed into their constituent morphemes prior to lexical access, and that polysyllabic words are similarly decomposed into their component syllables. Murrell and Morton (1974) showed that in a word list, learning task performance on a given item was facilitated in the same way by pretraining on a different derivative of the same root morpheme as by pretraining with the same word. Other studies have indicated that before a word is accessed from the mental lexicon it is stripped of syntactic (inflectional) suffixes (-s, -ed, etc.; Gibson and Guinet, 1971) and of noun- and adjective-forming (derivational) suffixes such as -ness and -able (Snodgrass and Jarvella, 1972).

Conjunct storage of words with different stress patterns in a comprehension lexicon seems, of course, to imply that lexical stress is unimportant for comprehension purposes.[6] Indeed, we usually hear stress errors as the right word with the wrong stress rather than the wrong word. A hearing error results only when the misplaced stress permits false segmentation, as in (16),

(16)   *He was a master of his craft, a pérfectionìst.*

which led a hearer to parse the last noun phrase as *a perfect shnist;* only after no entry for *shnist* could be located in the lexicon was the utterance reanalyzed and an error of lexical stress diagnosed.

Note finally that a lexicon structured along the lines suggested here and at the same time organized by left-to-right phonemic structure, as argued by Fay and Cutler, would perforce make use of a phonemic representation of a considerable degree of abstractness; in many cases, two derivatives from a single stem have quite different initial segments in their surface forms (for example, *analysis* and *analyze*). Abstract phonological representation at the lexical level was in fact suggested by Fay and Cutler on independent grounds, and is also argued by Fromkin (1976).

2. Errors of Phrase and Sentence Stress

Stress placement errors at levels higher than the word also occur with a reasonable degree of frequency; they include errors of stress within nominal compounds and other phrases, errors in placement of primary sentence stress, and errors in assignment of contrastive or emphatic stress. The degree to which these different types of errors are detected by the hearer differs; stress errors within the phrase often stand out with the same glaring obviousness as lexical stress errors, although they do not seem to occur as frequently. Examples (17)–(19) are typical:

(17) *The price of lettuce has just sky-rócketed.* (T: ský-rocketed)
(18) Q. *You ate a cookie, didn't you?*
      A. *No, pèanut bútter.* (T: péanut bùtter)
(19) *by averaging the six—the six scóres* (from Fromkin, 1973)

How do such errors arise? Two explanations seem possible. On the one hand, the stress shift might result from a simple exchange of stress features, since in the majority of cases only two words are involved, one with primary, the other with secondary or tertiary stress. No phonetic accommodation is involved, since within-word stress remains unaltered; the exchange might be considered to take place at a low level in the production process. On the other hand, the stress shift might be a consequence of an independent error involving, for example, a shift or exchange of grammatical marking, otherwise undetectable in any surface phonetic change; Fromkin (1976) cites cases in which the shift of a bound morpheme precipitates a change in stress pattern:

(20) *Làrry's Hýman pàper* (T: Lárry Hỳman's páper)
(21) *It's not only us who have scrèw lóoses* (T: scréws loòse)

The evidence available so far does not suffice to decide the issue. Nor does a significant amount of independent evidence exist that might shed additional light, although the malapropism data show a tendency for nominal compounds to substitute for other nominal compounds having stress pattern and one element in common (for example, *eár canàl* for *bírth canàl*, *máilbox* for *lúnchbox*, *ráilway stàtion* for *rádio stàtion*, *compúter prògram* for *TV́ prògram*), one nevertheless finds the occasional example of a noun–noun compound substituting for a noncompounded noun phrase, such as:

(22)   *I'll bring a big **pìcnic táble*** (T: pìcnic lúnch)

In (22) the stress pattern of the target is preserved although the compound *picnic table* would normally bear primary–secondary stress.

As with lexical stress errors, a phrase stress error is usually detected; hearing errors result only when the phrase stress is ambiguous, as it is in the following two examples:

(23)   *This result was recently réplicated by someone at the University of Minnesota in **children.***

(24)   *Mr. Milne came to Rothsay to impress upon this **prètty** leftwing gàthering....*

In (23) the speaker placed emphatic stress on *children* and failed to set off intonationally the prepositional phrase *by someone at the University of Minnesota*, with the result that a hearer parsed the sentence to include a constituent *the University of Minnesota in children* (compare, for example, *the University of Texas in Austin*). In (24) the noun phrase *pretty leftwing gathering* was parsed Adj–Adj–N rather than Adv–Adj–N, probably due to a rather greater than usual degree of stress on the adverb.

In contrast to phrase stress errors, misplacement of sentence stress is rarely detected by the hearer. There is a common-sense reason for this: Practically any word in a sentence can carry the primary stress, a fact well known to children who will play at stressing each word in a sentence in turn. A change in the location of the primary stress will lead to a change in the sentence's focus, and depending on the context may have considerable pragmatic effects, but it will not produce an anomalous sentence. Hence, it is possible that primary sentence stress is often misplaced, and that what the hearer understands is in consequence not what the speaker intended; but unless the misplacement is corrected, there is no way of knowing that an error has occurred. When it seems important to avoid misunderstanding by correcting the misapplied focus, the speaker will do so:

(25)   *I think that any **serious appróach**–any sérious approach to the study of grammar....*

(26)   *And what **Í'm saying**–what I'm sáying is....*

The assignment of contrastive stress can also be subject to error, either being applied to the wrong element, as in (27), or not applied when desired (28):

(27)   *They're not **psýcholinguists**–they're not psycholínguists.*

(28)   *If the child **had**–sorry, if the child hád and uśed an interpretation...*

Again, misapplied contrastive stress does not produce an anomalous sentence, but may create a contextual effect not desired by the speaker. Let me offer just one example of an uncorrected contrastive stress error, for which it is obviously necessary to supply an extended context. The speaker of (29) had found a particular fault with psychology, and had then in a short digression recounted an anecdote from chemistry exemplifying the same fault; he concluded this digression by saying:

(29) So *this* sort of thing happens in other fields.

Given the mutability of focal stress, it is advisable that I also mention that there was no question of any other *sort of thing* being at issue that might happen in other fields; in the context there was to this hearer's mind no doubt that the primary stress belonged on *other*. The extensive collection of further examples awaits a heightened sensitivity to pragmatic factors on the part of error collectors.

It has frequently been noted by speech error researchers that sentence stress interacts with other errors in some interesting ways. Boomer and Laver (1968) pointed out that slips usually involved the word bearing heaviest stress in a "tone group" (phonemic clause), especially as the origin of an intrusion, and furthermore that the two elements involved in a metathesis were nearly always of the same degree of stress (either both strong or both weak). Nooteboom (1969) claimed that both elements of an error are more often stressed items than unstressed. MacKay (1969) argued that in cases of "forward masking" (anticipation), the masking phoneme is always stressed, and attributed this to a higher level of activation of stressed phonemes in the utterance program. Certainly some element of intrusion from a highly stressed source is apparent in such cases as (30):

(30) and also **intempt**—also attempt to conclude—**incorrectly!**—that the child uses intonation to . . . .

But nearly all of MacKay's anticipation errors involved consonants, whereas the brunt of stress is actually borne by the vocalic nucleus of a syllable; if the level of physical activation is indeed the precipitating factor, it is unclear why the masking phonemes were not more often vowels.

Moreover, as Garrett (1975) has pointed out, many of the suprasegmental regularities exhibited by speech errors can be explained by reference to effects of grammatical category and surface structure; and a further confounding may exist in the degree of detectability of errors in stressed versus unstressed syllables. Work on hearing errors (Garnes and Bond, 1975) shows that the stressed syllable is usually perceived correctly, so that hearing errors consist chiefly in misreconstruction of unstressed syllables. This is not surprising, given the acoustic advantages of stressed syllables; unstressed syllables are often considerably compressed in running speech. It could be the case, therefore, that slips in unstressed syllables are in fact as common as those in stressed syllables, but are simply harder to detect; the hearer reconstructs the unstressed portions of the utterance as the speaker intended to say them rather than as they were actually said, that is, a hearing error prevents detection of a speech error.

It has also been observed (Fromkin, 1971; 1976; Garrett, 1975) that primary sentence stress often does not shift when the element that would carry it in the target utterance shifts; in (31) and (32), for example, the sentence stress pattern of the target is preserved although two words, one of which would have borne stress in the target sentence, have switched places:

(31)   *I can't believe that anyone didn't **stòp to thìnk** and pick up a Big Mac.* (T: didn't thìnk to stóp . . . .

(32)   *We might have been sending a Wall St. **subscription Journal** to Ánne.* (T: Wall St. Joùrnal subscription . . . .

However, on closer inspection it turns out that the stress pattern is preserved only when both the words involved in the shift are open class items. When closed class words shift or exchange, the stress moves with its bearer:

(33)   *. . . they don't know how far they **ìn are**.* (T: . . . how far ìn they are)

(34)   *Where do you suppose **áre they**?* (T: . . . they áre)

(35)   *Consider how **cóuld it** be.* (T: . . . how it cóuld be)

(36)   *You can turn it **ón back** now.* (T: . . . back ón now)

(37)   *Just ask me where the tools are. I know where **they're áll**.* (T: . . . where they áll are)

(38)   *But it didn't work **that way óut**.* (T: . . . work óut that way)

(39)   *Òne just* [dʒəst] *quéstion!* (T: Just òne quéstion)

This generalization holds for all the examples in my collection and for all those that I can find in the literature. (Fromkin, 1973, lists 35 examples of exchanges or shifts in which she asserts that the target sentence stress has not changed. Four of these involve closed class items, but in three cases the stress level of the elements involved seems to have been the same, while in the other case:

(40)   *I would like to **all remind** you . . .* (T: . . . to remind you all . . .)

it is hard to see how the stress pattern could have remained unaffected by the shift.) On the one hand, this finding supports the contention of Garrett (1975; 1976) that there is an interesting difference in the way open- and closed class items participate in speech errors. But it also appears to imply that stress "sticks" to a closed class word more than it does to an open class item. Many errors of the type in (33)-(39), however, are cases of contrastive stress (with the conspicuous exception of those involving verb particles, which may be said to bear a degree of stress belonging as much to the verb as to the particle, for example, *turn it ón, work óut*). Contrastive stress can stay behind when its carrier has been lost from the sentence:

(41)   *He acts differently depending on who **he ís**.* (T: . . . who he is wíth)

If, in fact, the regularity noted in examples (33)-(39) simply reflects the fact that closed class words rarely bear stress unless it is contrastive, and that the "stickiness" of the stress is a product of its contrastive function, then we might expect that contrastively stressed open class words would similarly carry their stress with them when they move. My collection does not, alas, contain examples that would decide this question one way or the other.

3. Errors of Intonation Contour

The preceding observation regarding inconspicuousness of focus assignment errors holds with even greater force for intonational errors. Intonation contours over and above sentence stress pattern depend on several diverse factors—whether the sentence embodies a statement or a yes–no question, references to the discourse context, the emotional state of the speaker. In certain instances, the contour can quite cancel out the meaning of the sentence—ironic tone of voice, for example, produces a conveyed meaning which is the converse of the sentence's literal meaning. As Pike (1945) trenchantly remarks: "If a man's tone of voice belies his words, we immediately assume that the intonation more faithfully reflects his true linguistic intentions" (p. 23). Should a speaker misapply an intonation contour, then, his audience will probably never diagnose an error, but instead will understand the utterance differently from the speaker's intention. Should the misunderstanding be profound, the hapless speaker can only protest: "but I didn't mean it that way."

One does, however, hear contours misapplied. In particular, a terminal contour may not be applied when it ought to be—the sentence is "left hanging"—or is applied when it ought not to be. The hearer's impression in the latter case is that the speaker has changed his mind and decided to add more (42), especially in order to remove unclarity or ambiguity (43), or anomaly of the sentence content (44):

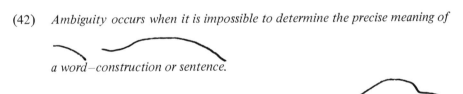

(42)   *Ambiguity occurs when it is impossible to determine the precise meaning of*

a word—construction or sentence.

(43)   *You think you understand and then later on you find you don't understand*

—what he's talking about.

(44)   *I hope it won't take more than two hours, but it might take—more than two*

hours.

As with all errors, the frequency of contour errors rises under conditions of (emotional) stress; what else could account for (45), uttered by an otherwise well-rehearsed participant in a production of *The Importance of Being Earnest:*

(45)   ... *a character which, according to his own brother's assessment, is....*

Some such errors are not simple to explain; in (46), for instance, a fall-rise contour appropriate for a phrase or clause boundary has been applied to half of a nominal compound:

(46)   *Now the basic notion of a process–state model is this.*

In such cases one is reduced to suggesting the possibility of a blend with another sentence pattern.

Finally, sentence intonation can be a valuable tool in explaining other errors. In (47) the intonation contour applied is that appropriate for a yes–no question, such as "Do you talk on the telephone with your right ear?" (a mind-boggling concept in itself, that):

(47)   *Do you talk on the telephone with which ear?*

The contour therefore argues in favor of an explanation of this error in terms of a blend with such an alternative question rather than, for example, simply as a wh-question in which a necessary movement rule has not been applied.

4. Summary

At various stages in the production of a sentence, suprasegmental values are assigned to the elements making up the surface string. Slips can occur at each stage, and the independence of the different suprasegmental operations is attested to by the differing character of the errors at each stage. Word stress errors, in which the wrong syllable of a polysyllabic word is emphasized, show a curious regularity—the erroneous stress pattern is usually that borne by a morphological relative. This evidence is supportive of a model of the mental lexicon incorporating morphological decomposition and conjunct storage of morphologically related words. Phrase stress errors, on the other hand, appear to arise at a level more near the surface, and to exhibit either metathesis of stress features or the effects of an independent error in grammatical marking. Shifts or exchanges of words usually do not affect the sentence stress pattern if open class words are involved, but closed class words carry their stress levels with them. Errors of focus (primary sentence stress) assignment and of contrastive stress are, for semantic and pragmatic reasons, far less detectable than other stress errors, as also are errors of intonation contour; however, it cannot be concluded that these do not occur. Sentence stress and intonation can be important factors in deciding the correct interpretation of other errors; error collectors are encouraged to pay greater attention to the suprasegmental features of utterances.

Notes

1. Many words in English have more than one possible stress pattern; American English often prefers one pattern for a particular word, British English another. Thus it is common to hear persons whose speech is subject to more than one dialectal influence produce a word such as *research* with differing stress patterns in successive utterances. Such cases, in which alternative stress patterns for the same word might reasonably be supposed to be familiar to the speaker, have been excluded from the present body of data—for example, *supine* (from Fromkin, 1973), *spectators.*

2. T (for target) represents the speaker's intended utterance.

3. Those utterances in Section I (A) of Table 1 that were corrected before the complete word was spoken are given as they were produced; where no correction was produced before the complete word was uttered none is given, but this should not be taken to imply that such utterances were not corrected—many of them were. Eleven examples in Section I (A), 7 in I (B), and 3 examples in Section II are from Fromkin (1971; 1973; 1976).

4. There appears to be no tendency for the distractor to have a higher frequency of occurrence in English than the target. Of the 59 errors in Table 1, the frequency of 48 was compared in the Kučera and Francis (1967) word count with the frequency of their distractor(s) (the remaining 10 pairs either did not appear or had the same orthographic surface form as, for example, *progress*). In 21 cases, the target was of higher frequency, in 28 cases the distractor, a nonsignificant difference ($\chi^2 = 1.00, p > .3$).

5. The question of how far morphological decomposition should go will be begged pending the availability of a larger body of pertinent data. It seems reasonable to suppose, for instance, that such a word as *responsible,* which although related to and derived from *response* has a semantic specification that is considerably different, might be accorded its own lexical entry. Aronoff (1976) suggests that "the lexicon is arranged according to stems, and that for each stem there is a slot for each canonical meaning, where 'canonical' means derived by regular [word formation] rules" (p. 45). Those derivatives that were formed by irregular rules, however, would be listed separately. It is interesting to speculate that when a complete categorization of word formation rules into regular and irregular is available, the lexical stress error corpus might not show any errors that would reflect a confusion between pairs or sets of words one of which was formed by an irregular rule.

6. Cutler (1976) found that sentence comprehension included tracking the suprasegmental contour to enable the direction of particular attention to the locations of stressed syllables, and suggested that this was compatible with lexical storage of words by stressed syllable. Subsequent research, however (Cutler and Fodor, 1979), has indicated that this result more probably reflects a search for the semantically more central portions of the sentence. Moreover, although in a lexical decision task, access is facilitated by prior presentation of a semantically related word (Meyer and Schvaneveldt, 1971), an unpublished study by David Swinney and myself shows that prior presentation of a word with the same stressed syllable in an auditory word comprehension task does not facilitate access. Lexical stress is probably not a necessary component of the information used for accessing a lexical entry.

References

Aronoff, M. 1976. *Word formation in generative grammar.* Cambridge, Massachusetts: MIT Press.

Boomer, D. S. & Laver, J. D. M. 1968. Slips of the tongue. *British Journal of Disorders of Communication, 3,* 2–12.

Cutler, A. 1976. Phoneme-monitoring reaction time as a function of preceding intonation contour. *Perception and Psychophysics, 20,* 55–60.

Cutler, A. & Fodor, J. A. 1979. Semantic focus and sentence comprehension. *Cognition, 7,* 49–59.

Fay, D. A. 1975. Some investigations of grammatical category in performance devices. Unpublished Ph.D. dissertation, Univ. of Texas at Austin.

Fay, D. A. & Cutler, A. 1977. Malapropisms and the structure of the mental lexicon. *Linguistic Inquiry, 8,* 505–520.

Fromkin, V. A. 1971. The non-anomalous nature of anomalous utterances. *Language, 47,* 27–52.

Fromkin, V. A. 1973. *Speech errors as linguistic evidence.* The Hague: Mouton.

Fromkin, V. A. 1976. Putting the emPHAsis on the wrong sylLABle. In L. Hyman (Ed.), *Studies in stress and accent.* Los Angeles: Univ. of Southern California. Pp. 15–26.

Garnes, S. & Bond, Z. S. 1975. Slips of the ear: Errors in perception of casual speech. In *Papers from the Eleventh Regional Meeting, Chicago Linguistic Society.*

Garrett, M. F. 1975. The analysis of sentence production. In G. Bower (Ed.), *Psychology of learning and motivation* (Vol. 9). New York: Academic Press. Pp. 133–177.

Garrett, M. F. 1976. Syntactic processes in sentence production. In R. J. Wales & E. C. T. Walker (Eds.), *New approaches to language mechanisms.* Amsterdam: North-Holland Publ. Pp. 231–255.

Gibson, E. J. & Guinet, L. 1971. Perception of inflections in brief visual presentations of words. *Journal of Verbal Learning and Verbal Behavior, 10,* 182–189.

Kučera, H. & Francis, W. N. 1967. *Computational analysis of present-day American English.* Providence, Rhode Island: Brown Univ. Press.

MacKay, D. G. 1969. Forward and backward masking in motor systems. *Kybernetik, 2,* 57–64.

Meyer, D. E. & Schvaneveldt, R. W. 1971. Facilitation in recognising pairs of words: Evidence of a dependence between retrieval operations. *Journal of Experimental Psychology, 90,* 227–234.

Murrell, G. A. & Morton, J. 1974. Word recognition and morphemic structure. *Journal of Experimental Psychology, 102,* 963–968.

Nooteboom, S. G. 1969. The tongue slips into patterns. In A. G. Sciarone, A. J. van Essen, and A. A. van Raad (Eds.), Nomen Society, *Leyden studies in linguistics and phonetics.* The Hague: Mouton. Pp. 114–132.

Pike, K. L. 1945. *The intonation of American English.* Ann Arbor: Univ. of Michigan Press.

Snodgrass, J. G. & Jarvella, R. J. 1972. Some linguistic determinants of word classification times. *Psychonomic Science, 27,* 220–222.

Taft, M. & Forster, K. I. 1975. Lexical storage and retrieval of prefixed words. *Journal of Verbal Learning and Verbal Behavior, 14,* 638–647.

Taft, M. & Forster, K. I. 1976. Lexical storage and retrieval of polymorphemic and polysyllabic words. *Journal of Verbal Learning and Verbal Behavior, 15,* 607–620.

Chapter 5

SLIPS OF THE TONGUE IN NORMAL
AND PATHOLOGICAL SPEECH

Ewa Söderpalm Talo

Department of Phonetics
University of Lund
Lund, Sweden

Since 1901, when Sigmund Freud published his *Psychopathology of Everyday Life* and suggested that slips of the tongue might tell us something about the "probable laws of the formation of speech," so-called spoonerisms have been the concern of many linguists in different countries. Spoonerisms have been collected for various reasons. Apart from the amusement they bring to their collectors, spoonerisms are analyzed by linguists who want to evaluate theories of language and learn more about the organization of language in the brain and the generation of utterances.

In the literature on slips of the tongue, there are numerous references to pathological speech pointing out the similarities between normal and pathological errors (Fromkin, 1971; Lashley, 1951; Linell, 1974). However, to my knowledge no research reported has been carried out specifically for systematic comparisons between slips of the tongue in normal speech and speech errors in aphasia. The purpose of the present chapter is to present a study now in progress comparing speech errors in normal and pathological (aphasic) speech in Swedish.

1. Definitions

A slip of the tongue is a deviation from what the speaker had in mind to say (Boomer and Laver, 1968). Somewhere along the generation of the utterance, a mistake is made, and the result is a lapse much to the surprise of the listener and the speaker himself. A slip of the tongue is not a mispronunciation due to faulty movements of the articulators (slurring), and it is not a mispronunciation due to faulty word knowledge (Nooteboom, 1969).

In adults with brain damage, there may exist articulatory disturbances of various kinds. It is sometimes very difficult to differentiate between these disturbances, which often look rather similar on the surface in the speech output. A variety of factors are, however, used clinically to differentiate between dysarthria, apraxia of speech, and literal paraphasia. Dysarthria represents a neuromuscular defect in executing speech movements, mostly due to bilateral cortical or subcortical damage. The speech organs may be paralyzed or weak and fail to produce a smooth speech output. The dysarthric patient knows what he wants to say and how to program the act, but he fails in the final stage of the motor program, and the result is slurred speech with poorly coordinated and imprecise articulatory movements. Dysarthric errors are fairly constant and predictable. The writing is unaffected. Dysarthric errors are not the concern of the present study.

Apraxia of speech is caused by unilateral cortical damage. The patient has difficulties in initiating speech, in making articulatory gestures voluntarily, although no muscular paralysis or weakness is present. The speech becomes laborious and the number of errors increase the more complex the articulatory gestures are. Writing is not affected.

Literal paraphasia is caused by unilateral damage in the cortex. There is a linguistic disorganization, resulting in errors in the choice and temporal ordering of the phonemes. The speech is often quite fluent but with frequent phonemic substitutions. Similar substitutions may also appear in the patient's writing.

2. Sampling

As has been pointed out by many linguists (Fry, 1969; Hill, 1972), there are various kinds of difficulties in collecting speech errors. They occur in spontaneous speech; they are seldom recorded and can rarely be repeated. Many errors are probably unnoticed, because we know what the speaker intended to say and this is what we hear. Sometimes we hear an error, but as we tend to listen and interpret according to the phonological pattern of our own language we probably miss many more. Sometimes errors are noticed but not recorded since it is not always possible to make notes at the time when they occur.

The corpus of normal errors in this study consists of about 200 slips of the tongue. The speakers are adults. The errors were collected by myself and by some of my friends, most of whom are linguistically trained. Only errors in spontaneous speech are included. Some radio and television speech slips are included but only from free discussions and never from read material.

The pathological speech errors (about 100 examples) were collected in therapy sessions in free conversation with aphasic patients. Most of the errors were collected by myself. The patients are between 37 and 76 years of age. Most of them have suffered cerebral vascular accidents causing aphasia. In one of the patients, a tumor was the cause of the aphasia.

3. Classification

Phonological, lexical, and syntactic errors were collected from normal and aphasic speech. Only the phonological errors are discussed in this paper. They were analyzed by the classification system as shown in Table 1.

TABLE 1: *Classification of Speech Errors*

I SYNTAGMATIC ERRORS

    I:1 Metathesis of phoneme (morpheme, word)

    I:2 Anticipation
        I:2 a = addition
        I:2 o = omission
        I:2 s = substitution

    I:3 Duplication
        I:3 a = addition
        I:3 o = omission
        I:3 s = substitution

II PARADIGMATIC ERRORS

    Substitution of phoneme (morpheme, word)

As is shown in the table, the errors are divided into two groups: syntagmatic errors and paradigmatic errors. The syntagmatic errors may be further divided into three categories: metathesis, anticipation, and duplication. Anticipations and duplications may be additions (a), omissions (o), or substitutions (s). Paradigmatic errors are all substitutions.

It will be noted that the term "duplication" is used rather than "perseveration," although the latter term is more frequently used in the speech error literature (cf. Fromkin, 1971; 1973). This is because "perseveration" is used in aphasiology in a different sense. Thus, in order to avoid terminological ambiguity in a study dealing with both normal and pathological speech, "duplication" seems to be a better choice.

The following examples illustrate the different error types.

    I:1. Syntagmatic Metathesis Errors
        (a) kontamination → *kontanimation* 'contamination'
        (b) hemfalla till knark → *hemfalla till krank* 'start using drugs'

(c) Kanada vann → *Vanada kann* 'Canada won'
(d) piloten [pi'lu:ten] → *politen* [pu'li:ten] 'the pilot'

Examples (a–d) are all metathesis errors from the normal sample. While this kind of error is quite common in the normal sample, it is very rare among the pathological errors. Both consonants and vowels can be involved.

I:2 Syntagmatic Anticipation Errors
   (e) insiktslöshet → *inslikslöshet* (I:2 a) 'lack of knowledge'
   (f) den brittiske biträdande ministern → *bittiske biträdande...* (I:2 o) 'the British deputy minister'
   (g) hur många som är socialdemokrater är oklart → *... socialdemoklater...* (I:2 s) 'how many are social democrats is unclear'
   (h) tänka på det → *känka på det* (I:2 s) 'think of it'

In these anticipation errors, (e) is an addition of an *l* to produce the first *sl* cluster. This might be an anticipation of the whole *sl* cluster that occurs later in the word or simply the addition to the earlier *s*. In (f) I have analyzed the omission of the *r* in the first word as an anticipatory omission due to the second word. In the anticipatory substitution in (g) the *l* in the last word is substituted for the *r* in the earlier word. Or, again, one might instead say that the *kr* is replaced by the anticipated *kl*. Many errors are ambiguous as to analysis in this way. Example (h) is, however, clearly a simple anticipatory substitution of *k* for *t*. Example (h) is one of the rare examples of anticipation in the pathological sample.

I:3 Syntagmatic Duplication Errors
   (i) det tror jag är hiskeligt viktigt → *... hiskeligt visk* (I:3 a) 'I think that is very important'
   (j) hade redan samlats till upprop → *... uppror* (I:3 s) 'had already come together for a meeting—for a riot'
   (k) det är så dyrt med julklappar → *... dulklappar* (I:3 s) 'Christmas presents are so expensive.'

These reveal duplication errors. Example (i) is a rather common addition, in that an *s* is added to form the *sk* cluster twice, and there seems to be a strong tendency to repeat *s* clusters. Such errors are frequent in the normal sample. Example (j) can be simply a duplication of the earlier *r* (perhaps a dissimilation because of the earlier *pp*?). It may also be an example of a "Freudian slip." The error was made by a television reporter after the three nonsocialist parties in Sweden had won the election. The leaders had come together to discuss the forming of a cabinet and many people expected serious difficulties. Example (k) is a substitution from the pathological sample.

II. Paradigmatic Substitution Errors
   (l) du passar bra in den frisyren → *... frisuren* 'that hair style suits you'
   (m) nu ljuger jag → *nu ljuter jag* 'now I lie'

Example (m) is from the pathological sample and represents the most common type of error in the pathological corpus.

As already mentioned above, very often an alternative analysis to the one I have suggested is possible. Should errors in voicing be analyzed as phoneme or feature errors, for example? Sometimes when only one phoneme is substituted, the output is a different but real word than the intended word. Is this then a phonological error or a word substitution error?

4. Conclusions

From the data analyzed so far, some tentative conclusions may be drawn. Although all kinds of errors occur in both the normal and the pathological corpus, there is a clear difference between the error types in the two groups, in a quantitative sense.

One problem is that the total number of utterances from which the pathological sample is drawn is much smaller than the number of normal utterances. While we expect the occurrence of speech errors by definition to be much bigger in aphasic speech, the error types seem to be fewer.

Syntagmatic errors are more common in the normal corpus, while paradigmatic errors prevail in the pathological material. Over 60 of all the errors in the pathological corpus can be analyzed as paradigmatic substitution errors. That is, the errors seem to be caused by factors other than the influence of surrounding (either already produced or later context) phonemic material. This must be compared to the normal corpus in which less than 20% were paradigmatic substitutions.

Temporal ordering of units seems to be a difficulty in the normal population, whereas the errors in the pathological sample reflect difficulty in choosing the correct unit or segment from the linguistic paradigm.

Another difference between the normal and the aphasic speakers that I found in my study relates to the speakers' awareness of their own errors. Normal speakers often either correct the lapse or by pausing indicate that they noticed it (see Nooteboom, this volume). Aphasic speakers seldom correct their errors. While there may be alternative reasons for this, one plausible reason is that the errors have been unnoticed by the speakers. I have checked this with aphasic speakers who have been explicitly asked to indicate every mistake they make. Very often, errors pass unnoticed. It is possible that the awareness of errors increases during language rehabilitation. If this is found to be so, upon further investigation, this could be used as an indication of therapeutic progress.

It is hoped that an increased knowledge of differences and similarities between speech errors made by normals and by aphasics will improve diagnostic and therapeutic work with language-disordered patients in the future.

References

Blumstein, S. 1973. A phonological investigation of aphasic speech. (Janua linguarum, 153). The Hague: Mouton.

Boomer, D. & Laver, J. (1968) 1973. Slips of the tongue. Reprinted in V. Fromkin (Ed.), *Speech errors as linguistic evidence*. (Janua linguarum, 77). The Hague: Mouton. Pp. 120–131.

Canter, G. 1973 Dysarthria, apraxia of speech, and literal paraphasia. Three distinct varieties of articulatory behavior in the adult with brain damage. Unpublished paper presented at the American Speech and Hearing Association convention, October 1973.

Freud, S. 1901. *Zur psychopathologie des alltaglebens*. Translated into English by Alan Tyson as *The psychopathology of everyday life*. New York: Norton, 1960.

Fromkin, V. 1971. The non-anomalous nature of anomalous utterances. *Language, 47,* 27–51.

Fromkin, V. (Ed.) 1973. *Speech errors as linguistic evidence*. (Janua linguarum, 77). The Hague: Mouton.

Fry, D. B. (1969) 1973. The linguistic evidence of speech errors. In V. Fromkin (Ed.), *Speech errors as linguistic evidence*. (Janua linguarum, 77). The Hague: Mouton. Pp. 157–163.

Hill, A. (1972) 1973. A theory of speech errors. In V. Fromkin (Ed.), *Speech errors as linguistic evidence*. (Janua linguarum, 77). The Hague: Mouton. Pp. 205–214.

Lashley, K. 1951. The problem of serial order of behavior. In L. Jeffress (Ed.), *Cerebral mechanisms in behavior*. New York: Wiley. Pp. 112–136.

Lecours, A. R. & Lhermitte, F. 1969. Phonemic paraphasias, linguistic structures, and tentative hypotheses. *Cortex, 5,* 193–228.

Linell, P. 1974. Problems of psychological reality in generative phonology. Reports from Uppsala University, Department of Linguistics, 4.

Nooteboom, S. G. 1969. The tongue slips into patterns. In A. G. Sciarone, A. J. van Essen, and A. A. van Raad (Eds.), Nomen Society, *Leyden studies in linguistics and phonetics*. The Hague: Mouton. Pp. 114–132.

Weigl, E. & Bierwisch, M. 1970. Neuropsychology and linguistics: Topics of common research. *Foundations of Language, 6,* 1–18.

Chapter 6

SPEAKING AND UNSPEAKING: DETECTION AND CORRECTION OF PHONOLOGICAL AND LEXICAL ERRORS IN SPONTANEOUS SPEECH

Sieb G. Nooteboom

Instituut Voor Perceptie Onderzoek
Eindhoven, The Netherlands

Department of Linguistics
Leyden University
Leyden, The Netherlands

> *... wir können in einen Sprechmechanismus*
> *hineinblicken der uns ohne das Versprechen*
> *volkommen geheimnisvoll geblieben wäre.*
>
> Meringer (1908)

Introduction

It is difficult, although perhaps not impossible, to design laboratory experiments capable of revealing the "mechanisms of the mind" that control spontaneous speech production.

This may at least partly explain the growing interest displayed by phoneticians, linguists, and psychologists in slips of the tongue, their own and others', which are really slips of the mind, betraying aspects of the mental control of speaking. Some recent attempts by psychologists to model the mental control structures for sentence generation make extensive use of such errors of speech as primary data (Garrett, 1975; Kempen, 1977).

Errors of speech are not only made, but are often also detected and corrected by the speaker, as in the following example taken from Fromkin (1973):

the firing of—uh—the hiring of minority faculty

As observed by Hockett (1967), the detection and correction ("editing") may either be covert, during the planning stages and before the speech is actually produced, or overt, after it has been produced. Laver (1969) distinguishes between a Planner, responsible for Hockett's covert editing, and a Monitor, dealing with the overt editing, driven by sensory, primarily auditory information on the speech already produced.

The covert detection and correction of errors in inner speech is hard to study empirically by means other than introspection. In contrast, the behavioral results of overt detection and correction of errors are there for us to observe and analyze. In this paper I will present the results of a first exploratory analysis of a number of corrections of errors of speech in part of the data published by Meringer (1908). The analysis was guided by four questions, which I thought to be sufficiently precise to be answerable and sufficiently broad to leave my mind open to unexpected observations. The questions are

1. How many speech errors made are corrected by the speaker?
2. At what point in the utterance does a speaker, after having made and detected an error, stop to make a new start for correction?
3. How far in the utterance does a speaker go back for a new start?
4. Are the answers to the above questions different for phonological and lexical errors?

From the results of this analysis, I will attempt to infer some properties of the mental control of speaking.

2. The Corpus

Meringer's collection of speech errors seems especially suited to answer the preceding questions, not only because it is "far superior to all other collections" by MacKay's criteria of extensiveness, context, validity, accuracy, documentation, and nonselective report (MacKay, 1970), but also because Meringer with very few exceptions included the corrections, if present, in his description of the speech errors.

My analysis was restricted to data from Meringer (1908) because at the time I had occasion to work on this I had no access to Meringer and Mayer (1895). I further limited the analysis to errors of selection of words and morphemes (*Mitklänge, schwebende Wortbilder, Nachklänge aus der Rede des anderen*), transpositions (*Vertauschungen*), anticipations (*Vorklänge*), and perseverations (*Nachklänge aus der eignen Rede*) of words, morphemes, phonemes, and phoneme clusters, as contained on pages 1–63 of Meringer's book. These classes of errors lend themselves to a clear bipartition into errors against whole words or morphemes (lexical errors) and errors against the phonological form of words or morphemes (phonological errors). I excluded a number of cases in which Meringer's classification of individual errors did not agree with my own. There remained 648 errors, 415 of which were corrected.

3. Percentages of Errors Corrected

Table 1 gives for seven classes of errors of speech the percentages of errors that, according to Meringer's description, were corrected by the speaker. I will assume that Meringer's unswerving attention to the collection of speech errors has not produced too much of a bias in favor of uncorrected or (more likely) corrected errors, or at least that the bias is similar for the different classes of errors.

TABLE 1. *Percentages of Corrections in Seven Classes of Errors of Speech*

	Selection	Anticipation	Perseveration	Transposition
Lexical errors	(n = 158) 59%	(n = 60) 80%	(n = 20) 55%	(n = 43) 18%
Phonological errors		(n = 224) 90%	(n = 101) 66%	(n = 42) 14%

The low percentages of corrected transpositions are easy to explain. If a transposition like *heft lemisphere* (Fromkin, 1973) is corrected immediately after the first phonemic error before the second error is made, it will automatically be classed as anticipation. Meringer includes such cases in his class of *Vertauschungen* only when the speaker (himself, or someone whose judgment he trusted) knew by introspection he was going to make a transposition: "Halt den Mund," said Frau Meringer, and then observed she had wanted to say, "Halt den Mund vor die Hand" instead of, "Halt die Hand vor den Mund."

The classification of corrected first halves of transpositions as anticipations may perhaps have contributed to the high percentage of corrected anticipations (and, for that matter, to the high percentage of anticipations in general, as compared to transpositions and perseverations). An additional or alternative explanation of the high percentage of corrected anticipations may be that the reoccurrence of the intruding segment, either in the inner speech or in the overt speech, increases the chance of error detection.

It is of interest that phonological errors are corrected at least as often as lexical errors. If possible harm to communication were the main criterion for correction, one would expect lexical errors to be corrected far more often than phonological errors. If, on the other hand, possible harm to linguistic orthodoxy were the main criterion, one would expect that phonological errors, which often lead to nonwords, would be corrected more often. If there is a difference it is rather in favor of the second possibility, but apparently the mental strategy (Laver's Monitor) dealing with the detection and correction of overt speech errors strives both for successful communication and linguistic orthodoxy.

At this point it should be made clear that although correction of speech errors by the speaker logically implies the detection of these errors by some control mechanism, this does not mean that the speaker is necessarily aware of either having made an error or correcting it. In many cases, errors and their corrections escape the conscious attention of both speakers and listeners. Apparently the covert and overt editing of speech is handled by relatively low level mental strategies that, in normal conversation, may occasionally reach the level of awareness, but often remain below it.

4. The Material Span between Error and New Start

Consider the following case:

*die **Waschen** mit dem Waschl–Ah! die Löffeln mit dem Waschl*

The first phoneme that went wrong is the /w/ of *Waschen*. The speaker could have detected that it was wrong at the moment of its production, stopped and made a new start, as in the following case:

im S(ommer)–im Winter

In the first case, however, the speaker goes on for five syllables or four words. It is difficult to establish whether the speaker has detected the error only at the moment he stops, or has detected it much earlier but nevertheless runs off some preprogramed unit before stopping and making a new start. If the moment of stopping is determined by a latency in detection only, one would expect a speaker to stop anywhere in the utterance without regard for the completeness of the unit in the process of being executed. If, on the other hand, the moment of stopping is determined by a desire to complete the programing unit under execution, one would expect the moments of stopping to coincide with, for example, word or phrase boundaries.

To see how long a speaker generally goes on speaking after an error before making a new start, I made frequency distributions of both the number of syllables and the number of words elapsing between the first phoneme that went wrong and the stop for a new start, for lexical and phonological errors separately (Figure 1). The zero columns stand for the cases where the syllable or word in which the error occurs is not completed:

syllable: *im S–im Winter*
word: ***be**–entsprechen Bezeichnungen*

It is of interest that, although a speaker sometimes stops before the word, or sometimes even before the syllable against which the error is made is completed, he never stops in the middle of another word. Thus, once he reaches the first word boundary after the error he will always stop at a word boundary. From Figure 1 it may be seen that a lexical error is corrected before the first word boundary in only about 10% of the corrections, a phonological error in somewhat less than 30% of the corrections. In all other cases, the stop for a new start is made at a word boundary, predominantly the first word boundary. This suggests that the moment of

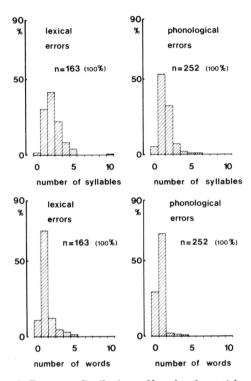

Figure 1: *Frequency distributions of lengths of material spans elapsing between the first wrong phoneme in a speech error and the stop for a new start. The zero column counts the cases in which the syllable or word containing the first wrong phoneme is not completed.*

stopping for a new start is not simply determined by the moment of error detection, but is generally also determined by an inhibition to discontinue the production of a word. This inhibition is apparently stronger for real, albeit wrongly selected, words than for nonwords resulting from phonological speech errors. The importance of the word as a programing unit of speech production is emphasized by the great majority of corrections made immediately after the first word is completed, in both lexical and phonological errors. Continuation after the first word is rare for phonological errors (about 10%), and less rare for lexical errors (about 20%). This is what one would expect, assuming that phonological errors are detected in a first check of the linguistic orthodoxy of the phonological form and that lexical errors are detected in a further check of the syntactic and semantic appropriateness of the phrase. The phrase length involved does not generally exceed five syllables and never exceeds five words. This may either mean that the chance of detection has decreased to zero after five words, or, if we assume that not all detected errors are also corrected, that the urge to correct has vanished after five words.

5. The Material Span Cancelled by the Correction

Someone said,

Ich will deine pflegmatische Nercheln–Nerven aufstacheln.

The first wrong phoneme is in the second syllable of *Nercheln*, the first syllable being correct. Yet the speaker includes the correct syllable *Ner-* in his correction, thus canceling the whole wrong word *Nercheln.* In the following case,

Das Wirtheis–haus heisst

only the second syllable is canceled. Such cases, in which a new start is made in the middle of a word, are extremely rare (less than 3% of all corrections), and even in those cases, the new start is always made at the beginning of a root morpheme that could also occur on its own as a content word.

In the great majority of cases (97%), the correction starts with the beginning of a word. This is not necessarily the word against which the error is made. It may also be an earlier word, as in the following example:

*Der Unterschied zwischen Typhus und **diagnostischen Scharfsinn** erfordert– zwischen Typhus und Tuberkulose erfordert diagnostischen Scharfsinn.*

Here the correction repeats three words that were never wrong, and the language material canceled by the correction comprises 15 syllables or six words. Figure 2 shows the frequency distributions of such material spans. It may be seen that here the material spans in lexical and phonological errors differ somewhat more than in Figure 1. The cause of this difference is brought out more clearly in Figure 3, pre- senting the frequency distributions of the number of syllables or words preceding the word in which the error is made but included in the correction. The zero col- umns stand for the cases in which the correction starts with the word against which the error was made. This is nearly always the case in corrections of phonological errors. Corrections of lexical errors quite often (42%) go further back in the utter- ance. Typical examples are the following:

*mit dem **Gitter**–mit dem Gesicht in dem Gitter für*
*die **Kellner** da–für die Gäste*
*wenn **mich**–wenn mann mich damals gefragt hätte so*
*verkehrt **er**–so verfügt er*
*auf **beschränkte**–auf geladene*
*nicht für zu **wenig**–für zu viel*

This difference in the structure of corrections of phonological and lexical errors suggests that the linguistic domain within which detection and correction of errors takes place is different for the two classes of errors. To explain this difference we have to assume that the mental strategy taking care of the detection and correction of overt speech errors differentiates between lexical and phonological errors. If the

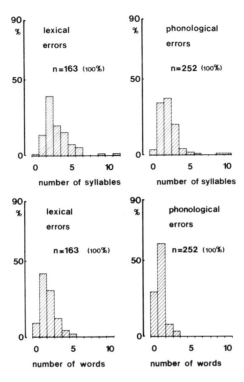

Figure 2: *Frequency distributions of lengths of material spans already spoken, but canceled by the correction. The zero column counts the cases in which the correction starts with a syllable or word that was not completed before. Cases in which correction does not start at a word boundary (less than 3% of all corrections) are excluded.*

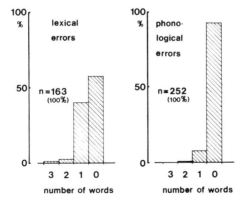

Figure 3: *Frequency distributions of the number of words preceding the word in which the error was made, but included in the correction.*

error is classed as phonological, there is no reason to go further back in the utterance, as the linguistic domain of phonological form is the word. If, however, the error is lexical, this might have induced changes in other parts of the phrase as in the following word selection error:

ein Monat—eine Woche

Note, however, that columns 1, 2, and 3 in Figure 3 concern only words that were not changed under the influence of the wrongly selected word (column 0). Apparently the speaker often prefers not to take chances, and would rather repeat the whole relevant phrase than to perform an extra check on the syntactic and semantic appropriateness of the phrase after insertion of the correct lexical item. In this way he betrays that, for example, combinations of articles and/or prepositions and nouns and combinations of adverbs and adjectives or verbs are operationally functioning as the domains of lexical insertion in the detection and correction of speech errors.

6. Discussion

Let me repeat, in summary form, the answers to the questions that guided our analysis of the corpus.

1. Sixty-four percent of all speech errors in the corpus are corrected. Anticipations are more often corrected than other speech errors. Phonological speech errors are slightly more often corrected than lexical errors.

2. Stops for a new start are predominantly made at the first word boundary after the error. Continuation after this first word boundary and before stopping always implies that the stop will be at another word boundary. Such continuation is less rare for lexical errors (20%) than for phonological errors (10%).

3. In corrections of phonological errors a new start is made practically always (93%) at the last word boundary preceding the error. In corrections of lexical errors, a new start is made relatively often (42%) at an earlier word boundary in the phrase, thus including in the corrections one or more words that were never wrong. These words always form a syntactically coherent phrase with the wrongly selected word.

To explain these data I envisage a mental strategy constantly monitoring the output speech, separately checking the phonological orthodoxy of words and the syntactic and semantic appropriateness of phrases. I assume this strategy to be fallible, thus accounting for the occurrence of noncorrected errors. If an error is detected, the timing of the command to stop speaking is determined by two competing forces, one stemming from the urge to correct the error immediately and the other from the urge to complete the word in the process of being spoken. If detection occurs before the first word boundary after the error, the first force may occasionally override the second. If detection is later, the second force always overrides the first, thus ensuring that no stop will be made in the middle of a word. The chance of detection has become zero after about five words. When an error is discovered while checking the phonological orthodoxy of word forms, the command to stop speaking will be followed by a command to go back to the word that went wrong, to correct its phonological form, and to start speaking again with that word. When a lexical error is detected while checking the syntactic and semantic appropriateness of the phrase, the command to stop will be followed either by a command to delete the wrongly selected word, to fill in the correct one and to restart the original program with the new word, or, in nearly half of the cases, to delete the phrase the wrongly selected word belonged to, make a new phrase, and start speaking this phrase. Phrases operationally functioning as domains of lexical insertion in the detection and correction of speech errors are generally of the most elementary kinds, such as combinations of articles and substantives, prepositional phrases, and adverbial phrases. The length of these phrases is limited to about five words, and is often less.

A more thorough analysis of the same and other data on the detection and correction of speech errors may further confirm, or dispute, the present conclusions and further refine our ideas on the mental control structure of the overt and covert editing of speech, and of speech production in general. It may also be worth comparing such data with data on the detection of errors in auditorily presented speech, as provided by Cole (1973) and Marslen-Wilson and Welsh (1977). If the structure in the two sets of data is sufficiently similar, one might propose the interesting possibility of studying properties of the mental control structure of speech production in a perceptual task. This would enable us to test hypotheses stemming from the observation of spontaneous speech production in well-controlled laboratory experiments.

References

Cole, R. A. 1973. Listening for mispronunciations: A measure of what we hear during speech. *Perception & Psychophysics, 13,* 153–156.

Fromkin, V. A. 1973. A sample of speech errors. In V. A. Fromkin (Ed.), *Speech errors as linguistic evidence.* The Hague: Mouton. Pp. 233–269.

Garrett, F. 1975. The analysis of sentence production. In G. Bower (Ed.), *The psychology of learning and motivation* (Vol. 9). New York: Academic Press. Pp. 133–177.

Hockett, C. F. 1967. Where the tongue slips, there slip I. In *To honor Roman Jakobson* (Vol. 2). (Janua linguarum, 32). The Hague: Mouton. Pp. 910–936.

Kempen, G. 1977. Man's sentence generator: Aspects of its control structure. Paper presented at the international colloquium "The Cognitive Viewpoint," Ghent, March 1977.

Laver, J. D. M. 1969. The detection and correction of slips of the tongue. Work in Progress 3, Department of Phonetics and Linguistics, University of Edinburgh.

MacKay, D. G. 1970. Spoonerisms: The structure of errors in the serial order of speech. *Neuropsychologia, 8,* 323–350.

Marslen-Wilson, W. D. & Welsh, A. 1978. Processing interactions and lexical access during word recognition in continuous speech. *Cognitive Psychology, 10,* 29–63.

Meringer, R. 1908. *Ausdem Leben der Sprache.* Berlin: V. Behr's Verlag.

Meringer, R. & Mayer, K. 1895. *Versprechen und Verlesen: Eine psychologisch-linguistische Studie.* Stuttgart: Göschensche Verlagsbuchhandlung.

Chapter 7

SEMANTIC SIMILARITY AS A FACTOR IN WHOLE-WORD SLIPS OF THE TONGUE

W. H. N. Hotopf

Department of Psychology
London School of Economics
London, England

As a psychologist interested in the mechanism of intentional behavior, I have been collecting slips of the tongue and of the pen for over 18 years. Much of this has been sporadic, but over shorter periods of time I have collected slips systematically in order to determine the frequency distribution of different categories of slip. My strategy in this was first to note every slip of the pen and every whole-word slip of the tongue I made myself over periods of 9 months and 1 year, respectively. This yielded 111 slips of the former and 96 of the latter. In order to check on the representativeness of my own examples, I then collected on a systematic basis every slip of the pen made by 24 students in a writing task. This, which I will call the Writing sample, yielded 413 slips of the pen of all kinds. As for whole-word slips of the tongue, insofar as circumstances made it possible, I recorded every slip that I noticed made by others over a 2-year period. This, the Daily Life sample, yielded 244 slips made by 111 different speakers. Up to then I had refrained from looking at the only collection of slips I had heard of at that time (1968), namely, that of Meringer. In order now, among other reasons, to test the reliability of this method of data collection (observation under everyday conditions), I turned to Meringer's two corpora (Meringer and Mayer, 1895; Meringer, 1908) and counted the frequency of his different categories of slips so as to compare them with mine. The agreement as to categories was extremely good. As to frequency distribution, there were some discrepancies, the interpretation of which has been rendered more difficult by the belated discovery that Meringer's published corpora of slips do not represent the complete sample of his total collection (Meringer and Mayer, 1895:v). Finally, I noted slips of the tongue made by 8 speakers who gave talks that had been tape recorded at a psychological conference. This, the Conference sample, yielded a further 125 whole-word slips of the tongue. It is not my purpose in this chapter to discuss the different categories of slips and their frequency distribution, but it is worth remarking that comparison of my own slips with those of others suggests individual differences in different speakers; and comparison of slips of the pen with slips of the tongue, and of the latter occurring in daily speech or when struggling to express complex ideas to a large audience, suggests that frequency of the different categories depends on the speech situations being studied. Furthermore, the proportion of slips of the tongue in the 3 collections of the speech of others that received a multiple classification ranged between 13% and 26%. This refers only to whole-word categories of slips, whether errors of order, such as anticipation, perseveration, or transposition, or of phonological or semantic similarity. These multiple-classification slips were practically all cases of dual categorization, although there were a few where a slip could be categorized under three different headings.

The discipline of experimental psychology tends not to favor data collected under uncontrolled conditions in the circumstances of everyday life. It was therefore encouraging to find such a degree of regularity as regards the different categories, if not their relative frequency of occurrence, into which over 97% of the slips could be placed. The next question was, would further regularities be found within these regularities, so as to increase one's confidence in the possible significance of what one is discovering? Tied up with this is the question as to whether the surface similarities upon which categorization is based conceal some significant differences. I wish to report this in the case of what I call "semantic group slips."

I understand semantic group slips to be ones where there is a close semantic similarity between error and target word. This category was the largest one among my own slips and in my Daily Life sample, constituting 34.6% of the former and 27.9% of the latter. It was the second largest in the Meringer sample, comprising 15.3% of the total. That it was not larger was due to the fact that Meringer did not notice the frequency of this type of slip until after the publication of *Versprechen und Verlesen*.[1] In the Conference sample, where errors of order were much more frequent than in the other collections, it formed, however, only 13.1% of the sample.

Excluding my own slips, there were in all 224 semantic group slips. Since in this, unlike the other categories, I was unable to discover a formal criterion, I shall have to describe them in an enumerative fashion. Of these slips 31.25% were ones in which error and target words stood in, to use Lyon's (1968) terms, complementary, antonymous, or converse relationships to one another. Examples are *early* for *late*, *unmassgebend* 'not standard' for *massgebend* 'standard,' and *husband* for *wife*. Co-hyponyms[2] of one another, such as color words (*red* for *black*), time words (*hour* for *week*), meal words (*breakfast* for *lunch*), words for parts of the body (*foot* for *finger*), greeting terms (*good evening* for *good morning*), names of months, of countries, and so on, comprised 44.6%. Another 24.2% stood in approximately hyponymous relation to one another, that is, they were dominated by a more distant and general superordinate so that error and target word were semantic cousins, as it were, rather than siblings. Examples of these are time words like *Saturday* for *January*, geographical terms like *Europe* for *Britain*, food words like *bacon* for *chicken*, relationship words like *uncle* for *husband*, instruments for measuring, as in Meringer's *Sieh auf's Thermometer wie viel Uhr es ist* 'Look at the thermometer and tell me what the time is,' and so on.

Before proceeding further, a few points should be made concerning the relationship between error and target words in semantic group slips. First, it is not the case that a particular semantic group is entirely determined by the sentential context in which the word occurs. Another word other than the error word, less closely related semantically to the target word, could in all cases have been substituted to produce a meaningful sentence. Second, if we conceive of a word being chosen by proceeding up a semantic tree and think some fault occurs in that process, it is odd that the error word should never[3] stand in a subordinate or superordinate relationship to the target word. One might have thought that this semantic search process would occasionally have got its levels wrong. Third, the relation between error and target word is always a contrastive one. There were no cases of the error word being a synonym of the target word, though synonyms do, as we shall see, play a part in slips.

So far I have only dealt with semantic group slips among slips of the tongue. What about slips of the pen? The evidence from whole-word slips of the pen is that the input to writing is the same as that to speech. About one-fifth of the whole-word slips of the pen in the Writing sample were cases of phonological similarity. As with slips of the tongue, there were also many cases of order errors of anticipation and perseveration. The incidence of slips is greater than in speech, and there is more evidence of disintegration of performance as shown, for example, in much more frequent cases of changes in form class between error and target word. With semantic group errors, however, the situation was different. There were only 10 of them in my Writing sample comprising no more than 3.7% of the sample, and all of them were multiply classified. It could therefore have been an accident that they took the form of semantic group slips at all. Similarly, there was only one semantic group slip among my own systematically collected slips of the pen.

What could this large and regular difference between the two word-production situations be due to? One possibility is that it is the amount of time required to find the right word. Obviously, much less is available when speaking than when writing because of the relative slowness of the latter activity[4] and the fact that it is much more self-paced. There are not, in the writing situation, the social pressures to get on with what one is saying that occurs with speech. Note, however, that this argument cannot be applied to errors of phonological similarity. These are, in general, as common in writing as they are in speech. Any model of speech production will have to take into account this difference between the two types of slip.

Now the time taken to produce a word immediately suggests Goldman-Eisler's (1958) theory concerning hesitation in speech. Is there any evidence that the error word in semantic group slips is a more frequently employed one and therefore one readier of access than the target word? To test this, I took a sample of 80 pairs of words from my Daily Life collection. These were words whose frequencies were given in the Thorndike-Lorge *Teacher's Word Book* and were not likely to be strongly atypical in frequency in comparison with my speaker population. In comparing these pairs of words for relative frequency, a slight but not statistically significant tendency for error words to be more frequent than target words was found: 45 being more common and 35 less common. As for the Meringer sample, taking 96 pairs of words for which word frequency norms were available in Meier's *Deutsche Sprachstatistik* (1964),[5] these were exactly divided between cases where the error word was more frequent and those where it was less frequent than the target word.

There can, however, be little doubt that in certain situations, a more frequent word is more likely to be spoken than a less frequent one. This can be seen in slips involving proper names of people. There were many cases in my collection of slips where a person in a particular role relationship to the speaker was called by the name of the previous occupant of that role, for example, addressing a new secretary or au pair girl by the name of the previous secretary or au pair girl, despite the intention to call her by her proper name. This also occurs in calling someone else's dog by the name of one's own dog, or calling a newly acquired dog by the name of some other dog one is more familiar with. These slips are like semantic group slips in that it is as though the newcomer were classified as being of a particular restricted class (like a semantic group) and then called by the name of another member of that class.

There is, however, another personal proper name slip that occurs widely. This is that of addressing or referring to a member of a group, which one frequently encounters, such as a family group, and saying instead of the intended name the name of another member of the group. Sometimes, indeed, one may run through a whole set of names until one gets the right one. Meringer also refers to this in *Aus dem Leben der Sprache,* and gives a number of instances of mixing up the names in his family group, calling his wife by the name of his dog, or being called by her by the name of their maid. I believe more restricted groupings than these may operate, having several instances of relations such as grandmothers or aunts saying the wrong name of members of sibling groups when referring to them in their absence. This may also be observed with the names of colleagues in small university departments. The numbers of these instances, however, fall short of what would be required for statistical tests to be considered. But what these cases do suggest is that when names in these ad hoc groups are of high and approximately equal frequency, then they are more likely to be confused with one another. It is as though constant and equally frequent use of the names in similar situations and similar verbal contexts has caused them to lose some of their distinctiveness. Could this also be the case with semantic group slips? To test this, the log frequencies[6] of error and target word in my 160 English word samples and 192 German word samples were compared. They yielded product moment correlations, respectively, of .543 (df = 78, $p < .005$, 1 tailed) and .64 (df = 46, $p < .001$, 1 tailed), showing that error and target words do tend to be of equal frequency, a finding that is consistent with Oldfield's (1966) theory that, in naming, the first choice in the search procedure is of a word-frequency class.

Now what this suggests is that semantic groups may, from the point of view of slips, be much narrower than linguistic considerations alone would suggest, being limited to words of approximately equal frequency within a particular speaker's vocabulary. For example, the semantic group of names of towns is obviously a huge class, but when we look at actual slips that Meringer reports, like *Wien* 'Vienna' for *Budapest,* or *München* 'Munich' for *Innsbruck,* or from the Daily Life sample, *Johannesburg* for *Capetown,* we can see that the actual group is likely to be much more limited than its description suggests. Similarly, we have closely related nationality nouns or adjectives, like *Japaner* for *Chinesen,* or *Czechisch* for *Magyarisch,* or animal words like *lion* for *tiger.* Other factors may assist the semantic group slip as in *Bucharest* for *Budapest,* which is clearly also a slip of phonological similarity. Again, associative factors, Freudian or otherwise, may facilitate a semantic group slip. Out of the five parts of the body slips that had eight different parts of the body as error or target word, the following is a good example. The speaker was concentrating on her argument, as she picked her way carefully in a very muddy lane, and said *I can't quite put my foot on it,* meaning of course *finger.* Family relationship slips also suggest these associative factors, particularly when the person referred to stands in a different relation to the speaker than to the listener. To give one out of a number of examples, a mother talking to her son referred to her daughter thus, *Some people are excellent liars. Your daughter* [X], *for example,* meaning *sister.* If my theory concerning similar frequency of error and target words in these kinds of slips is correct, factors of this kind will, of course, attenuate the correlation.

Another feature of semantic group slips to consider is their relation to syntactic form class. I have counted the distribution of these slips in the four major content form classes of verbs, nouns, adjectives, and adverbs. This is shown in Tables 1 and 2 for the English and German samples. There were rather few adverbs so I have included them with adjectives since they behaved in a similar fashion.

What is immediately striking about the tables is the relative rarity of verbs. These form only 3% of semantic group slips in the English sample and 8.9% in the German one, which it will be remembered, in contrast with the English sample, was a selected one. Ideally, one would like to compare their frequency of occurrence with that obtaining within general usage of the language. I have not, however, been able to find any statistics on this in German. The only possible source I know of, Meier's *Deutsche Sprachstatistik* (1964), does not give this information. As for English, I have only some unpublished data, sent me by the late Dr. Herdan, based on a count he carried out in certain English novels.[7] Adjusting his figure for comparability with mine shows that verbs formed 32.7% of the three form classes (verbs, nouns, and adjectives) that he distinguished. In order to be able to make comparisons for German as well, I counted for both language samples the frequencies in the different form classes of all other slips except blends and personal proper names for compari-

TABLE 1. *Distribution of Major Syntactic Form Classes among Semantic Group and Other Types of Slips in the English Samples*

	Semantic group slips		Other types of slip	
	Number	Percent	Number	Percent
Verbs	3	3.0	37	29.6
Nouns	81	80.2	80	64.0
Adjectives and Adverbs	17	16.8	8	6.4
Total	101		125	

TABLE 2. *Distribution of Major Syntactic Form Classes among Semantic Group and Other Types of Slips in the Meringer Sample*

	Semantic group slips		Other types of slip	
	Number	Percent	Number	Percent
Verbs	11	8.9	121	33.6
Nouns	58	47.2	212	58.9
Adjectives and Adverbs	54	43.9	27	7.5
Total	123		360	

TABLE 3. *Distribution of Major Syntactic Form Classes among Different Types of Semantic Group Slips in Combined Samples*

	Opposition slips		Hyponym slips	
	Number	Percent	Number	Percent
Verbs	6	8.6	8	5.2
Nouns	17	24.3	122	79.2
Adjectives and Adverbs	47	67.1	24	15.6
Total	70		154	

son with semantic group slips. These are also given in Tables 1 and 2,[8] and show not only that verbs are relatively rare among semantic group slips but that adjectives and adverbs[9] are much more common. The odds against these differences occurring by chance are very high and certainly statistically significant (for Table 1, $\chi^2 = 299.35$, df 2, $p < .001$; for Table 2, $\chi^2 = 95.11$, df 2, $p < .001$).

How should we account for these differences? One answer might be that in the process involved in realizing our intention to say a particular word, phrase, or clause by either saying it or by putting it in a buffer store in readiness for speech, more time may be allocated to selection of the verb and less to that of the adjective than is involved in selecting the noun. Could this be connected with verbs' greater morphological complexity and association with auxiliaries? If so, this might suggest that, on the average, more time must be spent in realizing verbs, making less time available for nouns or adjectives. But this would imply that in constructing a clause the verb would be considered first. This might agree with a case grammar approach, but would only apply to the abstract construction and not to lexical realization. An alternative suggestion is that the differences reflect the relative distribution of antonyms or hyponyms of high but equal frequencies in the different form classes.

Some evidence relating to this is provided by Table 3. This shows for both language samples combined[10] the numbers and proportions of words in the first and the other two subcategories of semantic group slips distinguished in the preceding discussion, that is to say, words standing in oppositional (i.e., converse, antonymous, or complementary) relationship to one another versus those standing in hyponymous relationship. Two-thirds of the first group are adjectives and adverbs, and nearly 80% of the second are nouns. The frequency of adjectives in the first group goes some way to explaining their much greater relative frequency among semantic group slips than among other slips.

Some light may be shed on this by considering the results of word association studies, so let us turn to these. Relations between stimulus words and associates in studies of free association differ in many ways from the relations between error and target word in slips of the tongue. The former yield many syntagmatic associations like *fish–swim, blue–sky, mother–love*,[11] and so on, whereas the latter never seem to do so.[12] Even where the association is not a syntagmatic one, the associate is far more frequently of a different form class from the stimulus word than the error is from the target word. Where they are both of the same form class and semantically similar to one another, they often cannot substitute for one another in many sentential contexts; this is rarely the case with slips. All this, of course, follows from the fact that if association operates in speech, then it would be constrained and not free association. The only area where there is strong similarity between slips of the tongue and free association norms is the one we have been discussing, namely, oppositional contrast. If we look at the Palermo–Jenkins free association norms for college students (Palermo and Jenkins, 1974), we find that where oppositional contrasts occur, and this is largely with adjectives, then such contrasts generally account for 50% or more of the association responses. In other words, the response frequency distribution curve is very steeply skewed. The same has also been found for German (Russell, 1970). Furthermore, Deese (1965) has shown that as far as adjectives are concerned, this relationship depends upon frequency of occurrence, there being a high correlation of .89 between log frequency of oppositional associates and log frequency of usage of the stimulus word. Since he also found that the frequency relationship between stimulus word and associate in cases of oppositional association was reciprocal, it follows that these pairs of words would be in similar frequency classes. This finding agrees with the correlation of frequency between error and stimulus word in semantic group slips that I mentioned in the preceding discussion. Indeed, there is also evidence (Postman, 1970) with regard to free association in general, and not just cases of oppositional contrast, that there is a significant relationship between the frequency of the stimulus word and that of the response word.

Hyponymous relationships between stimulus and response words are not nearly so prominent in free association word norms as are oppositional relationships. They occur for nouns, but so do many other forms of associational relationships. These others are probably the ones that are inhibited by the syntactical constraints operating in speech that I referred to earlier. Also, as was previously mentioned, the presumed hyponym classes operating in slips of the tongue may be much smaller than their logical definitions would suggest. Furthermore, semantic group slips of this kind may be assisted by thoughts or events noticed at the time of speech, to say nothing of those that may be multiply determined by phonological similarity, or perseveration, to mention the two main factors cooperating with semantic group.

There is one other difference between free association norms and slips of the tongue that is relevant to our discourse and that concerns synonymy. Approximately synonymous associates are given to stimulus words in free association, but this does not occur with semantic group slips. There is, however, a category of slips where this relationship may be found, and this is the category of blends. In the English sample, these are relatively rare (1.7% in the Daily Life sample and 4.6% in the Conference one). At 13.4%, they form a suspiciously large proportion of the Meringer sample.[13] Three different kinds of blends can be distinguished: distraction, semantic group, and synonym blends. The first includes cases where thinking of something else or seeing it at the moment of speech causes a compounding of the name of this distracting object with the word the speaker wished to speak. Of more interest to us at present are the other two kinds of blends. Semantic group blends, as the name suggests, are blends of two words that stand either in oppositional relationship or could be regarded as co-hyponyms.[14] If we include personal proper names, there were 11 of these. In agreement with the pattern for semantic group slips, none of these was a verb. On the other hand, there were 93 blends compounded of approximate synonyms like *in particulee* from *in particular* and *particularly*, or *überstaunt* from *überrascht* 'surprised' and *erstaunt* 'astonished.' Of these, 30.4% were verbs, a proportion, as Tables 1 and 2 show, closely similar to those for all slips other than semantic group ones in both the English and the German samples. This suggests that synonymous blends are indeed different from semantic group ones. How should we relate the two categories? The answer, I suggest, lies in distinguishing the stages during which the two kinds of slips arise, and I would like to conclude by a theoretical consideration of that part of the word production situation that is relevant.

A slip of the tongue, according to the *Shorter Oxford Dictionary*, is an "unintentional error or blunder in writing, speaking, etc."; and models of speech production generally start with a stage known as "intention," which is the idea that is to be expressed (Lashley, 1951; Laver, 1969; Fromkin, 1971). Now it has been suggested that the reason we do not produce synonyms in semantic group slips of the tongue is that to speak a synonym would not be a slip, since the sentence would be acceptable as conveying the meaning we intended. But this is to confuse the intention in terms of which a slip is defined with the intention to express a certain idea or meaning. Such a notion would imply that when we make a lexical slip we recognize that the word does not express our meaning and have therefore to find another word, a process that might be expected to take rather more time than is usually required for correcting a slip. Further, recognizing that a word does not express our meaning is not always easy to do because as the sentence proceeds we might find that in an indirect or roundabout way it is in fact doing that. And as Lashley showed in a well-known example, and as any linguist knows, the meaning to be attributed to a word may only be determined later in the sentence. But the intention in terms of which the word *slip* should be defined is not that of conveying a particular meaning, it is rather the intention to produce a particular word. When we make a slip, we know instantly that this was not the word we intended to say and may correct ourselves in mid-word, that is, before we have finished saying the word in question. If the speaker does not notice the slip and is told he has committed one, it is often the case that he will deny that he failed to say that particular word, not that he failed to convey a particular meaning. Of course, we may make an error in word-choice as opposed to a slip and correct ourselves, although the relation between our words and our meaning is often not at all close, as anybody who has struggled in writing to express his meaning exactly must know. I would therefore divide the initial intention stage in the model of speech production into at least two substages, the second of which is the intention to speak particular words.[15] Now the intention to speak a particular word is not equivalent to having that word. We generally know that we know a particular word or name, but have then to access it. Where this is most evident is in the tip of the tongue phenomenon. It is not surprising that the psychologist who best publicized this effect was the brother of Henry James, whose conversational hesitations were legendary. Now in speaking we may fail to access the word we intended, in which case we will use dummy words like *thingummyjig, what you call it, Dingsda, chose,* etc., or we may produce the wrong word. When we do that, we are in a situation similar to that of the speaker searching for the *mot juste,* in that we know the word we spoke was not the word we intended, but, of course, unlike the man in that situation, we very quickly access the word we want.

This reasoning applies not only to speaking words but also to thinking them or to holding them in a buffer store preparatory to speech. Meringer (1908), Hockett (1968), Laver (1969), and Hill (1972) have all reported detecting either a slip in thinking or one that they were about to commit in speech, and I, without knowing of this other evidence, have had the same experience.[16] What this means is that a word held in store is not the intended one and that this was recognized before it was uttered. Of course, it is theoretically possible that a word held in store may have deteriorated, and a popular suggestion is that this is an instance of short-term memory decay (Laver, 1969; Nooteboom, 1969). However, such a theory would not by itself adequately account for our ability immediately to correct the error. If, as we are saying the wrong word, let alone when we are about to say it, we realize it is not the word we intend, how could this wrong word be attributed to forgetting what we wanted to say?[17] We can, if we wish, call the presumed deterioration of the word held in store short-term forgetting as long as we recognize that the intention to speak that word has not, itself, been forgotten.

If we apply the preceding analysis to the two different categories of slips distinguished earlier, blends, which according to my data rarely occur, would be due to the coexistence, such as occasionally happens, of two different intentions—to say the words or phrases that got blended. Semantic group slips, on the other hand, will occur in the interval between forming the intention and producing the words, either in speech or in readiness for speech. If the word we intend to speak is highly associated with another word that meets the contextual constraints operating within the utterance, then, given a certain time limit, that other word may be produced instead. The error word needs to be a word of high frequency or one whose threshold for production is lowered by other events occurring at the same time for it to have the necessary short latency in response.

But how are we to account for the absence of synonymous semantic group slips of the tongue, given that, as word association norms show, words are associated with their synonyms? We have rejected the view that these would not be slips because they preserve the intended meaning, but it might still be argued that a speaker would not in such cases correct himself or indeed that if he did this would be regarded as a reformulation rather than a slip. Obviously, it is difficult to answer such an objection. One can only appeal to one's own experience. In nearly 20 years of interest in and observation of slips, I have never noticed this happening in myself nor heard it reported by others. Another, and to my mind more material, objection is that one-word synonyms are rather rare, at least as regards the kinds of words that figure in semantic group slips. There are very few synonyms for the proper names of towns or countries or days of the week, though German has two words for *Saturday* (*Samstag* and *Sonnabend*) and of course we have the alternatives of *England, Britain,* and *The United Kingdom.* Similarly, there are few synonyms for common nouns like *day, week,* and *year,* words for relations like *brother* and *aunt* or for the names of parts of the body, although with words for meals we do have the alternatives of *lunch* and *dinner,* or *dinner* and *supper.* On the other hand, as we have seen with blends, synonyms do occur in slips of the tongue. The comparative rarity of blends, according to my data, would testify to the comparative rarity of acceptable synonyms, but the rarity of synonyms among semantic group slips is evidently greater; in my data and in Meringer's they do not exist at all. A possible explanation might be that whereas a word we intend to speak may excite the production of hyponymous or oppositional associates, it will inhibit the production of ones of similar meaning. This is to suggest an extension to higher order units of the mechanism of lateral inhibition that operates to produce masking or reduction of contrast between contiguous units of the same kind in perception. The evidence for interference not only between similar acoustically coded consonants and vowels in short-term memory but also between semantically similar words in long-term memory suggests that such an extension might have wide explanatory value if it could be precisely formulated. This inhibition would not, of course, apply in free association because there is no intention of speaking the stimulus word.

At the start of this chapter, I declared that my purpose was to show that the collection of slips of the tongue by observation of everyday conditions was justified by certain regularities that the data revealed. The different frequencies of occurrence of semantic group slips between the speech and the writing situation, the rarity of those slips occurring with verbs and the greater frequency of adjectives, the relation between slips, form class, and synonymous, hyponymous, and antonymous classifications, as well as the frequency relationships between error and target words, go some way to justifying the method. They adumbrate laws of occurrence. How these are interpreted is, of course, another matter; it will not have escaped the reader that my interpretation as a psychologist pays more attention to performance variables than is perhaps customary in this growing area of research.

Acknowledgment

I would like to thank Dr. Jean Aitchison for her comments on an earlier draft of this chapter.

Notes

1. Meringer gives only 13 examples of semantic group slips in his first book. In his second book he wrote that "only after the appearance of *Versprechen und Verlesen* did I become aware of the frequency of this category" (Meringer, 1908:40). The category he was actually referring to included slips of phonological similarity. However, there is little difference in the proportion of the latter type of slip in his two books but a big difference in the semantic group category.
2. For the rest of the chapter, the word *hyponym* will be used to refer to co-hyponyms dominated by the same superordinate.
3. As always in slips research, there are exceptions. Meringer has *Obst* 'fruit' for *Äpfel* 'apples,' but this is the only exception in the entire collection of semantic group slips.
4. The one semantic group that occurred among my own slips of the pen is suggestive in this respect. This was when I quickly jotted down as a memo in my diary "Sen. H." for "S. Ken," these being my abbreviations for two different libraries in London.
5. Meier lists the frequency of each different form of a word. Where there was a modification due to case ending in one word but not in the other, then the unmodified form was taken for both. For example, with *vielleicht in der Stadt schöner als hier* 'perhaps nicer in the town than here,' instead of *auf dem Lande* 'in the country,' the frequencies taken were those for *Stadt* and *Land*. This only arose in very few cases.
6. Log frequencies were taken in order to normalize the distribution of word frequency. This was successfully accomplished both in relation to this and to the Meringer sample.

7. The novels were those of Aldous Huxley, Virginia Woolf, and Graham Greene.
8. Only slips where error and target word were of the same form class are included in the tables; further, all cases of multiple classification where one of the classes was semantic group were included among the semantic group slips and not among the other slips.
9. The figures for adverbs separately are 7.1% of semantic group slips and 1.4% for other slips (both samples combined). The adverbs in the sample were ones like *much* and *little, less* and *more, at the latest* and *at the earliest.* These were from the Meringer sample. There were no adverbial slips in the English sample.
10. The same trends were shown for both languages; hence, for simplicity of exposition they were combined.
11. Deese (1965:106) gives proportions of syntagmatic associations ranging from 21% in the case of nouns to 73% in that of adverbs.
12. Very occasionally a slip may occur where a word is inserted because it has strong syntagmatic association with the preceding word, as, for example, my saying *Exeter House* instead of *Exeter,* the former being the name of a block of flats I lived in for some years. Occasionally, also, particularly in slips of the pen, a word may be omitted; in other words, there is an anticipation slip in which the target word is displaced by the word following it.
13. This might, however, be due not to a selective interest on Meringer's part but to a language difference, reflecting perhaps the greater degree of word-compounding in German and greater inflectional complexity in its grammar.
14. *Wehr* from a blend of *mehr* 'more' and *weniger* 'less,' and *Beneinung* from *Bejahung* 'affirmation' and *Verneinung* 'denial' are examples of the oppositional relationship; and *Figari* from *Figaro* and *Kikeriki,* names of two comic papers, and *marmelite* from *marmalade* and *marmite* exemplify the co-hyponyms.
15. The intention to speak a particular word is not an intention simply to say the word but to produce it in a particular syntactic, semantic, and pragmatic context. The implications that the point of view adopted in this chapter have for a detailed model of speech production go beyond the scope of this chapter and will be developed elsewhere.
16. Two examples of semantic group slips from my own experience are detecting *kinaesthetic* for *auditory* before writing it, and *brush my teeth* for *cut my nails* before speaking.
17. Only in the much slower process of formulating sentences to write have I had the quite frequent experience of having a phonologically similar word in mind without being able to remember the originally formulated word that it had displaced.

References

Deese, J. 1965. *The structure of association in language and thought.* Baltimore, Maryland: Johns Hopkins Press.
Fromkin, V. A. 1971. The non-anomalous nature of anomalous utterances. *Language, 47,* 27–52.
Goldman-Eisler, F. 1958. Speech production and the predictability of words in context. *Quarterly Journal of Experimental Psychology, 96,* 9–10.
Hill, A. A. 1972. A theory of speech errors. In E. S. Firchow, K. Grimstad, N. Hasselmo, & W. A. O'Neil (Eds.), *Studies offered to Einar Haugen.* The Hague: Mouton. Pp. 296–304.
Hockett, C. F. 1968. *The state of the art.* The Hague: Mouton.
Lashley, K. S. 1951. The problem of serial order in behaviour. In L. P. Jeffress (Ed.), *Cerebral mechanisms in behaviour: The Hixon Symposium.* New York: Wiley. Pp. 112–136.
Laver, J. D. M. 1969. The detection and correction of slips of the tongue. Work in Progress, 3, Department of Phonetics and Linguistics, University of Edinburgh.
Lyons, J. 1968. *Introduction to theoretical linguistics.* London and New York: Cambridge Univ. Press.

Meier, H. 1964. *Deutsche Sprachstatistik*. Hildesheim, Olms Verlagsbuchhandlung.

Meringer, R. 1908. *Aus dem Leben der Sprache: Versprechen, Kindersprache, Nachahmungstrieb*. Berlin: Behrs Verlag.

Meringer, R. & Mayer, K. 1895. *Versprechen und Verlesen: Eine psychologisch-linguistische Studie*. Stuttgart: Göschensche Verlagsbuchhandlung.

Morton, J. 1964. A model for continuous language behavior. *Language and Speech, 7*, 40–70.

Nooteboom, S. G. 1969. The tongue slips into patterns. In A. G. Sciarone, A. J. van Essen, and A. A. van Raad (Eds.), Nomen Society, *Leyden studies in linguistics and phonetics*. The Hague: Mouton. Pp. 114–132.

Oldfield, R. C. 1966. Things, words and the brain. *Quarterly Journal of Experimental Psychology, 18*, 340–353.

Palermo, D. & Jenkins, J. J. 1974. *Word association norms*. Minneapolis: Univ. of Minnesota Press.

Postman, L. 1970. The California norms: Association as a function of word frequency in norms of word association. In L. Postman & G. Keppel (Eds.), *Norms of word association*. New York: Academic Press. Pp. 241–320.

Russell, W. A. 1970. The complete German language norms for responses to 100 words from the Kent-Rosanoff association test. In L. Postman & G. Keppel (Eds.), *Norms of Word Association*. New York: Academic Press. Pp. 53–94.

Thorndike, E. L. & Lorge, I. 1944. *The teacher's word book of 30,000 words*. New York: Columbia Univ. Press.

Chapter 8

TRANSFORMATIONAL ERRORS

David Fay

Department of Psychology
University of Illinois, Chicago Circle
Chicago, Illinois

At the heart of any theory of speech production will be an account of the relation between a grammar and the mental processes that issue in an utterance. From the work of Fromkin (1971; 1973) and others on speech errors, a picture has begun to emerge of a close correspondence between the linguistic descriptions of a grammar and the psychological states that underlie speech. For example, certain speech errors seem to be best explained by supposing that a speaker analyzes an utterance into linguistic units like Sentence, Noun Phrase, and Phoneme.

While much has been made of the evidence for linguistic units, there has been little discussion of how these units might be put together to make acceptable utterances. In a grammar, the units of a sentence are constructed and transformed by syntactic rules. The close correspondence between the linguistic units of a grammar and the psychological units of speech implies that there should be a parallel correspondence between linguistic rules and the psychological processes that create utterances.

Some evidence for the use of linguistic rules in speech production has been discovered by Fromkin (1973:Introduction). These rules have been primarily morphophonemic (e.g., the *a–an* alternation) or phonological (e.g., the rule deleting a word-final /g/ when it is preceded by a nasal), and not syntactic. It is natural to suppose, however, that evidence might exist also for the use of syntactic rules in the construction of utterances. In particular, we might hypothesize that the mental operations carried out in producing an utterance include transformations, a type of rule that lies at the heart of recent linguistic theory (Chomsky, 1975). We will call this the Transformational Hypothesis.

In this paper, evaluation of the empirical claims of the Transformational Hypothesis will be initiated. We will be concerned with arguments both for and against it.

We will show, on the one hand, that the hypothesis makes rich and explicit predictions about the existence of certain types of errors and that these predictions are confirmed by the data. On the other hand, we will discuss the construction of counterarguments to transformational analyses and show that, in at least one case, a counterargument is successful. It is hoped that these arguments will be just the first step in a thorough examination of the hypothesis.

1. The Case for Transformational Errors

In this section we will present arguments that utterances are constructed using transformations. The arguments will be supported by data from a collection of more than 4000 errors in spontaneous speech accumulated by the author over the past 5 years. In each case, the speech error was recorded along with the speaker's intuition, if available, about what the intended utterance, or target, was. Otherwise the target was constructed from the error and the context.

Before presenting the evidence, we will briefly review the structure of transformational rules since the details of their formulation will play a central role in our account. Consider as an example the optional rule of Particle Movement given in (1):[1]

(1)   SA: X - V - PRT - NP - Y
              1   2   3   4   5
        SC: 1   2   0   4+3   5
        Condition: Obligatory if 4 is a Pronoun.

This rule takes a copy of a Particle and places it to the right of an adjacent Noun Phrase, and deletes the original. It is this rule that distinguishes the derivation of (3) from that of (2); the condition on its application accounts for the ungrammaticality of sentences like (4).

(2)   *Mary threw out her boyfriend.*
(3)   *Mary threw her boyfriend out.*
(4)   **Mary threw out him.*

In general, a transformation consists of three parts: a Structural Analysis (SA), a Structural Change (SC), and conditions on the application of the rule. The Structural Analysis provides an abstract specification of the phrase markers to which the rule can apply. For example, Particle Movement can apply to any phrase marker that includes a sequence of elements identifiable as a Verb (V), followed by a Particle (PRT), followed by a Noun Phrase (NP). The variables X and Y indicate that the environment to the left and right of this sequence may be anything at all. The Structural Change states the changes the phrase marker undergoes when the rule applies. These changes are given in terms of three elementary transformations: deletion (0), adjunction (+), and substitution (Chomsky, 1965). Note that Particle Movement involves both deletion and adjunction. Conditions on the rule place restrictions on its application (e.g., that a rule cannot apply to an embedded sentence).

If we think of a speech production device as applying transformations to an underlying structure, we can make predictions about the ways in which the device can malfunction. Since the application of a transformation involves several steps, we should find errors that correspond to each step. In what follows, we will consider in turn each aspect of applying a transformation and show that the predicted error types occur.

Consider first the Structural Analysis of a transformation. Processing of this part of a rule can go wrong in three ways. First, the device applying the rule can misanalyze a phrase marker such that the rule applies when it should, but applies incorrectly. Second, the device may make an incorrect decision that the Structural Analysis of an obligatory rule does not fit a phrase marker when, in fact, it does; hence, the rule is not applied. Finally, the device may misanalyze a phrase marker so as to allow a rule to apply when it shouldn't.

An example of the first type of error is given in (5):

(5) E(rror): *Why do you be an oaf sometimes?*
 T(arget): Why are you an oaf sometimes?

(6) Q you PRES be an oaf sometimes WHY   Underlying Structure
 WHY you PRES be an oaf sometimes   WH-Fronting
 WHY PRES you be an oaf sometimes   *Subject Auxiliary Inversion
 WHY do+PRES you be an oaf sometimes   Do-Support
 Why do you be an oaf sometimes?   Morphophonemics

In this case, the Subject Auxiliary Inversion Transformation (henceforth SAI) has misanalyzed the structure to which it applies. As shown in the rough derivation given in (6), the rule fails to move the Verb along with tense marker to the left of the subject NP. In the intended utterance, both tense marker and Verb would be moved and the tense would be attached to the Verb by the rule of Affix-Hopping.

There are two virtues to this account. First, it explains why the word *do* shows up in the error when it was not in the target. Second, it explains the lack of tense on the Verb. These differences between target and error follow naturally as a consequence of a single mistake in applying a rule. Other examples of this sort are given in (7):[2]

(7) a. E: *Why did this be done?*[3]
 T: Why was this done?
 b. E: *If I was done that to ...*
 T: If that was done to me ...
 c. E: *What could have I done with the check?*
 T: What could I have done with the check?
 d. E: *How many's got theory?*
 T: How many has theory got?

The error in (7a) is of the same type as (5). In (7b) the passive rule has taken not the first NP after the Verb, but rather the second and moved it to subject position. With certain complex verbs (e.g., *take advantage of*) this is permissible, but not with the superficially similar sequence *do that to*. In (7c and d) SAI has incorrectly placed the main verb along with the auxiliary verb in front of the subject NP. What is common to all these errors is that a transformation has misanalyzed the structure to which it applies so as to move more or less material than should properly have been moved.

The second type of error in the analysis of phrase structure involves an incorrect decision *not* to apply a rule. This is illustrated in examples (8) and (9):[4]

(8) a. E: *Why it is—why is it that nobody makes a decent toilet seat?*
     b. E: *What it is that has to be welded?*
        T: What is it that has to be welded?
     c. E: *What she could do?*
        T: What could she do?
(9) a. E: *And what he said?*
        T: And what did he say?
     b. E: *Do you think it not works?*
        T: Do you think it doesn't work?
     c. E: *Look at those clouds are moving how fast.*
        T: Look at how fast those clouds are moving.
     d. E: *Linda, do you talk on the telephone with which ear?*
        T: Linda, which ear do you talk on the telephone with?

The errors given in (8) involve a simple inversion of two words from the target; hence, they could be explained away as exchange errors (Fay, 1977b; Garrett, 1975). However, no such simple account will do for the errors in (9). To see this, consider the derivation of (9a) given in (10):

(10) and Q he PAST say WHAT   Underlying Structure
      and WHAT he PAST say   WH-Fronting
      and WHAT he PAST say   *SAI (omitted)
      and WHAT he say+PAST   Affix-Hopping
      and what he said   Morphophonemics

What is interesting about this error is that the omission of SAI has created the conditions for the application of Affix-Hopping, a rule that would not have applied in the target utterance. In a derivation of the target, the tense marker would be placed before the subject by SAI. However, Affix-Hopping would be blocked from applying because the tense marker would not be adjacent to a Verb. Finally, Do-Support would apply. The same explanation holds for the error in (9b) except that the rule that fails to apply is Auxiliary Preposing,[5] rather than SAI.

Errors (9c and d) likewise provide support for the transformational account. In these cases, WH-Fronting has not applied so that the WH-phrases appear in their deep structure position. The placement of these phrases follows naturally from a transformational explanation since an element not moved by a transformation must remain in deep structure position. On any other account, it would have to be a coincidence that these phrases are misordered into just the position they occupy in deep structure, and apparently no other.

The third type of Structural Analysis error results in the application of a rule when it shouldn't apply, apparently because of a misreading of the phrase marker being analyzed. Some examples are given in (11):

(11) a. E: *How do we go!!*
     T: How we go!! (shouted as an athletic slogan)
  b. E: Speaker 1: *Am I 26 or 25?*
         Speaker 2: *26.*
         Speaker 1: *So am I–I mean, so I am.*
  c. E: Speaker 1: *Roben, you're dripping that on your pants.*
         Speaker 2: *Oh dear! So am I.*
     T: So I am.
  d. E: *Just ask me where the tools are. I know where they're all.*
     T: ...where they all are.
  e. E: *Where do you suppose are they?*
     T: Where do you suppose they are?
  f. E: *... but it didn't work that way out.*
     T: ...but it didn't work out that way.

In (11a) the rules of SAI and Do-Support have applied to an idiomatic slogan, which, although not a question, has a fronted WH-phrase. In (11b and c) SAI has applied to sentences with a fronted adverb *so*. Note that the resulting utterances are perfectly well formed but have a different meaning than the intended one. In (11d) Auxiliary Shift (Baker, 1971) has hopped the Verb *are* to the left of the quantifier *all*. However, this movement is not permissible when an element (in this case, *where*) has been moved from the position to the right of the Verb (see Baker, 1971, for a discussion of this restriction). In (11e) SAI applies to invert the subject and Verb in an embedded complement clause that is very unlike a structure that SAI would apply to. We will see in the following discussion that SAI often applies incorrectly to embedded indirect questions, which are syntactically very similar to direct questions (Baker, 1970). In this case, however, there are few similarities to direct questions.

In the final example, Particle Movement has apparently taken the Particle from the intransitive expression *work out* and moved it to the right of an adverbial Noun Phrase. While this is possible with other senses of *work out* which are transitive (e.g., *work out the solution* versus *work the solution out*), it leads to an unacceptable utterance in this case. Whatever the syntactic details that would prohibit Particle Movement from applying in this instance, it is clear that there are many similarities to environments in which the rule is applicable. In fact, there seems to be a generalization that rules will apply incorrectly to structures that are minimally different from structures to which they could correctly apply. Of course, a detailed study would be required to support this generalization.

Turning now to the Structural Change part of a transformation, we assume that the production device has correctly analyzed the phrase marker it is processing. Errors can still be made in carrying out the elementary transformations that comprise the rule. Consider, for instance, what is involved in a movement rule, such as Particle Movement. This type of transformation moves an element specified in the Structural Analysis to a new position in the phrase marker. As indicated earlier, this is done by first copying the element into a new position and then deleting the original. Since there are two elementary transformations involved here (adjunction and deletion), it is possible that only one will be performed. If the deletion operation is skipped, errors like those shown in (12) will result:

(12) a. E: *A boy who I know a boy has hair down to here.*[6]
         T: A boy who I know has hair down to here.
      b. E: *And when the Indians chew coca, which they chew coca all day long, they....*
         T: And when the Indians chew coca, which they chew all day long, they ....
      c. E: *Are those are for the taking?*
         T: Are those for the taking?
      d. E: *Do I have to put on my seat belt on?*
         T: Do I have to put on my seat belt?

To illustrate how these errors come about a derivation of (12a) is given in (13):

(13) A boy [I know a boy]...   Underlying form
           S
      A boy [WH + a boy I know a boy]...   *Relative Clause Formation
           S
      A boy who I know a boy ...   Morphophonemics

The Relative Clause rule copies a Noun Phrase within the clause to the front attaching a WH-marker at the same time. However, the second elementary transformation, deletion, is skipped leaving the Noun Phrase in its original deep structure position. Errors (12b), (12c), and (12d) result from incomplete application of Relative Clause Formation to a nonrestrictive relative, SAI, and Particle Movement, respectively. In each of these cases, the transformational account explains in a principled way the appearance of an extra element in deep structure position. This is most striking, of course, in the case of obligatory rules, as in (12a and b), since the duplicated element does not ordinarily show up in that position.[7]

Finally, we consider errors that violate conditions on transformations. One rule having a condition is SAI, which applies in direct, but not embedded (indirect), questions. The restriction is imposed by simply limiting the rule to main clauses. Violation of the restriction creates errors like those in (14):[8]

(14) a. E: *I know where is a top for it.*
     T: I know where a top for it is.
   b. E: *I don't know what's his problem.*
     T: I don't know what his problem is.
   c. E: *I wonder how can she tell.*
     T: I wonder how she can tell.

Similarly, there is a condition on the optional rule of Particle Movement, making the rule obligatory when the object NP is a Pronoun. Violation of this condition produces utterances like those in (15):

(15) a. E: *His secretary types up it.*
     T: His secretary types it up.
   b. E: *Can I turn off this?*
     T: Can I turn this off?
   c. E: *I'll check out it on 127.*
     T: I'll check it out on 127.

Tag Question Formation is also a rule with a condition on its application. Like SAI, it is restricted to the main clause of a sentence. Errors like those in (16) show that this condition is occasionally violated.

(16) a. E: *It's hard when there's pressure, isn't there?*
     T: ...isn't it?
   b. E: *That's the way it used to be, didn't it?*
     T: ...isn't it?
   c. E: *You're nursing him just because you missed him, didn't you?*
     T: ...aren't you?

Note that in each case, the tag is formed not on the main clause but on the subject Noun Phrase and Verb of the embedded clause.

Finally, the WH-Fronting transformation has a condition on it which Ross (1967: 114) calls the Left Branch Condition of the Pied Piping Convention. This condition states that no WH-phrase that is on the left branch of a larger Noun Phrase can be moved out of that phrase. Instead, the whole NP must be moved. Precisely this situation holds in the following error:

(17) E: *Go ahead and do what you're going to do else and I'll be there in a minute.*
     T: Go ahead and do what else you're going to do and ....

Ross's convention prohibits *what* from being moved out of the NP *what else*. Violation of this restriction results in *else* being left behind in its deep structure position.

The evidence we have presented here appears to support the claim that transformations are carried out as mental operations in speech production. To be clear about what has been claimed, it may be useful at this point to review the structure of the argument. Three hypotheses were necessary for the derivation of the empirical predictions that were checked against the error data. First, we assume the general notion of a transformational rule with an inner structure consisting of a Structural Analysis, a Structural Change, and conditions on the rule. Second, we assumed the existence of particular transformations in the grammar of English (e.g., Particle Movement). Finally, we assumed that transformations are mental processes and like all such processes are subject to malfunction. From these hypotheses we were able to make predictions about the existence of particular types of speech errors. The fact that the predictions were supported by the data adds strength to all three hypotheses and, in particular, to the third, which has not previously been thought to be particularly plausible, much less empirically supportable.

It cannot have escaped the notice of readers familiar with the complexity and variety of speech errors that many other explanations could be offered for the errors discussed here. However, it will not be possible to present a detailed defense of the transformational account given in this chapter. In part this is due to limitations of space, but it is also due to a paucity of data. Because of the observational, rather than experimental, nature of speech error data, error types that are necessary to attack or defend the transformational hypothesis are often simply not available. For example, it was pointed out in the preceding that the transformational hypotheses predicts that WH-phrases will be misordered into deep structure position when WH-Fronting fails to apply. Examples (9c and d) support this prediction, but it could be argued that these are cases of simple misordering, which is known to exist anyway (Fay, 1977b; Garrett, 1975). If so, we should observe errors in which WH-phrases misorder into non-deep-structure positions. Unfortunately, this alternative hypothesis is difficult to evaluate since there are so few examples in the data (just these two) of misordered WH-phrases.

The question of how the transformational hypothesis is to be evaluated is an important one, and we do not wish to imply that the scarcity of critical data makes it invulnerable. In order to demonstrate that the hypothesis is, in fact, open to attack we will develop one counterargument here. This example will also serve to illustrate the kind of challenges the transformational hypothesis must survive as more data become available.

2. A Counterargument

Consider the operations involved in the placement of tense within a sentence. Tense is generated in deep structure to the left of the Verb it is to be attached to (Chomsky, 1957). It is then moved to the right over the adjacent Verb and attached by the rule of Affix-Hopping. However, if some non-Verb intervenes between the tense and a Verb, the tense cannot be moved, and the rule of Do-Support inserts a *do* for the tense to attach to. Given these rules and a few others that were introduced earlier, we can predict from the transformational hypothesis a variety of errors that are found in the data.

We start with the observation that Affix-Hopping is a movement rule. From this it follows that either of the two elementary transformations (adjunction and deletion) may be omitted in applying the rule. If adjunction is skipped, the tense will be eliminated by the deletion elementary, and the utterance will become tenseless. The predicted errors $(N = 3)^9$ are found as shown in (18):

(18) a. E: *It's as if someone were turning it on and off as they come—came and went.*
  b. E: *Probably went under the radiator and melt—melted.*
  c. E: *Forster said in a talk I hear him give—gave—*
    T: Forster said in a talk I heard him give . . . .

On the other hand, if the deletion elementary is omitted the tense will be duplicated. There are no examples of the predicted sequence *do + tense V + tense* in the data; however, there are many cases in which tense is duplicated as a result of misapplication of other rules that move tense. For example, SAI can move tense to the left of a subject NP. If the deletion elementary in SAI fails to take place, the resulting utterance will have a tense on *do* and also an extra tense which is attached to the Verb by Affix-Hopping. Some examples $(N = 10)$ are given in (19):

(19) a. E: *Did he knew who you were?*
    T: Did he know who you were?
  b. E: *What did you wanted to say?*
    T: What did you want to say?
  c. E: *How long does that has to—have to simmer?*

Furthermore, the rule of Auxiliary Preposing, which was mentioned earlier, moves tense to the left of a negative marker and may also be only partially carried out. The result will again be duplication of tense as in the examples $(N = 6)$ in (20):

(20) a. E: *I didn't ate—.*
    T: I didn't eat until 7:30.
  b. E: *They didn't actually withdrew—you know, withdraw the needle.*
  c. E: *No, I didn't meant that.*
    T: No, I didn't mean that.

Finally, we predict that Affix-Hopping can misanalyze a structure to which it is applied. If the result is omission of the rule altogether, Do-Support will subsequently insert *do*. The resulting utterance will look like a well-formed emphatic (e.g., *John did say that* for *John said that*) and will be easily missed; it is no surprise, therefore, that no examples occur in the data. However, if the phrase marker is misanalyzed so that the rule can still apply, tense will attach not to the adjacent Verb to the right but to another element further to the right. This is illustrated by the errors $(N = 7)$ in (21):

(21) a. E: *He always know whats to say.*
        T: He always knows what to say.
      b. E: *It's cloudy out. Get darks early.*
        T: It's cloudy out. Gets dark early.
      c. E: *He's going to bite it if he get holds of it.*
        T: He's going to bite it if he gets hold of it.

These examples show that, with certain exceptions, the errors predicted by a transformational analysis of tense placement are represented in the data. The question now arises of how this analysis might be refuted. One avenue of attack might be to show that the transformations appealed to do not exist in the grammar of English. More generally, one could show transformational grammar to be incorrect. However, more modest aims are all that are required here. A demonstration that there is a simpler explanation for the data would be sufficient to undermine the transformational account. A simpler explanation, in this case, would be one that does not appeal to the transformational apparatus, yet predicts the data with equal facility. Ideally, the simpler hypothesis would also be more general in that it predicts other data that cannot be explained as the misapplication of transformations.

Consider the following alternative hypothesis. Suppose that abstract tense markers act like phonological segments in an utterance. Since it is known that these segments can be omitted, displaced, and duplicated (Fromkin, 1971) within an utterance, we predict that tense markers will show the same behavior.[10] In fact, the errors cited in (18)–(21) exhibit exactly these properties. What is more, there is a class of errors predicted by this hypothesis that is unexplainable in transformational terms. If tense markers duplicate freely, then they should appear redundantly not only when moved by a transformation as in (19) and (20), but in other cases as well. Examples of this type (N = 11) are presented in (22):

(22) a. E: *All we did was sat there....*
        T: All we did was sit there ....
      b. E: *He just hasta does–do something else.*
      c. E: *... and therefore tended to chose–to choose....*

In these errors the only rule that moves tense is Affix-Hopping, which cannot misapply in any one of the ways described previously to give errors of this sort. Of course, one could argue that these cases result from a double mistake in Affix-Hopping in which the tense is copied onto the wrong element and the deletion elementary is skipped as well. However, such an account would be completely ad hoc since we would expect double errors to occur with much lower frequency than single errors, and these obviously do not.

It seems then that tense markers exhibit all the same error types as do phonological segments and that we needn't resort to transformations to explain the pattern of errors. No doubt there are replies that the advocate of the transformational hypothesis could make; it is clear that the debate over the correct analysis of tense errors will not end here. Nevertheless, in this single case, the Transformational Hypothesis does not appear at present to provide the best account.

We have tried to show in this chapter that there is evidence for the Transformational Hypothesis. But we have also shown that, in at least one instance, what appears to be a set of transformational errors can be better explained in other ways. What remains is to determine whether the Transformational Hypothesis can survive a detailed analysis of the other data that appears to support it. If it can, we will have gained an important insight into the nature of speech production.

Acknowledgments

Some of the data presented here have appeared previously in Fay (1974; 1975; 1977a) and Foss and Fay (1975). The approach taken in this chapter owes much to the insights of Hausser (1971), who was, I believe, the first person to recognize transformational errors. Thanks are due Virginia Valian for comments on an earlier version of this chapter.

Notes

1. Throughout this chapter we will follow the notation given in Bach (1974).
2. Unless a statement is made to the contrary, the listings of errors in this section of the chapter include all examples of a given type in the author's data.
3. This example and the following one are taken from Hausser (1971).
4. There are five other errors like those in (8) in the data.
5. See Klima (1964) and Fay (1974) for discussion of this rule.
6. This example comes from Fromkin (1973:Appendix).
7. The transformational account also predicts that the elementary transformation of adjunction (copying) may be skipped in a movement rule. If it is, the deletion elementary will apply to eliminate the element that was to be moved. These errors will result in single words being missing from an utterance and will be very hard to distinguish from the simple omission of a word, which is a common (though unexplained) type of error. I have not done the detailed study that would be required to determine whether there is evidence for this type of error independent of word omissions.
8. There are two other errors of this type in the author's collection.
9. In this section, the number of errors in the data of a given type will be indicated in this way.
10. This is just what Fromkin (1974:Introduction) maintains in her discussion of this type of error.

References

Bach, E. 1974. *Syntactic theory*. New York: Holt, Rinehart & Winston.
Baker, C. L. 1970. Notes on the description of English questions: The role of an abstract question morpheme. *Foundations of Language, 6,* 197–219.
Baker, C. L. 1971. Stress level and auxiliary behavior in English. *Linguistic Inquiry, 2,* 167–182.

Chomsky, N. 1957. *Syntactic structures*. (Janua Linguarum, 4). The Hague: Mouton.
Chomsky, N. 1965. *Aspects of the theory of syntax*. Cambridge, Massachusetts: MIT Press.
Chomsky, N. 1975. *The logical structure of linguistic theory*. New York: Plenum.
Fay, D. 1974. Simplification in children's speech and the formulation of movement rules. Paper presented at the 1974 Summer Meeting of the Linguistic Society of America, July 26–28, Amherst, Massachusetts.
Fay, D. 1975. Some investigations of grammatical category in performance devices. Ph.D. dissertation, University of Texas.
Fay, D. 1977a. Transformations and speech production. Paper presented at the Forty-Ninth Annual Meeting of the Midwestern Psychological Association, May 5–7, Chicago, Illinois.
Fay, D. 1977b. Surface structure and the production of speech. Paper presented at the Forty-Ninth Annual Meeting of the Midwestern Psychological Association, May 5–7, Chicago, Illinois.
Foss, D. & Fay, D. 1975. Linguistic theory and performance models. In D. Cohen & J. R. Wirth (Eds.), *Testing linguistic hypotheses*. New York: Halsted. Pp. 65–91.
Fromkin, V. A. 1971. The non-anomalous nature of anomalous utterances. *Language, 47,* 27–52.
Fromkin, V. A. 1973. *Speech errors as linguistic evidence*. The Hague: Mouton.
Garrett, M. 1975. The analysis of sentence production. In G. Bower (Ed.), *The psychology of learning and motivation* (Vol. 9). New York: Academic Press. Pp. 133–177.
Hausser, R. 1971. A theory of systematic deviants. Report to NSF: On the theory of transformational grammar. Grant GS-2468, Emmon Bach and Stanley Peters, Principal Investigators.
Klima, E. 1964. Negation in English. In J. A. Fodor & J. J. Katz (Eds.), *The structure of language*. Englewood Cliffs, New Jersey: Prentice-Hall. Pp. 246–323.
Ross, J. R. 1967. Constraints on variables in syntax. Ph.D. dissertation, MIT. Reproduced by the Indiana University Linguistics Club.

Chapter 9

ON THE FREUDIAN THEORY OF SPEECH ERRORS

Andrew W. Ellis

Department of Psychology
University of Lancaster
Lancaster, England

The considerable volume of research into slips of the tongue that has taken place in recent years has been motivated by predominantly psycholinguistic, rather than psychoanalytic interests.[1] With the exception of Hockett (1967), most investigators have followed Boomer and Laver (1968:4) in assuming that "the mechanics of slips can be studied linguistically without reference to their motivation." This attitude may have been influenced by a desire to establish the study of speech errors as a distinct field of psycholinguistic enquiry, independent from psychopathology. This purpose has been successfully accomplished, to the extent that the psycholinguist may now look afresh at psychoanalytic theory to decide whether or not that theory is supported by the available evidence, and to consider the extent to which depth-analytic explanations are needed in addition to the mechanical–psycholinguistic explanations proposed more recently. That, in brief, is the aim of this chapter.

1. Freud's Theory

Freud's account of the processes responsible for generating speech errors is set out in his *Psychopathology of Everyday Life* (1941/1975) and in the *Introductory Lectures on Psychoanalysis* (1916-17/1974). Freud held that speech errors "arise from the concurrent action—or perhaps rather, the mutually opposing action—of two different intentions" (Freud, 1974:70). One of these two intentions is the meaning that the speaker consciously wishes to convey. A second, disturbing intention interferes with the conscious purpose, and the outcome of this conflict is a slip of the tongue. It is not necessary that the speaker should be unaware of the activity of the disturbing purpose within him before it reveals itself in the slip, although, as Freud states: "My interpretation carries with it the hypothesis that intentions can find expression in a speaker of which he himself knows nothing, but which I am able to infer from circumstantial evidence" (Freud, 1974:92).

Two examples can be given that illustrate Freud's mode of explanation. On one occasion a Professor remarked:

(1)   *"In the case of the female genitals, in spite of many Versuchungen* ['temptations']–*I beg your pardon, Versuche* ['experiments']...."

On another occasion, a President of the Lower House of Parliament who wanted to open the sitting said:

(2)   *"Gentlemen, I take notice that a full quorum of members is present and herewith declare the sitting closed."*

The interpretation of the disturbing intention in example (1) is self-evident, while of example (2) Freud states: "It is clear that he wanted to open the sitting (i.e., the conscious intention), but it is equally clear that he also wanted to close it (i.e., the disturbing intention). That is so obvious that it leaves us nothing to interpret" (Freud, 1974:73-74).

2. Lexical Substitution Errors

The index of parapraxes at the end of *The Psychopathology of Everyday Life* lists 94 slips of the tongue, 85 of which were made in normal speech (most of the remainder being taken from literary sources). By my estimation, 51 of these errors (60%) involve lexical substitution, that is replacing an intended word by an errror word, as in examples (1) and (2).

Lexical substitution errors have been studied recently by a number of scholars, including Nooteboom, 1969; Fromkin, 1971; Tweney, Tkacz, and Zaruba, 1975; Garrett, 1976; and Fay and Cutler, 1977. Their general experience is that the bulk of these errors fall into two broad classes. The first class comprises errors in which the substituting word is similar in phonological form to the intended word, as in examples (3) to (5) from Fay and Cutler (1977):

(3)   signal → *single*
(4)   confession → *convention*
(5)   suburbs → *subways*

The second class consists of errors in which the substituting word is related in meaning (semantically or associatively) to the word it replaces, as in examples (6) to (8) from the Appendix to Fromkin (1973):

(6)   Don't burn your fingers → ... *your toes*
(7)   I know his father-in-law → ... *brother-in-*....
(8)   small Japanese restaurant → ... *Chinese–I mean*....

All but two of Freud's lexical substitution errors can, in the writer's opinion, be classified as similar to the intended word in either form or meaning. On admittedly intuitive criteria, and including substitutions of proper names, I estimate there to be 22 semantic–associative substitutions in Freud's (1975) corpus, including example (2) and examples (9) to (12)–these are translations from the original German:

(9)   medicine → *chemistry*
(10)   see you more often → *see you more seldom*
(11)   retiring → *expiring*
(12)   I am the brother of → *I am the father of*

Twenty-seven of the remaining lexical substitutions involve similarity of phonological form between the intended word and the error word (errors showing similarity of both form and meaning have been classed as semantic-associative substitutions). These lexical form errors include example (1) and examples (13) to (17):

(13)   curable → *durable*
(14)   patriot → *idiot*
(15)   geschwind ('quickly') → *geschminkt* ('with make-up on')
(16)   unterbringen ('take in') → *umbringen* ('put an end to')
(17)   geeingnet ('qualified') → *geneigt* ('inclined')

Two lexical substitutions do not fall into either of the above categories. In these errors, the speaker replaces the intended word by a word present in the preceding verbal co-text. In example (18) the word *repay* had just been uttered by another speaker, as had the word *Matthäus* in example (19).

(18)   *Let me see, haven't you repaid me that–I'm sorry–I mean told me that already?*

(19)   At Kaufmann's → *At Matthäus*

Garrett (1976:244–245) notes two similar "situational errors," while the Appendix to Fromkin (1973) includes the related example (20):

(20)   Qu.   *When are you going to have the ale?*
        Ans.   With the dinner. → *With the beer.*

Thus, the lexical substitution errors that Freud adduces in support of his theory of conflicting intentions do not differ on formal or structural grounds from the errors analyzed by psycholinguists.

Freud (1974:59) claims that "the commonest slips of the tongue are when, instead of saying one word, we say another very much like it." This claim is surprising because it is not the experience of most investigators. Data from Hotopf (1968) and

Fay and Cutler (1977) indicate that lexical substitutions account for only 20-25% of speech errors, and in my own collection of slips, phonemic spoonerisms (anticipations, perseverations, and reversals of consonants or vowels) outnumber lexical substitutions by approximately three to one. Indeed, Freud later states more accurately that "the commonest, simplest and most trivial slips of the tongue are contractions and anticipations" (Freud, 1974:96). However, the fact that Freud was prepared to believe that lexical substitutions occur more frequently than other types of error may be taken as evidence for what Fromkin (1973:16) termed Freud's "unconscious filter." Fromkin meant by this that Freud, like everyone else, probably tended not to detect large numbers of errors, resulting in an error corpus biased in the direction of those slips that severely distort the speaker's intention.

3. Phonemic Spoonerisms

Further evidence of Freud's "filter" may be seen in his neglect of the simple spoonerism. Only 10 of Freud's errors (12%) are presented as spoonerisms. At least four of these are taken from Meringer and Mayer (1895), and only a few are analyzed in any depth. Those spoonerisms most amenable to the theory of conflicting intentions are the ones which result in a meaningful error product as in examples (21) to (23) taken by Freud from Meringer and Mayer (1895):

(21)   Eiweiss-scheibchen ('small slices of white bread') → *Eischeissweibchen* (lit. 'egg-shit-female')
(22)   Alabasterbüchse ('alabaster box') → *Alabüsterbachse* (*Büste* = 'breast')
(23)   Lotuskapitäl ('lotus-flower capital') → *Lokuskapitäl* (*Lokus* = 'W.C.')

Again, the errors Freud cites are formally and structurally the same as those reported by psycholinguists. Of errors like examples (21) to (23) Freud writes that "what results ...has a sense of its own ...the product of the slip of the tongue may perhaps itself have a right to be regarded as a completely valid psychical act, pursuing an aim of its own, with a content and significance" (Freud, 1974:61).

It can be noted at this stage that the lexical form and situational errors, and the phonemic spoonerisms, are the only errors (apart from the word blends which will be discussed later) that support Freud's contention that "the content of the disturbing intention may have nothing to do with that of the disturbed one" (Freud, 1974:89).

4. Freudian versus Non-Freudian Theory

Freud (1974:71) poses the question "Do all slips of the tongue require explanation in terms of conflicting intentions?" and provides his own answer, stating, "I am very much inclined to think so, and my reason is that every time one investigates an instance of a slip of the tongue an explanation of this sort is forthcoming. But it is also true that there is no way of proving that a slip of the tongue cannot occur without this mechanism." Elsewhere Freud writes: "I still secretly cling to my expectation that even apparently simple slips of the tongue could be traced to interference by a half-suppressed idea that lies outside the intended context" (Freud, 1975:127). It is clear from this last quotation that Freud did, on occasion, perceive errors for which he could not provide a satisfactory explanation in terms of conflicting intentions. Thus, his assertion that all slips of the tongue require a depth analysis amounts more to a statement of a priori belief than to an empirical generalization. It is certainly not falsifiable.

Most recent investigators have adopted a very different position, arguing either that Freudian explanations "are neither verifiable nor reproducible and are therefore to be discarded in a systematic analysis" (Nooteboom, 1969), or that Freudian slips of the tongue do occur, but constitute only a small proportion of observed errors (Fromkin, 1973:Introduction; Garrett, 1975).

Psycholinguists are currently evolving an information-processing model of speech production that, it is hoped, will be capable of providing a satisfactory account of the origins of speech errors. Within the model, lexical substitution errors are explained by reference to a hypothetical internal word store or lexicon. Syntactically organized messages coded in some (unspecified) semantic form are presented to the lexicon whose function is to match semantic–syntactic inputs to phonemic forms, hence making suitable words available to express the speaker's message or intention. Lexical substitutions occur, *ex hypothesi*, when an incorrect phonemic form is chosen as a result of similarity between it and the intended word. This theory is elaborated further in Fromkin (1971), Garrett (1975; 1976), Tweney, Tkacz, and Zaruba (1975), and Fay and Cutler (1977). To explain phonemic spoonerisms, one must postulate in addition a postlexicon phonemic buffer store within which preplanned stretches of speech are stored, and whose own mis-selections of phonemes from the stored array result in misordered instructions being sent to the articulatory mechanisms (Ellis and Myers, 1976; Shaffer, 1976; Ellis, 1979).

If such a model can be shown to be capable of simulating naturally occurring speech errors, then it will do so without recourse to a hypothesized secondary intention interfering with the conscious intention. Nevertheless, there is obviously a finite nonzero probability that processes of this sort would sometimes produce an output that appeared, entirely by chance, to indicate an unconscious disturbing purpose.

If it is once conceded that not all errors require explanation in terms of competing intentions, and if it can be shown that the supposedly Freudian slips are qualitatively indistinguishable from other, non-Freudian, errors, then the problem becomes, in essence, a statistical one. In the current state of the art the problem is, however, insoluble. Ideally, one would divide naturally occurring errors into Freudian and non-Freudian categories. One would then compare the observed frequencies in the two categories with the frequencies expected by chance alone. This would be done separately for each of the distinct types of speech error.

There are two major reasons why such a program cannot be implemented. First, there are no accepted criteria upon which to base the provisional division of errors into Freudian and non-Freudian categories (Freud did not consider it necessary that the apparent disturbing purpose should be a sexual one—the competing purpose is of a sexual nature in fewer than a quarter of the errors that Freud [1975] discusses).

The second problem concerns the specification of chance levels. As Garrett (1976:251) remarks, "Deciding on 'chance' is a nontrivial problem for speech errors." At a time when there is disagreement over procedures for estimating chance levels for relatively simple phonemic factors (see Shaffer's [1976] comments on MacKay [1970]), the prospect of agreed procedures for testing Freudian predictions seems remote.

The logic of the preceding argument applies only to those classes of error where Freudian and non-Freudian slips are formally comparable. There is, however, a class of errors for which this precondition is apparently not satisfied.

5. Word Blends

Word blends are familiar to students of speech errors through slips like example (24) from Boomer and Laver (1968):

(24)   *didn't bother me in the **sleast**...' slightest*

Here, the error form *sleast* is taken to be a blend of the two words *slightest* and *least*.

Psycholinguistic studies of word blends are unanimous in their agreement that the words that combine to form the error are often synonyms and are always equally appropriate in the context of the utterance (e.g., Fromkin, 1971; 1973:Introduction; Garrett, 1975; 1976). An explanation of blends in terms of the internal lexicon might propose that a set of semantic and syntactic attributes is presented to the lexicon, and that this set accesses not one, but two appropriate phonemic forms, both of which adequately express the intended meaning. A blend may then occur, possibly facilitated by the presence of common phonemes in the two rivals for output (MacKay, 1972).

However, 12 of the 15 slips of the tongue that Freud presents as word blends (or compromise formations) differ from conventional blends in that the two words allegedly involved are not synonyms, neither are they equally appropriate in the context of the utterance. Consider example (25), which Freud (1975:98) takes from Meringer and Mayer (1895):

(25)   "Ru. was speaking of occurrences which, within himself, he pronounced to be '*Schweinereien*' ('disgusting,' lit. 'piggish').' He tried, however, to express himself mildly, and began: 'But then facts came to "*Vorschwein*" [Ru. intended to say 'came to light' and should have used the word *Vorschein*. Instead he used the meaningless word *Vorschwein*]. Mayer and I were present and Ru. confirmed his having thought 'Schweinerein'."

Example (26) provides a similar instance:

(26) "A young man addressed a lady in the street in the following words: 'If you will permit me, madam. I should like to *begleit-digen* you.' It was obvious what his thoughts were: he would like to *begleiten* ('accompany') her, but was afraid his offer would *begleidigen* ('insult') her." (Freud, 1975:110).

Of these and similar slips Freud (1974:68–69) states: "Even these obscurer cases of slips of the tongue can be explained by a convergence, a mutual interference, between two different intended speeches." The implication of this for the psycholinguistic model is that two sets of attributes are presented to the lexicon, representing the conscious intention and the disturbing purpose, and that these have given rise to two phonemic words whose simultaneous availability causes them to be blended.

However, the evidence of these word blends is less compelling than it might appear at first sight. A number of the errors presented by Freud as compromise formations may be given alternative explanations. For example, a gentleman was offering his condolences to a young lady whose husband had recently died, and produced the following slip:

(27) *"You will find consolation in widwen [a meaningless word] yourself entirely to your children."*

The intended word here was *widmen* ('devoting'). *Widwen* is a nonword whose origins are sought by Freud in a suppressed thought that the young lady remained "a young and pretty widow (*Witwe*) who will soon enjoy fresh sexual pleasures" (Freud, 1975:113). An alternative interpretation of the slip, however, is as a simple phoneme perseveration, analogous with example (28) from the Appendix to Fromkin (1973):

(28) cortical → *corkical*

In other instances, for example, (25), the speaker's introspections reveal that the disturbing word that blends with the intended word had been in the speaker's thoughts before the utterance was produced. Arguably the disturbing word had been "spoken" subvocally, so that the intended word could have blended with a lingering phonemic trace of the disturbing word. Such errors would, indeed, be revealing as to the thoughts that the speaker wished to conceal, but those thoughts could not have been truly unconscious prior to manifesting themselves in the slip.

6. Final Remarks

Viewed critically, the evidence for Freud's theory of speech errors is not strong. Freud (1974:66) asks: "Was it, then, merely a deceptive illusion or a poetic exaltation of parapraxes when we thought we recognized an intention in them?" In the absence of strong evidence to the contrary, many will feel inclined to answer him in the affirmative (although in doing so they should ask themselves why psychoanalysts have been able to point out a number of instances of the use of speech errors by dramatists to reveal the hidden motives and desires of their characters).

Freud's formulations may be rejected on the grounds of current untestability, but they should not be rejected as vague, or as incompatible with an information-processing approach. Freud's theory can be translated into the language of modern speech production models without excessive difficulty. The theory requires that the cognitive system which molds semantic messages into phonemic form should be capable of processing two rival messages simultaneously (this requirement may conflict with current notions of limited-capacity processing, but it is not an impossible demand). Speakers should (sometimes) be unaware of cognitive–linguistic activity until its products are crystallized into phonemic form (data on subliminal perception may be given a similar interpretation). Also, following read-out from the phonemic response buffer, impending speech should be capable of being vetted for its lexical-semantic properties (cf. Baars, Motley, and MacKay, 1975; Motley and Baars, 1976). These and similar modifications of the existing model would suffice to incorporate into it all the requirements necessary to simulate Freudian slips of the tongue.

One thing is certain. While the perpetrators of Freudian slips may be just the hapless victims of chance, their inadvertent blunders will continue to raise an eyebrow and a knowing smile from those near enough to hear. I close with a few collectors items for connoisseurs of the Freudian slip of the tongue, psycholinguist or psychoanalyst.

(29)   *The psychology of success–sex*
(30)   (a female speaker) At least I've got my priorities right. → *At least I've got my proportions right.*
(31)   palace of antiquities → *palace of iniquities*
(32)   (from a politician) *I like Heath. He's tough–like Hitler–*(shocked silence from reporters)*–Did I say Hitler? I meant Churchill.*

Note

1. This chapter was written while the author was a postgraduate student at the University of Edinburgh, Department of Psychology.

References

Baars, B. J., Motley, M. T., & MacKay, D. G. 1975. Output editing for lexical status in artificially elicited slips of the tongue. *Journal of Verbal Learning and Verbal Behaviour, 14,* 382-391.
Boomer, D. S. & Laver, J. D. M. 1968. Slips of the tongue. *British Journal of Disorders of Communication, 3,* 2-12.

Ellis, A. W. 1979. Speech production and short-term memory. In J. Morton & J. C. Marshall (Eds.), *Psycholinguistics Series Vol. 2: Structures and Processes.* London: Elek & Cambridge, Mass.: MIT Press. Pp. 157-187.

Ellis, A. W. & Myers, T. F. 1976. The role of a phonemic response buffer in speech and short-term memory. Paper presented to Autumn Conference of the British Institute of Acoustics. September 1976.

Fay, D. & Cutler, A. 1977. Malapropisms and the structure of the mental lexicon. *Linguistic Inquiry, 8,* 505-520.

Freud, S. (1916-17) 1974. *Introductory lectures on psychoanalysis.* Translated by J. Strachey. Harmondsworth, England: Penguin Books.

Freud, S. (1941) 1975. *The psychopathology of everyday life.* Translated by A. Tyson. Harmondsworth, England: Penguin Books.

Fromkin, V. A. 1971. The non-anomalous nature of anomalous utterances. *Language, 47,* 27-52.

Fromkin, V. A. 1973. *Speech errors as linguistic evidence.* The Hague: Mouton.

Garrett, M. F. 1975. The analysis of sentence production. In G. H. Bower (Ed.), *The psychology of learning and motivation* (Vol. 9). New York: Academic Press. Pp. 133-177.

Garrett, M. F. 1976. Syntactic processes in sentence production. In R. J. Wales & E. Walker (Eds.), *New approaches to language mechanisms.* Amsterdam: North-Holland Publ. Co. Pp. 231-256.

Hockett, C. F. 1967. Where the tongue slips, there slip I. In *To honour Roman Jakobson* (Vol. 2). The Hague: Mouton. Pp. 910-936.

Hotopf, W. H. N. 1968. Unintentional errors in speech and writing as clues to the processes underlying word production. Mimeographed paper, London School of Economics.

MacKay, D. G. 1970. Spoonerisms: The structure of errors in the serial order of speech. *Neuropsychologia, 8,* 323-350.

MacKay, D. G. 1972. The structure of words and syllables: Evidence from errors in speech. *Cognitive Psychology, 3,* 210-227.

Meringer, R. & Mayer, C. 1895. *Versprechen und verlesen: Eine psychologisch-linguistische Studie.* Berlin: Verlag.

Motley, M. T. & Baars, B. J. 1976. Semantic bias effects on the outcome of verbal slips. *Cognition, 4,* 177-188.

Nooteboom, S. G. 1969. The tongue slips into patterns. In A. G. Sciarone, A. J. van Essen, and A. A. van Raad (Eds.), Nomen Society, *Leyden studies in linguistics and phonetics.* The Hague: Mouton. Pp. 114-132.

Shaffer, L. H. 1976. Intention and performance. *Psychological Review, 83,* 375-393.

Tweney, R. D., Tkacz, S., & Zaruba, S. 1975. Slips of the tongue and lexical storage. *Language and Speech, 18,* 388-396.

Chapter 10

VERIFICATION OF "FREUDIAN SLIPS"
AND SEMANTIC PREARTICULATORY EDITING
VIA LABORATORY-INDUCED SPOONERISMS

Michael T. Motley

Department of Communication
The Ohio State University
Columbus, Ohio

1. Introduction

Ever since Freud (1901) first popularized the suggestion that verbal slips may provide insights to cognitive processing, linguists and psycholinguists have examined slips of the tongue in pursuit of such insight. The verbal slip research since Freud has discounted Freud's original notions, however. Freud claimed that verbal slips are instigated by the global cognitive (and affective) state of the speaker, and that linguistic factors do not influence the outcome of the errors. Subsequent research has ignored the Freudian notion of influence by global cognitive states, while focusing on the linguistic factors that influence verbal slips. The present study, while based upon the recognition that linguistic factors most certainly influence verbal slip outcomes, is designed to pursue the possibility that the influences outlined by Freud may operate as well.

Freud explained verbal slips as a manifestation of a speaker's cognitive state. The claim was that verbal slips are semantically related to a cognitive state, or set, which is determined by personality and situational influences, and which may be independent of the cognitions associated with the speaker's intended utterance. To put it another way, Freud's view was that semantic influences (e.g., cognitive set) that are independent of a speaker's intended utterance can create a distorted utterance such that the mutilated outcome (i.e., verbal slip) more closely resembles the meaning of the (semantic) interference than the meaning of the originally intended verbal output. Although the notion of the "Freudian slip" has enjoyed intuitive popularity, there has been no replicable empirical evidence of the phenomenon, and there has been very little evidence of the specific speech encoding processes that could account for this type of verbal slip. More specifically, there has been no experimental evidence that the kinds of semantic considerations present in "higher," and presumably more remote, stages of encoding (e.g., semantic and presemantic stages) can distort the more immediate phonological or articulatory stages. Since evidence for Freudian slips has always been anecdotal, corresponding theories have always been *post hoc.*

Researchers have succeeded in artificially eliciting various types of slips of the tongue (MacKay, 1971; Motley and Baars, 1975a; 1976a; see especially Baars, this volume). Laboratory-generated verbal slips now allow a precisely replicable investigation of the potential of semantic factors (and/or cognitive set) to influence verbal slips. The present study investigates this question via a laboratory technique which elicits spoonerisms—the type of verbal slip in which phonemes are switched with one another (e.g., the intended utterance *blue chip stocks* accidentally spoken as *blue chop sticks*). The spoonerism has been an especially popular type of verbal slip for psycholinguistic research, partially because of the clarity of its mutilation (see MacKay, 1970; Motley, 1973).

This study employed the spoonerism elicitation technique developed by Motley and Baars (1976a). The basic procedure (to be detailed in the following section) consists of a tachistoscopic presentation of a word-pair list. The word pairs are read silently by the subject, with the exception of certain word pairs that are cued to be spoken aloud; these being TARGET word pairs designed by the experimenter to elicit spoonerisms. The target word pairs are preceded by INTERFERENCE word pairs (read silently), which are designed to resemble more closely the phonology of the desired spoonerism error than the phonology of the subject's intended target. (For example, the target *red bowl,* expected to spoonerize into *bed roll,* might be preceded by interference items such as *best rose* or *bets rode.*) This SLIP technique (Spoonerisms of Laboratory-Induced Predisposition) elicits spoonerisms on approximately 30% of the target word pairs attempted by the subject. (For details and variations of the technique, see Motley and Baars, 1976a. For an introduction to other laboratory techniques for eliciting various kinds of verbal slips, see Baars, this volume.)

While at the same time pursuing Freud's explanation of verbal slips, the present study was conceived primarily as an extension of earlier studies using the SLIP technique. Previous research with the SLIP procedure has demonstrated that spoonerism frequencies are affected by certain linguistic characteristics of the spoonerism error itself, independent of the characteristics of the target. Motley and Baars (1975a) demonstrated, for example, that spoonerism frequencies increase according to the transitional probability of the initial phoneme sequence of the error: Word-initial spoonerism frequencies increase for errors with higher word-initial phonotactic probabilities. Baars, Motley, and MacKay (1975) demonstrated that spoonerism frequencies increase according to the lexical legitimacy of the error, independent of the lexical characteristics of their targets: Spoonerism frequencies are greater for lexically legitimate errors than for lexically anomalous errors, regardless of their targets.

These earlier studies allowed conclusions regarding the probable linguistic characteristics of spoonerism outcomes. More importantly, however, these studies also allowed conclusions regarding the subjects' cognitive encoding operations during the SLIP task. Specifically, the cognitive processing that precedes the subject's eventual articulation involves not only a consideration of the target, but also an evaluative consideration of its recoded (spoonerized) phoneme sequence. Notice, for example, that subjects provided with an equal number of targets such as *long root* (/lɔŋ rut/ → /rɔŋ lut/), versus phonologically matched targets such as *lawn roof* (/lɔn ruf/ → /rɔn luf/), will produce a significantly greater number of slips on those targets that allow lexically legitimate spoonerisms (e.g., *long root* → *wrong loot* versus *lawn roof* → *rawn loof.* See Baars *et al.,* 1975). Since the targets themselves are similar in all respects, subjects' spoonerism behavior (e.g., favoring *wrong loot* over *rawn loof*) cannot be dependent in any direct way upon subjects' evaluations of the targets. Rather, the spoonerism behavior can be explained only by allowing that subjects considered the spoonerized version of the targets prior to articulation, and *evaluated* the corresponding phoneme sequences by applying the criterion of lexical legitimacy.

Thus, it appears that the SLIP errors manifest a sort of PREARTICULATORY EDITING process: The SLIP interference word pairs presumably create confusion within the phoneme sequencing process; this confusion multiplies the available choice of phoneme sequences accompanying the attempted articulation of the target (e.g., at least the target sequence and spoonerized sequence are potential choices); and the decision of which potential phoneme string will in fact be articulated is determined by "editing" (i.e., evaluating) the available choices. As for the analogous role of prearticulatory editing in natural speech encoding, Motley and Baars (1975b) offer the following explanation: Since phoneme sequencing in natural speech is typically quite efficient (e.g., Wickelgren, 1969), the edit probably performs a generally passive function, with activation occasionally being triggered by noise, or interference, within the phoneme-sequence information. When triggered, the editing mechanism evaluates the available phoneme-sequence options, approving for articulation the sequence which fits its editing criteria. Notice that phoneme sequence options that happen NOT to be the originally intended utterance might nevertheless satisfy the editing criteria. For example, the "error" *darn bore* (from intended *barn door*) would satisfy an edit based on phonotactic and lexical criteria. Thus, many natural verbal slips might result from prearticulatory editing APPROVAL of the utterance. Those situations in which verbal slips are linguistically anomalous must then represent failures within the prearticulatory editing operations. (This model of prearticulatory editing, both within the SLIP task and within natural psycholinguistic encoding, is presented in detail elsewhere; see especially Motley and Baars, 1975b. For a discussion of sources of interference within phoneme-sequencing operations, see Baars's discussions of "competing plans," this volume, and especially Baars, 1976. For a discussion of sources of failure within prearticulatory editing, see Motley and Baars, 1975b.)

As suggested in the preceding discussion, earlier studies of laboratory-induced verbal slips have suggested two criteria employed by prearticulatory editing operations—the phonotactic integrity of the phoneme sequence (Motley and Baars, 1975a) and the lexical integrity of the phoneme sequence (Baars *et al.*, 1975). The present study investigates the presence of additional prearticulatory editing criteria; specifically, SEMANTIC criteria.

Given a prearticulatory editing model, Freud's prediction of cognitive set influences upon verbal slip outcomes may be approached as a prediction of semantic criteria operating within the edit. That is, perhaps edited phoneme sequences are evaluated not only on the basis of phonotactic and lexical legitimacy, but also on the basis of their semantic legitimacy. Notice, however, that whereas phonotactic and lexical legitimacy are rather absolute (that is, a given phoneme sequence simply either does or does not satisfy the phonology and lexicon of the speaker's language), semantic legitimacy is relative. That is to say, we might consider the semantic fidelity of a phoneme sequence (assuming that the sequence is indeed phonotactically and lexically legitimate) in terms of its consonance with its immediate verbal context, or perhaps in terms of its consonance with the speaker's sociosituational context (which is a more "Freudian" interpretation), or even in terms of its consonance with some aspect of the speaker's personality (which is a yet more Freudian interpretation). These three levels of semantic editing are investigated within the present study. Experiment 1 investigates the influence of VERBAL semantic interference upon spoonerism outcomes. Experiment 2 investigates the influence of SITUATION-AL COGNITIVE SET upon verbal slip outcomes. Experiment 3 investigates the influence of PERSONALITY upon verbal slips.

2. Experiment 1[1]

2.1. *Hypothesis*

Frequencies of spoonerisms will be significantly greater for word-pair targets preceded by both semantic and phonological interference than for targets preceded by phonological interference only.

2.2. *Subjects*

Subjects were 44 experimentally naive students of an introductory communication course at California State University, Los Angeles. All were native speakers of American English.

2.3. Apparatus

The SLIP word pairs were tachistoscopically presented by a memory drum, each word pair being exposed for one second, with less than .10 second between exposures. The cue for subjects to speak aloud the target word pairs (and certain neutral "filler" word pairs) was a buzzer.

2.4. Stimuli

Two matched lists of 264 word pairs were constructed; one for the Semantic Interference treatment, and one for the Semantically Neutral treatment; they were identical except for their semantic bias items. Each word-pair list contained 20 target word pairs as potential spoonerisms, each target preceded by four interference word pairs. Target word pairs were designed to elicit lexically legitimate spoonerism switches of the words' initial consonants. For example, the target *bad mug* would be expected to spoonerize to *mad bug*. The interference preceding each target consisted of two word pairs containing phonological interference, and two word pairs containing semantic interference. The phonological interference word pairs were constructed such that the initial consonants and subsequent vowels of both words were identical to the corresponding phonemes of the expected spoonerism (e.g., phonological interference pairs *mashed buns* and *massive bus* for target *bad mug →* *mad bug*). The semantic interference word pairs (for the Semantic Interference treatment list only) were constructed such that their MEANING would be similar to that of the expected spoonerisms while independent of the meaning of their target word pairs (e.g., semantic interference pairs *irate wasp* and *angry insect* for target *bad mug → mad bug*). These semantic interference word pairs (of the Semantic Interference treatment list) were matched on the Semantically Neutral treatment list by word pairs that were similar in phonology (to their semantic interference "mates") but which were semantically independent of their corresponding target or expected spoonerism. (For example, the semantic interference words *irate wasp* and *angry insect* were matched by the semantically neutral *Irene's watch* and *angle insert,* for target *bad mug → mad bug.*)

The sequential order for each set of 4 interference word pairs alternated phonological–semantic interference items (beginning with semantic interference), with the semantic interference pairs cued to be spoken aloud. Each set of interference and target items was separated by four to seven neutral "filler" word pairs, some of which were randomly cued to be spoken aloud.[2]

A counterbalanced within-subjects design was employed. Each subject's trial consisted of a performance on the first half of one treatment's word list followed immediately by the second half of the other treatment's word list.

2.5. *Instructions*

Subjects were instructed to read the word pair list silently. Upon hearing the buzzer cue, subjects were to speak aloud the word pair which had accompanied the buzzer.[3]

2.6. *Results*

As predicted, the 44 subjects committed a significantly greater number of spoonerism errors for the Semantic Interference treatment than for the Semantically Neutral treatment. Specifically, 75 spoonerisms occurred under the Semantic Interference treatment versus 27 spoonerisms for the Semantically Neutral treatment, with 31 subjects performing in the predicted direction ($T[34] = 30$, 10 ties, $p < .001$; Wilcoxon Signed Ranks test). We may thus accept the hypothesis.

2.7. *Discussion*

Experiment 1 demonstrates that the subjects' speech encoding systems were sensitive to semantic influence from the "semantic interference" word pairs. Notice that since subjects in both treatments were considering the SAME targets, the differences in spoonerism frequencies cannot be due to an encoding evaluation of the target itself. Rather, the increased frequency of semantically biased spoonerisms must be due to some evaluation of the spoonerized phoneme sequence. That is, the subjects' encoding process must have involved an evaluation of recoded (i.e., spoonerized and perhaps alternative) phoneme strings, since the semantic bias relates only to the error OUTCOME, independent of the target.[4] These semantic evaluations of recoded phoneme sequences served either to inhibit the eventual articulation of semantically anomalous phoneme sequences or to facilitate the articulation of semantically appropriate phoneme sequences, or both.

As in the earlier SLIP studies, prearticulatory editing of recoded phoneme strings is evident in Experiment 1. In this case, however, the editing criterion is a semantic criterion. Moreover, the edit seems to base its semantic evaluation not so much upon what is semantically congruous with the target, but rather upon what is semantically congruous with the verbal context that accompanies the target. In effect, the semantic criterion overrides the target criterion.

Experiment 1, by demonstrating the ability of semantic criteria to override target criteria during prearticulatory encoding, comes close to demonstrating the effects proposed by Freud. As in Freud's theory, the SLIP task demonstrates that semantic interference may contribute to a distortion of the articulated phonology of a speaker's intended utterance, and that the distortion may result in an utterance whose meaning is closer to that of the semantic interference than to that of the intended utterance. There is, however, a primary difference between the type of verbal slip discussed by Freud and the verbal slips generated in Experiment 1. In Freud's verbal slip examples, the semantic interference is supposed to originate from "outside" of the total semantic context of the intended utterance. This condition was only partially present in Experiment 1, since the interference was verbal interference within the context of the task, and was in close proximity to the targets (although semantically independent of the targets). That is, the semantic editing criteria were established by the verbal context of the SLIP lists.

Experiment 2 seeks evidence of semantic editing criteria based not upon verbal context, but rather upon a more global "situational cognitive set." The procedure was similar to that of Experiment 1, except that the source of semantic interference was designed to be found not on the word lists, but rather within the treatments' situational environments. While being virtually a direct test of Freud's theory, Experiment 2 seeks an extension of the semantic editing criteria established by Experiment 1.

3. Experiment 2[5]

3.1. *Hypothesis*

Frequencies of spoonerisms will be significantly greater for targets yielding errors semantically congruous with subjects' situational cognitive set than for targets yielding errors semantically incongruous with subjects' situational cognitive set.

3.2. *Subjects*

Subjects were 90 experimentally naive male students of an introductory communication course at California State University, Los Angeles. All were native speakers of American English.

3.3. *Apparatus*

The apparatus was the same as that of Experiment 1.

3.4. *Treatments*

Subjects were randomly assigned to one of three treatment conditions designed to manipulate situational cognitive set (30 subjects per condition): One condition was designed to create a situational cognitive set toward electric shocks. For this Electricity Set treatment, subjects were attached to false electrodes ostensibly connected to an electric timer. Subjects were told that the timer was capable of emitting random, moderately painful, electric shocks; and that during the course of their task they may or may not receive such a shock. (No shocks were administered.) The Electricity Set treatment was administered by a male experimenter. A second treatment condition was created to establish a situational cognitive set toward sex. For this Sex Set treatment, the task was administered by a female confederate experimenter who was by design, attractive, personable, very provocatively attired, and seductive in behavior. The Sex Set treatment was administered in the absence of electrical apparatus. A Neutral Set control treatment was administered by a male experimenter in the absence of electrical apparatus.

3.5. *Stimuli*

Subjects in all treatments performed the SLIP task on the same word-pair list. Spoonerism targets were nonsense words for which a switch of initial consonants would create real words related either to electricity or sex. The word-pair list contained 7 targets designed to elicit spoonerism errors related to the Electricity Set (e.g., *shad bock → bad shock, vani molts → many volts,* etc.) alternated with 7 targets designed to elicit spoonerism errors related to the Sex Set (e.g., *goxi furl → foxi girl, lood gegs → good legs,* etc.).

Each target was preceded by three interference word pairs designed to create phonological bias toward the expected spoonerism error. For example, the target *bine foddy*—expected to spoonerize to *fine body*—was preceded by the interference word pairs, *fire bobby, five toddies,* and *line shoddy.*[6] Each set of interference and target items was separated by 4 to 6 neutral filler word pairs, some of which received randomly assigned cues to be spoken aloud. Interference words were semantically independent of expected spoonerisms. Interference and filler items consisted of both nonsense-word pairs and real-word pairs.

3.6. *Instructions*

Instructions were the same as for Experiment 1.

3.7. *Results*

As predicted, spoonerism frequencies were higher for the targets whose errors matched the treatments' cognitive set than for targets whose errors were unrelated to the treatment. The Sex Set yielded 76 Sex Errors and 36 Electricity Errors, the Electricity Set produced 69 Electricity Errors and 31 Sex Errors, and the Neutral Set allowed 44 Electricity Errors and 41 Sex Errors. Analysis determined these frequency differences between treatments to be statistically significant. Specifically, a significant interaction occurred between the Cognitive Set factor (Electricity, Sex, and Neutral Sets) and the Error Outcome (Electricity and Sex Errors) factor ($F[2,87] = 24.91, p < .001$; Two Factor ANOVA, Repeated Measures on One Factor). A test for simple main effects demonstrated a significant difference in the effect of the Error Outcome factor for the Sex Set ($p < .001$) and for the Electricity Set ($p < .001$), though not for the Neutral Set ($p > .25$); as well as a significant difference in the effect of the Cognitive Set factor for the Sex Errors ($p < .01$), and for the Electricity Errors ($p < .01$). That is, for the Sex Set, Sex Errors were significantly more frequent than were Electricity Errors, whereas the reverse was true for the Electricity Set, and no difference was found for the Neutral Set. These results support the hypothesis.

3.8. Discussion

Experiment 2 demonstrates that subjects' speech encoding systems were sensitive to semantic influence from their situational cognitive set. Notice again that since subjects in all treatments were considering the same targets, and since the situational bias related only to the spoonerism outcome, the differences in spoonerism frequencies cannot be due to an encoding evaluation of the target itself, but rather must be due to an evaluation of the target's recoded phoneme sequence. Again, the evaluation was based upon criteria independent of the target itself; and again, these evaluations of recoded phoneme sequences served to inhibit incongruous sequences and/or to facilitate congruous sequences.

As in Experiment 1, Experiment 2 presents evidence of prearticulatory editing of recoded phoneme strings on the basis of semantic criteria. In Experiment 2, however, the semantic editing criterion is oriented toward support for Freud's proposal that natural verbal slips may be facilitated by a cognitive set independent of the semantic context of an intended utterance. That is, it appears that a prearticulatory edit evaluated potential phoneme sequences in terms of their congruence with the speakers' situational cognitive set.

Thus, Experiment 2 provides strong support for Freud's view of verbal slips. Crucial to a more complete interpretation of Freud's view, however, is his claim that the cognitive state supposedly manifested by verbal slips is determined not only by situational factors (as in Experiment 2), but by more global personality factors as well. Experiment 3 examines the influence of a personality trait (sexual anxiety) upon verbal slip outcomes.

4. Experiment 3

4.1. Hypothesis

Frequencies of Sex Error spoonerisms within a situational Sex Set will be greater for subjects with high levels of sex anxiety than for subjects with low levels of sex anxiety.

4.2. Subjects

Subjects were 36 experimentally naive male students of an introductory communication course at The Ohio State University. All were native speakers of American English.

4.3. *Apparatus*

Apparatus was the same as that of Experiments 1 and 2.

4.4. *Treatments*

The independent variable, sexual anxiety, was operationalized as Mosher Sex-Guilt Inventory scores (Mosher, 1966). From a larger initial subject pool were selected 12 High Sex Anxiety subjects, 14 Medium Sex Anxiety subjects, and 10 Low Sex Anxiety subjects.[7]

Subjects within all treatment groups (High, Medium, and Low Sex Anxiety) performed the SLIP task under the conditions of Experiment 2's Sex Set. (A different female confederate was employed for Experiment 3.) All subjects performed the task on the same stimulus list.

4.5. *Stimuli*

The primary ("experimental") SLIP stimuli were 9 targets (and accompanying interference pairs) of the type employed for the Sex Errors of Experiment 2; that is, nonsense-syllable-pair targets capable of initial-consonant spoonerisms into real words related to the sexually provocative treatment situation. Secondary ("control") stimuli were 9 nonsense-syllable targets (and interference items) that were phonologically matched with the 9 experimental targets, but which would yield real-word spoonerisms semantically unrelated to the sex-oriented treatment condition. The 9 experimental and 9 control target–interference sets were presented in alternating order, each control and experimental set separated by approximately 5 neutral filler word pairs. The 18 targets (and certain filler items) were buzzer-cued to be spoken aloud.

4.6. *Instructions*

Instructions were the same as for Experiments 1 and 2.

4.7. *Results*

Analyzed data were DIFFERENCE scores for each subject—the frequency of his spoonerisms on experimental (sex-related) targets minus his frequency of spoonerisms on control (neutral) targets. (As suggested by Experiment 2, spoonerism frequencies were consistently higher for experimental targets than for control targets.)[8]

As predicted, High Sex Anxiety subjects committed a greater number of Sex-Error spoonerisms ($\overline{D}$ = 2.7) than did Medium Sex Anxiety subjects ($\overline{D}$ = 1.7), who committed a greater number of Sex-Error spoonerisms than Low Sex Anxiety subjects ($\overline{D}$ = 1.3). A Kruskal-Wallis One-Way ANOVA by Ranks indicates these differences to be statistically significant (χ^2 [2] = 10.84, $p < .01$). These results support the hypothesis of a positive relationship between sexual anxiety and sex-related spoonerism frequencies.

4.8. *Discussion*

Whereas Experiment 2 demonstrated that situational cognitive set may affect verbal slip outcomes, Experiment 3 demonstrates that within a single situational cognitive set, personality factors may also influence verbal slip outcomes. That is, since all subjects performed the SLIP task on the same targets and within the same sexually provocative conditions, the differences in error rates of sex-related spoonerisms may be attributed to the personality, or sex-anxiety, differences between the groups. Moreover, since virtually all subjects produced more sex-related errors than neutral control errors, it again appears that subjects edited impending phoneme sequences prior to articulation. Clearly, however, this prearticulatory edit was more critical for High Sex Anxiety subjects than for Medium or Low Sex Anxiety subjects. An explanation of these results, compatible both with Freud's theories and with a prearticulatory editing model, is that the "Sex Set" situation provided a series of verbal associations against which a prearticulatory semantic edit might seek verification, and that those associations were most salient for High Sex Anxiety subjects.

5. Conclusion

Experiments 1, 2, and 3 may be viewed as evidence of additional criteria for prearticulatory editing. That is, to the phonological and lexical criteria evidence in earlier studies, we may now add semantic criteria. Thus, the prearticulatory editing model would postulate that when noise enters a phoneme sequence during encoding toward articulation, the noise is treated by an evaluation (edit) of potential phoneme sequence options. This evaluation includes a consideration of the phonotactic, lexical, and semantic integrity of the phoneme sequences; rejecting those sequences that fail to meet the criteria, and "approving" for articulation a sequence that does meet the criteria. The approved phoneme sequence may be that of the original target; but since the edit criteria are linguistic criteria independent of the target, the approved phoneme sequence may be one other than that of the original target (i.e., may be a verbal slip).

Having found evidence of prearticulatory editing upon several criteria, we must wonder what is the source of these edit criteria. That is, what is the nature of the information against which phoneme sequences are compared during an editing evaluation? The issue is more complex for the semantic editing demonstrated in Experiments 1, 2, and 3 than for the earlier studies. Given the question, "Is phoneme string X PHONOTACTICALLY appropriate?," or "Is phoneme string X LEXICALLY appropriate?," an editor could make a simple yes-or-no decision. Moreover, this decision may be made simply on the basis of the linguistic parameters of the editor's language as a whole. That is, a given phoneme string simply either does or does not meet the phonotactic criteria of the language; and if it does, then it either does or does not represent an existing lexical entity within the language. Thus, since we have evidence that phonotactic and lexical prearticulatory editing decisions are not based upon comparisons with the target, we might conclude that the decisions are based upon comparisons with phonotactic and lexical information for the language as a whole.

However, given the question, "Is phoneme string X SEMANTICALLY appropriate?," an editor could not make a simple yes–no decision without further information. That is, phoneme sequences are not semantically appropriate or inappropriate on the basis of linguistic criteria alone, but rather are appropriate or inappropriate on the basis of contextual considerations. Whereas each phonotactic or lexical editing decision may be determined by reference to the same information, each semantic editing decision must be determined by reference to new information.

As for the source of reference information for semantic edits, the explanation implied by Freud seems plausible. Freud (1901:41) asserts that two factors influence verbal slips; a "stream of associations," and a "relaxation of the inhibiting attention [i.e., ego]." Within the context of Experiment 2, these factors would operate as follows: Situations involving threat of electric shock or a sexually provocative environment should produce a series of corresponding associations for practically all male subjects; those associations should serve as criteria for semantically oriented prearticulatory edits; and moreover, the SLIP task itself is sufficiently complex to create a diversion of attention and a corresponding relaxation of the inhibiting mechanism (see Corsini, 1977), so that the (otherwise inhibited) associations are then available for editing access (and production).

Experiment 3 follows the same pattern, with the association-evoking situation (i.e., Sex Set) constant for all subjects, and the inhibition–relaxation diversion (the SLIP task) constant for all subjects. Experiment 3, however, provides evidence for Freud's prediction that the strength of the stream of associations should be positively related to the amount of psychodynamic conflict being experienced by the individual. That is to say, the sexually provocative environment of Experiment 3 should have created more psychodynamic conflict for High Sex Anxiety subjects than for Medium or Low Sex Anxiety subjects, and this greater conflict should have produced a stronger stream of associations for the High Sex Anxiety subjects. Thus, Experiment 3's results may be explained in terms of the semantic edit criteria (i.e., the stream of associations) being more salient (to the prearticulatory edit) for the High Sex Anxiety subjects than for other subjects.

To explain the results of Experiment 1, we need only recognize (although disagreeing with Freud) that "streams of associations" are presumably instigated not only by situational contexts, but (at least) by verbal contexts as well (Collins and Loftus, 1975). Again, these associations may serve as the criteria for a semantic edit.

We may now readdress the more general question of the source of (all) prearticulatory editing criteria. As implied earlier in this discussion (and as discussed by Baars, this volume), the earlier demonstrations of prearticulatory editing suggested some sort of feedback operations, or "bottom-up" encoding processes, within the more commonly accepted "top-down" (semantic-lexical-syntactic-phonological-articulatory) encoding processes. With phonotactic and lexical editing, however, we could not be certain that the feedback reference was one that goes back up to higher, or earlier, encoding levels. Since the reference information for phonotactic and lexical decisions is static, it was at least possible (though intuitively unattractive) that this reference information enters the flow of control at stages lower than phonological encoding. In the case of semantic editing, however, we can be certain of a bottom-up feedback process to higher than postphonological levels of encoding. Since the semantic reference information is dynamic and situation-specific, and since the reference information may even be preverbal (in the sense of being independent of the verbal constraints of the intended utterance), the semantic edit must flow upward to a very high level of encoding. We may thus at least infer that the phonological and lexical edits likewise require feedback to higher (than postphonological) levels of encoding.

In summary, this study, while seeking evidence of semantic criteria in prearticulatory editing, has supported Freud's notion of verbal slips, although differing in certain particulars. Whereas Freud would claim that linguistic factors do not influence verbal slips, this study recognizes that linguistic factors do indeed influence verbal slip outcomes. Whereas Freud would claim that ALL verbal slips are semantic manifestations of a speaker's private cognitive-affective state, the present study makes no such claim (and this writer would expect such manifestations to be rare). Freud would claim that one's cognitive set is a direct cause of verbal slips, in that the cognitive set is responsible for the (stream of) association(s) that may be output, or articulated, if the inhibition (i.e., ego) is relaxed. The position of this report is that the more direct cause of verbal slips is noise or interference in the phonological encoding processes, with the associations provided by cognitive set (and verbal context) serving merely as reference information for the semantic phase of prearticulatory editing (and with that semantic phase being only one component of a larger series of prearticulatory editing operations). Freud's more general insight is one for which this study lends strong support: Semantic influences that are independent of a speaker's intended utterance can influence verbal slips to be closer in meaning to those semantic influences than to the originally intended utterance.

Acknowledgments

The author wishes to acknowledge the valuable comments of his colleague Bernard J. Baars on many of the issues raised in this chapter; to acknowledge Sandra Gary for her assistance with Experiment 2; and to acknowledge Carl T. Camden for his assistance with Experiment 3.

Notes

1. Experiment 1 has been reported in detail elsewhere. (See Motley and Baars, 1976b.)
2. These neutral control word pairs served as fillers to prevent the subjects from noticing a pattern by which to predict the cue for target word pairs.
3. A more complete and accurate account (e.g., for replication purposes) of the instructions and stimulus list is provided by Motley and Baars (1976b).
4. Motley and Baars (1976a) have demonstrated that these laboratory-generated spoonerisms are not the result of reading errors or other errors of the target's input into the encoding process, but rather are clearly the result of errors in attempting the target's articulatory output.
5. Experiment 2 is reported in detail elsewhere (see Motley and Baars, 1979).
6. The phonological pattern for these interference word pairs was constant for all targets. The pattern used was that of Motley and Baars (1976a).
7. "High" was defined as at least 1 SD above the mean, "Medium" as within ½ SD of the mean, and "Low" as at least 1 SD below the mean.
8. The difference between spoonerism frequencies for experimental targets and control targets was significant for each group ($p < .05$ for all groups). This partially replicates (and supports) Experiment 2.

References

Baars, B. J. 1976. The competing plans hypothesis: An heuristic approach to the problem of speech errors. Unpublished paper, University of California, Los Angeles.

Baars, B. J. & Motley, M. T. 1976. Spoonerisms as sequencer conflicts: Evidence from artificially elicited errors. *American Journal of Psychology, 83,* 467–484.

Baars, B. J., Motley, M. T., & MacKay, D. G. 1975. Output editing for lexical status in artificially elicited slips of the tongue. *Journal of Verbal Learning and Verbal Behavior, 14,* 382–391.

Collins, A. M. & Loftus, E. F. 1975. A spreading-activation theory of semantic processing. *Psychological Review, 82,* 407–428.

Corsini, R. J., 1977. *Current personality theories.* Itasca, Illinois: Peacock.

Freud, S. (1901) 1966. *Psychopathology of everyday life.* Translated by A. Tyson. London: Benn.

MacKay, D. G. 1970. Spoonerisms: The structure of errors in the serial order of speech. *Neuropsychologia, 8,* 323–350.

MacKay, D. G. 1971. Stress pre-entry in motor systems. *American Journal of Psychology, 84,* 35–51.

Mosher, D. L. 1966. The development and multitrait–multimethod matrix analysis of three measures of three aspects of guilt. *Journal of Consulting and Clinical Psychology, 30,* 25–29.

Motley, M. T. 1973. An analysis of spoonerisms as psycholinguistic phenomena. *Speech Monographs, 40,* 66–71.

Motley, M. T. & Baars, B. J. 1975a. Encoding sensitivities to phonological markedness and transitional probability: Evidence from spoonerisms. *Human Communication Research, 2,* 351–361.

Motley, M. T. & Baars, B. J. 1975b. Toward a model of integrated editing processes in prearticulatory encoding: Evidence from laboratory generated verbal slips. Paper presented to the Speech Communication Association, Houston.

Motley, M. T. & Baars, B. J. 1976a. Laboratory induction of verbal slips: A new method for psycholinguistic research. *Communication Quarterly, 24,* 28–34.

Motley, M. T. & Baars, B. J. 1976b. Semantic bias effects on the outcome of verbal slips. *Cognition, 4,* 177–187.

Motley, M. T. & Baars, B. J. 1979. Effects of cognitive set upon laboratory induced verbal (Freudian) slips. *Journal of Speech and Hearing Research, 22,* 421–432.

Wickelgren, W. A. 1969. Context-sensitive coding, associative memory, and serial order in (speech) behavior. *Psychological Review, 76,* 1–15.

Chapter 11

SPEECH PRODUCTION: CORRECTION OF
SEMANTIC AND GRAMMATICAL ERRORS
DURING SPEECH SHADOWING[1]

James R. Lackner

Department of Psychology
Brandeis University
Waltham, Massachusetts

The relationship between the linguistic structure of a message and its perceptual processing has become much better understood in recent years. In particular, it has been found that perceptual units in sentence comprehension are in part syntactically determined. By contrast, much less is known about the organizational units involved in sentence production; and that which is known has been derived primarily from studies of speech errors (Fromkin, 1971; MacKay, 1970). Several recent experiments have supported the conclusions drawn from these speech-error analyses and confirmed the existence of a supraword level of organization in speech production (Lackner and Levine, 1975; Shattuck-Hufnagel and Lackner, 1975). These studies raise the possibility of similar representational levels in sentence decoding during speech comprehension and in sentence encoding during speech production. The experiment to be described was addressed to this possibility; it makes use of the task of speech shadowing—the continuous repetition by a listener of a message that he receives over headphones—which involves both sentence comprehension and production.

The basis for this experiment is derived from earlier work. Shattuck-Hufnagel and Lackner (1975) found that subjects who were required to shadow sentences and word lists (constructed by rearranging the words of the sentences) could no longer keep up with the word lists as the rate of presentation was increased from three to six words per second although their performance was still quite good on the sentences. The inability to shadow word lists accurately at the higher rates of presentation was not due entirely to a recognition difficulty but was due in part to an inability to articulate the individual words rapidly enough. In related observations, Shattuck-Hufnagel and Lackner (1975) and Lackner and Levine (1975) found that the rapidity and temporal accuracy with which sentences can be spoken are much greater than for word lists constructed from the same sentences.

Most shadowers are "distant shadowers," the latency between the onset of the message and the onset of their response is on the order of 750 msec. Marslen-Wilson (1973) has confirmed the observations of Kozhevnikov and Chistovich (1965) that some subjects are "close shadowers" and can follow a message with latencies as small as 300 msec. In the Shattuck-Hufnagel and Lackner experiments the performance of both close and distant shadowers was augmented by the presence of syntactic structure in the message being shadowed.

It seems likely that at very low rates of stimulus presentation, for instance, one or two words/second, subjects can shadow on a word-by-word basis. However, at high rates of presentation, more and more reliance must be placed on syntactic characteristics of the signal in order to decode and encode it rapidly enough to maintain pace. Accordingly, it might be expected that at higher stimulus rates perceptual and production units will more nearly approximate each other. Furthermore, at high presentation rates there should be less capability to analyze in depth the semantic and syntactic structure of the message being shadowed, and there should be greater reliance on contextual cues extrapolated during the course of the shadowed message.

To test these predictions we measured as a function of rate of presentation the performance of subjects shadowing messages containing various kinds of semantic and syntactic errors. We were interested in whether subjects would show spontaneous corrections of anomalous material and whether the presence of anomalies would interfere with their ability to shadow. Our prediction was that at higher rates of presentation subjects would show many spontaneous corrections without realizing the material they were shadowing was anomalous. We also expected that subjects would not be disrupted (in relation to performance on normal sentences presented at the same rates) by the anomalies since we expected that at the fast rates the subject's speech output would be organized in supraword innervational patterns similar in scope to the supraword units in which he decodes the input message.

1. Method

1.1. *Subjects*

Twelve Brandeis students volunteered for paid participation. All were right-handed, native speakers of English without known speech or hearing defects.

1.2. *Stimuli*

Four different kinds of stimulus material were prepared: normal sentences, word lists, sentences with syntactic errors, and sentences with semantic errors. All stimuli were 25 words in length. Twenty sentences were constructed that contained grammatical errors; these errors included incorrect verb tense, incorrect verb number, incorrect comparative form, and substitutions of adjectival endings for adverbial endings and vice versa. Twenty additional sentences were constructed that contained semantic errors, these errors were of two kinds: A totally inappropriate noun had been substituted for another in the sentence; or a spoonerism had been constructed from a familiar adage by interchanging certain words, for example, *People who live in stone houses should not throw glasses.*

The stimuli with grammatical and semantic errors were recorded by a male speaker at four rates, 3, 4, 5, and 6 words/sec, five of each kind of stimulus at each rate. Each stimulus was rerecorded by the speaker until it was within ± .1 word/sec of the desired rate and until an independent judge thought it sounded smooth and natural. Sixteen normal sentences and sixteen word lists were also constructed to serve as control stimuli. The word lists were created by rearranging the words of the individual normal sentences into a nonsyntactic, nonmeaningful order. Four word lists and four normal sentences were recorded at each of the four presentation rates. A normal sentence and the word lists constructed from it were always recorded at different rates.

A master tape was prepared by cross-recording the experimental and control stimuli in such a fashion that the order of stimulus appearance was randomized across type of stimulus and rate of presentation. In addition, two "practice" sentences, one at 3 words/sec and one at 5 words/sec were placed at the beginning of the experimental order. Ten seconds of silence were left between individual stimuli.

1.3. *Procedure*

During the experiment the subject was seated in a sound insulated booth and wore a stereophonic headset. A microphone, positioned approximately 12 inches in front of the subject's mouth, fed a tape recorder that made a permanent record of his responses. The subject was instructed that he would hear a voice over the headset and that he should repeat as exactly as possible everything the voice said. It was emphasized that he should begin his response as quickly as possible and that he should repeat exactly what the speaker said while following as closely behind as possible. The experimenter warned the subject that the speaker's rate of speaking could vary considerably from one stimulus to the next, that sometimes the speaker would be saying lists of words, and that individual stimuli would be separated by 10 sec of silence.

The stimuli were presented at 70 ± 3 dB (re .002 dynes/cm²). Six subjects heard the stimuli in their left ear, the remaining six heard the stimuli in their right ear. At the end of the first half of the experimental order, the subject was given a 5-min rest break.

1.4. *Scoring*

The recordings of each subject's experimental session were transcribed onto master sheets containing the stimuli actually presented, and any deviations from these were noted.

2. Results

Our first analysis determined accuracy as a function of rate on the different kinds of stimuli. On this measure a perfect score means the stimulus was repeated exactly as it was presented. Table 1 presents the experimental findings. The entries represent the percentage of words correct for the different types of stimuli and the four rates of presentation. Each of 12 subjects received five examples of each stimulus type at each of the presentation rates.

At all rates of presentation, performance was significantly worse on the word-list stimuli compared with the other stimulus types. At 3 and 4 words/sec the accuracy scores on the normal sentences, sentences with semantic errors, and sentences with syntactic errors are not significantly different. However, at 5 and 6 words/sec shadowing is significantly more accurate on the normal sentences compared with the sentences containing semantic or syntactic errors.

TABLE 1: *Shadowing Accuracy: Percentage of Total Stimulus Words Correct*

Stimulus type	Presentation rate (words/sec)			
	3	4	5	6
Sentence (normal)	95	91	91	70
Sentence (grammatical error)	93	92	82	63
Sentence (semantic error)	97	92	74	64
Word list	69	58	38	19

TABLE 2: *Error Correction Rate (%)*

Sentence type	Presentation rate (words/sec)			
	3	4	5	6
Grammatical error	28.4	16.0	61.8	59.8
Semantic error	13.6	15.0	48.4	63.2

The incidences of corrections of syntactic and semantic errors as a function of presentation rate are summarized in Table 2. The entries represent the percentage of stimulus sentences containing grammatical errors and semantic errors in which corrections were spontaneously made to eliminate or compensate for the anomaly. Subjects made corrections for both types of errors at all rates of presentation, but the number of corrections was significantly greater for the stimuli at 5 and 6 words/ sec compared with the stimuli at 3 and 4 words/sec. At the higher presentation rates, the incidence of error correction approached or exceeded 50% for both syntactic and semantic errors. Corrections were not restricted to a few of the sentences of each error type but were made on 35 of the 40 sentences; moreover, all subjects exhibited corrections for both kinds of error stimuli.

3. Discussion

Several features of the results require elaboration. At low rates of stimulus presentation, 3 and 4 words/sec, shadowing performance was just as accurate on the sentences with grammatical and semantic errors as on the normal sentences; at the higher rates, 5 and 6 words/sec, performance was better on the normal sentences. This performance asymmetry arises because at the higher presentation rates subjects corrected a high percentage of the errors in the anomalous sentences; accordingly, accuracy of repetition of the anomalous stimuli necessarily decreased because the subjects in making a correction were no longer repeating exactly the stimulus sentence. Clearly, the presence of anomalies in the stimulus sentences did not serve as distractions that disrupted shadowing of the attended message. In this vein it should be mentioned that subjects uniformly expressed surprise when told later that many of the stimuli had contained errors. Some subjects actually denied that they could have been presented anomalous stimuli because they had "heard" the corrected version. This observation is reminiscent of the report of Lackner and Garrett (1973) that it is possible to bias systematically a subject's interpretation of a message that he is hearing without his being aware of the bias.

The results do not permit a conclusion that one type of error correction is more common than another; grammatical corrections were slightly more frequent, but that is not surprising since some of the semantic corrections required changes of more than one word or changes in the positions of several words, whereas many of the grammatical corrections involved single words. Occasionally in the three kinds of sentential stimuli (sentences with semantic errors, sentences with grammatic errors, and normal sentences), a word would be omitted that would have affected the grammaticality of the sentence. In most of these instances, other changes were made further on that compensated for the omission. Thus one of the most persistent aspects of performance on the shadowing task was the continual imposition of semantic and grammatical regularity to eliminate anomaly.

These observations can now be related to our original hypotheses. As expected, at high rates of stimulus presentation subjects "correct" deviant material without being aware that it is deviant. Marslen-Wilson (1975)[2] has also been studying whether close-shadowers correct anomalies in stimulus sentences; the anomalies he has used are all within-word errors consisting of inappropriate syllables, suffixes, or words. His close-shadowers also exhibit error correction but at a much lower incidence than our distant-shadowers. All but one of the stimulus rates that he employed are slower than ours, and his fastest rate corresponds to our slowest, so it is possible to extrapolate that at very low rates of presentation, 1 or 2 words/sec, subjects can shadow anomalous material with reasonable accuracy. Apparently, at slow rates of presentation subjects are able to perform a more detailed syntactic and semantic analysis of the stimulus material; but at higher presentation rates they cannot both recover full details of the stimulus and shadow, too (see also Marslen-Wilson, 1975).

When a subject accurately shadowed an anomalous sentence, he had two opportunities to detect the error: once when hearing it presented by the speaker and once when producing it himself. That he detects the anomaly neither time suggests either that he pays little attention to the auditory feedback from his own voice while shadowing or that the level of perceptual analysis performed on his own auditory feedback is no greater than that on the original input.

It was possible to demonstrate, *post hoc,* that the inability of subjects to detect the errors in the anomalous sentences at the higher presentation rates was dependent on the simultaneous demands of the shadowing task on comprehension and production. This fact was demonstrated very simply by having another group of 12 subjects listen to the same stimulus material and write down on a sheet of paper each anomaly that they could detect in the stimuli. At 3 and 4 words/sec, 91% of the anomalies were accurately transcribed without being corrected; at 5 and 6 words/ sec, 78%.

The experimental observations support the notion of a symmetry between levels of organization in speech comprehension and speech production because when a subject fails to detect an anomaly while hearing a sentence he also fails to detect it when reproducing it in his shadowing response. Similarly, if a subject shadowing an anomalous sentence corrects the error, he is unaware that a discrepancy exists between the sentence presented and the sentence he spoke. It cannot be concluded, however, that because the organizational units in comprehension and production share similarities, they also have a common neurological substratum. The different types of language impairments that follow injury to different cortical and subcortical areas suggest that comprehension and production have distinct but related neural representations.

Notes

1. Support for this study was provided by the Rosenstiel Biomedical Sciences Foundation and the Spencer Foundation.
2. The present study and that of Marslen-Wilson were conceived and undertaken independently.

References

Fromkin, V. 1971. The non-anomalous nature of anomalous utterances. *Language, 47,* 27–52.
Kozhevnikov, V. A. & Chistovich, L. A. 1965. Speech: Articulation and perception. *Joint Publication Research Service, 30,* 543. Washington: U.S. Department of Commerce.
Lackner, J. R. & Garrett, M. F. 1972. Resolving ambiguity: Effects of biasing context in one unattended ear. *Cognition, 1,* 359–372.
Lackner, J. R. & Levine, K. S. 1975. Speech production: Evidence for syntactically and phonologically determined units. *Perception and Psychophysics, 17,* 107–113.
MacKay, D. G. 1970. Spoonerisms: The structure of errors in the serial order of speech. *Neuropsychology, 8,* 323–350.
Marslen-Wilson, W. 1973. Linguistic structure and speech shadowing at very short latencies. *Nature, 244,* 522–523.
Marslen-Wilson, W. 1975. Sentence perception as an interactive parallel process. *Science, 189,* 226–228.
Shattuck-Hufnagel, S. & Lackner, J. 1975. Speech production: Contribution of syntactic structure. *Perceptual and Motor Skills, 40,* 931–936.

Chapter 12

CORRECTING OF SPEECH ERRORS
IN A SHADOWING TASK

Anthony Cohen

Department of Phonetics
University of Utrecht
Utrecht, The Netherlands

1. Introduction

It had always been my intention to follow up earlier work with some experiments introducing the technique of shadowing. The main reason for this was that inclusion of the study of the monitoring function in speech, as outlined by Laver (1973), seemed to provide a necessary complement to the study of speech errors as such.

It has been generally noticed by workers in this field that in spontaneous speech, more often than not, the errors produced are corrected by the speakers themselves. Nooteboom (1977; this volume) has made a special study of this aspect of speech errors on the basis of the material that Meringer (1908) himself provided.

Some work on this line has been carried out by Cole (1973) and Marslen-Wilson and Welsh (1978). Cole's study was restricted to investigating the detection mechanism of listeners whose task it was to screen the input of spoken texts containing deliberate mispronunciations, which could involve single distinctive features as well as complexes of two, three, and four distinctive features. As it turned out, listeners were poorer in detecting single feature mistakes than they were in any of the other categories. In fact, his work was done with the aim of testing the hypothesis that distinctive features play a decisive role in the recognition of words in ongoing speech. Marslen-Wilson and Welsh's study had a much more ambitious scope in that they tried to test the relative contribution of the so-called bottom–top and top–bottom strategies in the perception of connected speech and their possible interaction. Their results obtained in a detection task as well as in a shadowing task were weighed against other models of speech perception.

The present set-up is more ambitious than the Cole study and at the same time far less so than the Marslen-Wilson and Welsh approach. As it was my intention to follow up previous work with spontaneous speech (Cohen, 1966; Nooteboom, 1969) it seemed only natural to maintain the various categories of errors described there. These involved the major categories of anticipations, perseverations, and transpositions. The first two were generally found to prevail in so-called phonological errors, whereas transpositions included larger structures such as morphemes and words.

On this basis the stimulus material was drawn up in two parts: one consisting of phonological errors, involving anticipations and perseverations, derived from a collection of errors occurring in spontaneous speech; the other consisting of a choice of proverbs and proverbial expressions derived from a standard collection (Stoett, 1953). In a pilot test both types of material were presented to subjects in an error-detection task. The outcome, contrary to Cole's results, was that hardly any error went undetected. Contrary to the set-up in the Marslen-Wilson and Welsh experiment, I chose to inform subjects of the presence of errors in the input speech.

2. Method

2.1. *Stimulus Material*

The twofold choice of material, phonological and proverbial, was based on the supposition that in ordinary speech production speakers clearly execute a monitoring task to the effect that they screen their output for possible errors. In the case of so-called phonological errors in ordinary speech the span of attention, or chunk, in monitoring may be smaller than in the language material involving proverbial expressions. The latter are presumably programed in larger chunks, giving rise historically to transpositions of whole words, as, for example, in Dutch *hart onder de riem steken* versus *riem onder het hart steken,* which have both become acceptable for expressing the same intention (see Stoett, 1953).

Since in phonological errors, involving single phonemes or clusters, a number of distinctions could be made on the basis of previously collected material dealing with spontaneous speech, it seemed useful for gaining a better understanding of the various components of the complex experimental task to set up a number of subdivisions in the stimulus material. In all cases the errors were worked into a coherent text.

The first subdivision that obtruded itself for inclusion was the distinction between anticipations and perseverations. In ongoing speech it seems most likely for a subject in the experimental task to overhear an error involving a perseveration than an error of the anticipatory kind. In the latter case the error as such is not foreshadowed but seems to come out of the blue unless one hears more of the following speech material. On this supposition perseveratory mispronunciations were expected to be restored more often than errors of anticipation.

As a second obvious subdivision with regard to conspicuity, the distinction between vowels and consonants seemed indicated as a possible variable in subjects' behavior, in which vowels may be expected to stand out more, perceptually, than consonants.

A third subdivision was created by the span between cause and actual error where the variable was intra- or interword span.

Since the shadowing task involved listening, it seemed advisable to distinguish also between errors in stressed and unstressed positions on the understanding that errors in unstressed positions would be less clearly noticeable and, therefore, would be restored more readily. This distinction made up the fourth subdivision of phonological errors. As for the proverbs, only whole-word transpositions were involved; a distinction was made between transpositions that would lead to nonsensical utterances and those leading to semantically acceptable alternatives. (See, for example, the English *a stitch in nine saves time* versus *he has kin nor kith.*)

The general expectation was that subjects would tend to correct phonological errors to which they were exposed more readily than word transpositions.

2.2. *Experimental set-up*

In all, 24 subjects whose native language was Dutch took part in the experiment, most of whom were students of the English department of Utrecht University. The texts were presented binaurally over headphones to subjects seated in a sound-treated booth with a microphone in front of them. Subjects were given a trial run of about one minute without errors to get accustomed to the shadowing task. They were not paid for their services. They received the oral instruction to repeat as accurately as possible everything they heard, including possible mistakes. They were expressly told not to try to correct them. Each session consisted of four texts, the first three containing phonological errors, the fourth word transpositions. To obviate a possible sequential effect, the order of presentation was reversed for a number of subjects, who were given the word transpositions first.

3. Results

The three texts with phonological errors contained 10, 10, and 11 errors, respectively, giving $31 \times 24 = 744$ errors of which 448 were corrected against the instructions, constituting about 60%. The text with word transpositions contained 10 errors, giving $10 \times 24 = 240$ possibilities of which 36 were corrected against the instruction (15%).

Table 1 gives an overall display of the results obtained divided over the various types, whereas Figure 1 shows the results in a graphic form, indicating the percentage restored in hatched bars and the percentage of errors preserved in white bars.

TABLE 1: *Number of times subjects either restored or preserved various categories of mispronunciations to which they were exposed in a speech-shadowing task.*

	Restored	Preserved	Total
Phonological			
Anticipations	215	169	384
Perseverations	233	127	360
Vowels	102	90	192
Consonants	312	144	456
Intraword	275	85	360
Interword	173	211	384
Stressed	311	241	552
Unstressed	137	55	192
Transpositing			
Nonsensical	18	126	144
Semantically acceptable	18	78	96

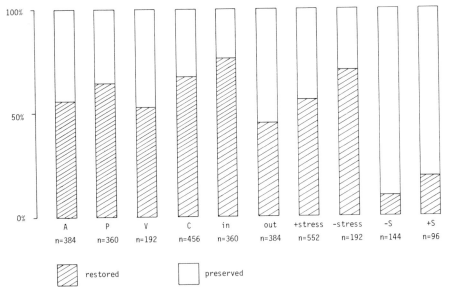

Figure 1. *Scores in percentage of errors restored (hatched bars) versus errors preserved (white bars) in the various categories of mispronunciations to which subjects were exposed in a speech-shadowing task. A = anticipations, P = perseverations, V = vowel, C = consonant, in = within a word, out = outside a word, +stress = stressed syllable, –stress = unstressed syllable, +S = semantically acceptable, –S = semantically unacceptable, n = total number of possible errors obtained by multiplying the number of subjects (24) by the number of errors of each category within the texts.*

3.1. *Anticipations versus perseverations*

There were 16 errors of anticipation, giving a total of 16 × 24 = 384 possible cases, against 15 errors of perseveration, giving a total of 15 × 24 = 360 possible cases. In line with expectation, errors of perseveration were restored more often than those of anticipation: 233 out of 360 (65%) versus 215 out of 384 (56%). This difference turned out to be significant (χ^2 = 5.918, df = 1, .02 > p > .01).

3.2. *Vowels versus consonants*

There were 8 vowel errors leading, to 8 × 24 = 192 cases for errors of which 102 (53%) were restored and 92 (47%) preserved. In the consonant category there were 19 errors, giving 19 × 24 = 456 cases, of which 312 (68%) were restored and 144 (32%) preserved. This difference was significant (χ^2 = 13.707, p < .001).

3.3. *Intraword versus interword interval*

There were 15 errors in which the cause and the error were within the same word (e.g., *probreem* instead of *probleem*), giving 15 × 24 = 360 possible cases of which 275 (76%) were restored and 85 (24%) preserved. There were 16 errors involving an interval beyond word boundaries (e.g., *uit de bos komt* instead of *uit de bus komt*), giving 16 × 24 = 384 cases of which 173 (45%) were restored and 211 (55%) preserved. This difference was significant (χ^2 = 76.174, p < .001).

3.4. *Stressed versus unstressed syllable*

There were 23 errors in stressed position, giving a total of 23 × 24 = 552, of which 311 (56%) were restored versus 241 (44%) preserved. In the unstressed position there were 8 cases, giving 8 × 24 = 192, of which 137 (71%) were restored and 55 (29%) preserved (χ^2 = 13.407, p < .001).

3.5. *Word transpositions*

Of the proverbs 6 cases involved nonsensical sequences of words, giving 6 × 24 = 144 cases, of which 18 (12%) were restored versus 126 (88%) preserved. The four remaining, giving 4 × 24 = 96 cases, involved errors that did not seriously affect meaning, of which 18 (19%) were restored versus 78 (81%) preserved. The difference here was not significant.

4. Discussion

The overall expectations were clearly fulfilled to the extent that phonological errors, against instructions, were restored in 60% of all cases. The same tendency was not at work in the word transpositions occurring in the proverbial stimuli, where only 15% were restored. Errors of anticipation were restored less frequently than perseverations, which seems to be in line with the expectation that in a shadowing task a subject would tend to overhear an error perseveration more readily than one in anticipation. The monitoring task seems to work more strictly in the case of consonants than in that of vowels, which may be due to the overall higher information involved in consonant phonemes.

As for the stressed versus unstressed position, it stands to reason that in a shadowing task it would be harder to perceive errors in unstressed syllables; therefore the so-called restoration rate in the output is bound to be higher than for stressed syllables.

With regard to the distinction between intra- and interword interval between origin and target, the high rate of restoration of errors within a word seems to fit in very well with the findings reported by Marslen-Wilson and Welsh (1978). In their experiment they also introduced a shadowing task, measuring response latencies in restorations, which clearly showed higher awareness of errors within a word recognition span. In other words there seems to be a subroutine at work in a speech processing task where the output screening is monitored on a word basis. It becomes particularly clear from their work that the shadowing technique constitutes a very interesting entrance to the ongoing processes in production and perception of continuous speech. It seems worthwhile to carry on this type of work with special emphasis on the various categories involved in errors of speech to which the present material gives rise.

As an extension, one can think of investigating response latencies to achieve further differentiation between the subdivisions already established as well as the type of restorations made in cases where the original text is not restored accurately. Furthermore, in accordance with Lackner (this volume), rates of speaking could be studied as an independent variable.

Acknowledgments

I wish to thank J. R. de Pijper, who took an active part in preparing the texts and setting up the experiment, and, in particular, B. Elsendoorn for his large share in running the experiment and carrying out the necessary calculations.

References

Cohen, A. 1966. Errors of speech and their implication for understanding the strategy of language users. *Zeitschrift für Phonetik, 21,* 177–181.
Cole, R. A. 1973. Listening for mispronunciations: A measure of what we hear during speech. *Perception and Psychophysics, 1,* 153–156.
Fromkin, V. A. (Ed.) 1973. *Speech errors as linguistic evidence.* The Hague: Mouton.
Laver, J. D. M. 1973. The detection and correction of slips of the tongue. In V. A. Fromkin (Ed.), *Speech errors as linguistic evidence.* The Hague, Mouton. Pp. 132–143.

Marslen-Wilson, W. D. & Welsh, A. 1978. Processing interactions and lexical access during word recognition in continuous speech. *Cognitive Psychology, 10,* 29-63.

Meringer, R. 1908. *Aus dem Leben der Sprache,* Berlin: V. Behr's Verlag.

Meringer, R. & Mayer, C. 1895. *Versprechen und verlesen, eine psychologisch-linguistische Studie.* Stuttgart: Göschense Verlagsbuchhandlung.

Nooteboom, S. G. 1969. The tongue slips into patterns. In A. G. Sciarone, A. J. van Essen, and A. A. van Raad (Eds.), Nomen Society, *Leyden studies in linguistics and phonetics.* The Hague: Mouton. Pp. 114-132.

Nooteboom, S. G. 1977. Speaking and unspeaking: The editing out of phonological and lexical errors in spontaneous speech. Paper presented to the working group "Slips of the Tongue and Ear," *Twelfth International Congress of Linguists,* Vienna, August 31-September 2.

Stoett, F. A. 1953. *Nederlandse spreekwoorden en zegswijzen 8.* Zutphen: Thieme & Co.

Chapter 13

LINGUISTIC EVIDENCE FROM
SLIPS OF THE HAND[1]

Don Newkirk   Edward S. Klima

The Salk Institute for Biological Studies   *Department of Linguistics*
La Jolla, California   *University of California, San Diego*
La Jolla, California

Carlene Canady Pedersen   Ursula Bellugi

The Salk Institute for Biological Studies   *The Salk Institute for Biological Studies*
La Jolla, California   *La Jolla, California*

Our research group has been studying the visual–gestural language evolved among deaf people in the United States: American Sign Language (ASL). What makes this language intriguing to one concerned with the general nature of language is that it has developed in a visual channel and is quite remote from spoken language, despite the fact that both spoken language and sign language coexist in the same communities. Because of the basic differences in the channels in which the language developed —the eye and the hands rather than the ear and the vocal tract—these studies promise to give important clues to the biological foundations of language.

It has become clear that the system of communication that is transmitted from one generation of deaf people to the next is not based on English in any essential way; that ASL has in fact evolved as an autonomous language of signs organized and modulated according to constraints and principles quite distinct from those that characterize the English language (Klima and Bellugi, 1979).

The differences between ASL and English do not range merely to differences in vocabulary and in sentence grammar. The signs of ASL are iconic to an extent not recognized in the words of any known spoken language. By this, it is meant that the overall form of a sign visually represents some salient physical or functional attributes of its referent. Until quite recently, in fact, the pervasive iconicity of signs led to their being regarded as holistically distinct symbols without any formal internal structure. The question of recurring formational components—indeed, of a unified sublexical structure—was almost completely ignored. Earlier writers focused on the outward form of the sign only to discuss the images that are generated by that form; a sign was considered to be merely a kind of icon for what it represented (Mallery, 1881; Wundt, 1921). This focus on the image and the icon apparently prevailed over any consideration of the internal structure of signs. In the 1960s and 1970s, however, linguists began to take a lively interest in studying the structure of signs (e.g., Stokoe, 1960; 1965; Battison, 1974; Friedman, 1977; Klima and Bellugi, 1979). While many questions of analysis still remain to be worked out, one fundamental point has been established: The sublexical structure of signs in this language formed by hands moving in space is, in one respect, not like that posited for spoken languages that have been studied so far. The form of typical monomorphemic sign in ASL does not lend itself at all well to an analysis into contrasting, sequentially segmentable elements analogous to the consonants and vowels that figure as the minimal differentiators of spoken words. Rather, according to the model posited by William Stokoe (1960, 1965), the forms of signs are distinguished by opposing values for simultaneously occurring attributes. Stokoe proposed a description of signs in terms of a limited set of formational elements that recur across signs, which include at the least information about the configuration of the hand or hands in making the sign, the location of the sign in relation to the signer's body, and the movement of the hand or hands. We have called these three parameters Hand Configuration (HC), Place of Articulation (PA), and Movement (MOV). Is this analysis only a result of the linguist's zeal for cataloging the subclassifying—for any class of functionally similar phenomena can in theory be analyzed into recurring parts and contrasting elements—or does it represent the internal organization of signs that is psychologically real for signers? The substance of this chapter is an investigation of the independence of the structural parameters posited for sign formation, a search for linguistic evidence from slips of the hand.

1. Linguistic Description of ASL Signs

1.1. *Hand Configuration*

The hand is a highly articulate organ. Its muscular structures permit differential extension, as well as flexion, at the individual joints of the thumb and fingers. Digits can extend, bend, contact, or spread apart; the thumb can assume variable positions with respect to the fingers; the hand can curve or close into an O shape. Handshapes are thus differentiated by the spatial configurations of the fingers and thumb; the digits may be arranged in a variety of ways, and may be held so as to form a vast array of static configurations.

The formational system of ASL, however, includes only a limited set of those handshapes permitted by the muscular structure of the hand. Stokoe's classification in the *Dictionary of American Sign Language* (DASL) lists 19 classes of Hand Configuration primes; each configuration class has criterial aspects and conditions of well-formedness. Figure 1 illustrates these basic hand configurations and the notational symbols used to refer to them.

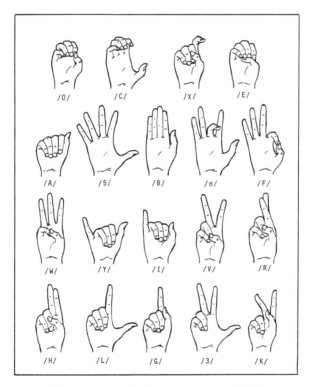

Figure 1: *Hand Configuration primes of ASL.*

1.2. *Place of Articulation*

The second major parameter of ASL lexical signs is the locus of a sign's movement, its Place of Articulation. The primes of Place of Articulation are defined with respect to particular locations and areas on and around the body within a delimited region we call the "signing space." The Place of Articulation primes include the whole face, upper face, nose and eyes, lower face, cheek and ear, neck, trunk, upper arm, lower arm, passive base hand, and the neutral area in front of the signer's head and body.

1.3. *Movement*

The third major parameter of sign structure, Movement, is the most complex dimension and has been the most difficult to analyze. We noted that in forming Hand Configurations the hands are highly articulate and capable of assuming a vast array of distinguishable static shapes; the hands and arms are even more versatile in producing distinguishable movements and movement contours in space. But just as the formational system of ASL limits the number of Hand Configurations to a relatively small number of all the physical possibilities, so does that system restrict the set of movement types.

The restricted set of basic movement types used in ASL signs includes directional movements (upward, downward, sideways, toward signer, to and fro, etc.), rotary actions of the wrist, local (hand-internal) movements (opening or closing of the hand configuration, finger-wiggling, etc.), and various interactions of the hands (converging, separating, contacting, linking, etc.).

The Movement parameter of signs can be described in terms of distinct Movement components, which can occur singly, in sequence, or simultaneously within single monomorphemic signs.

1.4. *Minor Parameters*

Functional attributes and potentials of the hands other than their shape are employed in the formational system of ASL. To describe fully a sign and distinguish it from all others, it is necessary to specify information about three additional dimensions of hand use: CONTACTING REGION (or focus), ORIENTATION, and HAND ARRANGEMENT. The contacting region specifies the areas of contactual or interactional focus on the hands in forming a sign, for instance, the fingertips, the palm, and so on. The number and identity of these contacting regions vary with the Hand Configurations. The hands as sign articulators may be oriented spatially in a limited number of ways, including palm upward, palm downward, palm toward the signer's body, tips upward, etc. There are three basic values for hand arrangement in ASL signs: Signs are made with one hand active, with two hands active, or with one hand acting on a passive base hand.

These dimensions of formation are termed minor parameters since they may be viewed as subclassifications of Hand Configuration;[2] whereas major parameters distinguish very large classes of signs, minor parameters distinguish limited sets of minimal pairs, yet are still significant in differentiating signs.

2. Linguistic Evidence from Slips of the Tongue

Analysts of spoken language have found important evidence supporting a segmental model of sublexical structure for words in a special set of exchange errors in language production called "slips of the tongue." Slips of the tongue have furnished useful insights into the hierarchical organization of spoken language (Fromkin,

1971; 1973; Garrett, 1975). The fact that whole word exchanges occur provides concrete evidence that words are ordered in language planning as discrete units that can misbehave independently of their phrase contexts. That single sounds are misordered attests to the independence of linguistic units smaller than whole words and syllables, that is, phonemes. That single features are misordered provides evidence of the independent existence of linguistic units at that level.

In addition to providing strong evidence of the reality of discrete elements at various levels in the planning of speech output, spontaneous speech errors provide evidence of regularities in the construction of words in specific languages. For instance, "although 'slips of the tongue' can be incorrectly uttered as 'stips of the lung,' it cannot be uttered as 'tlip of the sung' because the sound 'tl' is not allowed as the beginning of an English word" (Fromkin, 1973), although, as the spelling of the name of the Alaskan Indian language called Tlingit implies, it is acceptable in some languages.

3. Linguistic Evidence from Slips of the Hand

Slips of the tongue take their form from the essential form of words: Slips are misorderings of serially arranged components. The fact that slips can best be explained in terms of a sequential sublexical structure model for words makes them very useful in linguistic analysis. The signs of ASL, though, are highly iconic representational gestures, not composed of sequential segments, as far as analysts have found. We wondered whether anything like slips of the tongue could reveal anything about the internal structure of signs: If the "simultaneous" model of sign structure as posited by Stokoe has any psychological validity, spontaneous signing errors ought to have a character quite different from slips of the tongue. What exactly might one look like?

One morning in our laboratory, as two deaf people were conversing, one offered to get the other a cup of coffee. Asked what he would like in it, the other responded in signs, "CREAM AND BUTTER."[3] Astonished, the first asked if he really intended to put butter in his coffee. His friend, somewhat embarrassed, signed that he meant SUGAR, and had made a mistake.

This could have been simply a semantic slip, considering the similarity in meaning between the two notions. But we noticed that the error BUTTER and the intended sign SUGAR, both made with a two-fingered /H/ handshape and a repeated brushing movement, form a minimal pair differing only in the place where they are made: SUGAR is made on the chin; the error BUTTER, on the palm of the hand. CREAM, the first sign in the utterance, is also made on the palm of the hand, with its own handshape and movement. Thus, the unintended error shared formational components with two signs: the intended sign and a previous sign in the utterance. This alerted us to the possibility of studying the properties of unintended slips of the hand, and we began to collect such instances where more than one person was present to corroborate the slip. In addition, we had recorded hundreds of hours of signing for our studies in the structural properties of ASL, and we began to search through our videotapes for other slips of the hand.[4]

We observed certain errors in signing that were clearly not just instances of "sloppy" or incomplete signs. Sometimes signs occurred in whole or in part in some order different from what the signer intended; often the signer stopped and corrected himself after making an error, thus overtly indicating what he had intended to sign. While the items incorrectly produced were occasionally actual signs of ASL, far more often they were not; what we found were largely gestural forms characterizable as POSSIBLE ASL signs—formed from Hand Configurations, Places of Articulation, and Movements drawn from the restricted inventories particular to well-formed signs in the language, but not associated with any conventional meaning. These slips of the hand are, like slips of the tongue in spoken language, valuable as spontaneously occurring data from everyday signing behavior that provide clues to the structural organization of sign language for deaf signers.

4. The Corpus

Our working corpus of 131 signing errors was compiled from two main sources: 77 from careful viewings of videotapes of conversational narrative signing; 54 from reported observations by informants and researchers connected with the laboratory. Ninety-eight of the errors were judged by the signers who made them as deviant from their intended forms, either by immediate self-correction (43 errors) or by a later report during a review of the videotapes (55 errors). Further, all 131 errors were reviewed on several occasions by at least two native deaf informants and judged to be in fact unintended slips of the hands and not explainable as the sort of regular articulatory assimilation that occurs in fast ongoing signing, incidental lapses in muscular control (fumbled fingers), or individual mannerisms in signing. Many candidates for the corpus were rejected on just such grounds.[5]

The errors were first recorded for analytical purposes on videotape, either in the form of a direct copy from the videotapes on which they were observed, or as reconstructed from annotated transcriptions made by the observers; and secondly, in a specially devised notation system, in which ten descriptive aspects of the intended and signed forms could be clearly displayed and compared. The linguistic context in which the error occurred was recorded where it was available.

4.1. *Method of Analysis*

The signing errors were analyzed descriptively in much the same way as speech errors, but with special accommodation to the specific structural elements posited for signs. Unlike the sequentially ordered sound segments of words, the building blocks of signs are simultaneously realized values of parameters that constitute a sign: the major parameters, Hand Configuration, Place of Articulation, and Movement, and the minor parameters, hand arrangement, orientation, and contacting region.

For each of the errors, a parametric chart was drawn, which included values for all of the relevant structural aspects of both the intended signs and the forms actually produced. The errors were categorized according to which parameter(s) showed value substitutions; the type of exchange involved, whether metathesis, anticipation, or perseveration; and the degree of separation between the error sign and the source of the value substituted. In addition, the error signs were all evaluated by native signers as to whether they were REAL signs (with meanings different from those of the intended signs); POSSIBLE signs, that is, gestures composed of parametric values valid for the system and combined according to the structural rules of ASL, yet not currently associated with any conventional meaning (an English example is *snobe*, from an intended "snow on the globe," which does not violate any combinational rules of English, but is nonetheless not an actual word); or IMPOSSIBLE signs, that is, gestures composed of parametric values combined in such a way that particular combinational rules are violated (an English example might be *tlip* in the error *tlip of the sung*).

Let us use the following slip of the hand to illustrate our notation system: A deaf signer intended to sign "SICK[+], BORED" (an idiom somewhat equivalent to the English 'I'm sick and tired of it'). Instead he made the error illustrated in Figure 2.

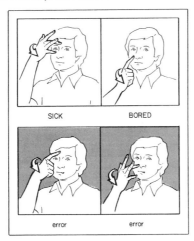

SICK   BORED

error   error

Figure 2. *Metathesis of Hand Configurations.*

In the notation we devised, the first sign intended is specified on the left side; the second sign intended is specified on the right side (see Table 1). Between Sign 1 and Sign 2 are columns indicating what was actually signed but with reference to what was intended; for example, Sign 1 was produced with all the characteristics of the intended sign SICK[+] except for the value for Hand Configuration, which was borrowed from Sign 2, BORED.

TABLE 1: *Example of Notation for Slips of the Hand*

Name of signer: DS
Intended: SICK[+], BORED ('sick and tired of it')
Location on videotape: VT II #449–453.

Parameter	Intended Sign 1		Signs produced		Intended Sign 2	
HA	1	O	1	11	11	O
PA	2	⌃	2	12	12	⌂
HC$_N$	3	$	3	13	13	$
R	4	$	4	14	14	$
HC$_D$	5	୪	15 G	5 ୪	15	G
O$_D$	6	T	6	16	16	T
O$_N$	7	$	7	17	17	$
M	8	a x	8	18	18	a x
M$_1$	9	$	9	19	19	$
HC$_F$	10	$	10	20	20	$

Sign 1   Sign 2

Exchange type: Metathesis of Hand Configuration
Lexical status: Possible sign
Degree of Separation: ø Signs intervening
The abbreviations in the Parameter column are expanded as follows:

HA   Hand arrangement (one-handed sign 'O'; two-handed sign with symmetrical Hand Configurations 'S'; base-hand sign with one hand acting on a passive base hand 'B')

PA   Place of Articulation

HC$_N$ Nondominant Hand Configuration

R   Relationship between the two hands

HC$_D$ Dominant Hand Configuration

O$_D$ Orientation of the Dominant hand

O$_N$ Orientation of the Nondominant hand

M   Movement type of the sign as a whole

M$_1$ Aspects of the Movement that are involved in the slip of the hand if such is not the total movement

HC$_F$ Final Hand Configuration (for signs whose Movement involves a change in Hand Configuration, where the final Hand Configuration is relevant in the slip)

(The symbol $ represents 'not applicable' or a 'default' value for a parameter. Actual prime values are specified by using symbols adapted from DASL notation.)

The information in Table 1 can be reconstructed as follows: The first sign intended was SICK[+], which is a one-handed sign (O) made with a bent mid-finger Hand Configuration /ඊ/ with the hand turned toward the signer (T), at the forehead (⌢), involving a twist of the wrist (a) while the hand is in contact (x): $[\,\text{ඊ}_{Tx}^{a}]$. The second sign intended is BORED, which is also a one-handed sign (O) made with a straight index-finger /G/ Hand Configuration with the hand turned toward the signer (T), at the nose (△), involving a twist of the wrist (a) while the hand is in contact (x): $[\triangle G_{Tx}^{a}]$.

The error is a metathesis in Hand Configuration (/ඊ/ metathesized with /G/). The sign SICK[+] is made with the handshape of BORED, and the sign BORED is made with the handshape of SICK[+] (see line HC_D of Table 1, items 5 and 15). Furthermore, the diagram makes clear the similarities between the two intended signs: Note that they are both one-handed signs (line HA), with the same orientation (line O_D), and the same movement (line M). The analysis and diagrammatic display help make clear precisely what occurred, and allows one to see at a glance the structure of the two intended signs, those aspects that have been switched in the error, the direction and nature of the error, and the similarities between the two intended signs.

5. Independence of Parameters

If signs were, as some previous investigators have thought, only holistic gestures without internal structure, we might expect signs to be organized (for production as well as in analysis) at a single primary level: that of the entire sign as a unitary object. If signs were so coded, involuntary deviations in performance from the intentions of a signer (aside from those resulting from temporary motor difficulties) should result in only whole signs being reordered. In fact, our corpus does include some exchanges of this type (9 out of 131 slips). For instance, a signer intending to sign "TASTE, MAYBE LIKE!" 'Taste it and maybe you'll like it,' signed instead "LIKE, MAYBE TASTE!"

Occasionally these whole sign exchanges involve components of compound signs. The signs THRILL and INFORM[+], for example, when joined together with a particular intonation, form a compound THRILL⌢INFORM[+] meaning 'news' or 'entertainment' (see Klima and Bellugi, 1979: Chapter 9). One signer intended to sign "LIST THRILL⌢INFORM[+] " when speaking of a 'list of news (items),' but erroneously began "THRILL LIST . . ." (self-corrected).

However, few of the exchanges in the corpus are whole signs exchanging as total units. Far more frequently (and more significantly, for the nature of signs and of constraints on their formational properties), a parameter value of one sign is erroneously realized in another sign.

In our corpus of slips of the hands, there are 65 instances of Hand Configuration prime value substitutions, 13 of Place of Articulation primes, and 11 of Movement components. The independence of these parameters may be most clearly examined if we can concentrate our discussion on instances where only one parameter (major or minor) has been affected in a slip; we will, for the most part, then, limit our attention to 44 "pure" substitutions in the Hand Configuration parameter, 4 in the Place of Articulation parameter, and 5 in the Movement parameter.

5.1. Metatheses

The best evidence for the independent coding of parameters comes from completed metatheses because these reveal all of the building blocks of the intended signs, some of which have been misordered in their production: No bit of structural material is lost in the linguistic output. In speech production, these completed exchanges of individual sounds between two words (nicknamed "spoonerisms" after the Reverend W. A. Spooner of New College, Oxford, who was famous for his special talent for making them) provide linguistic evidence that in the planning stages underlying the production of the speech string affected, both of the sound units involved were independently prepared for but at some prearticulatory level were somehow affected so as to become misordered in the final production. Thus, one can account for all of the sounds in the error *noble tons of soil*, uttered instead of the intended phrase "noble sons of toil," on an individual basis, because while neither *tons* nor *soil* is a word in the intended phrase, each of their component phonemes has a place in it: Only the sounds /s/ and /t/ are misordered.

Our corpus of sign production errors includes several examples of complete metatheses of sign-parts. Table 2 lists some completed metatheses according to the parameters involved and includes examples of exchanges of all three major parameters, Hand Configuration, Place of Articulation, and Movement, and of the minor parameter hand arrangement.

TABLE 2: *Slips of the Hand Resulting in Metatheses of Primes*

Parameter involved	Glosses	Values exchanges	
Hand Configuration	SICK$^{[+]}$$_{[sl:HC]}$ BORED$_{[sl:HC]}$	/ʊ/	/G/
	BE$_{[sl:HC]}$ CAREFUL$_{[sl:HC]}$	/B/	/K/
Place of Articulation	RECENTLY$^{[+]}$$_{[sl:PA]}$ EAT$_{[sl:PA]}$	/ʒ/	/ʊ/
Movement	IN$_{[sl:MOV]}$ FLOWER$_{[sl:MOV]}$	/X/	/X > X/
	TASTE$_{sl:MOV]}$ GOOD$_{[sl:MOV]}$	/X¨/	/X⊥/
Hand Arrangement	CAN'T$_{[sl:HA]}$ SEE$_{[sl:HA]}$	Base-hand sign	One-handed sign

Just as the *tons of soil* example showed how individual sounds could exchange places in the production of a speech sequence, each of the metatheses in our corpus represents the misordering of individual parametric values in the signs. For instance, in the example

$$\text{``SICK}^{[+]}_{[sl:HC]}\text{' BORED}_{[sl:HC]}\text{''}$$

(see Figure 2), only the values for the two intended Hand Configurations are exchanged, all other aspects of the signs remaining as intended. In a second example, when a signer intended to sign "BE CAREFUL," the sign $BE_{[sl:HC]}$ was made with the /K/ Hand Configuration intended for CAREFUL, while $CAREFUL_{[sl:HC]}$ was made with the /B/ Hand Configuration of BE. As Figure 3 shows, neither the Places of Articulation, Movements, nor any other parameters except Hand Configuration were affected.

The Place of Articulation metathesis between $RECENTLY^{[+]}$ and EAT in the sentence

$$\text{``(ME) RECENTLY}^{[+]}_{[sl:PA]}\text{ EAT}_{[sl:PA]}\text{ FINISH''}\qquad\text{'I just finished eating'}$$

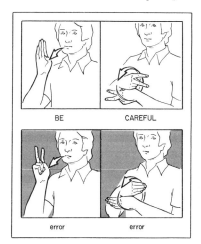

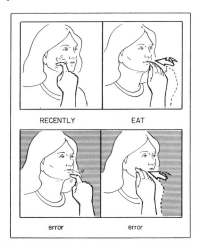

Figure 3. *Metathesis of Hand Configurations.*   **Figure 4.** *Metathesis of Place of Articulation.*

in a similar way supports the claim that Place of Articulation is an independent structural parameter in ASL. Figure 4 shows how the Hand Configurations, Movements, and orientations of the two signs were preserved, although $RECENTLY^{[+]}_{[sl:PA]}$ was made on the mouth, where EAT should have been, and $EAT_{[sl:PA]}$ was made on the cheek, where $RECENTLY^{[+]}$ should have been.

Values for the third major parameter (Movement) were exchanged in two metatheses. In one,

$$\text{``IN}_{[sl:MOV]}\text{ FLOWER}_{[sl:MOV]}\text{ ˆGROWˆPLACE''}\qquad\text{'In the garden'}$$

the single contact Movement of IN was replaced by the complex touch, move over, touch Movement of FLOWER, while FLOWER$_{[sl:MOV]}$ was made by a single touch in its accustomed Place of Articulation, all other values of both signs remaining constant; the Hand Configurations of the two signs are the same (see Figure 5a). The second Movement metathesis affected the two signs in the phrase "TASTE GOOD," both made in the same Place of Articulation, on the mouth.

"TASTE$_{[sl:MOV]}$ GOOD$_{[sl:MOV]}$"   'It tastes good'

The Movement of TASTE, a bouncing repeated contact, was exchanged with the Movement of GOOD, a single straight diagonal movement downward and outward from the mouth (see Figure 5b).

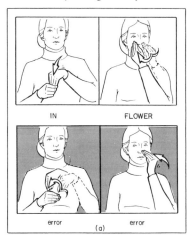 

Figure 5. *Movement metatheses.*

The minor parameter hand arrangement was the source of one exchange of values in a slip of the hand. A base-hand sign became a one-handed sign and vice versa, other parameters remaining as intended. The signer produced

"CAN'T$_{[sl:HA]}$ SEE$_{[sl:HA]}$."

CAN'T is a base-hand sign, made by striking the index finger of one hand down and past the tip of the index finger of the other hand; SEE is a one-handed sign, made with a /V/ Hand Configuration moving outward from the cheek.

Note that in CAN'T, the active hand and the base hand are both /G/ Configurations, with orientation palm downward (see Figure 6). In the error, when SEE acquires a base hand, it is not that of CAN'T that appears, but rather a copy of the Configuration and orientation of the active hand of SEE: a /V/ Configuration, palm up. Thus, there is symmetry in the error SEE$_{[sl:HA]}$, functionally parallel to the symmetry of Hand Configurations in the influencing sign CAN'T.

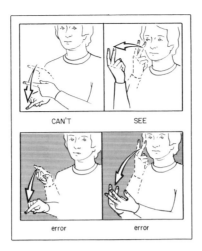

Figure 6. *Metathesis of hand arrangement.*

5.2. *Anticipations and Perseverations*

Completed metatheses of individual parameters clearly indicate the independent organization of these parameters in sign production. However, far outnumbering completed metatheses in our sign-error corpus (as in all reported corpora of speech errors) are the single-direction substitutions called "anticipations"—production errors in which some parametric value appears that is different from that intended, but identical to one appearing later in the signed sequence—and "perseverations"— production errors where a specific intended parametric value is replaced by one invoked in the production of a sign appearing earlier on in the sequence. In these types of articulatory element substitutions, while the overall amount of misordering may not be so striking to the eye as in metatheses, the net effect on the affected sign is equivalent: A gesture is produced whose holistic description is different in one element from that of the intended sign, and in most cases, different from any other conventional sign (thus ruling out lexical substitution as the cause of its appearance in the signed sequence); furthermore, each of the major structural parameters of Hand Configuration, Place of Articulation, and Movement is represented by a systematically valid prime, two of which are identical to those intended for the sign, the third being found in another sign in the string.[6]

Hand Configuration slips

The corpus includes 26 examples of Hand Configuration prime anticipations in which the Place of Articulation and Movement values remain as intended. In one example of Hand Configuration anticipation, a signer meant to produce "FEEL C-O-N-F-I-D-E-N-T THAT . . . ." The sign FEEL$_{[sl:HC]}$ was produced in the Place of

Articulation and with the Movement appropriate to FEEL, but with the Hand Configuration of THAT$_{[inf]}$ (see Figure 7a).

Another signer, intending to sign

"SIGN BASIS O-F POEM"   'The sign-language basis of the poem'

articulated SIGN with the /K/ handshape of POEM instead of the index-finger /G/ shape required (Figure 7b). In a third example, in the intended string "ONE THOUSAND CLOWN," the sign THOUSAND was produced with the handshape of CLOWN, a sort of "claw," replacing the required angular /B/ shape (Figure 7c).

The corpus also includes 20 examples of Hand Configuration-only perseverations.

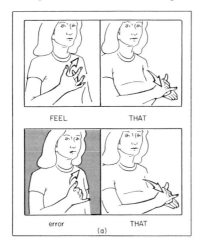
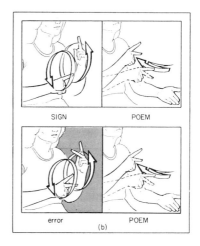

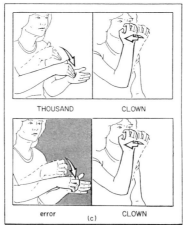

Figure 7. *Hand Configuration anticipations.*

In three of these, one or two signs intervened between the source of the Hand Configuration used and the sign in which it intruded. For instance, in the intended question

"YOU MEAN COFFEE MIXED WITH WINE?"

the proper Hand Configuration of WINE$_{[sl:HC]}$ was replaced by that of COFFEE$_{[inf]}$, although Place of Articulation and Movement were realized as intended. When another signer intended to produce the compound sign "JESUS^BOOK^SCHOOL," ('Bible school'), the active-hand /ʊ/ handshape in JESUS$_{[inf]}$ appeared in SCHOOL$_{[sl:HC]}$, which requires the full flat /B/ shape (the intervening sign BOOK was signed as intended with the required flat /B/ shape). The existence in our small corpus of such clear cases of Hand Configuration perseveration where linguistic material intervened between the two signs involved provides added evidence of the independence of the Hand Configuration parameter in the organization of signs.

Place of Articulation slips

Other major parameters also exhibit anticipations and perseverations as well as whole exchanges. In one of two Place of Articulation perseverations, an intended sentence included the list "MAN, FATHER, GIRL..."; the sign GIRL$_{[sl:PA]}$, properly made on the cheek, was made instead on the forehead, the Place of Articulation of FATHER$_{[inf]}$, while Hand Configuration and Movement were not affected (see Figure 8a). In the other example, when the signer intended to produce the sentence "STILL SOUND FUNNY" (It still sounds funny'), FUNNY$_{[sl:PA]}$, instead of being made in its required location on the nose, was articulated on the ear, the Place of Articulation for SOUND (Figure 8b).

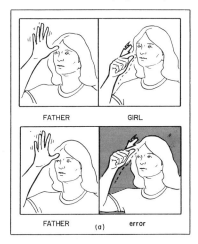

FATHER GIRL

FATHER (a) error

SOUND FUNNY

SOUND (b) error

Figure 8. *Place of Articulation perseverations.*

Movement slips

Examples of Movement prime slips are particularly interesting because of the great variety of Movement categories appearing in ASL signs—simple contact, brushing contact, orbiting revolution, axial rotation, opening or closing of the hand, and wiggling of the fingers are among the simple Movement primes that can be used to form signs.

Our small corpus includes ten examples of changes in Movements alone. One of these, a perseveration, was made when a signer intended to sign "(HE) PLEASE HELP" ('He will be glad to help'). The Movement for PLEASE is made by a circular brushing on the chest; HELP is made by one hand approaching the other from the bottom and lifting it up slightly: two acutely distinct types of Movement. In the error, however, the circular brushing of PLEASE$_{[inf]}$ was also used in HELP$_{[sl:MOV]}$, with the intended Hand Configuration and Place of Articulation remaining unaffected (see Figure 9).

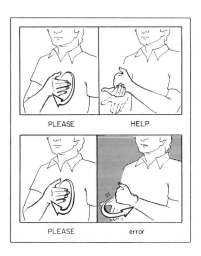

Figure 9. *Movement perseveration.*

In another example, a signer intended to sign

"EAT, TASTE PERFECT; DELICIOUS"   'I ate it and it tasted perfect; delicious'

Here, the simple contact movement of TASTE perseverated onto the sign PERFECT$_{[sl:MOV]}$, which is normally made with a circular movement followed by a holding contact.

Minor parameters.

There is in our corpus little evidence of slips involving only the minor parameter orientation. Of the three orientation-only slips, all affect only the base hand.[7] Two explanations present themselves: One is the small size of our corpus; the other is that orientation is not particularly autonomous in the structure of signs. Although orientation minimally differentiates a small number of otherwise similar pairs of signs (for instance, CHILDREN and THING, made with the same values for the major parameters, differ only in having palm-down and palm-up orientations, respectively), specific orientation may generally be tied inextricably to the other parameters and thus not exhibit structural independence.

Similarly, there are no clear examples in our corpus of signing errors based only on substitutions in the minor parameter contacting region. We will limit our discussion of this parameter, then, to its role in affecting the form of Hand Configuration slips (see the section on morpheme structure constraints).

The minor parameter hand arrangement shows considerably more independence. This parameter describes how many of the two possible articulators are used to make a sign and whether one or both are active; signs may be made with one hand active, with two hands active, or with one hand acting on the other as a base. The whole exchange of hand arrangement in "CAN'T$_{[sl:HA]}$ SEE$_{[sl:HA]}$" (Figure 6) is persuasive evidence of the independence of this parameter. The corpus also includes four examples of hand arrangement anticipations and four perseverations in which all other structural parameters preserve their values, but the number of hands used changes. In two anticipations, one-handed signs add a second active hand, under the influence of a following two-handed sign: For example, when a signer produced

"KING SAY, A-L-L GIRL MUST$_{[sl:HA]}$ TRY$_{[inf]}$"

the sign MUST$_{[sl:HA]}$, normally a one-handed sign, was made with an added hand, anticipating the two-handed arrangement of TRY (see Figure 10). In the second anticipation of this type, also involving the sign TRY as the hand arrangement influence, the signer, in signing "WILL TRY" ('I'll try') signed WILL$_{[sl:HA]}$ with both hands, producing a form much like the ASL sign meaning 'pay attention.' In both examples, the second hands added were identical in Configuration and Movement to the first, exhibiting the symmetry characteristic of two-handed signs in ASL (see Battison, 1974; Frishberg, 1975; Klima and Bellugi, 1979: Chapter 2, for discussions of symmetry in sign structure).

Two other anticipations change base-hand signs into one-handed signs. In one of these, the intended sequence was the compound sign "COOK^CHICKEN" ('fried chicken'). Here, the signer produced the component sign COOK$_{[sl:HA]}$ with one

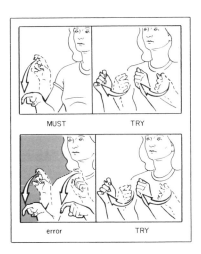

Figure 10. *Hand arrangement anticipation.*

hand, dropping the base hand apparently in anticipation of the one-handed hand arrangement of CHICKEN$_{[inf]}$.

Four hand arrangement perseverations show two-handed signs losing a hand or one-handed signs gaining a hand in straightforward ways. In one example, a signer intended the sentence

"CINDERELLA LOOK DEPRESSED, QUIET; 'WISH (ME) CAN GO'"
  'Cinderella looked depressed and quiet; (she said) "I wish I could go."'

However, he perseverated the two-handed hand arrangement of QUIET$_{[inf]}$ into the production of the normally one-handed WISH$_{[sl:HA]}$ (see Figure 11a).

In a second example, the signer intended to sign

"INTERESTING, (SHE) TEACHER"   'It was interesting that she was a
  teacher.'

She made the indexic (SHE)$_{[sl:HA]}$ with both hands instead of the normal one-handed sign (see Figure 11b). Again, when active second hands are added, they are symmetrical with the first. The corpus includes 13 additional examples of hand-arrangement changes involving major parameter changes as well, especially Place of Articulation.

The signing slips in our corpus, then, provide strong evidence for the independence of the three major structural parameters and for the minor parameter hand arrangement in sign language production.

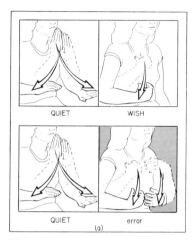 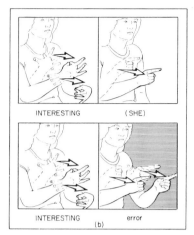

Figure 11. *Hand arrangement perseverations.*

6. Other Issues of Structural Organization

Analysis of slips of the tongue in spoken language has provided evidence that individual phonological segments are themselves coded as bundles of discrete features such as voicing, stridency, and nasality. A very small number of errors in our corpus suggest a possible feature-level analysis of handshapes of signs. The strongest evidence for this hypothesized "featural" level of structure is more highly restricted than that for the parametric level; not only do the examples have to show substitutions for specific parametric primes, but the resulting values should be different from either intended prime. In spoken English, an exchange that is strong evidence of feature misordering is the example "clear blue sky" transposed to *glear plue sky* (Fromkin, 1973). This is a metathesis of the single feature voicing; the voiceless /k/ became a voiced /g/, and the voiced /b/ became a voiceless /p/. Unequivocal examples of slips of the tongue involving only features (versus whole segments) are relatively rare in the various corpora that have been reported.

In order for a slip of the hand to count as the strongest kind of evidence for a feature substitution rather than a prime value substitution, the slip must be one in which the error was not an entire prime value of either sign but rather appeared to be composed of specific within-prime characteristics of one or both. For instance, suppose a signer intended to sign a sentence in which one sign had a spread flat hand /5/, and another sign had a nonspread two-finger hand /H/, but instead used a nonspread flat hand /B/ in the first sign and a spread two-finger hand. / V/ in the second sign (see Figure 12). The error might be described as a metatheses of values of a feature, for example, a putative feature "±Spread."

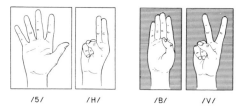

/5/   /H/   /B/   /V/

Figure 12. *Invented example of feature exchange (±Spread).*

6.1. Hand Configuration Features

Among the Hand Configuration substitutions in our limited corpus, very few qualify as feature substitutions rather than substitutions of whole prime values. We present two examples here as candidates. In the sequence

"MUST$_{[sl:HC]}$ SEE$_{[inf]}$"   'I must see about it'

MUST ordinarily would be made with the bent index finger /X/ Hand Configuration, and SEE with the nonbent /V/ Hand Configuration. In the error, MUST$_{[sl:HC]}$ was made with a bent /V/ Hand Configuration: the middle finger of /V/ was added to the index finger of /X/ but in the bent form (see Figure 13a). Here the +Bent quality of one Hand Configuration applied to another Hand Configuration.

As a second candidate for feature-level errors, in the intended sign phrase "REAL HARD," the signer articulated REAL$_{[sl:HC]}$ with an /X/ Hand Configuration, that is, a bent index-finger hand, anticipating the bent quality of the /V/ in HARD (Figure 13b). Because these are not straightforward slips of whole Hand Configuration primes, they offer some initial support for a feature-level analysis of Hand Configuration for ASL signs (for a suggested feature model for ASL Hand Configurations, see Lane, Boyes-Braem, and Bellugi, 1976).

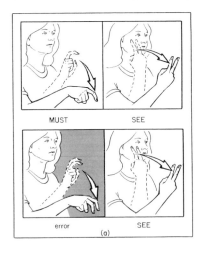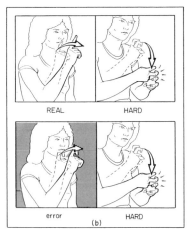

Figure 13. *Hand Configuration feature error.*

6.2. *Movement Clusters*

In our discussion of the Movement parameter, we used examples of entire move-ment substitutions (which could be combinations of movement components). The movements posited in the DASL can occur as sequential combinations (for example, contact–move–contact) or simultaneous combinations (movement away from signer while opening the hand). We call these combinations "movement clusters." Such movement clusters are sometimes involved in slips of the hand as whole movement substitutions, as in Figure 9, where a lifting movement is replaced by a circular brushing movement. But, some movement parameter exchanges appear to involve addition or deletion of parts of clusters, rather than whole movement substitutions.

For instance, a signer intended to sign the sentence

"(ME) HAVE BLACK WHITE TABLE TV."   'I have a black and white portable TV.'

but instead of making the sign BLACK$_{[sl:MOV]}$ with a simple lateral movement, he added the closing movement of WHITE$_{[inf]}$ while moving the hand sideways (see Figure 14). The visual impression of the resultant movement is not that of anticipa-tion of a whole movement type, but rather a hybrid (closing while brushing side-ways), combining aspects of movement from both intended signs.

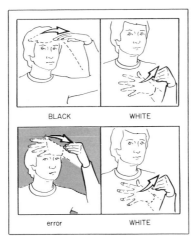

BLACK   WHITE

error   WHITE

Figure 14. *Movement cluster error.*

Another example occurred when a signer slipped in signing a translation of the song "Let Me Call You Sweetheart." The sign (ME) is made by a single contact of the index finger on the chest; the sign SWEETHEART in the song version is made by the hands in contact, the thumbs wiggling first on one side, then on the other side of the signing space. In the error, however, the sign (ME)$_{[sl:MOV]}$ was made not as a single contact but as a touch, move-over, touch movement on the torso. Here, as in the BLACK$_{[sl:MOV]}$ WHITE$_{[inf]}$ example, the resultant movement was not an exact copy of the influencing movement; rather, the movement cluster produced combined aspects of both intended forms.

In a similar example, this one a perseveration, the signer intended to produce the phrase "RED FLOWER." RED$_{[inf]}$ was signed as intended, with the index finger brushing downward across the lips while closing into an /X/ handshape. Then, instead of the proper form for FLOWER (that is, an /O/ hand making contact first on one side of the nose and then on the other), the signer made, in essence, the sign RED on either side of the nose (see Figure 15). Here, the simplex movement form of the intended sign FLOWER, that is, contact, was replaced within the two-touch pattern by the complex brushing-while-closing of RED.[8]

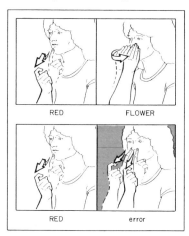

Figure 15. *Movement cluster error.*

In a final example of this kind, a signer produced the sequence

"BIRD$_{[inf]}$ RUN$^{[+]}_{[sl:PA,MOV]}$,"   'the bird ran away.'

BIRD is properly made by closing movements of the fingers while the hand is in contact with the chin; RUN is made by moving the hands away from the body while the index finger wiggles repeatedly. In the error, RUN$^{[+]}_{[sl:PA,MOV]}$ kept its wiggling movement, but was made instead on the chin and remained stationary rather than moving away from the face.

These four examples of movement-cluster interference illustrate the addition of movement to form a SIMULTANEOUS cluster, the addition of movement to form a SEQUENTIAL cluster, the REPLACEMENT of one movement type within a cluster by another movement type, and the deletion of movement to DECOMPOSE a simultaneous cluster. The types of slips that occur thus suggest that the individual values for movement within clusters are independently organized.

6.3. *Two-Part Signs*

Thus far in our discussion of slips of the hand, we have considered all simplex signs as single segments, simultaneously comprising a single Hand Configuration prime, a single Place of Articulation prime, and one or more Movement primes. Occasionally, component parts of unassimilated compound signs were independently affected in slips of the hands (for instance, in the whole sign exchange in "LIST THRILL^INFORM" and the movement metathesis in "IN FLOWER^GROW^ PLACE" described in the preceding section).

A small number of ASL signs that are not compound signs require two Places of Articulation in their specification (sometimes accompanied by a consequent change in orientation).[9] A sign such as TOAST, made with a bent /V/ hand contacting first the back of the hand and then the palm side, is not a compound, and yet could be considered as a two-part sign. Other such signs are SPAIN, PROGRAM, NUN, INDIAN, each requiring two specifications for Place of Articulation. Evidence from slips of the hand might bear on the question of whether such signs should be analyzed into two discrete parts.

Our corpus of slips provides three clear examples that would support an analysis of certain signs as having two-part structures. In two Hand Configuration slips and one Place of Articulation slip, only one part of a two-part sign was altered, leaving the other intact. In one example of this kind, a signer intended to sign the compound sign "CHEESE^TOAST" ('grilled cheese sandwich'); that sequence became scrambled, but in a very straightforward way. The intended sign CHEESE, a simplex sign, is made by one hand in a loose /5/ Hand Configuration mashing into the palm of a flat /B/ base hand. TOAST, a two-part sign, is made with an active bent /V/ hand touching first the back of a flat base hand, then its supinated palm. In the

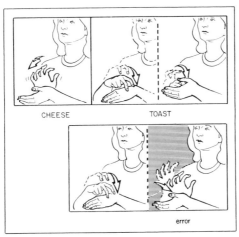

CHEESE   TOAST

error

Figure 16. *Slip involving a two-part sign.*

error, CHEESE, with its mashing movement, was skipped over; the first part of TOAST was produced as intended, and then, in the second part, the /5/ Hand Configuration of CHEESE was substituted for the bent /V/ of TOAST, with the simple-contact movement of the proper second half of TOAST preserved (see Figure 16).

Another such example occurred with the intended signs "PROGRAM DEAF" ('program for the deaf'); PROGRAM, like TOAST, involves two different locations (on the palm side of the hand and then on the back of the hand). Again, the two parts were treated as segmentable; the signer made the first segment of PROGRAM and then, instead of making the second contact on the back of the base hand, made a contact (still with the active /K/ hand of PROGRAM) on the cheek, the initial Place of Articulation of DEAF.

These examples in our corpus suggest some degree of independent planning for the two parts of such signs affected in slips (that is, two-part signs made in two Places of Articulation).

7. Morpheme Structure Constraints

The analysis of language production errors can provide evidence not only of the independence of individual structural elements at several levels in the planning process, but also of the persistence of the rules for combining these elements. Linguists studying spoken language errors have noted that "a slip of the tongue is practically always a phonetically possible noise" (Wells, 1951). Even if at some planning stage the individual sounds in a language are misordered, the combinatorial rules of that language persist in shaping the output in predictable, grammatical ways. It is the persistence of these rules, rather than physical impossibility, that renders forms like "tlip of the sung" highly unlikely. Furthermore, although there are many examples of actual words produced in slips, many more are meaningless though, for all linguistic purposes, possible forms.

7.1. "Actual" Sign Forms

Our corpus includes at least a dozen clear examples of actual, commonly used signs resulting from substitution of parametric values in intended signs with values from other signs. Table 3 categorizes these according to the parameter(s) involved, and shows that the meanings of the signs produced are usually far different from the meanings of those intended.

7.2. "Possible" Sign Forms

The overwhelming majority of slips in our corpus take the form of possible combinations of parametric values that happen not to have conventional meanings associated with them. One example of this kind comes from the anticipation of Hand Configuration in the slip

"FEEL$_{[sl:HC]}$ C-O-N-F-I-D-E-N-T THAT$_{[inf]}$ ···"

(see Figure 7a) where the Hand Configuration of THAT$_{[inf]}$ occurred two signs earlier as a substitute for the Hand Configuration of FEEL, resulting in a possible but nonexistent sign. Another example, this one a Place of Articulation substitution, involved the last sign in the sentence

"STILL SOUND$_{[inf]}$ FUNNY$_{[sl:PA]}$"

Instead of brushing downward twice on the nose, the sign FUNNY$_{[sl:PA]}$ was made by brushing downward on the ear, the location of SOUND$_{[inf]}$ as seen in Figure 8b. In a third example, a signer produced

"THAT CHARACTER$_{[inf]}$ MEAN$_{[sl:MOV]}$"   'That's the characteristic
      meaning'

The movement of CHARACTER$_{[inf]}$, a cluster of circling followed by contact, perseverated in the sign MEAN$_{[sl:MOV]}$ (see Figure 17). None of these three slips has

TABLE 3: *Actual Signs Produced in Slips of the Hand*

Parameter involved	Glosses	Sign(s) produced
Hand Configuration	CAN'T$_{[sl:HC]}$ SLEEP$_{[inf]}$	THAN
	BUT$_{[inf]}$ WHAT$_{[sl:HC]}$	CUT
	DEAF$_{[sl:HC]}$ WOMAN$_{[inf]}$	PARENTS
	HOME$_{[sl:HC]}$ WORK$_{[inf]}$	MENSTRUAL-PERIOD
	PAPER$_{[sl:HC]}$ GOOD⌢ENOUGH$_{[inf]}$	FILL$^{[M:habitual]}$
	MEET$_{[inf]}$ READY$_{[sl:HC]}$	DIFFERENT
Place of Articulation	BIRD$_{[inf]}$ RUN$^{[+]}_{[sl:PA,MOV]}$	WHO
	CREAM$_{[inf]}$ SUGAR$_{[sl:PA]}$	BUTTER
	RECENTLY$^{[+]}_{[sl:PA]}$ EAT$_{[sl:PA]}$	RED HOME
Movement	TASTE$_{[sl:MOV]}$ GOOD$_{[inf]}$	DELICIOUS
Hand Arrangement	WILL$_{[sl:HA]}$ TRY$_{[inf]}$	PAY-ATTENTION

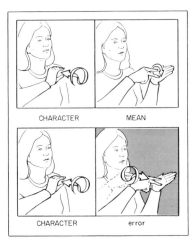

Figure 17. *Slip producing possible ASL sign form.*

any conventional meaning, but each can claim to be a possible sign in ASL, because
the values for each of the structural parameters utilized in them are chosen from
the catalog of possible values, and the final combinations of values are all allowable
under the structural constraints of ASL (see also Figures 2, 3, 5, and 6 for other
possible sign forms).

Some of the data from our corpus suggest how combinatorial rules can come
into play in shaping the final forms of slips of the hands. One category of constraints
governs the use of contacting regions for particular Hand Configurations in particular Places of Articulation. For example, a total listing of the contacting regions used
with the crossed-fingers /R/ Hand Configuration includes the tips of the extended
fingers, the heel of the palm, the back of the wrist, the palm side of the fist, and the
edges of the extended fingers. However, in signs made with one hand in contact
with the other, contact on the edges of the /R/ fingers is allowed only when both
hands are in the same Configuration, as in the two-handed signs READY and RELA-
TIVE.

In almost every case (39 out of the 44 Hand Configuration-only substitutions),
the choice of contacting region in the resulting sign form was determined by accom-
modating to constraints on contacting region use.[10] For example, sometimes when a
Hand Configuration is exchanged in an intended sign, the contacting region specified
for the intended sign is kept, because that used in the influencing sign is not compatible with the other specifications in the error sign. In the Hand Configuration
anticipation in the phrase "CAN'T$_{[sl:HC]}$ SLEEP$_{[inf]}$," when the /G/ Hand Configuration intended for CAN'T was replaced by the /B/ from SLEEP$_{[inf]}$, the contacting
region specification for CAN'T remained as intended, that is, on the extended
fingers. Here, with contact on the back of the fingers of the inactive hand, the full-
palm contacting region specified for the sign SLEEP is not allowed. There were 15
instances of such accommodation to contacting region constraints in our corpus.

In other cases, however, the contacting region specified for the influencing sign
is brought along with the Hand Configuration, because the contacting region speci-

Figure 18. *Contacting region substitution accompanying a Hand Configuration slip.*

fied for the intended sign is not compatible, in context, with the new Hand Configuration. For example, in the Hand Configuration metathesis between SICK[+] and BORED$_{[sl:HC]}$, the index-finger contact of BORED was not preserved when the Hand Configuration of SICK[+] was used (see Figure 2), since the contacting region for the bent middle-finger /8/ Hand Configuration is the tip of the middle finger. Index-finger contact with this Hand Configuration is ruled out.

In another example, the signer intended "DEAF WOMAN," and signed DEAF$_{[sl:HC]}$ with the Hand Configuration of WOMAN (see Figure 18). The intended sign DEAF has a /G/ Hand Configuration, with contact on the side of the index finger, for which a /5/ Hand Configuration was substituted; the index-finger contact was not maintained, but rather thumb-tip contact of the influencing sign was substituted. There were 17 instances of this type of contacting region accommodation in our corpus.

It is sometimes the case that in a context where a Hand Configuration is replaced in a slip, neither the contacting region specified for the intended sign nor that for the influencing sign is allowable. There were seven instances in our corpus where this was true; in the error forms produced, a new contacting region appeared, which was in fact compatible with the substituted Hand Configuration. For example, in a slip involving the compound BED^ROOM, the crossed-fingers /R/ configuration of ROOM$_{[inf]}$ replaced the flat /B/ configuration in BED$_{[sl:HC]}$. In this slip, the active /R/ hand made contact on the cheek at the tips of the extended fingers, the only contacting region allowable in this context.

There were only five instances out of 44 Hand Configuration-only substitutions where contacting region constraints were not observed. The remaining 39 accommodations to these constraints provide strong evidence of the persistence of such rules in the production of ASL signs and to their significance in the systematic linguistic structure for signers.

Another kind of constraint deals with a process of symmetricalization that oper-

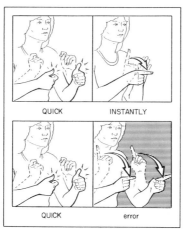

Figure 19. *Hand arrangement slip with symmetry of configuration and movement.*

ates in signs made with two active hands (see the preceding discussion of hand arrangement) such that both hands will exhibit the same Hand Configuration and Movement. This constraint, too, is almost always observed in slips of the hands. For example, a signer intended to sign "QUICK . . . INSTANTLY." QUICK$_{[inf]}$ is a symmetrical two-handed sign; the intended INSTANTLY is a base-hand sign, the dominant hand moving in an index-finger /G/ Hand Configuration on the palm of the inactive flat /B/ base. In the error INSTANTLY$_{[sl:HA]}$, the signer made both hands active, the two hands in /G/ Hand Configurations moving symmetrically without contact in the neutral signing area (see Figure 19).

In 21 out of 22 slips in our corpus where the affected sign was either already a two-handed sign in its intended form (13 cases) or made into a two-handed sign in the slip (8 cases), the symmetry constraint applied (see, for example, Figures 3, 6, 10, and 11). In the one exception, symmetry of Movement did occur even though symmetry of Hand Configuration did not. Such adherence to known structural constraints in slips provides supportive evidence of their psychological reality in normal language formation.

7.3. *"Impossible" Sign Forms*

As in speech error slips, nearly all of the signing slips resulted in actual but unintended signs or in forms that are possible but nonexistent in the language. There were, however, a few errors (five) in our corpus that were felt to be impossible, or extrasystemic gestures, that is, signs in which combinations of parametric values violate specific structural constraints of the language.[11]

For example, when a signer intended to ask "READY START?" ('Are you ready to start?'), the /R/ Hand Configuration of READY$_{[inf]}$ appeared in START$_{[sl:HC]}$, which is properly articulated with a straight index-finger /G/ Configuration inserted

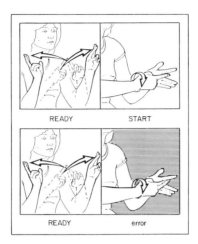

| READY | START |

| READY | error |

Figure 20. *Slip resulting in impossible ASL sign form.*

into the space between the index and middle fingers of the /5/ base hand. In this slip, the active hand in the /R/ Configuration made contact on the edges of the extended crossed fingers (see Figure 20). This contacting region, as we have pointed out, may be used with the /R/ Configuration only where the other hand also bears the /R/ shape. We suspect that it is the violation of this constraint that led our informants to classify the error form START$_{[sl:HC]}$ as an impossible sign form.

Although there are rare occurrences of slips that produce combinations of formational elements that are not allowable in ASL, and there are some slips that produce actual though unintended signs, the great majority of slips of the hand produce possible signs that accord with known rules for the combination of parameter primes. Such slips provide evidence of rules for combining abstract formational elements into meaningful units in the language.

8. Summary

The speech errors called slips of the tongue have furnished evidence for the combinational units and rules that constitute spoken language. We have found their counterparts, "slips of the hand," to provide equally valuable clues to the organization of sign language for deaf signers. As in the case of intrusion errors from short-term memory experiments (Bellugi, Klima, and Siple, 1974), the nature of the slips of the hand was captured readily by an analysis that treats the sign as a simultaneous composite of separately abstractable values. The units of organization affected by slips were occasionally entire signs; far more frequently (and more significantly from the point of view of the nature of signs and the constraints on their formational properties), a value of one sign is erroneously realized in another sign.

Spontaneous slips of the hand generally result in gestures that are not actual signs of ASL; most of these, in the judgment of deaf signers, are considered as possible but nonexistent signs in ASL. This strongly supports the hypothesis that signs are in fact coded (and not just analyzable) in terms of such parameter values. Those slips of the hand that are not actual ASL signs turn out to be for the most part combinations of parameter values that simply happen not to have a conventional meaning associated with them. That such slips should predominate is exactly what is predicted if slips of the hand do involve inadvertent substitutions and transpositions of parameter values.

Slips of the hand provide striking evidence for the psychological reality and independence of individual parameters of ASL: behavioral evidence from everyday communication that a sign is organized sublexically, and thus that this language of signs exhibits duality of patterning and arbitrary relationships between meaning and form.

Notes

1. This research was supported in part by National Science Foundation Grant BNS79–16423 and National Institutes of Health Grants HD13249 and NS15175 to The Salk Institute for Biological Studies. This is an expanded version of Chapter 5 in Klima and Bellugi, 1979. All illustrations were drawn by Frank A. Paul, copyright Ursula Bellugi.
2. Friedman (1977) treats orientation as a major parameter, coequal with Hand Configuration, Place of Articulation, and Movement. Her points of contact (our contacting regions) are introduced as a means for characterizing certain otherwise ambiguous values for orientation (pp. 43–49).
3. English glosses for ASL signs are represented in capital letters. The English word is merely used as a label for the sign and does not represent the full range of meanings of that sign in various linguistic contexts. Symbols for Hand Configuration primes are shown with drawings of the handshapes in Figure 1. Other notational conventions are found in the Appendix to this chapter.
4. An initial collection and analysis of sign errors was begun by Sharon Neumann Solow. We are grateful to Victoria Fromkin for her insightful discussions with us of slips of the tongue and hand.
5. Besides the intuitions of our informants, the evidence that the "slips" we are presenting are not assimilations can take several forms: In metatheses, there is a completed exchange of formational elements; in other cases, there may be intervening signs between the two signs involved in a slip. When there is a deviation from citation form performance between two adjacent signs, we can still differentiate slips of the hand from normal juncture assimilations. Slips typically involve switches of full parametric values throughout a sign; in a juncture assimilation, by contrast, a sign may begin as expected and show substitution of a value only in the end segment of a sign, substituting, for example, the Hand Configuration from the following sign.
6. Analysts of spoken language have identified other kinds of slips. One, a fusion of phonetic material from two (or more) words, is called a "blend." Blends differ from metatheses, anticipations, and perseverations in that the words involved do not occur in intended sequences, but rather are each possible choices of words that could fit into one position in the utterance, as in *recoflect* uttered as a blend of *recognize* and *reflect*. In our corpus are five clear cases of sign blends. One such blend combines a Place of Articulation value from

one sign with the active Hand Configuration and Movement from another. The signer produced "(HE) SEARCH[+], FIND (ME) QUICK/INSTANTLY." In this case, the active Hand Configuration and Movement values are taken from QUICK (the thumb flicks out from under the curled index finger), while the Place of Articulation is taken from INSTANTLY (the active hand rests on the tip of the inactive straight index finger).

A similar type of error, called a "haplology," differs from blends in that both signs involved were in fact found in the intended utterance, but were compressed into one syntactic slot in the error. An example from English is the utterance of *shrig soufflé* instead of the intended "shrimp and egg soufflé." There are five cases of this type of error in our corpus; in one, a signer intended the sentence "D-O-T THINK O-F SIGN BEFORE WRITE POEM." In the event, he telescoped the last two signs into a form consisting of the Hand Configuration of POEM (the thumb-and-middle finger /K/ Hand Configuration) with the Place of Articulation and Movement of WRITE (an oscillating outward brushing on the palm of the base hand).

Although blends and haplologies do not reflect the reordering of elements typical in metatheses, etc., they do reveal the persistence of constraints pertaining to ASL structure in that all the errors of these types in our corpus do in fact represent well-formed, potential sign-forms.

7. There was an additional possible example of an orientation metathesis where, in two base-hand signs requiring symmetrical orientations, the entire orientation specifications for the two signs—base and active hands together—seem to have been permuted.

8. In both these examples, the "two-touch" pattern (displaced iteration frame) has become separated from the more basic movement embedded in it. Of interest in the analysis of sign movement is the fact that, while displaced iteration has been recognized as an inflectional pattern in ASL (see Klima and Bellugi, 1979: Chapter 12) in which any lexical movement type may be embedded, this pattern has so far in sign analysis been systematically treated only with respect to the embedding of simple contact; in the Stokean analysis, as a sequence of touch-move over-touch, and in the Friedman reanalysis, as a unique value for the simultaneously specified contact dimension (i.e., double contact). The few instances of other movement types so embedded were treated by Stokoe exclusively as sequences of movement primes (e.g., in CHEERLEADER and TRANSFER 'move oneself'—two downward movements separated by sideways movement; in CHOICE—thumb and index closing while moving toward signer, twice, separated by sideways movement, etc.). Friedman does not mention such complex movements in her treatment of the movement parameter of sign structure, but a unified treatment of all such signs, in light of errors such as the ones described here, might separate the simplex movement and the displaced iteration frame as independent simultaneously appearing specifications.

9. These two-part signs differ from simplex two-touch (movement-cluster) signs in that they typically involve changes in prime-level specifications for their beginning and ending contacting points; in two-part base-hand signs, the base hand usually changes contacting region and/or orientation simultaneously with the movement of the active hand, as in PROGRAM and TOAST. Also included in this two-part category are two-hand symmetrical signs such as FRIEND (which figured in our third example of apparent segmentation) and HAMBURGER, where the hands exchange roles in the execution of the movement.

10. When a new sign is coined from an existing one by changing the Hand Configuration only, the point of contact of the new active Hand Configuration must be chosen from among the possible contacting regions for that Hand Configuration. For example, the /P/ Hand Configuration, when it is making sliding contact, makes this contact only at the tip of the middle finger. For a sign meaning 'profession' coined from an existing sign meaning 'field (of endeavor),' the active Hand Configuration /P/ makes contact with the tip of the finger rather than the side of the hand.

11. It is possible that the appearance of these few "impossible" gestures in our corpus and their virtual absence from other reported data is related to our sampling methods. Many reported studies to not use audio- or videotape recordings, but rely on reported or remembered errors.

Perhaps in memory one tends to accommodate what was perceived to what was expected, which may lead to a "filtering out" of impossible sounds or sequences. Much of our corpus was culled from videotapes; by editing, we copied the errors onto a single tape of slips, and extensively reviewed the actual occurrences both at normal speed and under slow motion. It could be that this process brought forth a few more examples of impossible signs. Alternatively, the occurrence of some impossible sign forms could reflect some relaxing of the forces of structural constraint.

Appendix: Notational Conventions

SIGN	English glosses for signs are indicated by full capital letters.
SIGN-SIGN	This indicates that two or more English words have been required to gloss a single sign.
SIGN⁀SIGN	This indicates that two signs are joined in a lexical compound and represent a complex sign.
(SIGN)	This indicates that a pointing sign has been glossed with its translation value. Note that signs glossed as "(HE)" and "(SHE)," for instance, have no formational distinction.
SIGN$^{[+]}$	This indicates that a sign cited in a slip had undergone a morphological process, for instance, an inflection for temporal aspect.
W-O-R-D	This indicates a fingerspelled English word.
SIGN$_{[sl:\ \ ]}$	This indicates a sign that has been affected in a slip. Abbreviations for the parameters whose values have been exchanged appear after the colon, as follows: HC (Hand Configuration); PA (Place of Articulation); MOV (Movement); and HA (Hand Arrangement).
SIGN$_{[inf]}$	This indicates the influencing sign in a slip.
SIGN/SIGN	This indicates a blend of two signs.

References

Battison, R. 1974. Phonological deletion in American Sign Language. *Sign Language Studies, 5,* 1-19.

Bellugi, U., Klima, E. S., & Siple, P. 1975. Remembering in signs. *Cognition: International Journal of Cognitive Psychology, 3* (2), 93-125.

Friedman, L. (Ed.). 1977. *On the other hand: New perspectives on American Sign Language.* New York: Academic Press.

Frishberg, N. 1975. Arbitrariness and iconicity: Historical change in American Sign Language. *Language, 51,* 696-719.

Fromkin, V. A. 1971. The non-anomalous nature of anomalous utterances. *Language, 47,* 27-52.

Fromkin, V. A. 1973. Slips of the tongue. *Scientific American, 229,* 109-117.

Garrett, M. F. 1975. The analysis of speech production. *Psychology of Learning and Motivation, 9,* 133-177.

Klima, E. S. & Bellugi, U. 1979. *The signs of language.* Cambridge, Massachusetts: Harvard Univ. Press.

Lane, H., Boyes-Braem, P., & Bellugi, U. 1976. Preliminaries to a distinctive feature analysis of handshapes in American Sign Language. *Cognitive Psychology, 8,* 263-289.

Mallery, G. (1881) 1972. Sign language among North American Indians compared with that among other peoples and deaf-mutes. In J. W. Powell (Ed.), *First annual report of the Bureau of Ethnology to the secretary of the Smithsonian Institution,* 1879-80. Reprint. The Hague: Mouton.

Stokoe, W. C., Jr. 1960. *Sign language structure.* Studies in Linguistics, Occasional Papers 8. Buffalo: Univ. of Buffalo Press.

Stokoe, W. C., Jr., Casterline, D., & Croneberg, C. 1965. *A dictionary of American Sign Language.* Washington, D.C.: Gallaudet College Press.

Wells, R. 1951. Predicting slips of the tongue. *The Yale Scientific Magazine, 26,* 9-30.

Wundt, W. (1921) 1973. *The language of gestures.* The Hague: Mouton.

Chapter 14

ON MERINGER'S CORPUS OF "SLIPS OF THE EAR"

Marianne Celce-Murcia

Department of English
University of California
Los Angeles, California

1. Introduction

In the late nineteenth and early twentieth centuries, Professor Rudolf Meringer of the University of Vienna published two volumes in German; namely *Versprechen und Verlesen* (hereafter referred to as *VuV*) with Karl Mayer in 1895 and *Aus dem Leben der Sprache* (hereafter referred to as *ALS*) in 1908. Even today these volumes constitute one of the psycholinguist's richest data bases for systematic production errors in speech and writing as well as reception errors in listening and reading. This chapter presents, translates, and analyzes the "slips of the ear" in Meringer's two-volume corpus. Meringer's phonological explanation concerning such errors is shown to be inadequate. Several additional important factors in the explanation of such errors are isolated and discussed. Some very detailed "slips of the ear" that I have collected in observing speakers of English are also included to support certain of the additional factors isolated and to illustrate the nature and extent of the data needed for a complete and accurate analysis of such errors.

2. Limiting Meringer's Corpus

Compared with Meringer's corpora for errors in speech, reading, and writing, the number of "slips of the ear" errors he collected is small indeed. He cited a total of 47 such errors in *VuV* and *ALS*. However, only 28 of these are drawn from natural speech and are thus suitable for further consideration in this chapter. The 19 errors excluded from detailed analysis are of three types:

1. Eight errors were excerpted from a volume on the German puppet theater, in which the comic character Kasperl commits many slips of the ear. These samples are clearly contrived and intended as a source of humor. It is interesting, however, to note how closely they follow Meringer's authentic slips of the ear. Therefore, I have listed them with English translations in Appendix A of this chapter.

2. Ten errors occurred while witnesses in a court of justice were listening to the oath and repeating it line by line before giving testimony. Since these errors occurred as attempts at repetition of a ritualistic formula rather than as errors in spontaneous speech and since the witnesses were probably very nervous under the circumstances, these errors are considered inappropriate data. However, the original oath and the errors occurring as attempted repetitions of it in court are listed and translated in Appendix B.

3. One error was made by a court stenographer, who wrote down something other than the actual oral testimony. We can assume a hearing error was involved; but since the situation requires two simultaneous activities (i.e., writing as well as listening), other factors could have played a role. This error is also cited and translated in Appendix B.

The remaining 28 errors, which we will examine more closely, occurred in natural speech and were committed by Meringer himself, his wife, his colleagues, or acquaintances and friends of his.

3. Meringer's Explanation for Slips of the Ear

In *VuV* (p. 157) under the heading "Wie man sich verhört" ('how people mishear'), Meringer provided the following explanation for slips of the ear, which I would like to present before citing any examples from his data.

> Der Vokal der Wurzelsilbe und die Vokale überhaupt werden am häufigsten richtig wahrgenommen.
> Auffallend ist dagegen, welche geringe Kraft die Consananten, sogar die anlautenden, dem Hörfehler entgegensetzen können. Für den Sprechenden ist der Wortanlaut sehr wichtig, weil von ihm in erster Linie die Erinnerung des Wortes abhängt, der Hörer ist aber oft nicht in der Lage ihn zu verstehn, was bei dem geringen akustischen Wert der Consonanten begreiflich erscheint, und sucht also lieber mit Hülfe der percipierten Silbenvokale das mangelhaft erfasste Wort zu erhaschen [Meringer and Mayer, 1895:157].

> The vowel of the root syllable and vowels in general are most frequently perceived correctly.
> In contrast it is striking what small effect the consonants, even those in initial position, have in deterring mistakes in perception. For the speaker the initial sound of a word is very important because in the first place his recall of the word depends primarily on it; the listener, however, is often not in a position to understand the initial sound. This is understandable because of the very slight acoustical value of the consonants. The listener, therefore, prefers to try to grasp the imperfectly understood word with the aid of the perceived syllable vowels [author's translation].

4. Analyzing Meringer's Corpus

From the preceding discussion we can deduce that Meringer felt that slips of the ear occur when the listener misperceives consonants while more or less correctly perceiving vowels in a given utterance. Before commenting in greater detail on Meringer's explanation, I would like to determine how many of his own 28 spontaneous errors can be explained by applying this principle. Even if we allow Meringer's generalization to account for loss and/or addition of consonants as well as substitution of consonants, only 5 of the 28 examples are accounted for. These 5 examples are:

(1)   Loss of word final /n/: Dr. Mayer understood "Feld im Meere" ('field in the sea-ocean') for "Feld in Mähren" ('field in Moravia'), *Vuv*, p. 157.

(2)   Substitution of word initial /b/ for /pf/ and loss of word final /d/: Meringer understood "Bär" ('bear') for "Pferd" ('horse'), *VuV*, p. 158.

(3)   Substitution of word initial /g/ for /b/ and word final /x/ for /f/: Meringer understood "Geruch" ('smell, odor') for "Beruf" ('occupation'), *VuV*, p. 158.

(4)   Loss of /r/ in the word-initial cluster and substitution of /k/ for /t/ in morpheme-final position: A waitress understood "Backhuhn" ('baked chicken') for "Brathuhn" ('roast chicken'), *VuV*, p. 158.

(5)   Possible substitution of syllable-final /k/ for /g/;[1] loss of postvocalic /r/: Drs. Adler and Pinter report that someone heard "Sack" ('sack, purse') for "Sarg" ('coffin'), *ALS*, p. 142.

If we weaken Meringer's phonological generalization to the extent that we allow minor variations in vowel length and/or quality, and also misperceived juncture boundary to play a role in accounting for slips of the ear, an additional 3 (or a total of 8 out of 28) errors are accounted for:

(6)   Substitution of morpheme-initial /f/ for /b/, stressed /ü/ for /ɪ/, and medial /g/ for /k/: Meringer understands "Ausflügen" ('to make an excursion') for "Ausblicken" ('to look outside'), *VuV*, p. 158.

(7)   Substitution of initial /h/ for /j/ and stressed /ü/ for /ü:/, loss of postnasal /g/ with corresponding readjustment of /ŋ/ to /n/: Dr. Much understands "Hühner isst" ('eats chickens') for "jünger ist" ('is younger'), *VuV*, p. 158.

(8)   Incorrect perception of juncture: Meringer understands "sind dumm" ('are dumb') for "sind um" ('are around' or 'have passed'), *VuV*, p. 158.

What of the 20 remaining slips of the ear? Some of them could have been squeezed into the above phonologically defined category, yet it seemed somewhat artificial to do so since other factors seem more important. The largest remaining category consisted of cases where a proper noun (i.e., a surname, a place name, or the name of a language) was confused with either a common noun (8 examples) or another proper noun (4 examples). Phonological factors played a role to be sure; however, they were not as systematic as in the previous examples, and involved other processes such as metathesis, loss or addition of one or more syllables, changes in stress patterns, and, in general, more extreme phonological variations.

4.1. *Proper Nouns Confused with Common Nouns*

(1)   (See the preceding section.)

(9)   Dr. Genzi Blaüme understood "Herrenhaus" ('manor-house') for "Eranos" ('a club or group')–i.e., "Gesellschaft"–in Vienna), *VuV*, p. 158.

(10) Meringer understood "Goethische" ('Goethean–pertaining to Goethe') for "kritische" ('critical'), *VuV*, p. 158.

(11) Dr. Adler understood "Elsass" ('Alsace') for "öfters" ('frequently'), *VuV*, p. 158.

(12) Meringer understood "Innsbruck" (i.e., 'the city in Austria') for "Dienstboten" ('servants'), *VuV*, p. 158.

(13) E. Bunzl understood "Russland" ('Russia') for "Ruhestand" ('retirement'), *ALS*, p. 142.

(14) Meringer understood "Hebra" ('Hebrew') for "Rehbraten" ('roast venison'), *VuV*, p. 158.

(15) Dr. Adler understood "Tyroler" ('people from the Tyrol') for "Philologen" ('philologists'), *VuV*, p. 158.

4.2. *Proper Nouns Confused with Proper Nouns*

(16) Meringer understood "Vetter aus Kroke" ('cousin from Kroke'[2]) for "Vetter aus Chicago" ('cousin from Chicago'), *VuV*, p. 157.

(17) Dr. von Boenicke understood "Löffler" ('a German surname') for "Lechthaler" ('a German surname'), *VuV*, p. 157.

(18) Dr. Adler understood "Kroaten" ('Croatians') for "Kosaken" ('Cossacks'), *VuV*, p. 158.

(19) Dr. Heberdey understood "Dumba war dagegen" ('Dumba'–a non-German surname–'was against it') for "Thun war dagegen" ('Thun'–a German surname pronounced /tun/–'was against it'), *VuV*, p. 158.

This last error brings us to a related category–i.e., the use of foreign words and expressions and their role in errors of misperception. In the Vienna dialect, such words and expressions are frequent–the two main source languages being French and Italian. The following four errors attest to the reality of this phenomenon (foreign surnames and place names could, of course, also be included in this category):

(20) Dr. Mayer understood "Bauernfeld" ('farmer's field') for "Bauern*feuilleton*" (Fr.) ('a series about farmers'), *VuV*, p. 157.

(21) Dr. Bormann understood 'Bahnen" probably ('railways') for "*Vulkane*" (It.) ('volcanoes'), *VuV*, p. 158.

(22) Meringer understood "*Ballett*" (Fr.) ('ballet') for "*Toilette*" (Fr.) ('W. C., lavatory'), *VuV*, p. 158.

(23) A waitress understood "ein *Diner*!" (Fr.) ('an elaborate meal') for "ein *Giardinetto*!" (It.) ('a dish made of fresh, mixed vegetables cooked together'), *VuV*, p. 158.

The remaining five slips of the ear represent progressively more extreme perceptual distortions that cannot be satisfactorily explained as problems due to sounds, proper names (unless one considers *Lysol* in Example 27 to be a proper name), or foreign borrowings. The explanation of these errors depends in large part on specification of the total conversational context as well as information about the interlocutors. Where Meringer provides such context (e.g., 27 and to some extent 26), I repeat it along with the example.

(24) Meringer understood "Durst oder Hunger" ('thirst or hunger') for "Verdruss oder Kummer" ('dismay or sorrow'), *VuV*, p. 158.

The expected phonological similarities occur in Example 24; however, it is difficult to determine the cause of the error without further context. The same thing is true of Example 25; i.e., without knowing what happened to the table, it is difficult to describe this error, which involves a loss of the subjunctive inflection on the modal auxiliary as well as phonological differences:

(25) Someone understood "Ihr Tischler soll einen Brand haben" ('Your table-maker must be crazy') for "Ihr Tischl sollte einen Rand haben" ('Your table—diminutive—ought to have a rim'), *ALS*, p. 143.

The preceding example and the following one also introduce a new factor—the use of idioms and colloquialisms in errors of misperception.

(26) Frau Meringer: Was fehlt ihm denn? ('What's wrong with him?')
      Frau L. von Frankl: Meschugge is er![3] ('He's crazy!')
      And Frau Meringer understood "Wie, verschiedenes?" ('How/Like what, different ones?') for what Frau von Frankl said, *ALS*, p. 143.

A background note for Example 27 is that *Seitel*[4] and *Krügl* are local measures for serving beer in Vienna. The former is a large glass that holds about ½ liter and the latter a large mug that holds about one liter of beer.

(27) Head waiter (to boy): 2 Seitel, 1 Krügl, rasch besorgen! ('Serve quickly') For this Meringer's wife heard "2 Seitel, 1 Krügl, Flasche Lysol!" ('a bottle of Lysol'), *ALS*, p. 142.

Meringer reports that his wife laughed over her hearing error and explained quite correctly that for her *eine Flasche Lysol* was a very familiar and immediate word-image because their eldest daughter was being washed with diluted Lysol at the time [*ALS:* 142-143]. In the final error from Meringer's corpus, one can speculate that a student customer wanted to study for half an hour in the restaurant, whereas the waitress, who is accustomed to taking orders for food, misheard the student's remark as an order for half a chicken:

(28) A waitress understood "halbes Huhn" ('half a chicken') for "halbe Stunde studieren" ('to study half an hour'), *VuV*, p. 158.

Without commenting further on these last five errors, I would like to report the eight slips of the ear that I have collected in English, two of which I report from written sources; one comes from an oral account provided me by the listener; and the other five I observed directly—even participating in four of them myself.

5. Errors of Perception in English

(E1) Preparing to board a British airliner, I handed my family's four tickets to the clerk at the counter. "How many miles?" he asked crisply. Surprised by the question, I was trying to estimate the mileage when he again asked, with obvious impatience, "How many miles?"

"How do you expect me to know the mileage to Amsterdam?" I muttered. "You run the airline."

The young Englishman shook his head. "No. No." he said. "In your party —how many miles and how many femiles?" [Reprinted from *Reader's Digest*, April 1977:128, with the permission of the publisher.]

Here dialect differences in phonology account for the misunderstanding. The American customer is initially unable to adjust to the Cockney substitution of /ay/ for /ey/. The latter vowel being the expected one in *males* in either standard British or American English. The very same vowel-based misperception occurred in the following slip of the ear, which was committed by a former foreign student advisor at an Arizona university during a conversation that he had with an exchange student from Australia.

(E2) Student: Can you tell me where I can find a /baysǝn/?
      Advisor: They're very rare in these parts nowadays. You can travel miles in the countryside and not see a single buffalo.
      Student: No, not a buffalo! I'm looking for a wash /baysǝn/ so I can wash my face and shave when I get up [Hector Guglielmo, personal communication].

(E3) Another dialect difference in phonological systems accounted for a misperception on my part. Several years ago while I was on a consulting job on the Navajo Indian Reservation, a local English teacher told me that he taught at the Indian school in /mɪni/ farms. I interpreted the location of the teacher's school to be *Mini-farms* (an analogy with *mini-bus, mini-skirt, mini-lesson,* etc.). It was not until a few days later, when I drove through a small village marked *Many Farms,* that I realized I had been misled by the speaker's dialect, which neutralizes the /ɪ/ ~ /ɛ/ distinction preceding nasal consonants.

(E4) My next example again involves a dialect difference and a proper name. During a conversation with one of my students, he made a reference to another student, Judy /gaf/, who had given him many good suggestions. "Who's Judy Gaff?" I asked myself, while continuing to converse with him. Somewhat later I realized that he was referring to Judy Gough, whose surname I always pronounced /gɔf/. Doug's California dialect, which lowers all open o's to /a/, was responsible for this momentary confusion on my part.

(E5) A more deviant misperception also involving proper names was committed by one of my students, ironically enough in a University of California, Los Angeles practical phonetics course. I was passing back quizzes to the class. The quizzes were in alphabetical order, and there were about 35 students in the class. When I called out "Margaret" for Margaret Kelly, Barbara Mason stretched out her hand. She thought I had said "Barbara." When I asked her how she had misheard "Margaret" as "Barbara," she said that she hadn't been listening closely, but that she knew I was getting close to the M's, and that it had sounded like her name.

(E6) (On the phone)

Charley: Hi. I'm at the Quality Inn near L.A. airport.

Marianne (a bit unsure of the name of the inn Charley mentioned): The Holiday Inn?

Charley: No, the *Quality* Inn.

Here, in addition to telephone distortion, the generalized American tendency to pronounce intervocalic /t/ in words like *Quality* as a flap, /d/, contributed to my initial confusion. The fact that the Holiday Inn is much better known to me than the Quality Inn also played a role.

(E7) (Setting: intermission at a concert that took place during the 1976-77 college basketball season. Gene Bartow was the UCLA basketball coach and speaker Y knows very little about music or musicians.)

X (addressing about four people, all of whom are somehow connected with UCLA): I don't like contemporary music. I don't even like Bartok [/bártɔk/).

Y (who listened in only on the second sentence): You don't like Bartow (/bártow/)? I can't stand him either. He's a lousy coach!

In this slip of the ear, we again have a phonological confusion involving proper names; however, it is very likely that what is more important in this case, is speaker Y's preoccupation with basketball and his ignorance concerning music and musicians.

(E8) One of the authors . . . once applied for an assistantship with a psychiatric research institute. At the appointed hour he reported to the director's office for his interview and the following conversation took place with the receptionist.

Visitor: Good afternoon. I have an appointment with Dr. H___. My name is Watzlawick (VAHT-sla-vick).

Receptionist: I did not say it was.

Visitor (taken aback and somewhat annoyed): But I'm telling you it *is*.

Receptionist (bewildered): Why then did you say it wasn't?

Visitor: But I *said* it was!

At this point the visitor was certain that he was being made the object of some incomprehensible but disrespectful joke, while as it turned out, the receptionist had by then decided that the visitor must be a new psychotic patient of Dr. H's. Eventually it became clear that instead of "My name is Watzlawick," the receptionist had understood "My name is *not* Slavic," which, indeed, she had never said it was [Watzlawick, Beavin, and Jackson, 1967:94–95].

In this error it appears that phonological factors and the sound of an unfamiliar surname (a foreign surname) along with the receptionist's readiness to expect people to say absurd or crazy things, especially if it is possible that they are Dr. H's patients, all contributed to the misunderstanding.

6. Discussion

Meringer's explanation for slips of the ear—that vowels are generally perceived correctly, whereas consonants can easily be confused because of their limited acoustical value—only accounted for at most 8 of the 28 spontaneous errors in his corpus and for at most 3 of the 8 errors in my small English corpus. Obviously, other factors are at work. Browman (this volume) who has collected over 200 slips of the ear committed by English speakers, feels that two origins of hearing errors are acoustic misanalysis and incorrect lexical decision. Furthermore, since 85% of the errors in her corpus involve single words only, she feels that the word is an important unit in speech processing. Garnes and Bond (this volume), who have collected almost 900 slips of the ear—also by English speakers—emphasize that listeners attempt to make sense of what they hear. They suggest four heuristics for speech processing:

1. Pay attention to stress and intonation—mismatches on this level are rare.
2. Pay attention to stressed vowels—such slips of the ear are rare compared with those involving consonants.
3. Find a word—the listener retrieves the best word match as soon as possible.
4. Find a phrase—give it a semantic analysis and edit it for morphological markers.

The second heuristic suggested by Garnes and Bond recalls Meringer's principle. Stressed vowels do seem basic: People who have suffered severe hearing loss can still hear and discriminate vowels but not consonants (Evelyn Hatch, personal communication). Thus vowels would seem to be a basic or given element in speech recognition, with consonants being the critical variables, i.e., the discriminators. When the misperception of a stressed vowel is the sole cause of a misunderstanding (there were no such errors in Meringer's corpus but see Examples E1, E2, E3, and E4), dialect differences may be the reason.

The 36 errors cited in the preceding section have shown us that there are many potential factors at work. In any given slip of the ear, two or more of the following 10 factors may be interacting:

1. Phonological misperception of consonant and vowel segments—loss, addition, substitution
2. Misperception based on loss, deletion, or substitution of entire syllables—especially if weakly stressed
3. Misperception of proper nouns
4. Misperception of foreign words and expressions (may include proper names)
5. Misperception based on phonological dialect differences (in English, vowels seem to be the main problem)
6. Misperception based on the listener's strong and immediate word-images
7. Misperception based on the listener's current preoccupations
8. Misperception based on what the listener expects or does not expect the interlocutor to say
9. Misperception based on the listener's lack of information (or incorrect information) with respect to the topic under discussion
10. Misperception based on the speaker's use of an idiom or a colloquialism

As more contextually detailed errors become available, this list will certainly be extended. For example, the precise role of semantic similarity in slips of the ear also needs to be explored since in 11 of the 36 examples cited in the preceding section, the intended expression and the misperceived expression share a close semantic relationship—that is to say, they belong to the same class (for instance, *Bär* ['bear']-*Pferd* ['horse']) as well as the proper names referring to people or places. Another two items seem to share a marginal semantic relationship (for example, *Meere* ['ocean, sea'] for *Mähren* ['Moravia']); here both the intended and the misperceived form have a locative, geographical reference.

This notion of semantic similarity perhaps holds a clue to the large number of proper nouns (i.e., personal names and place names that occurred in the preceding slips of the ear. There were 17 errors involving proper nouns: 8 confused a proper noun with a common noun and 9 confused proper nouns with other proper nouns. These last 9 errors, especially, show a high degree of semantic similarity—for example, one woman's name for another, one hotel name for another, etc. In addition, proper nouns share a number of syntactic features that set them apart from common nouns, such as article usage. However, on the basis of the errors cited in this chapter, it would not be wise to overdo the notion of semantic similarity since 23 of the preceding 36 slips of the ear are semantically unrelated (for example, *Beruf* ['occupation']-*Geruch* ['odor, smell']); in such semantically anomalous cases—apart from the strong phonological similarities—the misheard form and the intended form often share certain other grammatical and discourse features—such as having the same part of speech or, as in the case of the German *Beruf*-*Geruch* pair, having the same grammatical gender—i.e., masculine. Such syntactic and discourse features must also be studied in greater detail.

Furthermore, the whole notion of interaction among the various possible factors must be analyzed. For example, it seems intuitively correct to predict that German *Bär* and *Pferd* will be misperceived more easily than their English equivalents *bear* and *horse* due to the former pair's combined phonological and semantic similarities. Likewise, since proper names are so frequently misheard and since foreign borrowings also cause similar problems, we can expect foreign proper names to play a role in slips of the ear (see, for instance, Examples 19 and E8).

The final question to be raised (perhaps it ought to have been the first) is why slips of the ear should be collected and studied at all. Four reasons come to mind:

1. If we understand more completely why and how errors of misperception occur, this will help us to reconstruct the strategies listeners use to process the stream of speech.

2. If further investigation shows us that discrimination of all the vowel sounds of a language in context is basic to speech processing, this becomes an important part of mastering listening comprehension in a foreign language. That is to say, vowel discrimination would form the base, and then consonant discrimination added to that would encourage normal acoustic processing strategies in the foreign language.

3. Machine recognition of human speech will be advanced by studies in this area.

4. Such errors provide a contemporary reenactment of certain phonologically based language changes that occurred in the past due to widespread errors of misperception. For example, many English words that originally ended in a velar fricative $/x/$ now are pronounced with a final $/f/$, for example *enough, tough, laugh, rough*, etc. For similar reasons a number of juncture changes have also occurred so that phrases such as *a napron* and *a nadder* became *an apron* and *an adder,* respectively.[5]

7. Conclusion

It is hoped that the information provided along with my eight slips of the ear in English and the information that Meringer provided with error 27 have convinced the reader that this type of detailed reporting is absolutely essential if we are to understand how and why slips of the ear take place. A mere listing of X being misperceived as Y misleadingly limits the study of slips of the ear to an analysis of phonological–acoustical and lexical factors. A sizable corpus of detailed contextualized errors must be amassed, and it is very likely that the work of the ethnomethodologists such as Sachs, Schegloff, and Jefferson (1974), who have studied the structure of conversation, would be a useful source to consult in such an undertaking.

Another important consideration is that the amount of adequately documented data that any one individual can collect firsthand is limited to his or her observations of conversations or events, wherein the listeners who misperceive are him- or herself and/or close acquaintances. (In this way, important background information can be provided regarding the person who misheard a given utterance, and the one who misheard can be asked follow-up questions.) Many people, therefore, will have to become involved in collecting and sharing more fully documented errors. A better sampling of languages is also required since the currently available data for analysis are mainly from English (i.e., Browman [this volume] and Garnes and Bond [this volume] with some also from German, i.e., Meringer's corpus.

Acknowledgments

I am grateful to Mr. and Mrs. Ernest Burgbacher and Professors Werner Leopold and Terence Wilbur for having helped me translate some of the more difficult items and passages in Meringer's corpus. Any errors that remain, however, are solely my responsibility.

Appendix A: Slips of the Ear in the German Puppet Theater

The 8 slips of the ear cited by Meringer that are committed by Kasperl, a comic character in German puppet-theater plays, come from *Vergleichende Deutsche Puppenspiele,* edited by Kralik and Winter, pages 136, 204, 225, etc. They are cited by Meringer in *VuV* on page 159. Kasperl understands:

1. "Leimsieder" ('glue-maker') for "Einsiedler" ('hermit')
2. "Schuster und Schneider" ('cobbler and tailor') for "Wurzeln und Kräuter" ('roots and herbs')
3. "Trompeter" ('trumpeter') for "Don Pedro"
4. "Marianna" for "Diana"
5. "Liesel" ('nickname for Louise or Elisabeth') for "Hiesel" ('could be a Southern dialect form for a small house or it could be a surname')
6. "Abg'röst" (This is a strange past participle. The infinitive could be *abreisen* ('to go away') or *abrüsten* ('to disarm, dismantle'). In either case the participle is ungrammatical.) for "Arrest" ('detention')
7. "Wagen" ('car, cart') for "Magen" ('stomach')
8. "Schnellwage" ('steelyard'—i.e., a special weight-measuring device currently spelled *Schnellwaage.*) for "Schildwache" ('sentinel')

Appendix B: Immediate Repetition or Dictation Indicates a Possible Slip of the Ear

All of the following examples are from *ALS,* page 142. H. Gross tells Meringer of the listening errors that occur during the taking of the oath by witnesses in court. The oath reads:

> Ich Schwöre bei Gott, dem Allmachtigen, Allwissenden eine reinen Eid, dass ich über alles, was ich bei Gericht befragt werde, die reine Wahrheit und nichts als die Wahrheit aussagen werde – so wahr mir Gott helfe!

> I swear to God, the almighty, the all-knowing, a chaste oath, that concerning every thing that I will be asked by the court I will speak the unadulterated truth and nothing but the truth – so help me God! [author's translation]

1. Instead of "einen reinen Eid" ('a chaste oath'), people repeated:
   a. "Keinen Eid" ('no oath')
   b. "eine Kleinigkeit" ('a trifle')
   c. "einen Meineid" ('perjury')
   d. "Reu und Leid" ('regret and sorrow')
   e. "Dreieinigkeit" ('the Trinity')
2. Instead of "Bei Gericht befragt werde" ('will be asked by the court'), someone repeated:
   "nicht befragt werde" ('will not be asked')
3. Instead of "nichts als die Wahrheit" ('nothing but the truth'), someone repeated: "und nix die Wahrheit" ('and no truth').
4. Instead of "reine Wahrheit" ('unadulterated truth'), someone repeated: "keine Wahrheit" ('no truth').
5. Instead of "ich schwöre, so wahr mir Gott helfe!" people repeated:
   a. "Ich wahre so schwer mir Gott helfe!" (– in Vienna dialect it's probably – 'I would be so heavy as God helps me.')
   b. "Ich helfe, so schwer mir Gott wahrt!" ('I help as hard [as] God inspires me.')

Finally, H. Gross also reported to Meringer that during a session for the verbal testimony "Gehirn blutreich" ('brain rich-in-blood, brain very bloody'), the court stenographer wrote down instead "Gehirn gut und weich" ('brain good and soft').

Notes

1. The reported substitution of syllable-final /k/ for /g/ in this item assumes that the German dialect(s) of both the speaker and listener involved in this slip of the ear do not have the morpheme-final devoicing rule, which systematically changes all morpheme-final occurrences of /b/, /d/, and /g/ to /p/, /t/, and /k/, respectively. Many Southern dialects do not have this rule. It is also possible that the speaker and the listener represent different dialects—i.e., one has the devoicing rule, the other doesn't. If this were the case, this error can be considered potentially similar to Examples E1, E2, E3, and E4.
2. I have been unable to track down this place name.
3. Meringer's version of this line in the dialogue is spelled *Meschugge,* with an umlauted *u*. This was probably a typographical error. The usual spelling contains no umlaut.
4. Werner Leopold (personal communication) informs me that the standard German equivalent for this Viennese term is *Seidel* ('beerstein').
5. Ironically, one of the reasons Meringer gave in *VuV* for studying speech errors was that they might turn out to be the cause of certain historical sound changes. Perhaps he was never able to support this hypothesis because he concentrated on speech errors rather than on errors of misperception, which do play a limited role in historical sound changes.

References

Carr, Edward. 1977. A pronounced difference. *Reader's Digest,* April 1977. P. 128.

Meringer, R. 1908. *Aus dem leben der sprache: Versprechen, kindersprache, nachahmungstrieb.* Berlin: B. Behr's Verlag. Pp. 142–143.

Meringer, R. & Mayer, K. 1895. *Versprechen und verlesen: Eine psychologische-linguisticische Studie.* Stuttgart: G. J. Goschen'sche Verlagshandlung. Pp. 157–159.

Sacks, H., Schegloff, E., & Jefferson, G. 1974. A simplest systematics for the organization of turn-taking for conversation. *Language, 50,* 4.

Watzlawick, P., Beavin, J. H., & Jackson, D. D. 1967. *Pragmatics of human communication: A study of interactional patterns, pathologies, and paradoxes.* New York: W. W. Norton. Pp. 94–95.

CHAPTER 15

PERCEPTUAL PROCESSING: EVIDENCE FROM SLIPS OF THE EAR[1]

Catherine P. Browman

Department of Linguistics
New York University
New York, New York

Paradigms of speech perception generally include references to a number of levels involved in the understanding of speech. Levels such as features, phonemes, syllables, words, and phrases have all been assumed to be important in perceptual processing, although different researchers have stressed the importance of different levels. Investigation into the details of perceptual processing has so far focused primarily on the lower levels of features and phonemes. Descriptions of the higher-level processing are generally of the black-box type, in which the levels are named and only described in broad terms. Explicit descriptions of the manner in which higher levels interact with lower levels are notably lacking. The purpose of the present chapter, then, is to examine in detail the interaction of the higher level of lexical decision with the lower level of acoustic analysis, by relating patterns of segmental misperceptions to the internal structure of words.

1. General Description of the Data

A slip of the ear occurs when the listener misperceives the speaker's utterance, for example:

speaker produced *fuel flask*
listener perceived *field glasses*

In this chapter, only those aspects of slips of the ear, or misperceptions, that pertain directly to the interaction of word structure and segment identification will be thoroughly discussed. In order to give the reader a feel for the data, however, I will first present a general description of the corpus.

The present analysis is of 222 misperceptions collected by the author, friends, relatives, etc. during the course of casual conversation. The misperceptions range from a single feature change in a single word (*van→fan*, i.e., *van* was misperceived as *fan*), through multiple feature changes across several words (*popping really slow→ prodigal son*), to substantial deletions and insertions of entire words (*go to the car and get the tuna→get my car tuned up*). Over half the misperceptions involve nominal utterances by the speaker. Only a few misperceptions result in nonsense items; quite likely this is a consequence of reporting bias. That is, most nonsense misperceptions probably elicit a *what?!* response from the listener, and are immediately forgotten. Generally the misperceptions are either semantically or syntactically anomalous, again probably a reporting-bias phenomenon. That is, only those misperceptions that violate some syntactic constraint or that do not make sense will be noticed and consequently recollected.

Of the misperceptions, 85% involve a single word only (*Barcelona→carcinoma*). I have argued elsewhere (Browman, 1976b) that this fact plus other distributional properties of the corpus suggest that the word is a particularly important unit in speech perception, and hence that a further investigation of the role of the word in perceptual processing should be fruitful. About 40% of the single words involved in single word errors are of two syllables (*simple→sinful*), a third are of one syllable (*Fudge→French*), a quarter are of three syllables (*Majorca→Malaga*), and a tenth are of four syllables. About a quarter of the vowels are misperceived, and a third of the consonants.

2. Word Structure and Segment Errors: Distribution of Errors

In order to test the effect of word structure on segmental errors, I created a composite of words by summing over all the words in the corpus. If a single misperception extends over more than one word, it contributes each of the words to the composite. Thus *fuel flask→field glasses* contributes two words to the composite; *popping really slow→prodigal son* contributes three words. A total of 164 words form the polysyllabic composite; the 182 monosyllabic words are summed separately. The polysyllabic composite has three syllables: initial, final, and medial, where medial is contributed only from three- and four- syllable (and greater, if any) words. In order to test the effect of stress, each composite syllable is a sum either of all stressed syllables in that position of the word or of all unstressed syllables in that word position. For each syllable, the initial consonant (if any), vowel, and final consonant (if any) are included in the analysis. Syllable-initial consonants also include consonants from those cases where syllabification is indeterminant: In *sylla-ble,* the *ll* is considered to be the initial consonant of the second syllable. Figure 1 shows the distribution of errors for each position of the polysyllabic and mono-

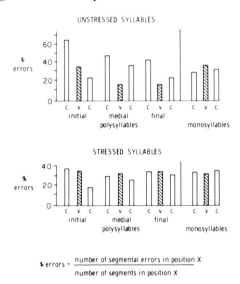

$$\% \text{ errors} = \frac{\text{number of segmental errors in position X}}{\text{number of segments in position X}}$$

Figure 1: *Overall error rates by position within composite.*

syllabic composites, considering stressed and unstressed syllables separately (see the Appendix to this chapter for a discussion of the methods used to match the utterances and misperceptions on the segmental level).

Consider first the distributions of errors for unstressed syllables in polysyllabic words, the top left figure. There is a definite word position effect, with the error rate progressively decreasing toward the end of the word. Within each syllable, there is a higher error rate for consonants than for vowels (except for the final consonant in initial syllable). Moreover, syllable-initial consonants have more errors than the corresponding syllable-final consonants. Notice that these generalizations are not true for the unstressed monosyllables shown in the top right figure; the error rate seems about the same for consonants and vowels, and for initial and final consonants. In fact, the unstressed monosyllables share the distributional properties of stressed monosyllables.

Consider now the stressed composites in the lower portion of Figure 1. The word position effect is apparently neutralized, with approximately the same error rate across the word. Moreover, within each syllable the vowels and consonants have about the same error rate (again with the exception of markedly fewer errors in the final consonant of the initial syllable). There is still a slight within-syllable effect with syllable-initial consonants having a somewhat higher error rate than syllable-final consonants. The stressed monosyllables, shown in the lower right of the figure, display the same error rates as in the stressed polysyllables, with perhaps a slight reversal of the within-syllable consonant effect.

Comparing the upper and lower portions of Figure 1, we see that monosyllables (whether stressed or unstressed) and stressed syllables (whether part of a polysyllabic or a monosyllabic word) have remarkably uniform error rates: Regardless of word position, about 30% of the segments are in error. (In this corpus, please note that the absolute figures are meaningless—only the relationships between the error rates can be taken seriously.) For unstressed syllables, and to a lesser extent for stressed syllables, the syllable-final consonant is less in error than the syllable-initial consonant, especially for initial syllables. This effect is nullified or slightly reversed for monosyllables. The consonants in unstressed syllables from polysyllabic words are much more frequently misperceived than their stressed counterparts; curiously, the opposite is apparently true for vowels. But I am not inclined to seriously compare stressed and unstressed vowels; since most of the unstressed vowels are coded as schwas, and since wherever possible in the analysis syllables are matched in terms of stress, one would expect fewer errors for unstressed schwas than for the stressed vowels, which are more highly differentiated. Thus the major difference between the effect of stressed and unstressed syllables on segment perception occurs in polysyllabic words, in which consonants in unstressed syllables are misperceived more often than in stressed syllables, and misperceptions in unstressed syllables are affected by position within the word.

It seems immediately obvious from an examination of the data that there are two sources of error—acoustic misanalysis and lexical decision. Assuming that the initial processing of the acoustic signal involves some sort of feature analysis, it seems probable that a misperception such as *van→fan* is a simple failure of the low-level feature analyzer, whereas it seems unlikely that the low-level analyzer would fail so grossly as to produce an error such as *clean teeth by tonight→my tea butter knife*. Instead, the severity of the errors probably results from the choice of the wrong word, i.e., lexical decision. The choice of the wrong word may be triggered by a relatively simple single misanalysis by the acoustic processor; this possibility, however, is difficult to either confirm or refute at present. In any case, assuming the existence of two origins of errors, the question arises as to possible differential effects of word structure on the two kinds of errors.

Assuming the preceding general model of perceptual processing, the acoustic errors should be characterized by a higher proportion of single feature errors than the lexical decision errors. That is, when the wrong word is chosen, the errors should be more severe and have more multiple feature changes. From this starting point, it becomes feasible to tease out the number of acoustic errors and lexical errors at each position in the word, and thus to determine the effect of word structure separately for each.

Consider the description of a corpus of perceptual errors depicted in Figure 2. By counting, we know N (the total number of segments), E (the number of segmental errors or misperceptions), S (the number of segments with single feature errors), and M (the number of segments with multiple feature errors). We want to determine A (the number of segments with acoustic errors) and L (the number of segments with lexical errors). That is, we want to determine the probability of an acoustic error, $p(A)$, and the probability of a lexical error, $p(L)$. (I shall approximate

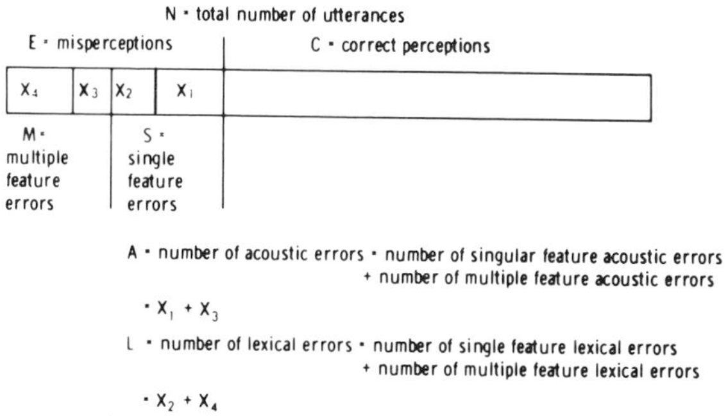

N • total number of utterances

E • misperceptions   C • correct perceptions

X_4	X_3	X_2	X_1	

M •
multiple
feature
errors

S •
single
feature
errors

A • number of acoustic errors • number of singular feature acoustic errors
                                + number of multiple feature acoustic errors
• $X_1 + X_3$

L • number of lexical errors • number of single feature lexical errors
                              + number of multiple feature lexical errors
• $X_2 + X_4$

Figure 2: *Distribution of lexical and acoustic errors in terms of single- and multiple-feature errors.*

the probability, p, of an event by its percentage of occurrence, and consequently will use $p(X)$ to refer both to the probability of occurrence of X, and the percentage of times X occurs in the observed data.)

From counting, we know the percentage of all the errors that are single feature errors (= the probability of a single feature error given an error):

$$p(S|E) = \frac{S}{E} = \frac{x_1 + x_2}{x_1 + x_2 + x_3 + x_4}$$

We also know the probability of an error

$$p(E) = \frac{E}{N} = \frac{x_1 + x_2 + x_3 + x_4}{x_1 + x_2 + x_3 + x_4 + C}$$

We define the percentage of acoustic errors that are single feature errors (= probability of a single feature error given an acoustic error) as

$$p(S|A) = \frac{x_1}{A} = \frac{x_1}{x_1 + x_3}$$

We further define the percentage of single feature errors that are acoustic errors (= probability of an acoustic error given a single feature error):

$$p(A|S) = \frac{x_1}{S} = \frac{x_1}{x_1 + x_2}$$

Finally, the probability of an acoustic error is

$$p(A) = \frac{A}{N} = \frac{x_1 + x_3}{x_1 + x_2 + x_3 + x_4 + C}$$

Then it is true that

(1) $p(S|A)\, p(A) = p(S|E)\, p(E)\, p(A|S)$

To show that equation (1) is true, substitute using the preceding definitions:

$$\frac{x_1}{A} \cdot \frac{A}{N} = \frac{S}{E} \cdot \frac{E}{N} \cdot \frac{x_1}{S}$$

Canceling appropriately then yields

$$\frac{x_1}{N} = \frac{x_1}{N}$$

Further, define the percentage of lexical errors that are single feature errors:

$$p(S|L) = \frac{x_2}{L} = \frac{x_2}{x_2 + x_4}$$

Define the percentage of single feature errors that are lexical errors as:

$$p(L|S) = \frac{x_2}{S} = \frac{x_2}{x_1 + x_2}$$

Note also that:

$$p(L|S) = 1 - p(A|S)$$

since

$$p(L|S) = \frac{x_2}{x_1 + x_2}$$

$$p(A|S) = \frac{x_1}{x_1 + x_2}$$

and $p(L|S) + p(A|S) = \dfrac{x_2}{x_1 + x_2} + \dfrac{x_1}{x_1 + x_2} = \dfrac{x_1 + x_2}{x_1 + x_2} = 1$

Finally define the probability of a lexical error as

$$p(L) = \frac{L}{N} = \frac{x_2 + x_4}{x_1 + x_2 + x_3 + x_4 + C}$$

Then, using the preceding definitions, it is true that:

(2) $p(S|L)\,p(L) = p(S|E)\,p(E)\,(1 - p(A|S))$

Finally, if one assumes that an error is either an acoustic error or a lexical error but not both, then

(3) $p(A) + p(L) = p(E)$

Given equations (1), (2), and (3), one can solve for the probability of an acoustic error:

(4) $p(A) = p(E)\,\dfrac{p(S|L) - p(S|E)}{p(S|L) - p(S|A)}$

Therefore, to determine the probability of an acoustic error $p(A)$, we need only plug in appropriate numbers for the variables on the right. Now we know $p(E)$ (percentage of errors) and $p(S|E)$ (percentage of single feature errors) by counting the data. Therefore we only need to determine $p(S|L)$ (percentage of lexical errors that are single feature errors) and $p(S|A)$ (percentage of acoustic errors that are single feature errors). Both these probabilities were estimated from other data as follows.

To determine $p(S|A)$, I calculated the percentage of single feature errors for a set of 16 consonants from a study by Wang and Bilger (1973). The consonants, in both initial and final positions of nonsense syllables (sets CV1 and VC1), were presented at several S/N ratios and the (mis)perceptions recorded. Because of the use of nonsense syllables, this data seemed a good approximation of purely acoustic errors. To estimate $p(S|L)$, I calculated the percentage of single feature errors in a confusion matrix of 24 consonants, where the number of confusions was determined by the overall frequency of occurrence of each consonant in the language. This confusion matrix approximated the number of single feature errors between randomly matched phonemes. Since the extreme form of lexical decision as an origin of error claims that the perceived segment bears only a random relation to the uttered segment, this seemed a reasonable approximation to $p(S|L)$. The feature set displayed in Table 1 was used for the estimation of both $p(S|L)$ and $p(S|A)$, as well as for the SLOE analysis itself.

The probabilities thus determined happily supported the original intuition that acoustic errors should have more single feature errors:

$p(S|A) = .47$
$p(S|L) = .22$

From the SLOE data, using consonants only,

$p(E)\ \ \ = .30$
$p(S|E) = .42$

TABLE 1. *Feature Set*

Consonants	Features					
	place	manner	voice	nasal	lateral	sibilant
p	L	S	–	–	–	–
t	A	S	–	–	–	–
k	V	S	–	–	–	–
b	L	S	+	–	–	–
d	A	S	+	–	–	–
g	V	S	+	–	–	–
f	L	F	–	–	–	–
s	A	F	–	–	–	+
v	L	F	+	–	–	–
z	A	F	+	–	–	+
θ	A	F	–	–	–	–
ð	A	F	+	–	–	–
ʃ	P	F	–	–	–	+
ʒ	P	F	+	–	–	+
tʃ	P	S	–	–	–	+
dʒ	P	S	+	–	–	+
m	L	S	+	+	–	–
n	A	S	+	+	–	–
ŋ	V	S	+	+	–	–
l	A	X	+	–	+	–
r	A	X	+	–	–	–
j	P	X	+	–	–	–
w	L	X	+	–	–	–
h	G	X	–	–	–	–
ɾ	A	S	+	–	–	–
ʔ	G	S	–	–	–	–

and hence, substituting in Equation (4),

$$p(A) = .24$$

Finally, since $p(A) + p(L) = p(E)$,

$$p(L) = .06$$

That is, in the present corpus, about a quarter of the consonants have acoustic errors, and 6% lexical errors.

Given these base probabilities of acoustic and lexical errors, it is possible to determine how the percentages of acoustic and lexical errors differ for different positions within the word. The percentage of acoustic errors $p(A)$ was computed for each word position and stress type using equation (4), but with position-specific values for $p(E)$ and $p(S|E)$. The $p(E)$ values used were those displayed in Figure 1; the

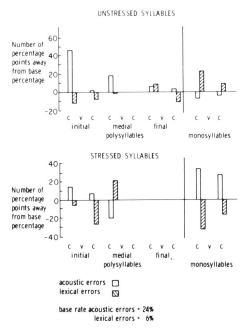

Figure 3: *Error rates for lexical and acoustic errors (consonants only).*

$p(S|E)$ values were the percentage of single feature errors for each position and stress type considered separately. Once the $p(A)$ values were determined, $p(L)$ values were computed using the formula $p(A) + p(L) = p(E)$, where all the percentages were position-specific. By graphing the position-specific $p(A)$ and $p(L)$ in relation to the overall expected values, as in Figure 3, the distribution of errors over the word can be seen separately for lexical and acoustic errors. Again, the exact percentages are meaningless: It is only the relationship between the various positions that is important. Note also that, although $p(A)$ and $p(L)$ are inversely related for the data set as a whole, and also for each specific position, it is still possible for the overall distribution of the acoustic errors and lexical errors to vary independently because the values of $p(E)$ vary from position to position.

Consider first the unstressed polysyllabic composite in the top left portion of Figure 3. The acoustic errors show the same decreasing error rate from left to right that we saw in the overall error distribution (again, with the exception of the final consonant in the initial syllable). Notice, too, the same relative increase in acoustic errors for syllable-initial consonants over syllable-final consonants as occurred for the errors overall. But note that the lexical errors do not show the left-to-right distribution of the acoustic errors. Instead, there are relatively more lexical errors word-medially than in initial and final positions of the word. The unstressed monosyllables, shown in the upper right of Figure 3, have yet another pattern, with lexical errors relatively decreasing and acoustic errors relatively increasing from left to right. There are also relatively more lexical errors and fewer acoustic errors for the unstressed monosyllables.

The pattern for the stressed polysyllabic composite in the lower portion of Figure 3 is less clear, largely because half of the positions did not have enough errors to be computed (I selected 15 as the cutoff point). The acoustic errors appear to decrease from left to right just as for the unstressed. There also appear to be fewer errors syllable-finally, as with the unstressed. In each position, the stressed consonants have relatively fewer acoustic errors than the unstressed. Again, the lexical errors show a different pattern, although with the three positions including the consistently anomalous final consonant in the initial syllable, it is unclear what the pattern is. The stressed monosyllables have exactly the opposite pattern as the unstressed monosyllables—acoustic errors decreasing and lexical increasing from left to right, and acoustic errors relatively increased and lexical errors decreased.

Discussion

The distribution of lexical errors, at least for unstressed syllables in polysyllabic words, correlates nicely with the effects of word structure on lexical retrieval as evidenced by tip-of-the-tongue data and memory tasks. In the present data, lexical errors are at a minimum at the beginning and end of a word. Brown and McNeill (1966) showed that the initial grapheme of a word is frequently remembered in the tip-of-the-tongue phenomenon, even though the entire word is not retrievable. Rubin (1975) and Browman (1976a; 1978) extended these results to include several graphemes both word-initially and word-finally. Horowitz, White, and Atwood (1968) showed experimentally that initial and final phonemes are better cues for word retrieval than are medial phonemes. Thus the same pattern is evidenced in strictly lexical retrieval data and in the lexical errors in the slips of the ear.

Note, however, that the similarity of patterning for the two kinds of data must be explained in terms of selective attention rather than in terms of strengthened memory traces. That is, the relative importance of word-terminal segments must be due to increased attention to the acoustic information word-terminally rather than to increased clarity or strength in storage. If the latter hypothesis were correct, one would expect the serial-position effect in the misperception data to be the inverse of the actual effect. That is, if word-terminal segments were more strongly or clearly stored, then they should tend to be retrieved regardless of the information supplied by the acoustic signal, thereby introducing more lexical errors word-terminally rather than fewer. But the mechanism of selective attention provides that the beginnings and ends of words will be attended to more closely and hence more accurately perceived and retrieved, regardless of whether the focus of attention is the memory trace (in TOT) or the incoming signal (in SLOE).

The structure of lexical errors in unstressed monosyllables is less straightforward. There are more lexical errors in unstressed monosyllables than in stressed monosyllables, which makes sense given that the unstressed monosyllables include grammatical words. One would expect grammatical words to be strongly affected by the syntactic analysis and choice of lexical items, and hence more likely to introduce lexical errors. However, while the stressed monosyllables show the expected pattern of fewer lexical errors word-initially, the unstressed monosyllables have more errors word-initially. I have no particularly constructive explanation for this reversal, except to suggest that unstressed monosyllables may effectively be a portion of a larger unit.

The stressed syllables in polysyllabic words have an even less clear relationship to the general lexical error structure. Mostly this is due to lack of data: Only half of the consonantal positions have enough data to be analyzed reliably. But of the remaining three positions, the final consonant in the first syllable shows the fewest errors, rather than falling between the word-initial position and the following consonant. Recall that this particular position has been anomalous throughout the analysis. The anomaly may reflect the smallness of the data set, or it may be an additional wrinkle in the patterning of lexical errors. Both a larger corpus of perceptual errors and a finer analysis of TOT data (to check for a similar pattern) would help settle this point.

The distribution of the acoustic errors can be resolved into separate patternings, most of which can be directly related to aspects of the acoustic signal. There are fewer acoustic errors on stressed syllables than on unstressed syllables in polysyllabic words, probably because of the greater prominence of the stressed syllables. The increased duration and intensity of stressed syllables yield a stronger signal; these plus the intonation extremes associated with stress may additionally cause greater attention to the acoustic signal by the acoustic analyzer. On the other hand, stressed monosyllables have relatively more acoustic errors than unstressed monosyllables. This apparent anomaly is probably due to the differing definitions of stress for polysyllables and monosyllables. A stressed syllable in a polysyllabic word is stressed in relation to the other syllables in the word; a stressed monosyllable is stressed relative to other words in the phrase, and hence probably has a high information content. Given that most of the stressed monosyllabic errors comprise an entire misperception, the patterning of acoustic errors for monosyllables can be interpreted as being a result of reporting. That is, an acoustic error on a word with potentially high information content (a stressed word) will disrupt communication more, and hence be more likely to be noticed and reported. Most of the polysyllabic words are probably stressed words in this sense, too. (Recall that over half of the misperceptions involve nominals.)

For all syllables except unstressed monosyllables, consonants in final position have fewer errors than consonants in initial position. This pattern of misperceptions is very likely due to differences in the acoustic signal between initial and final consonants. Broad and Fertig (1970) showed that formants two and three have a greater frequency change syllable-finally than syllable-initially. Lehiste and Peterson (1961) demonstrated that, except for /e/ and /i/, the transition to the final consonant was of greater duration than the transition from the initial consonant. Both of these findings suggest that a consonant in syllable-final position is more clearly represented in the acoustic signal than one in initial position, and hence should be easier to perceive. Moreover, the syllabic nucleus provides a variety of specific cues for final consonants and not for initial consonants. Voiced final consonants are associated with a lengthening of the vowel (see, for example, Peterson and Lehiste, 1960). The same study showed that final fricatives are also accompanied by vowel lengthening. Final nasals cause much more nasalization of the vowel than initial nasals. Note that these effects are relatively independent of the vowel quality. Therefore, whether or not the vowel is correctly identified, there is information about the final consonant over a greater span of the acoustic signal than for the initial consonant. Again, the increased amount of information should improve perception of final consonants.

Let us now return to the question posed at the beginning of this chapter, concerning the interaction of the lexical decision level with the acoustic analysis level. The model schematized in Figure 4 explicitly accounts for all but one of the major regularities of the perceptual errors. The strength of the acoustic signal varies in relation to syllable structure and word structure: There is more information syllable-finally and word-terminally. The output from the acoustic analyzer retains the within-syllable strength relationships, but has a changed word pattern, with strength increasing from the beginning to the end of the word. (This changed word pattern is the only portion of the model neither explicitly described nor related to other evidence; it will be treated at greater length in the following discussion.) The segment recognizer attends selectively to different portions of the incoming acoustic analysis,

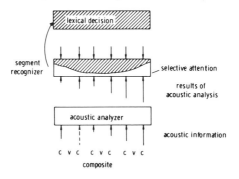

The length of the arrows represents the relative strength of the information (longer=stronger).

Stress adds length (=strength) to every arrow associated with the affected syllable.

The dashed arrow (- -) represents less certainty about the acoustic information.

Figure 4: *Processing model (details for consonants only).*

with more attention being paid to the beginning and the end of the word than to the middle. The segment recognizer provides input for the lexical decision; in turn, the lexical decision affects the segment recognizer.

The major regularity of the data still left hidden in a black box is the decreasing error rate for acoustic errors throughout the word. Patterns in the acoustic signal do not account for the decreasing rate. The portion of the acoustic signal likeliest to account for the regularity seems to be duration. That is, if the duration of the syllables (or consonants) increases throughout the word, then the increasing strength of the acoustic signal should mean decreasing numbers of acoustic errors. A study by Oller (1973) using intervocalic consonants (open syllables) suggested that consonant duration does not increase throughout the word, but instead decreases from initial to medial syllables and then increases again word-finally. An informal study by the author using closed syllables confirmed this finding. Four native American-speaking subjects read the words *compassion* versus *incomplete,* and *condition* versus *reconcile* (each word was in the frame "say _____ again"). In every case, the medial syllable was no longer than the comparable initial syllable; again, in every case, the syllable-initial /k/ was not longer in the medial syllable than in the initial syllable. Thus duration cannot account for the decreasing error rate.

Apparently, then, the decreasing error rate reflects the mechanism of the acoustic analyzer itself. The most obvious hypothesis is that the analyzer works from left to right in sequential temporal order, and then recycles at the word boundary. It could be, for example, that knowledge of the expected form class yields finely detailed phonotactic constraints that continually reduce the class of possible segments as the word is processed. But it is impossible to test this hypothesis using the present analysis. Although previous analyses suggested that the window over which analysis proceeds is the word, this is by no means certain—and, of course, if the window is not the word, then the hypothesis no longer holds as stated. Moreover, to test the left-to-right hypothesis, it is necessary to differentiate it from other plausible hypotheses, such as that processing begins with stressed syllables and proceeds from there, either in a sequential fashion or spreading in both directions from the stressed syllable. To differentiate these hypotheses, it is crucially important to know the relationship of the errors to the rhythmic pattern of the words, as well as to the word boundaries. Thus, future analyses must decompose the composite of words into separate rhythmic patterns.

Acknowledgments

My thanks to Peter Ladefoged, Ian Maddieson, Pam Munro, Sandra Thompson, Marcel van den Broecke, and particularly Louis Goldstein for various forms of aid and comfort throughout the production of this study. My especial thanks to Ron, Lloyd, Doug, and Scott for returning the PDP-12 to some semblance of working order, again and yet again.

Appendix

In order to find segmental errors, it is necessary to match the phonemes in the utterance and in the perception. Since slips of the ear include many insertions and deletions, and also many segmental changes, the matching was done using a set of interactive computer programs developed by the author and Louis Goldstein for the PDP-12 computer in the University of California, Los Angeles's Phonetics Laboratory. Because deletions and insertions of syllables or words are extremely difficult to detect automatically, an initial pass of syllable matching was performed by the humans. Because computers are faster and more consistent than humans at applying complicated algorithms to a large amount of data, the rest of the matching was done automatically.

The first pass of syllable matching was trivial so long as the utterance and the perception had the same number of syllables (where a syllable was defined in terms of its nucleus, i.e., a vowel or syllabic *l, r, n,* or *m*). In this case, matching proceeded left to right, first syllable to first syllable, etc. If a syllable that occurred in the utterance was deleted in the perception, or a syllable was added in the perception, then syllables were matched to maximize similarity, in the judgment of the person doing the matching (in this case, the author). Here, too, matching was constrained to proceed from left to right, although, of course, syllables could be skipped. That is, no metathesis of syllables was permitted in the matching scheme. For example:

Utterance:	*fuel*	*flask*			
	↓	↓			
Perception:	*field*	*glasses*			
U:	*popping*	*really*	*slow*		
	↘	↘ ↓	↓		
P:	*pro*	*di gal*	*son*		
U:	*go*	*to the car*	*and get the tu*		*na*
	↓	↓ ↓		↓	↓
P:	*get*	*my car*		*tuned*	*up*

Throughout this discussion, underlined syllables have no match.

After the initial pass of syllable matching, the programs took over. Segment matching proceeded from the clearest cases to the least clear cases. First, only matching syllables were considered. Moreover, only consonant clusters and vowels in the same positions within the syllable were compared. That is, the vowel of the utterance U was matched with the vowel of the perception P, the segments in the initial cluster of U with those in the initial cluster of P, and the segments in the final cluster of U with those in the final cluster of P. Within any cluster, order was ignored. First, all segments that were identical in the cluster in U and in P were matched. Then the remaining nonidentical segments in the cluster were matched, using the criterion of maximizing the total number of features in common between the U cluster and the P cluster. Only in the case that two or more ways of matching the nonidentical segments resulted in equal maximization was order invoked. In such a tie, the pattern of matching the segments that retained the most order information beginning from the left was chosen. For example:

sprain → freight (an imaginary example)

```
s preɪn
  | | | |
f reɪ t
```

Then any *r, l, m,* or *n* still unmatched were checked for metathesis across the vowel. That is, if one of these segments occurred in the initial cluster of one syllable, and in the final cluster of the matched syllable, then the two segments were matched. After this pass, the three examples given in the preceding section would now be matched as follows:

fuel flask → field glasses

```
fjul  flæsk
| ||  |||
f ild glæ  səz
```

popping really slow → prodigal son

```
p apɪŋ rɪ li̲ slou
| |||  || | |
pradɪ gəl  s ʌn
```

go to the car and get the tuna → get my car tuned up

```
gou tə ðə  kar ænd gɛt ðə tu  nʌ
||     | \ |||          || |
gɛt    maɪ kar          tund ʌp
```

Next, the consonants in those syllables that were deleted or inserted (i.e., whose nucleus was deleted or inserted) were considered. If more than one syllable was deleted (or inserted) in a row, only the first and last were considered for possible consonantal matches. The segments from the initial cluster of the first unmatched syllable were compared to the unmatched segments from the final cluster of the immediately preceding syllable (i.e., for insertions, the initial cluster of the inserted syllable in the perception was compared to the final cluster of the syllable in the utterance after which it was inserted, and vice versa for deletions). Similarly, the segments from the final cluster of the last unmatched syllable were compared to the unmatched segments in the initial cluster of the immediately following syllable. As before, matches were made first on the basis of identity and then on the basis of common feature maximization, with order information breaking any ties. Thus:

fuel flask → field glasses

```
fjul   flæ sk
| ||   ||| \
f ild  glæ  sǝz
```

popping really slow → prodigal son

```
p apɪŋ  ɪɪ  li  slou
| |||   || /  | /
pradɪ   gǝl  sʌn
```

go to the car and get the tuna → get my car tuned up

```
gou tǝ ðǝ  kar  ænd gɛt ðǝ tu  nʌ
|| /  | \ |||      || / |
gɛ t   maɪ kar         tund ʌp         (final match)
```

Next the same procedure was followed for any unmatched segments in the matched syllables. That is, unmatched segments from the initial cluster of a matched syllable were compared with unmatched segments from the final cluster of the immediately preceding matched syllable; similarly, the final cluster was compared to the initial cluster of the immediately following syllable. As usual, segments were matched on the basis of identity first, and then common feature maximization. For example:

to zero → his ear off

before:
```
       tǝ   zi   rou
       ||    |    |
       hɪz  ir   af
```

after:
```
       tǝ  zi rou
       || / | / |
       hɪz  ir  af
```

We skated → it's eighty

before: wi   skeɪrəd
            | |||
          ɪts   eɪɾ i

after: wi   skeɪrəd
           | ⁄ |||
         ɪts   eɪɾ i

Finally, in case any consonants remained unmatched, the following procedures were applied. First, another pass was performed for the deletions and insertions, where the same positions in the same deleted (or inserted) syllables were considered as for the first pass. This time, however, the unmatched segments from the initial cluster of the deleted or inserted syllable were compared with unmatched segments from the initial cluster of the immediately following syllable, as opposed to the final in the preceding syllable. Analogously, segments from the final cluster were compared with those from the final cluster of the immediately preceding syllable. Both identity and common feature maximization were used.

fuel flask → field glasses

    fjul   flæsk
    | || ||| \\
    f ild glæ <u>səz</u>

Then another pass was performed for the matched syllables. Any unmatched segments preceding the vowel were compared with any following the vowel, again using identity and then feature maximization.

fuel flask → field glasses

    fjul   flæsk
    |↖ ||| \\
    f ild glæ <u>səz</u>   (final match)

popping really slow → prodigal son

    p apɪŋ ri <u>li</u> slou
    | ||| ||⁄ |✗
    pradɪ gəl sʌn   (final match)

230 Catherine P. Browman

Throughout all the analyses, if a consonant (non-*h*) was matched with *h* in an earlier pass, and that consonant could be matched to an identical consonant on a later pass, then the later result was chosen. This exception was intended to account for aspiration. Thus:

loop hole → *loo pole*

before: lup hol
               || |||
               lu   pol

after: lup hol
               || \ ||
               lu   pol

Note

1. The research was conducted while the author was a graduate student in the Department of Linguistics, Phonetics Laboratory, University of California, Los Angeles.

References

Broad, D. J. & Fertig, R. H. 1970. Formant-frequency trajectories in selected CVC-syllable nuclei. *Journal of the Acoustical Society of America, 47,* 1572-1582.

Browman, C. P. 1976a. The natural mnemopath: Or, what you know about words you forget. *UCLA Working Papers in Phonetics, 31,* 62-67.

Browman, C. P. 1976b. Slips of the ear—misperceptions as clues for processing. Paper presented at Ninety-first meeting of ASA, Washington, D.C., April 1976.

Browman, C. P. 1978. Tip of the tongue and slip of the ear: Implications for language processing. *UCLA Working Papers in Phonetics, 42.*

Brown, R. & McNeill, D. 1966. The 'tip of the tongue' phenomenon. *Journal of Verbal Learning and Verbal Behavior, 5,* 325-337.

Horowitz, L. M, White, M. A. & Atwood, D. W. 1968. Word fragments as aids to recall: The organization of a word. *Journal of Experimental Psychology, 76,* 219-226.

Lehiste, I. & Peterson, G. E. 1961. Transitions, glides and diphthongs. *Journal of the Acoustical Society of America, 33,* 268-277.

Oller, D. K. 1973. The effect of position in utterance on speech segment duration in English. *Journal of the Acoustical Society of America, 54,* 1235-1247.

Peterson, G. E. & Lehiste, I. 1960. Duration of syllable nuclei in English. *Journal of the Acoustical Society of America, 32,* 693-703.

Rubin, D. C. 1975. Within word structure in the TOT phenomenon. *Journal of Verbal Learning and Verbal Behavior, 14,* 392-397.

Wang, M. D. & Bilger, R. C. 1973. Consonant confusions in noise: A study of perceptual features. *Journal of the Acoustical Society of America, 54,* 1248-1266.

Chapter 16

A SLIP OF THE EAR: A SNIP OF THE EAR?
A SLIP OF THE YEAR?

Sara Garnes   Zinny S. Bond

Department of English   *Department of Speech and Hearing Science*
The Ohio State University   *Ohio University*
Columbus, Ohio   *Athens, Ohio*

1. Introduction

In Ogden Nash's poem "Eh?" (1961), he says "My ears persuade me she said 'Xenophon,' not 'zen is fun.'" And he refers to a "female movie addict" who complains "that this year's award winning song is not as good as one of its predecessors, "Pork Loins in the Fountain.'" He attributes the "mishearings" illustrated in his poem to old age and accompanying hearing impairment. His mishearings, however, strongly resemble some of the data that we have collected over the past few years, which mishearings or misperceptions we have labeled "slips of the ear" (see, for example, Garnes and Bond, 1975; Bond and Garnes, 1975).

A slip of the ear is most felicitously shown by citing the two mishearings of the phrase "a slip of the ear" as given in our title. On one occasion, the phrase was misheard as *a snip of the ear* (showing the confusion of a nasal with a liquid; on another occasion, the mishearing was *a slip of the year* (with a palatal glide inserted).

The errors discussed in our previous publications occurred in everyday conversations. The misspellings and mislexicalizations (anomalous, yet phonologically related, representations of lexical items) that we have also collected provide evidence that slips of the ear are neither transient nor isolated occurrences. As will be shown below, a study of slips of the ear may lead to new insights regarding eight other linguistic phenomena. Its relevance to understanding the processes of speech perception continues, however, to be our greatest interest.

2. Slips of the Ear in Related Fields

Our data base consists of about 900 examples of misperceptions that have occurred in conversational speech. The examples are frequently collected under less
than ideal circumstances. Ideally, we are third party observers; the speaker is mis-
understood by the hearer; the hearer reports what he or she thinks is heard, for
example, *I'm hoping to get Mandarin Chinese **food** from the wife of my golfing
partner → **flu?**[1]* When the hearer misstates what we have heard the speaker say, we
note what was said, what was heard, the dialects spoken, the circumstances surrounding the conversation, and the date. Optimal conditions do not always obtain;
for example, we may be one of the participants in the conversation and lack a neutral third-party observer. In such cases, the error may be due to a slip of the tongue
rather than a slip of the ear. Thus, the criteria we have imposed on our collection
are similar to those used by Fromkin (1971) in recording slips of the tongue.

Several laboratory experiments replicate our data. For example, Bond (1976a;
1976b) has shown that nasal and liquid environments interfere with vowel identification. The present study shows that of the 37 simple vowel errors (see Table 1), 24
occur in the environment of liquids or nasals.

Based on our analysis of slips of the ear, we hypothesized that in speech perception, a listener attempts to make sense out of what he hears. An experiment to test
this under controlled laboratory conditions obtained the predicted results (Garnes
and Bond, 1977). In the experiment, the stimuli were synthesized versions of the
sentences:

(1) Here's the fishing gear and the (bait).

(2) Check the calendar and the (date).

(3) Paint the fence and the (gate).

Fourteen different second-formant hubs were used as the first consonant in the last
word. These fourteen stimuli were spliced in as the last word in each of the three
carrier sentences. Listeners were asked to indicate on prepared answer sheets which
of the three words they thought they heard: *bait, date,* or *gate.*

The results show that listeners did report anomalous sentences such as *Check the
calendar and the **bait**.* When the F2 hub, however, fell in the cross-over range between /b/ and /d/, or between /d/ and /g/ the listeners, not surprisingly, identified
the ambiguous stimuli as those most semantically "natural," that is, *Check the
calendar and the date* ($p < .005$, Wilcoxon matched-pairs signed ranks one-tailed
test).

When listeners cannot make sense of what they hear, their typical reaction is to
question the reader, "Did you say ____?" There are, however, different kinds of
data that show that hearers may instead attempt to reinterpret what they hear and
actually attempt to process their misperceptions. Examples of such responses are
given in the following:

Misspellings. The college student who misspelled *intstrument* (for *instrument*) may have misheard that word as in the misperception of *pants* for *pans* in *What kind of pans did you use?* It is of course impossible to know whether he ever used the correct spelling.

Children's Misunderstandings. The following reported conversation reveals how children attempt to make sense of a misperception or a correct perception that they cannot understand.

> Mother: "What did you learn in Sunday School today?"
> Child (5 years old): "We talked about the acts of God."
> Mother: "Tell me more."
> Child: "Oh you know—the ax of God—it's like a hatchet."

The Sunday School Teacher may very well have simplified [ækts] to [æks] a word the child probably understood better than the intended "acts."
Children apparently misinterpret formulaic speech in a similar way:

a. of thee I sing → "of thee icing" (reported by D. Stampe).

b. one nation under God, indivisible → "one nation under dog, indivisible"

c. Gladly, Thy cross I'd bear → "Gladly, the cross-eyed bear" (reported by P. Hopper).

d. Take then thy wife and child and flee into Egypt → "Take then thy wife and child and flea into Egypt" (reported by P. Hopper).

In a similar vein, Bill Fisher reports that his sister once asked, "What's a round-eyed virgin?" after hearing "round yon Virgin" in "Silent Night."

Folk Etymologies. The strategy of making sense out of what one hears or mishears is manifested in folk etymologies, such as the "renaming" of *asparagus* as *sparrow-grass.* This is not surprising since *grass* is in the same semantic sphere as *asparagus* (it is green and grows in the ground). *Sparrow* may be somewhat odd and unexpected in this context, but it is a familiar lexical item (if *crab grass,* why not *sparrow grass?*).

Jokes and Cartoons. Like speech errors, slips of the ear surface in verbal humor, as the following examples show:

a. A child draws a picture of an airplane containing passengers and a pilot. When asked to explain it, the child says: "Oh, that's Mary and Joseph on the flight to Egypt with Pontius the pilot" (source, I. Lehiste).

b. Jules Feiffer shows an interview with former President Ford.
Voice: "Describe your views on civil rights."
Ford: "Who's Cybil Rice?"

TABLE 1. *Classification of Misperceptions in Casual Speech*

	Number	Total number
I. Errors involving single consonants		200
1. Single feature change Example: *Let's look for the **cape** → . . . **cake.***	113	
2. Consonant deletion Example: *The **nodes** of the moon → The **nose** . . .*	32	
3. Consonant insertion Example: *braise → braids*	34	

4. More than one feature change
        Example: *All of the members of the group **grew up** in
        Philadelphia → . . . **threw up** . . .*
	21	

II. Errors involving single vowels		37
Example: *How do you spell **since**? → Which do you mean, **cents** or **sense**?*		
III. Multiple errors within one word		250
1. Two consonant errors Example: ***raised** chocolate doughnut → **glazed** . . .*	31	
2. Two vowel errors Example: ***Hero** sandwich → **harrah** sandwich*	1	

3. Vowels and consonants
        Example: *He has a garage for repairing **foreign** cars →
        . . . **falling** cars*
	145	

4. Syllable deletion Example: *I teach speech **science** → . . . speech **signs***	48	

5. Syllable insertion
        Example: *Many a father has been **greeted** by a roller skate
        on the driveway → . . . **created** . . .*
	25	

IV. Metathesis		38
Example: *Speech **science** → speech **sinus***		
V. Multiple word errors		226

1. Word substitutions
        Example: *He doesn't **mow** his own **lawn** → He doesn't **blow**
        his own **horn.***
	16	

2. Syllable deletion Example: *This is **mystery** dressing → . . . **Mr.** Dressing*	19	

	Number	Total number
3. Syllable insertion Example: *Good news! We got our **Task Force Grant** → ...our **Tennis Court** grant.*	14	
4. Function word errors (plus other changes) Example: *You **swallowed** a watermelon → You **smiled at** a watermelon.*	18	
5. Word boundary shift Example: *There's some **ice tea made** → There's a **nice team mate**.*	39	
6. Word boundary deletion Example: *He works in an **herb and spice** shop in the village. → What's an **urban spice** shop?*	74	
7. Word boundary addition Example: *Maybe we ought to give up **descriptive** linguistics →... **the script of** linguistics*	46	
VI. Miscellaneous		139
1. Homonyms Example: *He's going to Iowa U →... Iowa you...*	8	
2. Mislexicalizations Example: *This will shed **some light** on the problem → ... **sun light**...* (Can also be analyzed as change of one feature)	74	
3. Foreign Example: *(Latvian) nokrita 'fell down' (III pret.) → nopirka 'bought' (III pret.)*	37	
4. Media errors	20	
Total errors of misperception in corpus		890

Feiffer obviously recognizes that phonetic elements may be involved (even if he is unaware of this) since in this cartoon "civil" becomes "Cybil" (just as in a slip in our collection 'savor' → *saber*) and /rays/ becomes /rayts/ by obstruent cluster formation (as in the real misperception *braise* → *braids*).

   c. A "Berry's World" cartoon shows President Ford asking an aide: "What did you say this meeting is about, the CRIME rate or the PRIME rate?"

Berry also shows that cartoonists are aware of slips of the ear dependent on a simple consonantal feature change.

d. The character, Gilda Radner, in the TV show "Saturday Night Live" produces various "slips" such as

Russian Jewry → "Russian jewelry"

Free elections in China → "flea elections in China."

These "constructed" slips involving /l/ and /r/ confusions or substitutions are similar to actually occurring ones. One can add to the humorous examples many Archie Bunkerisms like "chloresteroil" for 'cholesterol' and "groinecologist" for 'gynecologist' which are both possible misperceptions or malapropisms that could occur off the television screen.

Puns. Puns, of course, all involve some kind of word play whether intentional or accidental, sophisticated or "groaners," and these often show the same kinds of phenomena under discussion.

a. "When is a door not a door?"
"When it's ajar."

This pun, which depends on the single word *ajar* versus the noun phrase *a jar,* is not unlike other misperceptions which result from incorrect insertion of word boundaries (see Table 1, item V. 7). Another example of a pun that depends on word boundary insertions is (b).

b. Groucho Marx: "When shooting elephants in Africa, I found the tusks very difficult to remove; but in Alabama, the Tuscaloosa."

Fiction. Not only cartoonists and humorists, but dramatists and novelists use possible perceptual errors and new lexicalizations. In Carson McCullers (1949) *The Member of the Wedding,* Frankie says, "What is your candy opinion?" instead of 'candid opinion.'

Michener (1974) explains the etymology of the name Picketwire River in *Centennial* as derived from the French Purgatoire River. The *Centennial* settlers now have a river name that is bimorphemic with the added benefit of both morphemes being "down to earth."

Malapropisms. Malapropisms share certain phonological features with their intended targets, as well as being semantically incongruous. The classic malapropism, "Allegory on the banks of the Nile" is quite similar to utterances such as "They've had several conflictions with the Symphony and the Scandinavian Club"; in this example, the noun *conflict* is redundantly nominalized with a Latinate suffix. Similarly, the example, "That's my analogy of the situation" involves a resemblance between the malapropism *analogy* and the intended word, *analysis.* Though malapropisms obviously involve more than the sorts of similarities explicable solely in terms of "slips of the ear," the basic phonological similarity that is a prerequisite for an "effective" malapropism is very similar to observed misperceptions.

Half-rhymes. As Zwicky's (1976) recent analysis of half-rhymes in rock music shows, composers and/or lyricists are aware of distinctive feature specifications of segments. Half-rhymes exhibit the same feature changes as do slips of the ear. *Forsake* rhymed with *rape* and *dark* rhymed with *heart* resemble slips such as 'cake' → *cape* and 'coke' → *coat*. Similarly, the rhyme *man* with *sand* is akin to slips such as 'can' → *can't*. It might be suggested, then, that perceptual confusability—which is one of the features of speech that makes slips of the ear possible—is also taken into account in creating half-rhyme.

These eight areas—misspellings, children's misunderstandings, folk etymologies, jokes and cartoons, puns, fiction, malapropisms, and half-rhymes—all show general awareness of the reality of misperceptions.

3. Data Classification

We have classified the data into some fairly primitive categories, summarized in Table 1, which shows the classification scheme, an example of a perceptual error in each category, and the number of errors of that type we have observed in the data.

The categories progress from simple to complex; simple errors involve single feature changes, for example, from a labial to a velar plosive as in 'Let's look for the cape' → *Let's look for the cake?* Complex errors often involve simple errors as well. For example, 'Skipper's treat' → *Trick or treat?* involves not only simple feature changes but also the insertion of a word boundary, the deletion of the possessive marker, and the change of the suffix *-er* to a conjunction *or*. We have not tabulated simple examples that occur in complex examples.

4. Speech Perception

Errors in the perception of casual speech provide unique insight into the mechanisms of speech perception. There are three quite strong implications concerning speech perception to be drawn from the data: (*a*) Speech perception is primarily an active, rather than a passive, process;[2] (*b*) listeners employ grammatical information in speech perception on the phonological, lexical, and syntactic level;[3] (*c*) speech perception employs heuristic strategies, rather than being describable purely in terms of operations defined for a grammatical description. Four strategies are suggested by our data. The first may be stated as: Pay attention to stress and intonation patterns. In our corpus, there are only a handful of errors in which the stress and intonation pattern is inaccurately reported, for example, 'kétchup' → *a chíp;* 'róll up' → *patról*. More typically, the perceived suprasegmental pattern matches the spoken pattern. A second strategy may be stated as: Pay attention to stressed vowels. Errors involving the perception of stressed vowels are rare, occurring most often in the context of consonants that would tend significantly to affect the formant pattern of the vowels.[4] There is a third heuristic that seems to be used by listeners: Find a word. Listeners seem to scan the signal for possible lexical items. In the example, *I had this appointment...* which was interrupted by the hearer saying *disappointment?* the listener reacts appropriately to a message that he believes is going to convey something quite serious. He does this on the basis of an hypothesized lexical item, in this case, an erroneous one. The impression this gives is that the lexical item was arrived at as a "best match" as soon as the speaker's phrase *this appointment* was available. Finally, one other strategy is used: Find a phrase. This probably also involves the first strategy. The listener segments the spoken sequence into phrases that can at least roughly be identified on the basis of stress and intonation (Bond, 1976c). These phrases must then be given some semantic analysis, "edited" for appropriate morphological markers, and probably ultimately unified into a semantic representation of the utterance. The "find a phrase" strategy is suggested by observing that there are virtually no examples of word boundary or metathesis errors that cross phrasal boundaries. Therefore, phrases must form perceptual units rather early during the speech perception process. The four examples that violate the suggested strategy involve interjection or vocative expressions, such as *Geez, really* → *Disraeli?* and *Mom, he did it* → *Mommy did it?*

5. Conclusion

We have summarized the data on misperceptions of casual speech and indicated several research areas that we have only briefly mentioned here. We believe that these areas of investigation will be better understood when seen from the perspective provided by slips of the ear. Closer investigation from this point of view will undoubtedly shed *sun light* (from 'some light') on the possibilities.

Notes

1. The arrow should be read, "heard as."
2. Whether or not feature detectors, as suggested by Abbs and Sussman (1971), are employed in some part of the normal speech perception process is not an issue which we can speak to on the basis of our data. However, active hypothesizing on the part of the listener concerning the intended message is certainly part of the speech perception process. No other explanation is possible for misperceptions which quite radically restructure the message, for example, *Say, there's Pier I imports* → *Beer wine imports?*
3. On occasion, however, listeners report hearing phonetic sequences that are possible but nonexistent in English, for example, /θoun/ and /ɛʃər/. The tendency here is perhaps not surprising when we consider that adding a word to the lexicon is a common enough occurrence.
4. Note that in Table 1 there are 200 single consonant errors as opposed to only 37 stressed vowel errors.

References

Abbs, J. H. & Sussman, H. M. 1971. Neurophysiological feature detectors and speech perception: A discussion of theoretical implications. *Journal of Speech and Hearing Research, 14,* 23–36.

Bond, Z. S. 1976a. Identification of vowels exerpted from neutral and nasal contexts. *Journal of the Acoustical Society of America, 59,* 1229–1232.

Bond, Z. S. 1976b. Identification of vowels exerpted from /l/ and /r/ contexts. *Journal of the Acoustical Society of America, 60,* 906–910.

Bond, Z. S. 1976c. On the specification of input units in speech perception. *Brain and Language, 3,* 72–87.

Bond, Z. S. & Garnes, S. 1975. Implications of misperceptions in conversational speech. Paper given at the Eighth International Congress of the Phonetic Sciences, Leeds.

Dubé, A., Franson, J. K., Murphy, R. E., & Parins, J. W. (Eds.). 1976. *Structure and Meaning.* Boston: Houghton Mifflin.

Fromkin, V. A. 1971. The non-anomalous nature of anomalous utterances. *Language, 47,* 27–53.

Garnes, S. & Bond, Z. S. 1975. Slips of the ear: Errors in perception of casual speech. *Proceedings of the Eleventh Regional Meeting of the Chicago Linguistic Society,* 214–225.

Garnes, S. & Bond, Z. S. 1977. The relationship between semantic expectation and acoustic information. In *Proceedings of the Third International Phonology Meeting,* Vienna, 1976.

McCullers, C. 1949. "The member of the wedding." New York: New Directions.

Michener, J. A. 1974. *Centennial.* Random House, Inc. New York.

Zwicky, A. M. 1976. Well, this rock and roll has got to stop. Junior's head is hard as rock. *Proceedings of the Twelfth Regional Meeting of the Chicago Linguistic Society,* 676–697.

Chapter 17

BIAS AND ASYMMETRY IN SPEECH PERCEPTION[1]

Louis Goldstein

Instituut Voor Perceptie Onderzoek
Eindhoven, The Netherlands

1. Introduction

1.1. *Asymmetries in Speech Perception*

Patterns of errors made by listeners when identifying auditorily presented speech sounds have frequently been studied to help in understanding the speech perception process. Such research has ranged from the work of Miller and Nicely (1955) who examined errors made in the perception of nonsense CV syllables under various conditions of noise and filtering, to recent investigations of perceptual errors that occur in normal conversation (Garnes and Bond, this volume; Browman, this volume). A common thread running through such research is the assumption that the more confusable a pair of speech sounds is, the greater their similarity with respect to the perceptual system. These similarities have been analyzed, by various techniques, into dimensions or features of perceptual similarity (for example, for consonants, see Miller and Nicely, 1955; Singh and Black, 1966; Shepard, 1972; Wang and Bilger, 1973; Wish and Carroll, 1974; Goldstein, 1980).

The concept of similarity employed by these studies is a symmetric one—the similarity between segment A and segment B is the same regardless of which is the stimulus, and which is the response. However, a casual perusal of the confusion matrices in published experiments reveals that this assumption is not always supported by the number of confusions in the data. For example, in the Miller–Nicely confusion matrices, /θ/ is reported as /f/ more frequently than /f/ is reported as /θ/. Such asymmetries have generally been attributed to a bias in favor of reporting some segments more than others. As such, this response bias has been considered irrelevant to the underlying similarity between the segments in question, and various techniques have been employed to remove such effects from confusion matrices (as will be discussed in the following section) in order to analyze the pattern of symmetric similarities.

Other kinds of investigations have required the removal of a response bias component from a confusion matrix before conducting some major analysis of the pattern of confusions. Verbrugge *et al.* (1976) wanted to examine various hypotheses about the effect of different presentation conditions on error rate in vowel recognition. Looking only at the change in error rate from condition to condition, it is impossible to know whether the change in error rate is due to a change in the inherent distinctiveness of a vowel, or to a change in the tendency to give certain vowels as a response. Verbrugge *et al.* employed one of the models to be discussed in the following section (that of Luce, 1959) to separate a change in response bias from a change in degree of ambiguity. Another example of this problem can be seen in Goldstein (1977), who has shown that the relative error rates for a set of consonants in the Miller–Nicely data is similar to the relative error rates for these consonants in a word and phrase recognition task. It could not be concluded, however, whether this similarity was to be explained in terms of the relative ambiguity of the consonants, or of their relative response biases (or both). Finally, Janson (1977) has shown that asymmetries in the confusion of Dutch vowels (in the data of Klein *et al.*, 1970) can be explained by a bias that is plausibly related to the fact that the range of F2 covered by the vowels in the experiment differed substantially from the range normally encountered in Dutch.

Clearly, there is a need for an appropriate model to separate out bias and symmetric components in a confusion matrix. Part of the purpose of this chapter is to compare the results of two different models for finding the bias in a confusion matrix—the linear model proposed by Luce (1959) and the nonmetric model proposed by Holman (1979). These models will be discussed in detail in the following section.

While the experiments noted in the preceding (and others) have attempted to remove bias from confusion matrices without interpreting it, it is possible that this bias is itself of some interest. Let us assume that bias can be shown to be reliable across different experiments, using the same stimuli, under different listening conditions. If this were the case, then this bias ought not to be discarded in an investigation of the perceptual system, as it would be potentially valuable information as to the working of the system itself. For example, reliable bias in perceptual confusions would differentiate speech perception and production systems with respect to errors. Shattuck-Hufnagel and Klatt (this volume) have shown that confusions among segments in speech production (i.e., speech errors involving single segments), tend to be extremely symmetric (with only one or two isolated asymmetries). They show that there is essentially no bias in their (speech error) data.

Asymmetries in perception are also important to examine from the point of view of helping to explain some of the asymmetries that can be observed in phonological processes (both historical and synchronic) commonly found in languages. For example, many languages have a rule (or have undergone a historical process) whereby a /k/ is palatalized to /tʃ/ before an /i/. However, examples of the converse (/tʃ/ becoming /k/ before /i/), are quite rare. Similarly, many languages undergo a process whereby syllable-final (or word-final) obstruents are devoiced, but a rule voicing syllable-final obstruents is, again, quite rare. It is possible that reliable asymmetries in speech perception can be shown to be related to such asymmetric processes.

Finally, on analogy to word recognition experiments, we might expect that frequency of occurrence of a segment in speech would be responsible for a bias in perception. The recognition threshold for a given word can be shown to be a function of its frequency of occurrence (see Howes, 1957). A common explanation for this lowered threshold is that there is a response bias to emit common words as responses, regardless of the stimulus. While the details of the explanation are quite varied (see, for example, Goldiamond and Hawkins, 1958; Savin, 1963), some notion of response bias is implicated in the explanation. We might, then, expect that subjects in a phoneme recognition task would also show a tendency to choose as responses those phonemes that occur most frequently in the language. Any reliable bias in perception should be compared, therefore, with data on frequency of occurrence.

1.2. Bias Models of Asymmetry

We will distinguish in the following discussion between two types of bias models —metric and nonmetric. Metric bias models attempt to relate the observed data in a confusion matrix to a set of underlying symmetric and bias parameters by means of a linear equation. The nonmetric model assumes only a monotonic relationship between the underlying parameters and the observed data. The best-known metric model is that proposed by Luce (1959). To explicate this model, let us consider a confusion matrix of n objects, in which p(xy) represents the number of times the stimulus x is reported as response y. Let each row of the matrix represent a particular stimulus and each column represent a particular response. Thus, confusions of x with y are represented by p(xy), and confusions of y with x by p(yx). Correct responses for the set of stimuli are represented by p(1,1)...p(x,x)...p(n,n). If we divide the entries in each row of such a matrix by the total number of times each stimulus was presented, then for each entry in a given row, p(xy) represents the PROPORTION of times stimulus x is reported as response y. The essence of the Luce model is that the probability p(xy) can be represented as the product of a symmetric function on x and y and a bias function on y. This is shown in equation (1) (a scale factor in the denominator of (1) has been left out of the equation for the sake of expository simplicity):

(1) $p(xy) = b(y) \cdot s(xy)$

where $s(xy) = s(yx)$

Thus, this model assumes that any observed asymmetry between p(yx) and p(xy) can be accounted for by a difference in the relative response bias of x and y, b(x) and b(y), respectively. We refer to this as the metric response bias model.

It would seem plausible that asymmetric properties in a confusion matrix could be due to differences among stimuli in terms of their tendency to be confused, as well as differences among responses in terms of their tendencies to be produced. Thus we might consider modeling this situation by adding another bias function (b') to (1), representing the confusability of each stimulus, as in (2):

(2) $p(xy) = b'(x) \cdot b(y) \cdot s(xy)$

However, Holman (personal communication) has shown that any set of data that can be modeled by (2), with both response and stimulus confusability biases, can be modeled equally well by (1), with only a response bias. This can be shown as follows:

(2a) $p(xy) = b'(x) \cdot b(y) \cdot s(xy)$

$$= \frac{b'(y)}{b'(y)} \cdot b'(x) \cdot b(y) \cdot s(xy) \text{ by multiplying by } b'(y)/b'(y)$$

(2b) $= \dfrac{b(y)}{b'(y)} \cdot [b'(x) \cdot b'(y) \cdot s(xy)]$ by rearranging factors.

In (2b), $b(y)/b'(y)$ defines a new function that depends on the response only. It differs from the original functions b and b', but it represents all the asymmetrical information in a single function on y. This is true because a $b'(x) \cdot b'(y)$ in equation (2b) is a symmetric quantity, that is, it has the same value for p(xy) as for p(yx). In a parallel way, it can be shown that all the asymmetric information in b' and b can be represented in a new bias function defined only on stimuli. This function will be $b'(x)/b(x)$, or the reciprocal of the response function. Thus, mathematically there is no unique solution, in the metric model, for representing the asymmetry of the matrix in terms of bias functions. A response bias can be modeled as a stimulus bias with the appropriate change in the symmetric component, and vice versa. The bias functions will simply be reciprocals of one another.

Although stimulus and response bias models are mathematically equivalent, in terms of fit to the data, it can be demonstrated that the response bias model is more useful than the stimulus bias model for confusion matrices in which each row sums to 1. As noted in the preceding discussion, stimulus and response bias models of the same data will differ in terms of their symmetric component. Crucial to this argument is the value of the model for the similarity component of the diagonal elements (the so-called self-similarities) $s(xx) \ldots s(yy) \ldots s(nn)$. Either the stimulus or response model will predict that the value of a diagonal entry p(xx) will be equal to $b(x) \cdot s(xx)$. We can interpret b(x), as before, as a response bias, a tendency for x to occur as a response regardless of the stimulus. The self-similarity term can be thought of as representing the relative distinctiveness of a given item. An item with a large $s(xx)$ can be considered to be very distinct; it tends not to be involved with other items in confusions, either as stimulus or response. A low value of $s(xx)$ can be interpreted as a relatively ambiguous item—it enters into confusions readily— either as stimulus or response.

Let us consider two diagonal entries in a confusion matrix $p(x_1 x_1)$ and $p(x_2 x_2)$, such that $p(x_1 x_1) > p(x_2 x_2)$, and see how this situation could be represented in stimulus and response bias models. $p(x_1 x_1) > p(x_2 x_2)$ means, of course, that there are more correct responses for stimulus x_1 than for stimulus x_2. In the response bias model, this inequality could be predicted in one of two ways. If, in general, there are more x_1 responses (not including the diagonal) than x_2 responses, then $b(x_1)$ will be greater than $b(x_2)$. Thus, the differences in the bias components are in the same direction as differences in the diagonal values, and the self-similarity parameters will vary so as to predict just the right magnitude of difference between $p(x_1 x_1)$ and $p(x_2 x_2)$. If, however, there are generally more x_2 responses than x_1, $b(x_2)$ will be greater than $b(x_1)$ and $s(x_1 x_1)$ will have to be greater than $s(x_2 x_2)$ in order to account for the diagonal entries. Thus, in this model, the relationship between the diagonal entries and the response totals in the off-diagonals conspire to determine the best $s(xx)$ values in an intuitively plausible way—a stimulus that has a lot of correct responses, but is not reported frequently as a response to other stimuli will be considered to be a distinctive, nonambiguous stimulus, with a low response bias.

The situation is rather different for the stimulus bias model, however. For this case, again, let us examine two diagonals $p(x_1 x_1) > p(x_2 x_2)$. If x_1 has more correct responses than x_2, then x_1 also has fewer confusions than x_2 since row sums must add to 1. Thus, assigning a low stimulus bias $b(x_1)$ to x_1 on the basis of the fewer confusions would make the WRONG prediction about the number of correct responses, since the same $b(x_1)$ will appear both in the diagonals and the off-diagonals of a given row. $s(x_1 x_1)$ will thus have to be inversely correlated with $b(x_1)$ to produce the right number of correct responses of $p(x_1 x_1)$. For data with equal row sums, $s(xx)$ will always turn out to be negatively correlated with $b(x)$, since $b(x)$ cannot simultaneously describe the tendency of a stimulus to be both correctly perceived and confused. Thus, for a set of data with equal row sums, a response bias model is more convenient because it allows us to calculate a bias function and a set of self-similarities that are, at least in principle, independent of one another.

The nonmetric bias model also represents a confusion matrix in terms of two sets of underlying parameters—a bias function, b, and a symmetric function, $s(xy)$. Unlike the metric model, however, the nonmetric model does not make an assumption about the particular form of the function that relates the parameters b and s to the data, $p(xy)$; it only assumes that $p(xy)$ is monotonic on b and s, in the sense that (3) is assumed to be true:

(3)   If $s(xy) \geq s(wz)$ AND $b(x) \leq b(w)$ AND $b(y) \geq b(z)$

this implies:

$p(xy) \geq p(wz)$

Thus, this model makes the following prediction about the relationship between the cells xy and wz of the confusion matrix. If the symmetric component of xy is greater than that for wz and the bias for y is greater than the bias for z, and the bias for x is smaller than the bias for w, then there should be more confusions p(xy) than p(wz).

The model attempts to order objects on b, and pairs of objects on s(xy), such that the number of violations of (3) is minimized. It should be noted that this model only makes a prediction about the inequality between two of the cells in the matrix, just in case the conditions in (3) are met; if these are not met, NO prediction is made. The bias function in this model is both a stimulus and response bias—one can think of the objects (phonemes in this case) as being ordered on this function in such a way that those objects with low values on the bias function tend to be responded to as objects with high values on the bias function more often than vice versa. Put another way, objects with high bias values tend to intrude on objects with low bias values. The model uses only the confusions in the original matrix; it does not use the data on the diagonal at all. Thus, no estimates of self-similarities are produced by this model, and there is no problem in the relationship between the bias function and the self-similarities, as was encountered in the metric stimulus bias model.

The metric bias model is stronger than the nonmetric model, in that it assumes a particular, linear relationship between the underlying parameters and the observed data. This stronger model implies the weaker nonmetric model, in the sense that the b and s parameters derived in fitting the metric model should still fulfill (3), assuming that the model is appropriate to the data. This follows because the linear function assumed by the metric model is a monotonic function on b and s. Thus, it is possible to show the inappropriateness of the metric bias model for a particular set of data by showing that the b and s parameters from the metric model of a given data set lead to a substantially greater number of violations of (3) than does the nonmetric model that reduces such violations to a minimum.

In the analysis to be described in the following section, metric and nonmetric bias models will be fitted to the same perceptual confusion data. The models will be compared. At the same time, the confusion data are chosen so as to allow assessment of the reliability of the obtained bias functions. Thus, we will be able to compare metric and nonmetric models both with respect to violations of (3) and with respect to the reliability of the obtained bias functions. Moreover, any reliable bias obtained will be interpreted with respect to general asymmetric linguistic processes, and will be compared with frequency of occurrence.

2. Method

2.1. *Data: Confusions*

The perceptual confusion data published by Wang and Bilger (1973) was chosen for analysis. This data includes confusion matrices for four different sets of syllables referred to as CV1, VC1, CV2, and VC2. Each set of 16 syllables was presented under two different listening conditions. In one of the listening conditions, syllables were presented with background white noise at various S/N levels (this is referred to in the following section as the N condition). In the other condition (referred to as Q), syllables are presented without background noise at a variety of low signal levels. The particular consonants involved in these syllables are shown in Table 1. Note that the CV1 and VC1 sets include the identical set of consonants—they differ only in the position of the consonant. CV2 and VC2 sets include the English syllable-initial and syllable-final consonants that were not included in the CV1 and VC1 sets, and thus are not identical to one another. The vowels in all sets were /i/, /a/, and /u/. Each of the eight confusion matrices represents data summed over subjects, vowels, and S/N level.

TABLE 1. *Consonants Used in the Wang and Bilger (1973) Experiment for Each of the Four Conditions*

CV1 VC1	p	t	k	b	d	g	f	θ	s	ʃ	v	ð	z	ʒ	tʃ	dʒ
CV2	p	b	tʃ	dʒ	l	r	f	s	v	z	h	h^w	w	j	m	n
VC2	p	b	g	m	n	ŋ	f	θ	s	ʃ	v	ð	z	ʒ	tʃ	dʒ

For each syllable type, the data in the noise and quiet conditions constitute potential tests for the reliability of extracted bias functions. It is easy enough to imagine that differences between these two presentation conditions are sufficient to introduce some differences in bias. However, there would not be much theoretical interest in a bias function that was not even reliable across conditions as similar as these.

2.2. *Data: Frequency*

In order to test the hypothesis that the biases obtained in perceptual confusions would correlate with the frequency of occurrence of the consonants, data on consonant frequency were tabulated. Four different sets of frequency of occurrence data were obtained, one set from Carterette and Jones (1974), and three sets from Roberts (1965). Carterette and Jones recorded spontaneous, informal speech of children and adults, transcribed this speech, and established phoneme frequency counts based on the transcriptions. For adults, the sample included 15,964 words of spoken speech, based on 24 speakers. From their totals for adults, the overall frequency of occurrence for consonants was obtained.

Roberts (1965) recorded a speaker reading sentences that included the 10,000 words in the Horn (1926) word count. These words were then transcribed and the frequency of occurrence of phonemes in the word list was determined. The frequencies of occurrence of the phonemes in the language were then computed on the basis of their frequencies in the words of this sample, and the frequency of occurrence of these words in the language, as reported by Horn (1926). From this phoneme count, the overall frequency of occurrence of consonants and the frequency of occurrence of consonants in word-initial position were obtained. In addition to the frequency of occurrence in the language of these consonants, the frequency in the Horn corpus was also noted. This can be considered a measure of LEXICAL frequency, rather than a measure of frequency of occurrence, that is, it is an estimate of the frequency of occurrence of the phonemes in a hypothetical dictionary of English in which each word is represented once.

2.3. *Analysis*

For each of the Wang and Bilger confusion matrices, the entries in each row were divided by the row totals, yielding estimates of row conditional probabilities. The resulting matrices were submitted to two computer programs. A program written by E. Holman found the best solution for the nonmetric model. The program converged within 15 iterations for all data sets analyzed. The second program, written by T. Wickens, used an iterative procedure to find the maximum-likelihood metric response bias model for a given set of data that included a diagonal. The program generally converged in less than 30 iterations, although for one of the data sets (CV2Q), the self-similarities were still changing slightly after 100 iterations.

3. Results

3.1. *Metric versus Nonmetric Bias Models*

The rank order of the consonants in the bias functions was quite similar for metric and nonmetric models. Rank order correlations (Kendall's tau) between metric and nonmetric biases are shown in Table 2 for each of the eight confusion matrices. Each correlation is significant at better than the .01 level.

The following procedure was used to test the appropriateness of the metric bias model for the data. For each data set, we calculated the percentage error for predictions made by the metric bias function under the assumption of monotonicity (made in equation 3). The nonmetric bias program was used to make this calcula-

TABLE 2. *Kendall's Tau for Correlation of Metric and Nonmetric Bias Functions*[a]

CV1N	.70	(.001)	CV1Q	.46	(.007)
VC1N	.70	(.001)	VC1Q	.80	(.001)
CV2N	.67	(.001)	CV2Q	.52	(.003)
VC2N	.72	(.001)	VC2Q	.70	(.001)

[a]Associated significance levels in parentheses.

TABLE 3. *Percentage of Predictions of Inequalities in Data That Are Incorrect*[a]

	Within-data		Across-data	
	Metric bias	Nonmetric bias	Metric bias	Nonmetric bias
CV1N	.150	.110	.225	.214
CV1Q	.286	.173	.287	.271
VC1N	.079	.060	.129	.126
VC1Q	.108	.087	.143	.145
CV2N	.186	.150	.466	.508
CV2Q	.240	.197	.460	.467
VC2N	.111	.088	.184	.253
VC2Q	.124	.099	.231	.294

[a]Results are shown for bias functions derived for metric and nonmetric models. Bias functions are used to predict data from which they have been derived (within-data) and data for contrasting noise condition (across-data).

tion. The percentage error was compared to the comparable value for the nonmetric bias function. The results are shown in the left-hand columns of Table 3. It is clear that there are more violations of monotonicity for the metric than for the nonmetric bias, for all matrices. However, the differences are rather small for all data sets except CV1Q.

In some sense, the nonmetric biases must have an advantage in the preceding comparison, since they are actually calculated so as to minimize the particular quantity being compared. A better analysis, therefore, would involve comparing violations of monotonicity for a bias function when used to predict not the original data it was based upon but the data of the paired confusion set, having the same syllables in a different noise condition. Thus, bias functions generated for the quiet condition data sets were used to predict the noisy condition data and vice versa. The percentage violations of monotonicity for these across-data-set comparisons are shown in the right-hand columns of Table 3. These results show a rather different pattern from the within-data-set comparisons. For the CV1 data sets, there are slightly more violations of monotonicity for the metric bias. For VC1 sets, differences are exceedingly small, one favoring the metric, the other the nonmetric. For CV2 sets, the across-data violations are so numerous (about half) that this data is largely irrelevant. (We will return to this case.) Finally, for CV2 sets, there were substantially fewer violations for the metric model. Thus, the metric solution for the VC2 data seems to be producing bias functions that are more reliable across-data than the bias functions produced by the nonmetric procedure. Moreover, since the within-data-set violations are not much larger for the metric model than for the nonmetric, the advantage of the metric solution does not seem to come at the expense of making many more errors in predicting the original data. Thus, the stronger assumptions of the metric model seem appropriate to the confusion data at hand. Its monotonic fit to the data cannot be considered worse than that of the nonmetric model. Since the metric model also has the advantage that the analysis provides an estimate of the self-similarity, or distinctiveness, of all the consonants, in addition to the bias function, it is the metric solutions that we will analyze in detail in the following sections.

3.2. *Reliability of the Metric Bias*

To test the hypothesis that the bias for a particular type of stimulus material would be reliable across presentation conditions, the metric bias functions from noise and quiet conditions were rank correlated (using Kendall's tau). Correlations for the four syllable types are shown in Table 4, along with associated significance levels. The sets clearly differ from one another in terms of reliability of bias. CV1, VC1, and VC2 sets all show highly significant correlations, whereas the CV2 set shows almost no correlation at all. It is odd that this set, with more nasals and approximants and fewer stops and fricatives than CV1, should have no reliable bias across noise and quiet conditions. However, as we shall see, the CV2N and CV2Q sets behave differently from the other matrices in a number of ways.

TABLE 4. *Kendall's Tau for Reliability of Metric-Derived Bias Across Conditions of Noise and Quiet*[a]

CV1N–CV1Q	.63	(.001)
VC1N–VC1Q	.64	(.001)
CV2N–CV2Q	.17	(.184)
VC2N–VC2Q	.53	(.002)

[a]Associated significance levels in parentheses.

TABLE 5. *Kendall's Tau for Correlation between Frequency and Bias*[a]

	Carterette and Jones		Roberts general		Roberts word-initial		Roberts lexical	
CV1N	.20	(.140)	.22	(.121)	.13	(.236)	.47	(.006)
CV1Q	.21	(.130)	.23	(.112)	.04	(.411)	.41	(.014)
VC1N	.45	(.008)	.43	(.01)	.45	(.008)	.58	(.001)
VC1Q	.24	(.096)	.29	(.057)	.34	(.032)	.51	(.003)
CV2N	.12	(.260)	.22	(.128)	.17	(.184)	.22	(.128)
CV2Q	.028	(.441)	-.10	(.293)	.03	(.429)	.16	(.200)
VC2N	.33	(.036)	.37	(.075)			.45	(.008)
VC2Q	.27	(.075)	.27	(.075)			.45	(.008)

[a]Associated significance levels in parentheses.

3.3. *Correlation of Bias with Frequency*

The rank correlations of metric biases and consonant frequencies are shown in Table 5, for all eight sets of consonants. Correlations are given for each of the four frequency measures discussed in the preceding section. Rank correlations are used, because the relationship between frequency and bias did not seem to be linear, either with the raw frequencies, or with log transforms of the frequencies. The hypothesis that reliable response bias would be a function of consonant frequency is partially supported by these results. For all eight sets of data, the highest correlations with bias are found for the lexical frequencies. Correlations of bias with lexical frequencies are significant for all four VC data sets and for CV1N. Correlations are marginally significant for CV1Q and, once again, virtually nonexistent for CV2N and CV2Q. VC syllables, in general, seem to show better correlations with frequency than CV syllables. VC1N has the best correlations with frequency, showing significant correlations with frequency of occurrence measures, as well as the single largest correlation with lexical frequency. VC1Q, VC2N, and VC2Q show some marginal correlations with frequency of occurrence, and the CV sets show no correlation at all with frequency of occurrence, as opposed to lexical frequency.

The hypothesis that response bias is due in part to frequency is strengthened by comparing the pattern of correlations to the patterns of goodness of fit of the model to the data, as shown by the percentage of monotonicity errors in Table 3. The percentage of violations of monotonicity is smaller for those data sets that show good correlations with frequency—the VCs. The three data sets that have marginal or no correlation with frequency also have the greatest percentage of errors in Table 3—CV1Q, CV2N, and CV2Q. Thus, it seems that the greater the degree to which a bias function fits a set of data, the greater the correlation of the bias with frequency. This certainly supports the notion that phoneme frequency is an important determinant of reliable response bias.

Two analyses were undertaken to determine whether the reliable bias for a given syllable set could be considered to be exhausted by frequency, or whether there were some additional components of this bias. The first analysis was to use the phoneme frequencies themselves as the bias function, and to calculate, using the nonmetric bias program, the percentage of violations of monotonicity for this frequency bias function. These percentages can then be compared to the values for the across-data-set predictions of the metric bias functions, previously discussed, in Table 3. If frequencies are as good at predicting a given set of data as the biases from the paired data set, this would imply that there is nothing but frequency that is reliable in the bias. The percentage of errors of frequencies are shown in Table 6. Comparing these values to those in Table 3 for cross-set predictions, it is clear that, in general, frequencies show more errors. The percentage of errors in predicting VC1N for the word-initial Roberts frequencies is the same as that for the VC1N bias, but in every other case, frequencies are worse than metric biases in predicting the data. Thus, this seems to indicate that there is more than frequency that is reliable in the bias.

The other procedure for deciding whether frequency exhausts the reliable bias is to partial frequency out of the bias functions of the noise and quiet sets of a given syllable type and to see if they still correlate significantly. Since we wanted to use frequency ranks rather than real values (given the linearity problem), we required some procedure for doing partial rank correlations. To approximate this, a Pearson correlation was performed, but using the ranks of frequency and bias as the values of the variables being correlated. This procedure essentially corresponds to a Spearman rank-order correlation. The correlation of these ranks, before and after partialling out frequency ranks, is shown in Table 7. The significance levels noted there should be regarded with some caution, given this partialling procedure. It is clear that the biases of noisy and quiet conditions for a given syllable type are still highly correlated, even after partialling out lexical frequency, the one that correlates best with the biases.

3.4. *Other Interpretations of Bias*

In order to determine what else is reliable in response bias, besides frequency, let us examine the actual bias functions themselves. In Table 8, the consonants are listed from left to right in order of decreasing bias, for each set of data. Let us first examine the bias for VC1N. The three voiceless stops /t,p,k/ show the highest bias and are followed closely by the three voiced stops and /s/: /g,s,b,d/. Thus, except for /s/, the high end of the bias function includes all and only the stop consonants, with the voiceless ones showing higher bias than the voiced ones. This reflects the rank of these consonants in terms of their likelihood to occur in the world's languages. Phonologies of 700 languages of the world in Ruhlen (1975) support the following claims: If a language has either stops or fricatives, but not both, it is much more likely to have stops; if it has either voiced or voiceless stops, but not both, it is much more likely to have voiceless stops. Moreover, if a language has only one

TABLE 6. *Percentage of Predictions of Inequalities in Data That Are Incorrect*[a]

	Carterette and Jones	Roberts general	Roberts word-initial	Roberts lexical
CV1N	.299	.345	.321	.244
CV1Q	.376	.421	.462	.312
VC1N	.179	.200	.129	.169
VC1Q	.256	.243	.231	.168
VC2N	.284	.320	.290	.252
VC2Q	.343	.322	.280	.238

[a] Results are shown for frequency ranks used as bias functions.

TABLE 7. *Partial Correlation (r) of Bias Ranks, after Partialling Out Frequency Ranks*[a]

	Zero-order		Carterette and Jones		Roberts general		Roberts word-initial		Roberts lexical	
CV1N–CV1Q	.82	(.001)	.81	(.001)	.81	(.001)	.82	(.001)	.75	(.001)
VC1N–VC1Q	.82	(.001)	.82	(.001)	.80	(.001)	.80	(.001)	.65	(.004)
CV2N–CV2Q	.31	(.130)	.31	(.142)	.41	(.069)	.36	(.102)	.27	(.176)
VC2N–VC2Q	.73	(.001)	.69	(.002)	.69	(.002)	.69	(.002)	.59	(.010)

[a] Zero-order rank correlations (Spearman's) are also given (see text).

TABLE 8. *Bias from Metric Analysis*[a]

	1	2	3	4	5	6	7	8	9	10	11	12	13	14	15	16
CV1N	p	f	v	dʒ	t	g	s	z	d	b	k	ʃ	tʃ	θ	ð	ʒ
CV1Q	v	p	t	f	d	b	z	g	dʒ	tʃ	s	ʃ	ʒ	k	θ	ð
VC1N	t	p	k	g	s	b	d	v	ʃ	dʒ	f	ð	z	tʃ	θ	ʒ
VC1Q	p	k	t	s	g	d	f	ʃ	dʒ	v	tʃ	θ	b	ʒ	ð	z
VC2N	l	h	m	f	s	r	j	p	w	hʷ	dʒ	n	tʃ	z	v	b
VC2Q	z	s	m	f	p	l	b	r	v	dʒ	tʃ	hʷ	h	j	n	w
VC2N	s	p	n	ŋ	m	g	θ	b	dʒ	v	f	tʃ	ð	z	ʒ	ʃ
VC2Q	p	s	g	f	n	m	v	tʃ	dʒ	b	ŋ	θ	ʃ	ð	ʒ	z

[a] Consonants are ordered from left to right in order of decreasing response bias.

fricative, it is more than likely to be /s/. Let us, oversimplifying for the present discussion, assume that the phonological naturalness of a given segment is directly related to its frequency among the languages in the world. Greenberg (1966) has shown that such distributional facts correlate with other criteria for "markedness" or naturalness, such as those discussed by Jakobson (1942), or Trubetzkoy (1958). The bias for VC1N seems to coincide with this scale of phonological naturalness.

Unfortunately, what is phonologically natural also tends to occur frequently in English. Greenberg (1966) has shown that this is not true just for English—in a variety of unrelated languages, markedness or naturalness of a segment was found to correlate with frequency of occurrence within the language. It is very difficult, therefore, to separate naturalness factors from frequency, in order to determine which, or both, is responsible for bias in VC perception. For example, let us define a variable that can, in a limited sense, be considered to be an indication of phonological naturalness: [1] for all fricatives and [0] for all stops. (Affricates are considered fricatives in this analysis.) This variable rank-correlates with lexical frequency ($\rho = .53, p < .02$). If one looks at the pattern of residuals after partialling frequency (lexical) out of the bias function for VC1N, the consonants are no longer completely systematically ordered according to phonological naturalness. However, there is still a significant correlation of the feature stop with bias, even after partialling in this way ($r = .68, p < .002$, although, again the significance level should be regarded with some caution). Moreover, turning this around, there is still a substantial correlation of bias with lexical frequency after partialling out the feature stop ($r = .63$, $p < .01$), the feature voice ($r = .74, p < .001$), or both features voice and stop ($r = .58, p < .02$). Thus, as far as can be determined at this point, lexical frequency and phonological naturalness are correlated but have separable effects on perceptual bias.

For the VC1Q set, the bias is similar to that for the VC1N set, except that /b/ has a very low bias, rather than being with the other stops at the top of the bias function. Moreover, the effects of frequency and phonological naturalness are more hopelessly intertwined in the VC1Q case. Partialling out frequency makes the correlation of bias with the stop feature not significant.

More problematic results for the quiet conditions seem to be the rule in this data. For quiet conditions, in general, the bias functions fit the data worse than for the corresponding noise condition (see Table 3). This should not be surprising, since there are many fewer errors in the quiet conditions, and therefore, the error distribution will be noisier, or less well determined. Thus, more problematic bias results in the quiet condition is somewhat less troubling than it would be in the noise condition.

There is a major objection to the phonological naturalness analysis made in the preceding section. As noted (in the Introduction), many languages devoice stops in final position. Unfortunately for the present analysis, such devoicing is possible in English. The distinction between voiced and voiceless final stops is often, in fact, cued by the length of the final vowel, rather than voicing in the consonant itself. (See Lisker, 1974; Javkin, 1976.) Thus, it is possible that the stimuli in the Wang and Bilger experiment included devoiced final stops. They may have tended to be reported as voiceless stops more than vice versa (this is the implication of their relative positions in the bias hierarchy) because they actually were produced somewhat between fully voiceless and fully voiced final stops. Without the acoustic data from the experiment, it is not possible fully to resolve this point.

There is another point for which it would be useful to have the acoustic data for the syllables used in the Wang and Bilger experiment. It is possible that the final stops were released, and perhaps even followed by a very short vowel, if the reader was trying to articulate them very clearly. If this were the case, the somewhat unusual acoustic marking might somehow be responsible for the bias in favor of the stops.

Returning to an examination of other interpretations of bias in the data, the bias in the VC2N condition also shows an effect of phonological naturalness. This stimulus set includes three stops—/p,b,g/—and three nasals—/m,n,ŋ/. These six consonants are included in the first eight positions of the bias function. Again, the voiceless stop has a higher bias than the voiced ones. Nasals are also common segments in the languages of the world, and in fact, there are languages (such as Peking Chinese) where the only syllable-final consonants are nasals. Thus, the fact that nasals have high bias once again supports the association of the bias function with phonological naturalness. The results for the corresponding quiet condition are, again, less clear. Both /b/ and /ŋ/ have considerably lower values of bias in the VC2Q condition than in the VC2N condition.

Unlike the situation for VCs, it is very difficult to find a phonological naturalness interpretation of the bias for CV1N or CV1Q. In fact, it is very difficult to find any interpretation of the bias other than the somewhat weak correlation with frequency. The fricatives /θ,ð,ʃ,ʒ/ seem to be at the extreme weak end of the bias continuum for both CV1N and CV1Q. However, it is not clear how to interpret this. Similarly, there seems to be a preference for grave or noncoronal consonants at the high bias end of the continuum. Again, no explanation suggests itself. Similarly for CV2N and CV2Q, there is no obvious interpretation of the bias. The CV2 biases, as we see, are also not reliable, do not correlate with frequency, and have high proportions of errors in predicting the inequalities in the data. In addition, there is very little variability in the actual metric bias values assigned within each of these conditions. Thus, it seems that there is only weak, uninterpretable, unreliable bias for these syllables. Possible reasons for this will be outlined in the following discussion.

3.5. *Self-Similarities*

One of the reasons for preferring the metric bias model, as outlined in the preceding section, is that it is possible to obtain a measure of the relative distinctiveness (or ambiguity) of the consonants, in addition to a measure of bias. This measure of distinctiveness—the self-similarities—was also reliable in the data analyzed. The

TABLE 9. *Kendall's Tau for Correlation between Self-Similarities across Noise and Quiet Conditions[a]*

CV1N–CV1Q	.85	(.001)
VC1N–VC1Q	.82	(.001)
CV2N–CV2Q	.45	(.04)
VC2N–VC2Q	.76	(.001)

[a] Associated significance levels in parentheses.

TABLE 10. *Kendall's Tau for Correlation of Bias and Self-Similarities for Each Data Set[a]*

CV1N	.53	(.002)	CV1Q	.59	(.001)
VC1N	.65	(.001)	VC1Q	.93	(.001)
CV2N	.58	(.001)	CV2Q	.70	(.001)
VC2N	.70	(.001)	VC2Q	.85	(.001)

[a] Associated significance levels in parentheses.

correlations between the noise and quiet conditions are shown in Table 9. Even the CV2 data shows a marginally significant reliability for self-similarities as opposed to bias. However, as it turns out, these self-similarities are highly correlated with the bias functions. This makes them very difficult to interpret independently. The rank correlations of the biases and self-similarities for the eight data sets are shown in Table 10. It should be noted that these correlations are higher, in every case, for the quiet condition than for the corresponding noise condition. It is not clear why this is the case, although it suggests the following: The computation of bias may be more heavily dependent on the relative sizes of the diagonals in conditions in which there are relatively few errors, than in conditions in which there are relatively more errors. Clearly, in conditions with few errors, differences among consonants, in terms of total number of responses, are going to depend very heavily on differences in the diagonal elements.

The consonants in each of the eight conditions are rank-ordered by self-similarity in Table 11. It is quite similar, of course, to Table 8, since the biases and self-similarities are quite highly correlated. One way to interpret the self-similarities is to see how they differ from the bias functions. Comparing Tables 8 and 11, the most obvious difference is in the position of sibilants, particularly, /tʃ/ and /ʃ/. These consonants have very low biases, but in every condition but one, the rank of /tʃ/ and /ʃ/ is higher in self-similarities than in biases (in the one exception, VC1Q, /ʃ/ has the same rank in both). This suggests that while there is very little response bias in favor

TABLE 11. *Rank Order of Self-Similarities*[a]

	1	2	3	4	5	6	7	8	9	10	11	12	13	14	15	16
CV1N	p	dʒ	g	s	t	d	ʃ	z	tʃ	f	v	k	ʒ	b	θ	ð
CV1Q	p	t	d	g	dʒ	z	tʃ	f	s	b	ʃ	v	k	ʒ	θ	ð
VC1N	s	t	p	k	g	b	d	ʃ	ʒ	v	tʃ	z	f	dʒ	θ	ð
VC1Q	k	p	t	s	g	d	f	ʃ	dʒ	tʃ	θ	v	ʒ	b	z	ð
CV2N	l	m	j	r	p	tʃ	s	n	dʒ	h	w	z	f	hʷ	b	v
CV2Q	s	z	m	p	l	f	r	dʒ	tʃ	h	b	j	n	v	hʷ	w
VC2N	s	p	ŋ	m	n	g	tʃ	b	dʒ	θ	ʃ	f	ʒ	v	ð	z
VC2Q	p	s	g	f	n	m	tʃ	dʒ	ŋ	ʃ	v	b	θ	z	ʒ	ð

[a] Consonants are arranged from left-to-right in order of decreasing self-similarity.

of /tʃ/ or /ʃ/, they are relatively unambiguous consonants. This is certainly a plausible result, and therefore suggests that the model may, in fact, be separating out response bias from relative ambiguity, as it should be.

4. Discussion

We have seen that the metric response bias model is reasonably appropriate for consonant confusion data, that there are reliable biases in consonant perception, especially for VC syllables, and that such biases can be shown to correlate either with lexical frequency or with phonological naturalness, or both. There are still a number of interesting issues raised by the biases found in CV and VC perception. Foremost among these is the question of why there is a difference between CVs and VCs in terms of bias. The bias function for VCs seems to fit the monotonic bias model better than that for CVs; the bias seems more generally reliable for VCs (CV2, it should be recalled, was very unreliable); and the bias seems more interpretable for VCs (both in terms of frequency and phonological naturalness). What can account for these differences?

There are different types of explanations for the CV/VC distinction, depending on whether we think the bias is related to a perceptual preference for phonologically natural sequences or to a lexical frequency effect. It should be noted, of course, that our phonological naturalness account of these biases does not explain (in the sense of providing proximal causes) why an individual's behavior in a perceptual experiment ought to reflect the distribution of consonants in the world's languages. The account suggests the possibility that this perceptual behavior may form part of the basis for the universal tendency, but no attempt is made, at this point, to explain why an individual's perceptual system should show this bias. Such an explanation would show, for example, how the detailed acoustic structure of the stimuli could account for the observed biases. Such an analysis is not presently possible. The CV/VC distinction would presumably be explained in such a framework, on the basis of differences in acoustic structure of consonants in syllable-initial and syllable-final positions.

Let us examine the frequency account for the consonant bias before attempting to see how this account can accommodate the CV/VC distinction. Certain consonants can be said to be more expected than others, on the basis of our language experience. When faced with an ambiguous stimulus, we choose the response that is more expected on the basis of this long-term experience. This has been modeled as a change in resting activation for recognition units, depending on their frequencies (see Morton, 1964). While such models have been mainly proposed to account for word recognition, there is no reason not to extend them to segment recognition as well.

There is a major problem with the frequency account of consonant bias as outlined in the preceding. In the current analysis, bias correlates significantly with lexical frequency, but generally does not correlate well with frequency of occurrence. This is certainly not what would be predicted by the kind of model proposed to account, for example, for the word-frequency effect. Expectancy should be a function of the actual frequency of experience. This discrepancy, along with the CV/VC distinction, suggests the following model to account for consonant bias. Let us suppose that, when presented with a relatively ambiguous nonsense stimulus, the listener's strategy is to sort through possible words that could plausibly include the ambiguous stimulus. The consonant decision is then made by determining which consonant is included in the greatest number of these plausible words. This model would predict, generally, a correlation of response bias with lexical frequency. Let us assume, in addition, that when listening to CV stimuli, the listeners sort through words whose BEGINNINGS are consistent with the stimulus, whereas, for VC stimuli, listeners sort through words whose ENDINGS are consistent with the stimulus. We could then predict the observed bias difference between CVs and VCs. English speakers are much better at listing words that end with a particular VC# than they are at listing words that begin with a particular #CV. (Baker, 1974.) If part of the listener's strategy in the CV and VC recognition task is to match either the beginnings or endings of words (respectively) with the stimuli, then subjects' superior ability in the latter case could result in a much more stable frequency bias.

The model we have suggested for accounting for the difference in bias between CVs and VCs is, admittedly, rather baroque. However, it could, in part, be tested. For example, one could examine individual differences in ability to produce words in a Baker-type task. To the extent to which degree of lexical frequency bias can be correlated with ability in the word-finding task, this would support the theory outlined.

Finally, it is interesting to speculate on why there does not seem to be any bias in speech production errors (as reported by Shattuck-Hufnagel and Klatt, this volume) comparable to the bias in perceptual errors. Of course, a trivial explanation for this difference could claim that the difference is due to the perceptual results being based on isolated nonsense syllables, or being based on experimental, as opposed to naturally occurring errors. There is no way, at present, to rule out these possibilities. There are two interesting explanations that are worth considering, however. The first of these would relate the difference to differences between perception and production. In perception, a listener is always faced with uncertainty. She or he is attempting to map some internal categories onto an ambiguous external signal. Biases help listeners decide how to make their choices. They narrow down the list of alternatives. In fact, since words and phonemes do differ in frequency of occurrence, a comprehension strategy involving response bias in favor of frequent items would lead to the correct response more often than would a strategy without such a bias.

In short, speech perception can be seen as hypothesis generation, and bias is one of the many ways that context and knowledge of the world guide this process. Errors in perception are simply hypotheses that happened to be incorrect. Speech errors, on the other hand, are not hypotheses about anything. Speakers generally know what it is they want to say. If we view bias in perception as part of the hypothesis-generating system, there is no reason to find it in production.

The preceding explanation for the difference between errors in speech perception and production is reasonable, as long as the bias we are discussing is, in fact, useful for the hypothesis-generating system. A frequency bias fulfills this requirement. However, a bias in favor of phonologically natural segments would not seem to be terribly useful to a perceptual system. Thus, there is no explanation for why there should be this kind of bias in perception but not in production (if, in fact, such a bias could be separated out from frequency). The explanation may lie in the fact that most speech errors (about 80%) tend to involve syllable-initial consonants. While we do not understand why this is so, the failure of bias to show up in speech errors may be because they are mostly syllable-initial consonants, a position that shows only weak bias in perception as well. An examination of exclusively syllable-final consonant errors might reveal bias in production, comparable to the phonological naturalness bias in perception.

Acknowledgments

I wish to thank Eric Holman for spending many hours discussing bias models and providing various programs. Tom Wickens supplied useful comments and programs. I had helpful discussions with C. P. Browman, Peter Ladefoged, and Ian Maddieson.

Note

1. This research was supported by the National Institutes of Health, and was conducted at the Phonetics Laboratory, Department of Linguistics, University of California, Los Angeles.

References

Baker, L. N. 1974. *The lexicon: Some psycholinguistic evidence.* UCLA Working Papers in Phonetics 26.

Carterette, E. C. & Jones, M. H. 1974. *Informal speech.* Los Angeles: Univ. of California Press.

Goldiamond, I. & Hawkins, W. F. 1958. Vexierversuch: The logarithmic relationship between word-frequency and recognition obtained in the absence of stimulus words. *Journal of Experimental Psychology, 56,* 457–463.

Goldstein, L. M. 1980. Categorical features in speech perception and production. *Journal of the Acoustical Society of America, 67,* 1336–1348.

Goldstein, L. M. 1977. Perceptual salience of stressed syllables. *UCLA Working Papers in Phonetics, 39,* 38–60.

Greenberg, J. H. 1966. *Language universals.* The Hague: Mouton.

Holman, E. 1979. Monotonic models for asymmetric proximities. *Journal of Mathematical Psychology, 20,* 1–15.

Horn, E. 1926. *A basic writing vocabulary.* University of Iowa Monographs in Education 4. Iowa City, Iowa.

Howes, D. H. 1957. On the relationship between intelligibility and frequency of occurrence of English words. *Journal of the Acoustical Society of America, 29,* 296–305.

Jakobson, R. 1942. Kindersprache, aphasie, und allgemeine Lautgesetze. *Selected writings I.* The Hague: Mouton. Pp. 328–401.

Janson, T. 1977. Asymmetry in vowel confusion matrices. *Journal of Phonetics, 5,* 91–96.

Javkin, H. 1976. The perceptual basis of vowel duration differences associated with the voiced/voiceless distinction. *Report of the Phonology Laboratory, Berkeley, 1,* 78–92.

Klein, W., Plomp, R. & Pols, L. C. W. 1970. Vowel spectra, vowel spaces, and vowel identification. *Journal of the Acoustical Society of America, 48,* 999–1009.

Lisker, L. 1974. On "explaining" vowel duration. *Glossa, 8,* 223–246.

Luce, D. 1959. *Individual choice behavior.* New York: Wiley.

Miller, G. & Nicely, P. 1955. An analysis of perceptual confusions among English consonants. *Journal of the Acoustical Society of America, 27,* 338–352.

Morton, J. 1964. A preliminary functional model for language behavior. *International Audiology, 3,* 216–225.

Roberts, A. H. 1965. *A statistical linguistic analysis of American English.* The Hague: Mouton.

Ruhlen, M. 1975. *A guide to the languages of the world.* Palo Alto, California: Stanford Univ. Press.

Savin, H. 1963. Word-frequency effect and errors in the perception of speech. *Journal of the Acoustical Society of America, 35,* 200–206.

Shepard, R. N. 1972. Psychological representation of speech sounds. In E. E. David and P. B. Denes (Eds.), *Human communication: A unified view.* New York: McGraw-Hill. Pp. 67–113.

Singh, S. & Black, J. W. 1966. Study of twenty-six intervocalic consonants as spoken and recognized by four language groups. *Journal of the Acoustical Society of America, 39,* 635–656.

Trubetzkoy, N. 1958. *Grundzüge der Phonologie.* Göttingen: Vandenhoeck und Ruprecht.

Verbrugge, R. R., Strange, W., Shankweiler, D. P., & Edman, T. R. 1976. What information enables a listener to map a talker's vowel space? *Journal of the Acoustical Society of America, 60,* 198–212.

Wang, M. D. & Bilger, R. C. 1973. Consonant confusions in noise: A study of perceptual features. *Journal of the Acoustical Society of America, 54,* 1248–1266.

Wish, M. & Carroll, J. D. 1974. Applications of individual differences scaling. In E. C. Carterette and M. P. Friedman (Eds.), *Handbook of Perception* (Vo. 2). New York: Academic Press. Pp. 449–491.

Chapter 18

THE LIMITS OF ACCOMMODATION: ARGUMENTS FOR INDEPENDENT PROCESSING LEVELS IN SENTENCE PRODUCTION

Merrill F. Garrett

Department of Psychology
Massachusetts Institute of Technology
Cambridge, Massachusetts

Among the most compelling aspects of speech error data are those in which the phonetic shape of elements involved in errors accommodates to the error-induced environment. Boomer and Laver (1968), Fromkin (1971), Nooteboom (1967), and several others have all commented on cases like those of examples (1) through (8) which illustrate various modes of this phenomenon:

(T = target, intended utterance)   (A = actual utterance)

(1)   T: It certainly runs out fast.   A: . . . *run outs fast.*
      /z/   /s/

(2)   T: Even the best teams lost.   A: . . . *team losts.*
      /z/   /s/

(3)   T: a language acquisition problem. A: . . . *an anguage lacquisition. . . .*

(4)   T: easily enough   A: *easy enoughly*

(5)   T: marsúpial   A: *musárpial*

(6)   T: Norman Róckefeller   A: *Norman Féllarocker*

(7)   T: It makes the air warmer to breathe. A: . . . *the wárm breather to air.*

(8)   T: Wheáties is the breakfast of cham-   A: *Breákfast is the Wheaties of cham-*
      pions.   *pions.*

I wish first to comment on what seems a particularly striking case of accommodatory phenomena, that in example (9), and to contrast it with what seems a striking failure of accommodation, example (10), given the existence of (9) and similar cases.

(9) T: I don't know that I'd know one if   A: ... *that I'd hear one if I knew it.*
      I heard it.

(10) T: I haven't sat down and written the   A: ... *satten down and writ the letter*
      letter yet.   *yet.*

I want, then, to suggest that the contrast of cases like (9) and (10) can best be accommodated by the postulation of distinct levels of sentence processing that roughly correspond to the different error mechanisms ("exchange" versus shift-anticipation–perseveration) involved. Finally, I want to provide some additional distributional evidence (from errors of anticipation and perseveration) that bears on the putatively distinguishing characteristics of word-exchange errors.

There are a number of straightforward, but very important, observations to be made given cases like (1) through (8). The first point, of course, is the demonstration that such errors provide for an ORDERING among the processes that give rise to utterances. Specifically, they show that the error locus (and presumably the locus for normal processes of comparable type) for cases like examples (1) through (3) must precede those processes that determine the particular phonetic form of tense and number morphemes or of the indefinite article; and similarly, that the processes of word production that assign stress and vowel quality are posterior to the locus of errors like (4) through (6). Finally, the fact that appropriate phrasal stress is preserved for word exchanges has prompted the observation that such stress must be represented independently of the particular lexical content of a phrase at the point where errors like (7) and (8) occur. I have argued elsewhere (Garrett, 1975) that these same facts have implications for theories of error mechanisms that assign a causal role to relative levels of activation in the motor system. If the activation level of the motor representation for a phonetic element is stress-correlated, such variations in level of activation cannot be implicated in error production for those error types that show accommodation of the sort in (4) through (8).

The moral of all the accommodation cases seems to be statable in terms of representations that are in some measure independent of the particular phonetic shape of the intended utterance. Word stress is appropriate for error-induced forms because there is a computationally effective representation of the regularities of stress that is not tied to particular lexical entries, and similarly for the phonetic shape of certain morphemes. On the face of it, regularity is the key to such independent representation—and hence to the accommodatory process. On those grounds, one might have expected the error in (9) to have had the form in (9)′

(9)′ ... that I'd know one if I heard it → that I'd hear one if I knowed it

rather than the form it did have, in which the appropriate irregular form of *know* appears.

We can accommodate such a "lexically dependent" adjustment of an error form in two ways. Either we may assume that the error occurred at a stage PRIOR to the point at which the phonetic form of words is determined, or we may assume that, in general, the accommodatory mechanisms have access to the lexical inventory. While the latter move is not incompatible with the facts of accommodation reflected in errors like (1) through (8), it is certainly not of the same spirit. More to the point, the existence of errors like (10) poses a real problem for such a characterization of accommodatory processes in errors. In (10), the assumption that the level at which accommodatory processes (of the sort we appeal to for an explanation of errors like [1]-[8]) have access to lexical information would lead one to expect an "accommodation" like that in (9), that is, (10)':

(10)' I haven't sat down and written the letter yet → I haven't sat down and write ...

Errors like (10) are, in short, not compatible with the view that (9) and similar errors should be explained by the postulation of a single processing level that, is, as it were, "responsible for" the final phonetic shape of output, including lexically dependent features.

It appears that one must, therefore, appeal to the notion that the errors of (9) occur at a processing level distinct both from that responsible for the accommodations of (1) through (8) and that responsible for errors like (10). I have argued elsewhere (Garrett, 1975; 1976) that several properties of error distributions seem best accommodated by the postulation of two levels of syntactic processing, one of which gives rise to errors of word exchange, and the other to errors in which bound morphemes SHIFT their attachment. I will not review those arguments here, but will simply run through a set of observations about the consequences of that claim. Consider the error in (11)

(11) I wanted to eat my beans first → *I want to eated m ...*

That error, like (10), appears to be a shift of a bound morpheme. If some sort of accommodatory process could apply one might expect (11)'

(11)' I wanted to eat my beans first → ... want to ate ...

(Note that if this had been an exchange of words [or stems], instead of a shift error, the appropriate form of *eat* would be predicted, just as for the appropriate form of the verb *know* in [9].)

The particular sort of errors being discussed here are not common. I have only the two examples cited, (10) and (11), in which there is a morpheme shift for an irregular form. There is, moreover, one counterexample that I know of (see the following discussion). There are, however, other somewhat more commonly occurring errors involving affixal elements that seem to have an import similar to that of (10) and (11), namely (12) through (15).

(12) T: I already took a bath.   A: *I already tooken a bath.*

(13) T: Sometimes I have put it in the   A: *Sometimes I have putten it....*
          drawer.

(14) T: I had forgotten about that.   A: *...forgot abouten that.*

(15) T: ...pointed out...   A: *...point outed...*

(16) T: So she's got her sights set on a   A: *...her sets sight....*
          college presidency.

For (12), the intruding participle probably comes from a competing alternate expression ("I've already taken a bath."). Examples (14) and (15) show the relatively common case in which an inflectional morph is shifted to a stem that does not inflect. The point of these examples is simply to indicate, contra the force of a lexically sensitive accommodation, that shift errors attach morphemes to stems without regard to any factor other than word boundaries and word form—in particular, without regard to the lexical identity or even the grammatical category of the error site.

I mentioned earlier that there is one counterexample to this claim, namely, Fromkin's well-known example, *Rosa always date shranks.* If this is, as it appears to be, a shift of the tense morpheme from the intended *dated* to *shrink* with an attendant accommodation of the resultant *shrink + past* to *shrank*, it would be flatly incompatible with the assumptions about morpheme shifts I have made in the analysis of (10) and (11). Unfortunately, I cannot offer a compelling alternative analysis of this error. It would, of course, suit the position I am exploring if the form of the error were "slightly" different—for example, "...always /dejt šrejnks/...." rather than "/dejt šrænks/"—that is, if it were a sound error of perseveration. That this might be a sound error or that it is some currently unknown exoticism are the only rationalizations that occur at the moment, and, however uncomfortably, I will just have to live with this empirical fly in my theoretical ointment until some additional cases are manifest. It is perhaps foolishly exigent to expect error data to be tidy, given the conditions of its acquisition, but I might have wished for a better score than 2-1 in spite of that.

There are, however, some additional observations that bear on the plausibility of a distinction between processing levels as the preferred vehicle of explanation for the contrast of (9) with (10) and (11). The pivotal point may be whether affixal elements and irregular forms have, at the error locus, been specified, or whether they remain to be specified as a function of phrasal features and lexical constraints. In terms of the distinction I argued for in Garrett (1975), that would correspond to the difference between the "positional" and "functional" levels of sentence processing. If that is roughly correct, one would expect the following: Errors that occur at the positional level (for example, morpheme shifts, and exchanges within phrases that violate grammatical category) should NOT show lexically dependent adjustments of form, whereas those errors that occur at the functional level of processing (e.g., word substitutions and exchanges between phrases that honor grammatical category) should show such adjustments. I have one somewhat dubious example of the former, namely (16), and several examples of the latter, namely (17) through (20):

(17) T: She offends his sense of how the   A: *He offends her sense....*
world should be.

(18) T: She wanted to get Roger to let   A: *... to let him cut her hair.*
her cut his hair.

(19) T: A bunch of us were teasing him.   A: *... him were teasing us.*

(20) T: I thought *I* was finishing your   A: *I thought **you** were finishing my*
beer!   *beer!*

Ideally (for the argument I am making), (16) is a within-phrase stranding error (note the abandoned plural affix) for which the lexically dependent accommodation (i.e., the emergence of the participial form *sighted*) does not occur. The case is weak because (*a*) it could be a sound error; and (*b*) the speaker did not continue past the utterance of *sight* so that we could be certain that the phrase was complete.

The cases in (17) through (20) are, however, clear enough and frequent enough (there are 34 such cases in the MIT corpus). Here we have exchanges that should show appropriate adjustments of form since they occur, by hypothesis, at a level that affords the required description of the error elements. Hence, the pronouns should have the form appropriate to their error induced phrasal environments—just as for the case of the verbs *know* and *hear* in example (9); 33 of the 34 cases do show the appropriate form. Note particularly that in (20) the form of the auxiliary is also adjusted to the moved pronoun; this is the case for the two other errors of this type where such a change could be detected.

Needless to say, it would be desirable to have more examples of the cases I have been discussing. Languages other than English should prove more fruitful sources of data.

Methodological Epilogue

The final points I want to make are not directly connected to the issue of accommodation. Rather, they bear on the arguments I have earlier appealed to in order to support the distinction between "functional" and "positional" levels of processing in the analysis of speech errors. The principal features of contrast are the phrasal membership of error elements and their grammatical role within their intended phrases—this latter factor I have assessed in terms of whether grammatical category is or is not honored in the interaction of sentence elements involved in an error. In addition, the correlated variable of degree of separation (in words) of error elements was considered. For exchanges of words (or stems) between phrases, correspondence of grammatical category seems very strongly to be the rule, and this is most particularly marked in those error elements of different clausal membership or where the errors occur over a span of several words. Exchanges of morphemes or sounds occur primarily within a phrase, and accordingly, grammatical category of the error words much more often differs than corresponds, and the interacting elements are rarely separated by more than a word. On these grounds and a number of others that seemed related, I argued that the errors so distinguished arose from processing at two distinct levels, both of which are concerned with aspects of the syntactic structure of sentences. In the preceding section in which I discussed accommodatory phenomena, I used that distinction between processing levels to explain what seem to me conflicting error patterns, and I rationalized that conflict by an appeal to putative differences in the description of sentence elements available at the two hypothesized levels of sentence processing. Thus, a good deal of the picture of sentence production processes that I have argued for turns in one way or another on the strength of observations about the correspondence of grammatical category for error elements.

One problem with the facts as I have presented them is readily apparent. If errors that exchange sounds (or groups of sounds, whether they have a morpheme analysis or not) are constrained to occur (for whatever reason) only between contiguous or nearly contiguous words, then the chance that such errors will obtain between words of differing grammatical category (or members of different phrases) will surely be less than for error interactions that may obtain over greater distances. Thus, the genuinely causal factor, one might argue, is simply propinquity, not grammatical role or phrasal membership.

There are a number of drawbacks to such an alternative line, not the least of which is the lack of any account of why propinquity is more significant for sound errors, for instance, than for word errors. It is not my purpose to marshal such arguments here, however. Rather, at this point I simply wish to present the facts arrayed in Tables 1 and 2 for consideration.

These tables present features of the distribution of anticipatory and perseveratory sound errors (there are a few included that seem to involve morphemes), for instance, (21) through (32).

(21) *If he says, "here's looking at you babe," take your foot out of the stirrups and wallop him in the chollops.*
       (chops)

(22) *The juice is still on the table. Is that enuice?*
       (enough)

(23) *I dreamt that he droke both arms.*
       (broke)

(24) *They first put on a coat of prime, and then a proat of...*
       (coat)

(25) *... experiences become much more exportant than anything else.*
       (important)

TABLE 1. *Anticipation-Perseveration Errors: MIT Corpus Sample 1 (n = 155) and Sample 2 (n = 65)*

Interacting elements are			Grammatical categories of interacting elements		
			Same	Different	
Within the same phrase			39	78	117
Separation in words	0	Sample 1	22	48	
		Sample 2	8	24	
	1	Sample 1	7	3	
		Sample 2	2	3	
In different phrases			29	74	103
Separation in words	0	Sample 1	1	21	
		Sample 2	1	5	
	1	Sample 1	4	20	
		Sample 2	3	4	
	2	Sample 1	11	10	
		Sample 2	3	3	
	3 or more	Sample 1	4	4	
		Sample 2	2	7	
			68	152	220

(26) *... so that I can start the stape back up.*
                              (tape)

(27) *I don't understand the order at or.*
                              (all)

(28) *He wants to take the G.O.P. nominowation away from Ford.*
                              (nomination)

(29) *One bure cures a bad dinner.*
            (beer)

(30) *The currenth month is...*
            (current)

(31) *... that's forward masking; baskward masking is...*
                              (backward)

(32) *What's your schedule this week?*
       I'm frine—I'm fine. I'm free all this week.

TABLE 2. *Anticipation-Perseveration Errors* [a]

Interacting elements are	Grammatical categories of interacting elements		
	Same	Different	
Within the same phrase	19	43	62
Separation in words 0	12	42	
Separation in words 1	7	1	
In different phrases	20	34	54
Separation in words 0	2	6	
Separation in words 1	9	12	
Separation in words 2	5	9	
Separation in words 3 or more	4	7	
	39	77	116

[a] From Fromkin (1973) corpus, categories A, B, D. E. F, G. J, and K; (n = 116).

Table 1 shows the correspondence of grammatical category for error source and target as a function of phrasal membership and separation (in words). Two "samples" from the MIT corpus are given; the first is for errors collected prior to January 1974, and the second is for errors collected from January 1974 to August 1977. Table 2 presents comparable facts for errors from Fromkin's (1973) published corpus.

The properties of the anticipation–perseveration errors seem to me to provide a convincing counterweight to the worry that the correspondence of grammatical category for word exchanges between phrases is a happenstance of their greater separation, for here, more often than not, the error elements come from different phrases, at varying separations, and they are of different grammatical category more often than they are of the same category. The contrast in "respect for grammatical category" is particularly clear for the error interactions that span clausal boundaries. For word exchanges there are virtually no such cases that do not have corresponding categories; for the anticipation–perseveration errors (n = 336), there are 44 cases that cross clause boundaries, and 21 of these violate grammatical category. One might also note that the anticipation–perseveration errors indicate that the tendency of the sound exchange errors to occur WITHIN a phrase and to be adjacent is neither accidental nor a necessary feature of sound errors.

One other feature of the anticipation–perseveration errors that is worth mentioning is the occasional involvement of closed-class vocabulary items in these errors (42 cases of the 336). In this they contrast sharply with sound-exchange errors. Most of these cases are interactions between an open- and closed-class vocabulary item, rather than interactions between two closed-class items. What seems to be a very powerful constraint on exchange of words (correspondence of category) or exchange of sounds (confined to open class) seems of much lesser importance to the system that gives rise to errors of anticipation and perseveration.

The arguments involving accommodatory—or apparently accommodatory—phenomena considered in the first part of this chapter seem to me, if they can be elaborated and supported by a sufficient number of cases, to provide strongly persuasive grounds for a view of the sentence production process as a set of interacting levels of analysis, with the computational activity internal to each such level proceeding largely in independence of the outcome of others. The grosser distributional facts that I discussed in the second part also seem to indicate such a view. Together these, and many similar sorts of facts not discussed here, make a case for a serious examination of the consequences of such a characterization of the production process.

References

Boomer, D. S. & Laver, J. D. M. 1968. Slips of the tongue. *British Journal of Disorders of Communication, 3,* 2–12.

Fromkin, V. A. 1971. The non-anomalous nature of anomalous utterances. *Language, 47,* 27–52.

Fromkin, V. A. (Ed.). 1973. *Speech errors as linguistic evidence.* The Hague: Mouton.

Garrett, M. F. 1975. The analysis of sentence production. In G. Bower (Ed.), *Psychology of learning and motivation* (Vol. 9). New York: Academic Press. Pp. 133–177.

Garrett, M. F. 1976. Syntactic processes in sentence production. In R. G. Wales & E. C. T. Walker (Eds.), *New approaches to language mechanisms.* Amsterdam: North-Holland. Pp. 231–255.

Nooteboom, S. G. 1967. *Some regularities in phonemic speech errors.* Annual Progress Report 2. Eindhoven, The Netherlands: Instituut voor Perceptie Onderzoek.

Chapter 19

TOWARD A UNIFIED MODEL OF SLIPS OF THE TONGUE[1]

Gary S. Dell

Peter A. Reich

Department of Psychology
University of Toronto
Toronto, Ontario

The topic of slips of the tongue is certainly as hoary as any other topic in the history of psychology. Nevertheless, until the publication of Fromkin (1971), this area was considered something to be taught as a part of Freudian theory, and thus was considered out of the mainstream of modern cognitive theory. More than any other study, Fromkin's work brought to our attention the logical structure of the data, and its relationship to both linguistic and psychological models of language processing. The conference in Vienna is evidence of the newly widespread interest and research in this area. Suddenly more and more new and different facts about slips of the tongue have been emerging, and along with them theories about what must be true of language production processing in order to account for these facts. So far, the various proposals do not yet add up to a unified picture of language production. It is the goal of this chapter to present a single unified model that accounts for the many diverse facts about slips of the tongue, both ancient and newly discovered.

One can talk about three different categories of slips-of-the-tongue phenomena. Analogous to a distinction made by Miller and Selfridge (1953), we shall refer to these three types as zero-order, first-order, and second-order phenomena. Most of the data discussed by Fromkin (1971), Hockett (1967), and Wells (1951), for example, are zero-order data. This information is derived by collecting slips of the tongue and sorting these slips into nominal categories. From the work of such authors, we have the distinctions among replacement slips, blends, and haplologies.

Within replacement slips, we have the distinctions among anticipation, transposition, and substitution (in the last one, the origin is unknown), and we know that such slips may involve units that vary in size from phonemic features through phonemes, clusters, syllables, morphemes, words, phrases, and even clauses.

More recently, authors have been discussing the relative frequencies of these nominal categories. These can be described as first-order data. One such fact is that slips that result in high-frequency consonant clusters occur more often than slips that result in low-frequency or "impossible" clusters (Wells, 1951; Fromkin, 1971). Other first-order facts are that initial phonemes are more often involved in slips than final phonemes (MacKay, 1970), stressed syllables are more often involved in slips than unstressed syllables (Boomer and Laver, 1968), the reversing phonemes in transposition slips are closer together than the target and origin phonemes in anticipation slips (Cohen, 1966), and so forth. Such information must be accounted for in any complete, unified model of slips of the tongue.

Recently, yet a third type of data is becoming known and discussed. This type concerns the fact that the rates of various types of slips can be affected by extralinguistic experimental conditions. This is what we term second-order data. Some of these facts are as simple as the fact that when you speed people up they make more slips (MacKay, 1971). Other second-order facts are more interesting. When you speed people up, the number of perseverations may increase to a greater extent than the number of anticipations (Cohen, 1966; Dell, 1974). When people slip while they are expecting to utter nonsense syllables rather than words, the number of slips to nonsense syllables is greater than when they are expecting to utter words (Baars, Motley, and MacKay, 1975). A unified model of slips of the tongue must be able to account for these contingent frequency phenomena as well.

By a unified model, we mean one that will not only account for the three types of slips of the tongue data, but a model that will be linguistically adequate in the sense that it will handle all types of constructions known to occur in natural language, and one that will explain other types of language data, such as the tip-of-the-tongue phenomenon and the type of information we are now learning in experiments on semantic memory.

Our model will be described in two parts. The first part concerns the linguistic structure postulated to be stored in long-term memory, and the second part concerns the processing of information on that linguistic structure. First we will describe this model; then we will describe how the model produces various zero-, first-, and second-order slips-of-the-tongue phenomena.

The language structure we postulate for our model is based on the relational network structure first postulated by Lamb (1966). Although this formalism is considerably less well known than transformational grammar, it has been proved mathematically to be adequate to the task, and possibly even superior (Bourgida, 1978). It has been shown to be amenable to such psychological considerations as multiple central embedding (Reich, 1969; Reich and Dell, 1977; Christie, 1976), language acquisition (Reich, 1970c), and the tip-of-the-tongue phenomenon (Smith, 1976). It has been the framework for a number of extensive linguistic analyses as well (see, for example, Sampson, 1970; Bennett, 1975; Johannesson, 1976). Furthermore, it is relatively compatible with network models being developed in artificial intelligence and semantic memory research (see, for example, Collins and Loftus, 1975; Schank, 1975; King and Anderson, 1976).

While more complete descriptions of the system are available elsewhere (see, for example, Reich, 1970a; 1970b; Lockwood, 1972), a brief description here is necessary to understand what follows. The basic relations on which any language system is based are CONCATENATION, which describes the linear sequence of elements of an utterance, DISJUNCTION, which describes the set membership relations among linguistic elements, and CONJUNCTION, which allows multiple factors simultaneously to influence linguistic output. Each node in a relational network represents one such relation. Different node types are represented by different node shapes. A triangle represents concatenation; a square bracket represents disjunction; and an inverted triangle represents conjunction. Thus in Figure 1 the triangle labeled A

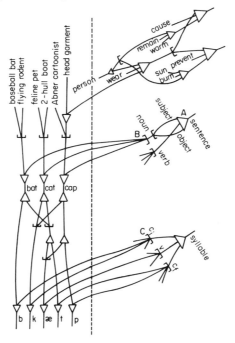

Figure 1: *Fragment of relational network grammar.*

describes the (simplified) fact that a sentence consists of a subject followed by a verb followed by an object. Similarly, the disjunction node labeled B indicates the set of all nouns, and the disjunction node labeled C represents the set of all initial consonants.

Most users of this framework find it useful to organize the patterns that emerge in this network framework into two types. The structures shown to the right of the dashed line in the figure are the tactic patterns. These patterns define the major constructive organization of language—the general rules. Most users find it useful to talk about at least three relatively independent tactic patterns—one for phonology, one for syntax, and one for semantics. The phonological tactics describe the buildup of phonemic features into phonemes, clusters, syllables, and rhythm groups; the syntactic tactics describe the buildup of morphemes into words, phrases, clauses, sentences, and transsentential structures. The semantic tactics describe the knowledge of the real world that is used by any language user to comprehend an utterance. People working in artificial intelligence refer to this information as FRAMES or SCENARIOS.

The network structure to the left of the dashed line is the realization portion. From the point of view of this chapter, we may refer to this portion as the lexicon or vocabulary. Unlike the organization of lexical entries in a transformational grammar, information in a relational network vocabulary is both more extensive and more interconnected. It is more extensive in that it includes not only words, but idioms (Makkai, 1972), cliché phrases, and whole memorized texts, such as the American Pledge of Allegiance. In principle, episodic memory is also represented here. It is also more interconnected, in that whenever two vocabulary items share any features in common, there is a path connecting the items through these features. In the figure *bat* and *cat,* since they rhyme, share an entire structure in common, whereas *bat* and *cap* are connected somewhat more distantly through the shared /æ/.

Words are not only tied together at the phonological level. Set memberships in the syntactic tactics connect all words of the same syntactic class, whereas set memberships in the semantic tactics connect all words of the same semantic class. Common opposites such as *hot* and *cold* are not only connected by being in the same semantic and syntactic classes; they are also connected in the vocabulary section by the fact that the definition of one will include the other and by the fact that collocational phrases such as "hot and cold" are stored as stock phrases in their entirety.

Language production in such a network system consists of signals running through the network. Signals flow from semantics to phonology, ultimately connecting at the bottom of the network to the muscles that are involved in articulatory movements. Feedback signals through the same network are used to guide timing. Several different systems of processing have been proposed (Reich, 1970; Christie, 1975; Smith, 1976). Thus far, none produce other than ideal speech. The modification of this system proposed in this chapter involves making the signal system somewhat "leaky." Superimposed over the system of signals previously developed is a general system of SPREADING ACTIVATION. Just as the structure we are using to describe linguistic facts has justification independent of any considerations of slips of the tongue, so has spreading activation. The use of similar notions to explain verbal behavior goes back as far as Wundt (1900). Recently, spreading activation has been proposed by a number of investigators as a way of explaining reaction time data in experiments involving search of long-term memory (Collins and Loftus, 1975; King and Anderson, 1976; Neely, 1976).

The system of spreading activation that we propose can be defined by the following 10 principles.

ACTIVATION. At any given time each node in the network has associated with it a (positive or negative) number, which represents the amount of activation on that node at any given time.

SPREADING. During each time step, a certain fraction of the activation on any node will spread from that node to all nodes directly connected with it.

SUMMATION. During each time step, the total amount of activation on a node will be incremented by the sum of all activations coming in from nodes to which it is most directly connected.

DECAY. During each time step, the total amount of activation on a node will be decremented by a certain percentage of the activation at the previous time step.

NOISE. During each time step, the total amount of activation on a node will be incremented or decremented by a (normally distributed) random amount.

SIGNALING. When a construction is to be produced, it is given a high amount of activation. At the same time, the next construction to be produced will be given anticipatory activation, which will be a certain fraction of the main activation signal. The construction to be produced after the next construction will be signaled an amount equal to the same fraction of the signal going to the next construction, and so on, in exponentially decreasing fashion.

SATISFACTION. When a construction is output, the activation on the wire associated with that output is set to zero.

CONSERVATION. Although the amount of activation in the system will vary from time step to time step, over the long run the total amount of activation in the system will remain relatively constant. This is accomplished by balancing the amount of signaling and spreading against the amount of satisfaction and decay.

COMPETITION. When it is time for one of a set of constructions to be produced, that construction is produced that has the highest activation.

RATE. The rate of speech production can vary independently of content of the production being produced.

It is not at all obvious how this proposed linguistic network structure combines with spreading activation to produce slips of the tongue. To test our intuitions that spreading activation does result in slips of the tongue, we simulated a small portion

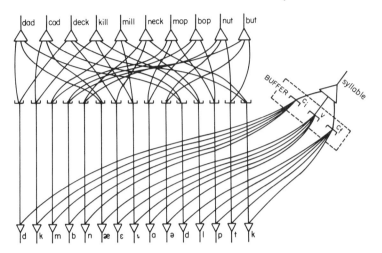

Figure 2: *Fragment of grammar used in computer simulation of model.*

of the unified model on the computer. Figure 2 shows the simple network structure that was used. This structure encompasses 10 words and their connection to a simple syllable phonology. The phonology indicates five possible initial consonants, followed by five possible vowels, followed by five possible final consonants. Thus, although there are only 10 words, the phonology allows 125 different syllables.

The program randomly selects words from its vocabulary and attempts to say them until instructed to stop. Given the severely limited network it had to operate on, the simulation produced almost all the types of zero-order categories. There were phoneme anticipations (*bop deck → dop deck*), phoneme perseverations (*cad deck → cad keck*), phoneme transpositions (*but neck → buck net*), word anticipations (*mill dad → dad dad*), word perseverations (*dad mop → dad dad*), word transpositions (*nut kill → kill nut*), word substitutions (*deck, mop bop → deck dad bop*), and blends (*deck/kill → dill*). There were even errors that looked as if they should have been haplologies, although the way this preliminary simulation was programed, it could not drop a syllable (*deck cad neck → dad neck neck*).

It is easier to describe the results and say that it does work than it is to describe how it works. The three disjunction nodes that indicate the possible phonemes in the three different positions in the syllable can be thought of as a buffer between the lexicon and the phonological tactics. When a word is about to be uttered, its constituent phonemes begin to be activated at each of the positions in the phonemic buffer. As the time to utter the word approaches, these signals increase in intensity, until the actual time for that word to be uttered, when normally those phonemes will have the highest activation and the word will be correctly produced. However, at the same time, the phonemes for the next syllable of the same stress will also be in the buffer, although at a lesser intensity. If random noise reduces the strength of activation of the primary signal or increases the strength of activation of the secondary signal, or both, the relative strengths of two phonemes competing for the same slot in the syllable may be reversed, in which case the wrong phoneme would be output.

Once a phoneme is output, the value of that phoneme will be set to zero. But it doesn't stay there for long. There is still reverberation in that part of the network, so, in fact, the activation of that phoneme will slowly decay. It will, however, decay faster than a phoneme that had not been satisfied. If an anticipation slip had been made without causing the speaker to stop and start again, then the next time that slot in the syllable was to be output there would be two possibilities. The already uttered phoneme may be still stronger than the phoneme that it replaced, in which case it will be uttered again, and a pure anticipatory slip would be the result. If, however, its activation was now less than that of the replaced phoneme, then the replaced phoneme will be output, and the total result would be a transposition slip. Thus, basic zero-order data can be accounted for.

As we turn our considerations to first-order data, in which the frequencies of the various types of events are considered, things begin to get more interesting. The relative frequencies of anticipation, perseveration, and transpositions can be matched by adjusting the relative values of three parameters of the model—the amount of spreading, the amount of anticipation, and the satisfaction value. Thus, the simulation of the correct frequencies of these basic types is essentially ad hoc and not very interesting. However, as we turn to editing and similarity phenomena, the power of this unified model begins to become apparent.

1. Prearticulatory Editing

Most investigators from Freud to the present have suspected that speech errors tend to create meaningful expressions. Thus, when former United States President Johnson spoke of his secretary of state as Dean Risk instead of Dean Rusk, one cannot help but think that the status of /risk/ as a meaningful word is hardly random. Baars, Motley, and MacKay (1975), using an experimental technique developed by Motley and Baars (1975a), showed that everyone's intuitions were correct, when they demonstrated that there is a genuine tendency for speech errors to create lexical items. More specifically, they found that phonemic transpositions were more likely when the resulting combination of phonemes was a word pair (*darn bore* → *barn door*), as opposed to a nonword pair (*dart board* → *bart doard*). This suggests that errors having lexical status are somehow more acceptable than nonword errors. They hypothesized that some sort of lexical editor checks each planned phoneme sequence prior to articulation and rejects the sequence if it is not a word.

Motley and Baars (1975b; 1976; 1979) have also found evidence for many other editorial processes in speech production. They found that slips are biased toward creating common phonemes and phoneme combinations (transition probability editing); slips tend to create synonyms to other words in the speech stream (seman-

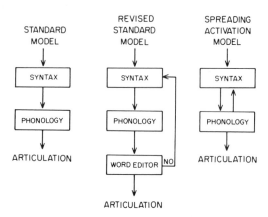

Figure 3: *Three models of language production.*

tic editing); slips even create expressions relevant to the extralinguistic context, as was observed when male subjects attended to by a provocative female experimenter had a greater tendency to spoonerize *goxi furl* into *foxy girl*. Fromkin's (1971) observation that morphophonemic alternations /s-z/ and /a-an/ agree with error outcomes rather than intended outcomes can also be seen as an editing phenomenon, this time at a morphophonemic level. Clearly, there seems to be much evidence that speech production involves a complex set of editorial operations occurring at all levels of language (Motley and Baars, 1975c). We claim that editing is not as complex and diverse as it appears.

Most language production models have held that the levels or components of the grammar are strictly ordered as in the left of Figure 3. For a process such as lexical editing to occur, it is required that information from a high level (for example, word level) be utilized after the units at the lower level have been spelled out (for example, phoneme level). One method of dealing with this is to add a new editorial component to speech production as is shown in the middle of Figure 3. But this would be wasteful since the editor, the lexical editor in this case, must contain the same knowledge as does the component where words are selected. Clearly, the component dealing with words should also be the component that acts as a lexical editor. If these functions are merged in one component, however, it is required that information flow bidirectionally between them. We claim that the spreading of activation between superordinate and subordinate linguistic units automatically produces editing. In the case of lexical editing, the spreading of activation implies the flowing or reverberation of activation between a superordinate word level and a subordinate phoneme level. An activated set of phonemes that corresponds to a word is continually reinforced by reverberation with a single word node because most of the activation from the phonemes converges and sums up at that node. A set of phonemes lacking lexical status would not reverberate with a single word node, and gradually the set would be replaced by a set that did correspond with a word.

In order to check our intuitions that spreading would indeed accomplish editing, we examined the errors from the simulation. Errors that created words were found to occur much more often than chance. When we adjusted the amount of spreading, we found that the greater the amount of spreading, the greater the tendency for word errors. Also, single phoneme slips that resulted in nonword outcomes were more likely if the resulting phoneme combination had a high transition probability among its phonemes. Thus the simulation acts as if it edits both for lexical status and for transition probabilities among phonemes.

The spreading of activation at all levels of a network grammar should result in editing at all levels, including the semantics and above. Spreading can be seen as a hypothesis regarding the mechanism of editorial biases in slips. With this view, however, one need not speak of "editors" at all, only of the natural processes of speech production.

2. Similarity Effects

Similarity plays an important role in determining the frequency of slips. The more similar a given unit is to an intended unit, the more likely the given unit or a part of it will replace the intended unit or a corresponding part of it.

Similarity is defined in terms of a grammar. Phonemes are similar when they share features or syllabic position; words can be similar in many respects—by sharing phonemes, syntactic function, having similar meaning, etc. In relational network grammar, similar units are represented by nodes at the same level that have many and/or relatively close connections between them.

Turning to the question of why and how similar units slip, there have been a number of proposals. Fromkin (1971) has suggested that semantically related words are substituted for each other because of a reversal or poor specification of semantic features, which results in the selection of incorrect yet related words (for example, *good → bad*). Word substitutions usually involve words of the same syntactic class. Fromkin argued that this could occur because content words are inserted into slots in an already generated syntactic function. At the level of the phoneme, MacKay (1970) and Nooteboom (1969) reported that similar phonemes tend to slip with each other more often than dissimilar ones. According to MacKay, this occurs because of a tendency for similar phonemes mutually to inhibit each other. This reciprocal inhibition is seen as a necessary process in production in order that phonemes be kept distinct.

One of the most important similarity findings is the repeated phoneme effect. MacKay (1970) reported that phonemic transpositions are more likely when the phonemes either before or after the reversing ones are identical, as in *bat cap → cat bap,* where the vowel sound /æ/ is repeated and follows the reversing phonemes. He explained this effect by assuming that prior to articulation planned phonemes are modified, or contextually integrated, so that each phoneme is fitted to go with those adjacent to it. As the words *bat cap* are planned, /b/ is modified to go with a following /æ/; /æ/ is modified to go with a preceding /b/ and a following /t/; and so on. After contextual integration, both the /b/ from *bat* and the /k/ from *cat* are fitted to go with a following /æ/. Thus, these modified initial consonants can fit in either word quite well, a situation that makes for order confusion, hence errors.

Although a variety of mechanisms have been proposed for similarity effects, spreading activation can account for these effects as well. Just as editing involves spreading between super- and subordinate units, similarity effects result from spreading between coordinate units—or units at the same level. How does this occur? The connections between similar units act as pathways for spreading. The more direct the connection and the greater the number of connections, the greater the tendency for activation to flow from one unit to another. A good analogy is two pitchers containing water at different levels. If they are connected by a siphon, their levels will begin to equalize. The greater the capacity of the siphon, the quicker their levels will equalize. Similarly, in our model, as the competing unit "robs" more and more activation, there is an increasingly greater chance that it will replace the intended unit, either wholly or partially.

Let us discuss two such effects in more detail. First, it has often been reported that when a competing word is substituted for an intended word (for example, *second Hungarian Rhapsody → second Hungarian restaurant*) or the two words are blended (for example, *rhapsody/restaurant → restody*), the words tend to be similar in sound (Fromkin, 1971; Dell and Reich, 1977). This is accounted for by activation spreading between the words by phonemic pathways. As the intended word is planned, activation spreads to its constituent phonemes. These phonemes send out activation as well, and the upward component of this spreading activates similar sounding words in addition to reactivating the intended word. When these similar sounding words send out activation to their phonemes, the stage is set for the substitution of an entire word, or a blending of the intended and competing words. We examined all the word substitution errors made by the simulation, and found that it was the case that the greater the number of shared phonemes between the intended and competing word, the greater the likelihood of the substitution.

The repeated phoneme effect is also accounted for by spreading activation but in a radically different fashion than that proposed by MacKay (1970). Assume that one is about to say *bat*, with *cap* the next intended word. *Bat* is given a high level of activation, and *cap* somewhat less. As activation spreads from *bat* to its phonemes, some of this activation enters the *cap* node via the repeated /æ/. This increases the activation level of *cap* by a significant amount because of the assumption that activation adds up at nodes. The increased activation on *cap* boosts that of its phonemes, making the /k/ for /b/ substitution more likely. In other words, the repeated phoneme creates a pathway for spreading between the words. We tested the repeated phoneme effect on the simulation by having it say two-word combinations with either zero, one, or two repeated phonemes, and found that errors were more likely the greater the number of repeated phonemes.

In some conditions, the spreading activation explanation for the repeated phoneme effect makes different predictions from those of the contextual integration hypothesis. According to the latter hypothesis, the repeated phoneme should induce slips only in those phonemes directly adjacent to the repeated ones, because these adjacent phonemes alone are integrated with the repeated phoneme. The spreading activation hypothesis claims that repeated phonemes in planned words should increase the probability of any phonemes in the words slipping, regardless of their position with respect to the repeated phoneme. Thus, spreading activation predicts that slips such as *take my bike → bake my bike* (Fromkin, 1973) are more likely because *take* and *bake* share the final /k/, even though the phonemes nearest the slip differ. An informal analysis we have done on Fromkin's collection of slips seems to support this prediction.

Thus many diverse first-order facts about slips of the tongue can be explained by spreading activation. Next we shall argue that spreading activation seems to account for some second-order facts as well.

3. Speaking Rate

It has long been known that when people speak too fast they make many slips of the tongue. There are a number of possible reasons why speaking quickly is difficult (see MacKay, 1971, for one proposal). The spreading activation model appears to account for at least part of this effect. Because spreading is a process that takes place over time, the amount of spreading that occurs as each word is planned is dependent on the speaking rate. Slow rates allow for much spreading before each word is said; fast rates allow for hardly any. Since spreading is the mechanism for editing, one would expect that the large number of errors associated with fast rates may be, in part, because there is little time for editing.

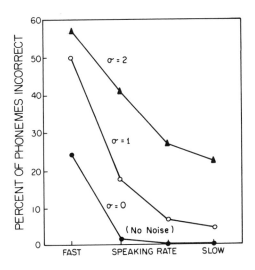

Figure 4: *Simulated influence of speaking rate and noise.*

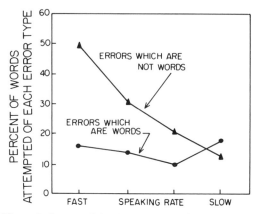

Figure 5: *Output of simulation showing lexical editing.*

In the simulation, we found speaking rate to be an important determiner of the number of errors. This can be seen in Figure 4, where the percentage of erroneous phonemes is plotted as a function of speaking rate and noise level. Clearly, rate has a large effect, and this is true whether there is noise or not. If the speaking rate effect is largely due to spreading, one would expect not only that errors are less likely when the rate is slow, but also that certain types of errors are more affected than others. In particular, lexical editing should operate more at slower rates than at faster rates. This prediction can be seen more clearly in the output from the simulation in Figure 5. Here the percentage of word and nonsense errors is plotted as a function of speaking rate. At fast rates, most of the errors create nonwords. As the simulation's speech slows down, however, the number of nonword errors is drastically reduced, whereas the errors creating words remain at a constant level. So the amount of lexical editing is directly related to the speaking rate. Notice that this interaction of lexical editing with speaking rate suggests that the simulation's editing occurs exactly as was proposed by Baars, Motley, and MacKay (1975)—namely, by the suppression of nonword outcomes rather than by the facilitation of word outcomes.

Although the simulation model engages in more lexical editing at slower speaking rates, it remains an open question whether this occurs in real people. The prediction, nevertheless, is testable. In fact, there is a variety of predictions from the model dealing with the properties of slips occurring at various speaking rates. Not only is it predicted that editing should vary as a function of rate, but similarity effects should also be influenced, since these effects are also seen as tied to spreading. It would be a simple matter to test these predictions in an experimental setting by having people speak short phrases at various rates. The slips created will, of course, be somewhat artificial, but they should tap processes of speech production that cannot be studied through the analysis of naturally occurring slips.

The clear separation between syntax and phonology that exists in the hypothesized linguistic structure used in this model helps to explain another second-order effect. This is the fact that when people expect their output to be nonsense strings, they do not lexically edit (Baars, Motley, and MacKay, 1975). This is equivalent to "turning off" or disconnecting the higher levels from the phonology. There is independent evidence that people can accomplish this "turning off." This appears to be exactly what happens in glossolalia, when people in certain Pentecostal and possibly other religious sects speak in what they consider "spiritual languages" (Samarin, 1972).

In conclusion, there are three aspects of this proposed model that commend it to us. The first aspect is that both the proposed linguistic structure and the notion of activation spreading are conceptual frameworks that have independent motivation in related fields of inquiry. The second aspect is that seemingly diverse phenomena in the area of slips of the tongue seem to be understood within a unified framework. Finally, the model makes new empirically testable predictions, and thus appears to be leading us to an even greater understanding of this most interesting area of human behavior.

Note

1. This research was supported in part by a grant from the Canada Council. For more detail on this model, see Dell (1980).

References

Baars, B. J., Motley, M. T., & MacKay, D. G. 1975. Output editing for lexical status from artificially elicited slips of the tongue. *Journal of Verbal Learning and Verbal Behavior, 14,* 382–391.

Bennett, D. C. 1968. English prepositions: A stratificational approach. *Journal of Linguistics, 4,* 153–172.

Boomer, D. S. & Laver, J. D. M. 1968. Slips of the tongue. *British Journal of Disorders of Communication, 3,* 1–12.

Bourgida, A. 1978. Formal aspects of stratificational theory. In M. Paradis (Ed.), *LACUS Forum 4.* Columbia, South Carolina: Hornbeam Press. Pp. 391–400.

Christie, W. M. 1976. Evidence concerning limits on central embeddings in English. *Forum Linguisticum, 1,* 25–37.

Cohen, A. 1966. Errors of speech and their implication for understanding the strategy of language users. *Zeitschrift für Phonetik, 21,* 177–181.

Collins, A. M. & Loftus, E. F. 1975. A spreading activation theory of semantic processing. *Psychological Review, 82,* 407–428.

Dell, G. S. 1974. Tongue twisters. University of Toronto Master's thesis.

Dell, G. S. 1980. Phonological and lexical encoding in speech production. Ph.D. dissertation. Univ. of Toronto.

Dell, G. S. & Reich, P. A. 1977. A model of slips of the tongue. In R. J. DiPietro & E. L. Blansitt, Jr. (Eds.), *LACUS Forum 3.* Columbia, South Carolina: Hornbeam Press. Pp. 448–455.

Fromkin, V. A. 1971. The non-anomalous nature of anomalous utterances. *Language, 47,* 27–52.

Fromkin, V. A. 1973. *Speech errors as linguistic evidence*. The Hague: Mouton.

Hockett, C. F. 1967. Where the tongue slips, there slip I. *To honor Roman Jakobson* (Vol. 2). (Janua linguarum, 32.) The Hague: Mouton. Pp. 910–936.

Johannesson, N. L. 1976. *The English auxiliaries: A stratificational account*. Stockholm: Almqist & Wiksell International.

King, D. W. & Anderson, J. R. 1976. Long-term memory search: An intersecting activation process. *Journal of Verbal Learning and Verbal Behavior, 15*, 587–606.

Lamb, S. M. 1966. *Outline of stratificational grammar*. Washington, D.C.: Georgetown Univ. Press.

Lockwood, D. G. 1972. *Introduction to stratificational linguistics*. New York: Harcourt Brace Jovanovich.

MacKay, D. G. 1970. Spoonerisms: The structure of errors in the serial order of speech. *Neuropsychologia, 8*, 323–350.

MacKay, D. G. 1971. Stress pre-entry in motor systems. *American Journal of Psychology, 84*, 35–51.

Makkai, A. 1972. *Idiom structure in English*. The Hague: Mouton.

Miller, G. A. & Selfridge, J. A. 1953. Verbal context and the recall of meaningful material. *American Journal of Psychology, 63*, 176–185.

Motley, M. T. & Baars, B. J. 1975(a). Laboratory induction of verbal slips: A new methodology for psycholinguistic research. Paper presented to Western Speech Communication Association, Seattle.

Motley, M. T. & Baars, B. J. 1975(b). Encoding sensitivities to phonological markedness and transition probability: Evidence from spoonerisms. *Human Communication Research, 2*, 351–361.

Motley, M. T. & Baars, B. J. 1975(c). Toward a model of integrated editing processes in prearticulatory encoding: Evidence from laboratory generated verbal slips. Paper prepared for Speech Sciences Division, Speech Communication Association Convention, Houston.

Motley, M. T. & Baars, B. J. 1976. Semantic bias effects on the outcomes of verbal slips. *Cognition, 4*, 177–188.

Motley, M. T. & Baars, B. J. 1979. Effects of cognitive set upon laboratory induced verbal (Freudian) slips. *Journal of Speech and Hearing Research, 22*, 421–432.

Neely, J. H. 1976. Semantic priming and retrieval from lexical memory: Evidence for facilitory and inhibitory processes. *Memory and Cognition, 4*, 648–654.

Nooteboom, S. G. 1969. The tongue slips into patterns. In A. G. Sciarone, A. J. van Essen, and A. A. van Raad, (Eds.), Nomen Society, *Leyden studies in linguistics and phonetics*. The Hague: Mouton. Pp. 114–132.

Reich, P. A. 1969. The finiteness of natural language. *Language, 45*, 831–843.

Reich, P. A. 1970(a). Relational networks. *Canadian Journal of Linguistics, 15*, 95–110.

Reich, P. A. 1970(b). The English auxiliaries: A relational network description. *Canadian Journal of Linguistics, 16*, 18–50.

Reich, P. A. 1970(c). A relational network model of language behavior. Unpublished Ph.D. dissertation. University of Michigan.

Reich, P. A. & Dell, G. S. 1977. Finiteness and embedding. In R. T. DiPietro and E. L. Blansitt, Jr. (Eds.), *LACUS Forum 3*. Columbia, South Carolina: Hornbeam Press. Pp. 438–447.

Samarin, W. J. 1972. *Tongues of men and angels*. New York: Macmillan.

Sampson, G. 1970. *Stratificational grammar*. The Hague: Mouton.

Schank, R. 1975. The structure of episodes in memory. In D. G. Bobrow and A. Collins (Eds.), *Representation and understanding: Studies in cognitive science*. New York: Academic Press. Pp. 423–450.

Smith, R. 1976. Cognitive networks. Unpublished bachelor's thesis. New Haven: Yale University.

Wells, R. 1951. Predicting slips of the tongue. *Yale Scientific Magazine, 26*, 9–30.

Wundt, W. 1900. *Völkerpsychologie I: Die Sprache*. Leipzig: Engelmann.

Chapter 20

MONITORING SYSTEMS IN THE NEUROLINGUISTIC
CONTROL OF SPEECH PRODUCTION

John Laver

Department of Linguistics
University of Edinburgh
Edinburgh, Scotland

The chief benefit of the past decade of research into slips of the tongue is that it has provided a fresh approach to the question of how the brain controls the production of spoken language. It might seem reasonable to expect a synthesis to emerge, bringing together ideas from linguistics, psychology, and neurophysiology. The distance still seems formidable, however, between the cognitive modeling undertaken by psychologists and linguists, on the one hand, and the more directly empirical standpoints of researchers investigating neurophysiological mechanisms. To take one example: Miller, Galanter, and Pribram (1960:26-27) characterize Norbert Wiener's "cybernetic hypothesis" as asserting that "the fundamental building block of the nervous system is the feedback loop." Fromkin's "utterance generator," described in one of the best articles on slips of the tongue (Fromkin, 1971:50), contains no feedback loops at all.

The problem lies at least partly in the descriptive metalanguages used in the modeling. The metalanguage of formal linguistics does not necessarily lend itself effectively to the task of facilitating the making of complementary statements in the metalanguage of neurophysiology. If linguistic models of the brain's control of speech performance are to court not only psychological validity but also potential neurophysiological realizations, eventually, then the adoption of a suitable metalanguage is clearly desirable.

A very useful lead toward a "neurolinguistic" metalanguage, which could permit compatible statements by linguists, psychologists, and neurophysiologists, was given a number of years ago, in neurophysiology itself, by McCulloch and Pitts (1943). They discussed the description of the activity of neuronal networks in terms of the logic of propositional calculus:

The "all-or-none" law of nervous activity is sufficient to insure that the activity of any neuron may be represented as a proposition. Physiological relations existing among nervous activities correspond, of course, to relations among the propositions; and the utility of the representations depends upon the identity of these relations with those of the logic of propositions. To each reaction of any neuron there is a corresponding assertion of a simple proposition. This, in turn, implies either some other simple proposition or the disjunction, or the conjunction, with or without negation, of similar propositions, according to the configuration of the synapses upon and the threshold of the neuron in question [McCulloch and Pitts, 1943:117].

Propositional logic is thus a suitable metalanguage for discussing the activity of any given neuron, in the sense that for any given firing threshold, the state of the neuron is completely accounted for by a statement of the condition of all neurons whose activities are prerequisites for that state. McCulloch and Pitts developed this argument further, and made it clear that wider psychological operations, because of their necessary dependence on the neuronal make-up of their underlying neurophysiological mechanisms, could also suitably be discussed in terms of propositional logic:

To psychology, however defined, specification of the net [namely, the neuronal network concerned in any particular cognition, perception, or state] would contribute all that could be achieved in that field—even if the analysis were pushed to ultimate psychic units or "psychons," for a psychon can be no less than the activity of a single neuron. Since that activity is inherently propositional, all psychic events have an intentional, or "semiotic" character. The "all-or-none" law of these activities, and the conformity of their relations to those of the logic of propositions, insure that the relations of psychons are those of the two-valued logic of propositions. Thus in psychology, introspective, behavioristic or physiological, the fundamental relations are those of two-valued logic [McCulloch and Pitts, 1943:131–132].

This chapter briefly presents a model of the speech producing system, to be explained more fully elsewhere, and based on findings from research on slips of the tongue, which makes use of a descriptive metalanguage embodying the concepts of propositional, Boolean logic. The logical relations posited to obtain between the various neurolinguistic functions, and between their component subfunctions, will be those of simple propositions, conjunction, inclusive and exclusive disjunction, and negation. By linking the different neurolinguistic functions in a relational network, it is possible to emphasize the specification of the relations between any given function and the logically prior functions that supply the prerequisite conditions for its operation. Control strategies of the brain are thus accounted for, in the discussion offered in this chaper, as the ways in which interaction between the posited neurolinguistic functions is either facilitated or limited by the hypothesized network of logical relations.

A major focus of this chapter is the nature of the monitoring systems for the detection and correction of errors in program construction and execution. The choice of such terms as "monitoring," "detection," "correction," and "error," with their strongly cybernetic flavor, is not accidental: The interesting problems of neurolinguistic performance are those of control. Cybernetics, as the science of all possible control systems, has a number of concepts of special relevance to the discussion of these problems. Among the most useful cybernetic concepts applicable here are the notions of the feedback loop and the feedforward link, together with the notion of error as a discrepancy between desired action and performed action.

This cybernetic conception of error will be particularly valuable in modeling neurolinguistic performance. Such a definition is wider than that usually used in research on slips of the tongue. The literature on tongue slip data characteristically discusses slips that either result in nonexistent linguistic forms or that substantially distort the semantic sense of the utterance. Slips of this sort certainly fall within the wider definition, of a discrepancy between desired and performed action; but also included would be, say, choices of lexical candidates that are only slightly imprecise in terms of the speaker's cognitive intention. A listener would have no evidence of any inadequacy of performance on the part of the speaker if such an "error" were not corrected. The virtue of the broad cybernetic definition of error is that processes of mental editing, where the degree of semantic appropriacy of a linguistic candidate is used as a criterion for its inclusion in or exclusion from a linguistic program, can be shown to be exploiting exactly the same monitoring mechanisms as are used for the detection of incipient slips of the tongue in the more customary definition. Broadening the definition of error to mean "inadequate performance" thus unifies normal language processing and tongue slip detection in a single system.

In order to capitalize upon relevant cybernetic ideas, the logical relations of the control systems that make up the neurolinguistic model are symbolized by a diagrammatic cybernetic network, rather than by the conventional algebra of propositional logic. The two representations are notationally equivalent, but the cybernetic network is not only mnemonically easier to understand, it also conveniently allows a global statement to be made of the overall relationships of the model assembled in a single diagram.

Four principal neurolinguistic decision-making functions are posited. These are IDEATION, LINGUISTIC PROGRAMING, MOTOR PROGRAMING, and MONITORING (Laver, 1969; 1970; 1977). An initial indication of their serial relationship is shown schematically in Figure 1.

In Figures 3 to 7, the neurolinguistic functions are diagramed in networks as "boxes" (of largely unknown internal strategy), connected to each other by lines, either directly or (more often) through one or more "gates." The gate symbols—the AND gate, the INCLUSIVE OR gate, and the EXCLUSIVE OR gate—specify the logical relations between the boxes they connect. The inputs to each gate represent the prerequisite conditions that must logically obtain before the box to which the gate supplies the input can carry out its prescribed function. Conventions for interpreting the gate symbols, and line-junctions, are given in Figure 2. Such symbols are often used for representing two-valued Boolean relations in electronic circuitry, for

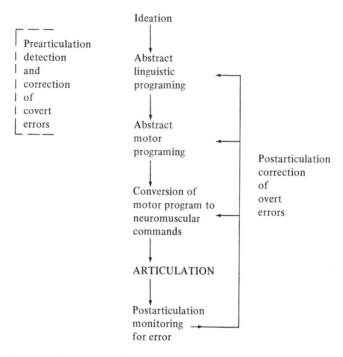

Figure 1: *Schematic outline of neurolinguistic functions.*

instance, and are thus particularly suitable for incorporation in a cybernetic network of this sort. They have been used in linguistic notation before, in writings on stratificational grammar. Equivalent devices are also used in writings on systemic grammar.

For convenience of exposition, the diagram of the total performance process has been initially broken down into four sections. These will be briefly discussed in turn as follows: Figure 3 shows the linguistic programing section, whose function is to construct an abstract linguistic program suitable for expressing the cognitive structure of the ideation concerned. Figure 4 shows the initial stage of the motor programing section, where a motor program of abstract motor schemata is produced, designed to express the linguistic program just constructed. Figure 5 shows the final stage of the motor programing section, where the program of abstract motor schemata is converted, in the light of sensory information about current states of the vocal apparatus, to the actual neuromuscular commands that result in the public articulatory performance audible to listeners. Figure 6 shows the stage where a component of the monitoring function scans the published performance for any error—that is, for any discrepancy between the intended utterance and the utterance actually performed. Monitoring for error in the preutterance stages of program construction is shown as an integral part of those stages. All subcompo-

1. Boolean logical relations and "gate" symbols

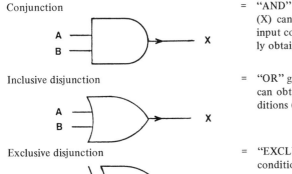

Conjunction = "AND" gate: The output condition (X) can obtain if and only if *all* the input conditions (A, B) simultaneously obtain.

Inclusive disjunction = "OR" gate: The output condition (X) can obtain if *any or all* the input conditions (A, B) obtain.

Exclusive disjunction = "EXCLUSIVE OR" gate: The output condition (X) can obtain if and only if *one only* of the input conditions (A, B) obtain.

2. Summary of the relations between input and output conditions

(1 = condition obtains; 0 = condition does not obtain.)

Conjunction		Inclusive disjunction		Exclusive disjunction	
Inputs	Output	Inputs	Output	Inputs	Output
A B	X	A B	X	A B	X
1 0	0	1 0	1	1 0	1
1 1	1	1 1	1	1 1	0
0 1	0	0 1	1	0 1	1
0 0	0	0 0	0	0 0	0

3. Symbols for nature of input conditions

a = positive condition

b = error condition

c = absence of error condition

4. Symbol for line-junctions

no junction

junction

Figure 2: *Symbol convention for Boolean network of logical relations.*

nents of the monitoring function are shown on the various diagrams as boxes printed in black, with white lettering. Associated gate symbols are printed similarly.

The four different sections are then finally combined in an overall diagram, in Figure 7. This shows not only the global and individual relationships of the different functions, but also includes the logical network utilized by the monitoring function in recycling detected overt errors to the lowest appropriate program construction level for correct reprograming.

A number of preliminary points need to be made before embarking on the exposition of the model. First, following William James (1890), it is assumed that ideation is to be distinguished from the linguistic resources that are exploited to construct expository linguistic programs. If this were not so, it would be difficult to understand how one linguistic program could be judged as semantically more appropriate for the expression of a given cognitive apprehension than a different but fairly similar program. This is not to oppose a potentially high degree of inter-action between the two functions, but no provision is made in the model offered here for the possible influence of the linguistic programing function on the idea-tional function.

Second, a distinction between LANGUAGE and MEDIUM (Abercrombie, 1967) is assumed. That is, a distinction is drawn between those features of neurolinguistic performance that should be seen as common to all mediums of language and those that are specific to the motor aspects of a particular medium. In this way, the model preserves its relevance for the operations involved not only in speaking, but also in writing, and in any other linguistic medium. Pathological data supports this position in that patients who can write but not speak, or speak but not write, demonstrate the retention of their linguistic ability in the absence of a medium-specific motor ability.

Third, the neurolinguistic operations suggested are seen as relevant to the per-formance of a single molar program of spoken communication. Previous work has shown, using evidence from the distribution of pauses (Boomer, 1965) and speech errors (Boomer and Laver, 1968; Fromkin, 1971), that molar programing, where a stretch of speech "is handled in the central nervous system as a unitary behavioral act, and the neural correlates of the separate elements are assembled and partially activated, or 'primed,' before the performance of the utterance begins" (Boomer and Laver, 1968:9), is very probably. The tone group, or phonemic clause, often coterminous with the syntactic clause, seems the best candidate for such molar programing, on the evidence of the preceding articles.

Fourth, a number of basic resources of the neurolinguistic system have been left out of the diagrams, partly for legibility. For example, every level of performance needs access to either or both long-term memory and short-term memory. Similarly, ATTENTION and MOTIVATION could be thought to have a potentially universal in-fluence on the components of the network. Appeal could be made to these two factors to explain variability in the efficiency of components. If attention is accept-able as a viable concept, then fluctuations in the degree of attention devoted to the operation of given components on different occasions could be responsible for some erratic performance. Also, variability in the efficiency of monitoring components might sometimes be attributable to changes in their operational thresholds, brought about by variations in the degree of motivational pressure felt by the speaker to communicate with his listener in a precise manner. Factors of social context would presumably be influential in this way. Access to memory, attention, and motivation is assumed throughout, although not explicitly diagramed.

Finally, it may be helpful to summarize the basic rationale underlying the construction of a model concerned at least partly with the covert correction of covert errors. The incidence of overt errors in speech seems surprisingly low, given the large volume of speech we each produce every day. The assumption is made here that the neurolinguistic speech production system is subject to more frequent inadequacies of performance, and that it has an integral monitoring system for the detection and correction of still covert errors in programing, which is efficient enough for such errors only occasionally to reach the level of overt articulatory performance. The assumption is buttressed by the notion of linguistic performance as a skilled and creative activity. That linguistic performance, particularly of cognitively novel and precise formulations, is creative is indisputable. That skill should be the partner of creativity in the continual, progressive refinement, before articulation, of expository linguistic programs seems highly plausible. One might say that skill can be defined as behavior that is prone to error where error is quickly detected and corrected. highest degree of skill is then seen in the situation where error is normally intercepted and corrected while still covert, in the programing processes prior to the overt, public stages of performance. That such behavior can be identified by the observer as skilled, rather than as automatic and incapable of error, will reside in the fact of a slight but necessary and publicly visible fallibility. A small number of errors must occasionally elude the internal monitoring mechanisms that have to be posited, and become overt. Their subsequent overt correction, and logically prior detection, then constitute the empirical data that support the formation of explanatory hypotheses about the characteristics of the covert programing and monitoring processes whose normal functioning successfully reduces the incidence of overt errors in everyday speech to a low level.

The Descriptive Model

The Linguistic Programing Section (Figure 3)

The first posited responsibility of this section, once the output of the ideation process has been established by Box 1, and stored in short-term memory, is to activate a number of linguistic candidates of tentative semantic suitability for the expression of the ideation. It is the function of Box 2 to do this, and the function of Box 3 to arrange them in a number of tentative linguistic programs. We know that

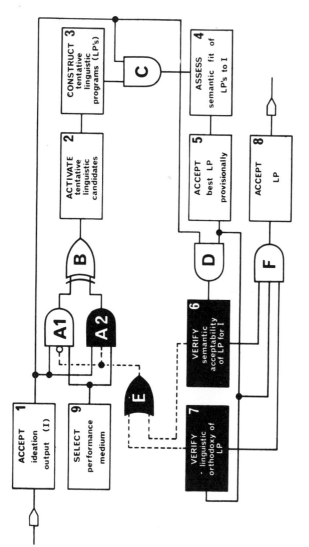

Figure 3.

more candidates are activated than are finally spoken, from blending errors widely reported, such as Fromkins's (1971:40):

the importance of adjoicent rules   ('adjacent' + adjoining')

and Laver's (1970:67):

he behaved as like a fool   ('like a fool' + 'as if/though he were a fool')

For Boxes 2 and 3 to perform their function, prerequisite information is not only the cognitive structure of the ideation, supplied by Box 1, but also the fact that the performance is intended eventually to be spoken rather than written. The implications of choice of medium will be more substantial later in the performance process, but even at the level of linguistic programing, the choice is influential—the language of speaking is, after all, not the same as the language of writing. The necessary conditions for Boxes 2 and 3 starting to work are symbolized by gate A1—the "absence of error" input is explained in the following section. When the conditions at A1 are satisfied, gate B will operate, on a single input.

The next task is the first editorial task: It is necessary to decide which of the constructed linguistic programs is most suitable for expressing the idea. The function of Box 4 is to assess the semantic suitability of each of the tentative programs, and arrange them in a hierarchy of goodness-of-fit. To do this, Box 4 has to be attributed major decoding and comparator powers. It also has to have access to the output of Box 1. The function of Box 5 is merely to pick the most highly valued program from the top of the hierarchy established by Box 4. That this program is the most suitable program so far constructed does not necessarily mean that the program is adequate by whatever criteria the standards of the occasion of conversation impose. It is the responsibility of Boxes 6 and 7, the first of the subcomponents of the monitoring function, to make the decision about adequacy. Mistakes such as the spatiotemporal confusion reported by Nooteboom (1967:14):

the two contemporary, er—sorry, adjacent buildings

would normally be rejected by Box 6 as semantically unsuitable for the expression of the idea. The error reported in the preceding section:

he behaved as like a fool

would normally be rejected as linguistically unorthodox by Box 7. In either case of unsuitability, an error signal would be sent through gate E to gate A1, the necessary "absence of error" condition for A1 would become inapplicable, and as an AND gate it would block. The conditions for A2 would then become applicable, however, and it would become the alternative entry for recycling, allowing the constructional process of Boxes 2 and 3 a second attempt to provide an adequate program, in the first example, in this model, of a feedback loop. (Some mechanism is needed here, not yet specified, for arranging that when A1 blocks, the serial output from Box 1 begins again at its starting point.)

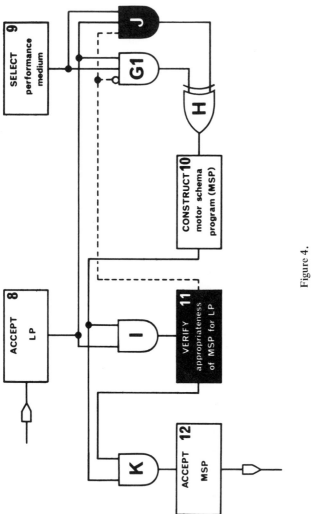

Figure 4.

Box 6, which like Box 4 must be attributed considerable decoding and comparator abilities, may reject programs for a variety of reasons: The candidates may be semantically nearly right, but on the occasion not precise enough; or the program accepted by Box 5 may be a misconstructed program unacceptably distorting the semantic sense of the communication. But there is an interesting additional possibility (Laver, 1977:150). In the finite time taken to construct a linguistic program to match the idea, the idea might itself have changed, for any one of a variety of reasons. Given that Box 6 has access to the current output of Box 1, a change of mind of this sort will lead to rejection of the linguistic program in exactly the same way as with other types of inadequate performance.

When the monitoring function is satisfied with the adequacy of the linguistic program for the expression of the ideation (and it may normally be satisfied on the first pass, on many occasions of undemanding conversational speech), the linguistic program is accepted by Box 8, through the AND gate F, and stored in short-term memory.

One of the features of the model presented here is that once a linguistic program is accepted by Box 8, its suitability is not challenged again until after the fact of articulation. This is possibly an unrealistic position, and is a consequence of the mainly serial flow of the model. In reality, one might prefer to believe that parallel access is more likely, and that decisions once taken are potentially subject to re-scrutiny.

The Motor Programing Section (Figure 4)

The operation of this section is straightforward. The task of Box 10 is to construct a program of abstract motor schemata, in the appropriate performance medium, for the expression of the chosen linguistic program. The relevant information comes to Box 10 through gates G1 and H. Box 11 checks on the suitability of the constructed motor schema program and rejects it if inadequate. When error is registered by Box 11, G1 blocks and gate J permits reentry to the program construction process. Errors of serial order, such as Fromkin's (1971:39):

Ralebais for 'Rabelais'

may be thought likely to arise here. However, it would not be appropriate to conclude that all errors involving only consonant- or vowel-sized segments are necessarily attributable to this section. For instance, one tongue slip reported by Fromkin (1971:41) was:

a kice ream cone for 'an ice cream cone'

It is clear that a morphophonemic adjustment took place here after the malfunction that caused the misplacing of the segments. Since such a morphophonological process must be applied in the linguistic programing section, then, logically, the misordering of the segments took place there also. We are thus faced with the situation,

in trying to use data from speech errors to construct a model of the speech generation process, of a given sympton of malfunction having multiple potential causal
locations.

Once Box 11 is satisfied, then Box 12 accepts the motor schema program and
stores it in short-term memory. The same comments apply to the "non-challenge-
ability" of acceptance of a program by Box 12 as applied to the case of Box 8.

The Neuromuscular Conversion Stage of the Motor Programing Section (Figure 5)

The function of this stage is to design and execute a program of neuromuscular
commands to the articulators that will embody the motor sequence specified by the
preceding section. To do this, three types of information are needed by Box 15.
The first, available from Box 12, is the specification of the motor schema program.
The second is that the neuromuscular sequence for the preceding molar neurolinguistic program has been completed—this information is available from Box 14. The
third is information from continuous auditory, tactile, and kinesthetic–propriocep-
tive reports about the current disposition of the vocal apparatus, from Box 13.

When all three conditions for gate L1 are satisfied, Box 15 operates; and, retrieving the stored motor schema program from short-term memory, produces the
neuromuscular commands that give rise to the audible articulatory performance of
the utterance.

It is necessary to distinguish between this neuromuscular stage and the earlier
abstract motor planning stage. The problem of motor equivalence, where a small

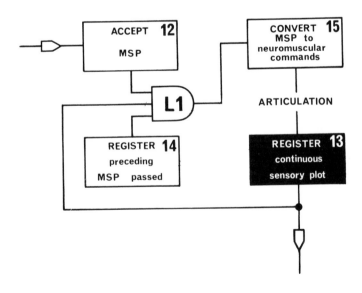

Figure 5.

number of nearly unique articulatory states have to be reached from a potentially almost infinite number of starting points, depending on the momentary spatial disposition of the vocal organs, makes it quite impossible for the brain to store all the necessary varieties of neuromuscular command patterns. It seems plausible that we store a more limited number of more abstract forms in long-term memory, together with strategies for taking account of the current muscular status of the vocal apparatus and for designing appropriate series of neuromuscular commands to move the apparatus to the next desired configuration or trajectory (MacNeilage, 1970:186; Laver, 1977:151).

In retrieving the motor schema program from short-term memory, the operation of Box 15 may be a fertile source of error. The large number of psychological experiments that have been carried out on short-term memory are relatively unanimous in showing that confusions tend to occur between items co-present in storage that share characteristics (Laver, 1977:152). Fromkin (1971:30–31) shows that voiceless fricatives interact, as in

> *alsho share* for 'also share'

as do approximants

> *blake fruid* for 'brake fluid'

and vowels

> *fash and tickle* for 'fish and tackle'

Boomer and Laver (1968:7) showed that the interaction of similars is effective in terms of syllable place, in that initial segments replace initials, medial replace medials, and finals replace finals. They also showed that stressed syllables interact with other stressed syllables, as a tendency, and that unstressed syllables preferentially affect other unstressed syllables.

The confusion of articulatory features reported by Fromkin (1971:36) may also be attributable to this source of error, as in

> *tebestrian* for 'pedestrian'

The Postutterance Monitoring Function (Figure 6)

It is the function of this component of the monitoring function to establish what utterance was actually performed, and to assess whether any discrepancy exists between the actual performance and the one that was intended.

Since adequate performance cannot be taken for granted, the monitoring function has to operate on the basis of sensory information supplied by Box 13 about the details of the articulatory performance. Boxes 16, 17, and 18 successively establish the performed motor schema program (that is, the motor schema program that would be taken to underlie the actually performed articulatory program); then the performed linguistic program; and finally the ideation that would be taken to underlie the performed linguistic program.

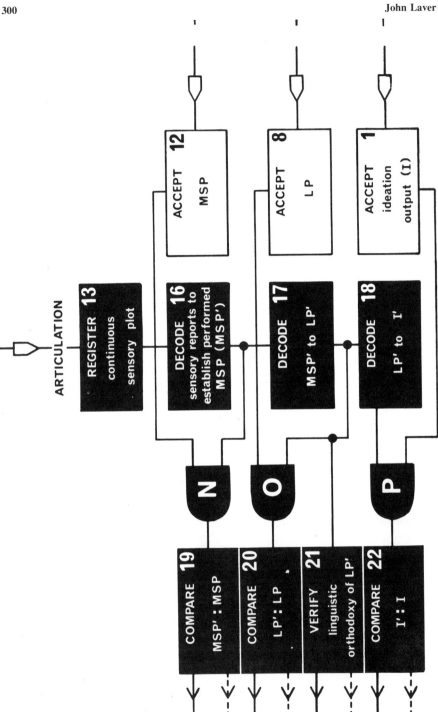

Figure 6.

The neurolinguistic system is now in a position to establish the fact and level of any error.

Box 19 compares the performed with the intended motor schema program. If any discrepancy is registered, then logically the error must have been introduced by the operation of Box 15, since Box 19 compares the outputs of Boxes 12 and 16.

Box 20 compares the performed with the intended linguistic program. If any discrepancy is registered, when Box 19 registers no error, then logically the error must have been introduced by Box 10, since Box 20 compares the outputs of Boxes 8 and 17.

Box 22 compares the performed with the intended ideational content of the utterance. If any discrepancy is registered, when Boxes 19 and 20 register no error, then the error must have been introduced by the linguistic programing section, since Box 22 compares the outputs of Boxes 1 and 18. The additional possibility exists here that, as earlier with Box 6, in the finite amount of time taken to program the utterance, the ideation may itself have changed. Changes of mind and slips of the tongue due to inadequate performance of the linguistic programing section would be treated identically by the monitoring system at this point.

Boxes 19, 20, and 22 are all comparator functions. In any such function in this model, the computation time needed to allow the necessary comparison of two sides of an equation to be made is unlikely to be negligible. Overt errors in speech are often corrected (and hence, detected) very quickly indeed. This prompts speculation about possibilities of economizing on postutterance monitoring latencies. If none of the necessary computation for postutterance monitoring was able to start until sensory information about the actual articulation was available from Box 13, then it would be difficult to understand how the brain manages to correct some overt slips so rapidly: There doesn't seem to be enough time for all the computation to be carried out. One possible time economy is provided by the notion of the feedforward link, and by the concept of presetting of perceptual systems.

In the model offered here, information about intended performance is available well in advance of articulation, at every point in time where a program is accepted and put into short-term memory storage. The outputs of Boxes 1, 8, and 12 is thus available to be fed forward to Boxes 22, 20, and 19 respectively, well ahead of the point in time when the actual comparisons will be made. Any necessary decoding, or reading off of indexation, that might be involved can therefore proceed in advance of the arrival of the later information about the articulated performance.

The time economy envisaged in this discussion concerns operations of a fairly high degree of cognitive complexity: Presetting any cognitive system to expect to perform on an anticipated set of data is likely to abbreviate the computation time necessary for that cognitive task. Presetting can be achieved at a lower perceptual level as well, however. It seems not impossible that another degree of time economy might be achieved by presetting the perceptual detectors involved in the earliest registration of the articulatory performance.[1] The network suggested here would have to be amended to include a link from Box 12 to Boxes 13 and 16 to incorporate this possibility.

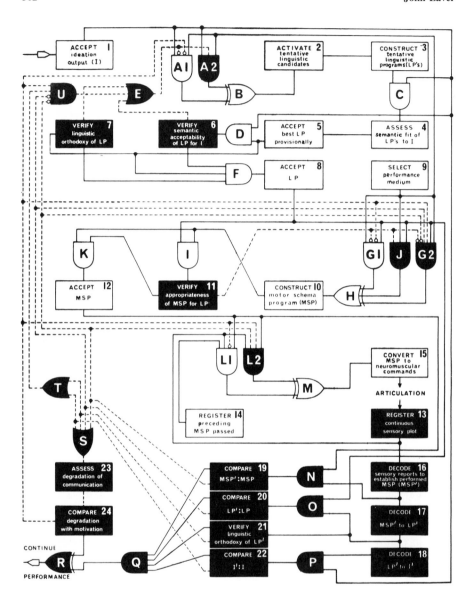

Figure 7.

Box 21 is the counterpart, in the postutterance monitoring section, of Box 7. Errors of linguistic unorthodoxy, such as the slip mentioned earlier

he behaved as like a fool

that had eluded the attention of Box 7 would presumably normally be caught by Box 21.

Postutterance Error Correction (Figure 7)

If Boxes 19 to 22 each produce a positive "no error" output, then all the conditions for the AND gate Q are satisfied, and articulatory performance continues. However, if even one of those boxes registers an error, then gate Q blocks, and the alternative route through gate S to Boxes 23 and 24 has to be traversed before the decision to continue articulatory performance or to halt it can be taken.

The function of Box 23 is to assess the degree of degradation the communication is likely to suffer as a result of the registered error. Box 24 then decides whether it is desirable to take any corrective action, in the particular circumstances of the occasion of conversation, about the error. If the decision is to allow the slip to pass without correction, then articulatory performance continues. So failure to correct a slip is not to be equated with failure to detect the slip (Laver, 1969:141). If it is decided that the slip should be corrected, then the first consequence is that the resultant "error" signal from Box 24 blocks gate L1, where "absence of error from Box 24" is a necessary condition. This is the articulation-halting mechanism.

When it is decided to correct an error, all the information for redirecting entry to the lowest necessary level of program construction is already available in the differential decisions of Boxes 19 to 22.

If Box 19 is the only one to register an error, then reentry automatically is directed through gate L2. Since registration of error by Box 19 means that the error was introduced by Box 15 (or that Box 13 gave false information, as in anesthetic intervention experiments), reentry through L2 will allow reuse of the adequate motor schema program previously accepted by Box 12, and will allow Box 15 another opportunity to achieve a satisfactory performance. The crucial effect of a delay of 180 msec in delayed auditory feedback experiments may be partly a reflection of the fact that when Box 13 gives misleading auditory information, and the brain establishes through the monitoring function that the apparently inadequate articulatory performance was due to an error being introduced after Box 12, then this is the typical latency for the lowest-level error-detection and articulation-halting mechanism to operate. The apparent stammering that often results from delayed auditory feedback would then reflect the repeated transmission of an adequate motor schema program from Box 12 through the remainder of the neuromuscular conversion section.[2]

If Box 20 registers an error while Box 19 shows no discrepancy, then reentry is directed through G2 to Box 10. If, on reconstructing the motor schema program, another error is created and detected by Box 11, then the feedback loop through gate J is used, and recycling occurs locally until Box 11 is satisfied.

If either Box 21 or Box 22 registers an error, then reentry is directed through gates T, U, E, and A2 to the beginning of the linguistic programing section.

Conclusion

The questions that this model provokes are interesting. For example, are errors that have their source at different levels corrected at different latencies? If slips of the tongue are the result of ephemeral malfunctions of some particular part of the model, does the permanent malfunction of that part of the model plausibly cause a recognizable speech pathology? Is it possible to manipulate experimentally the thresholds of the subcomponents of the monitoring function? Would one gain more extensive insight into the speech-producing system by attempting to rewrite the model as a computer program?

Modeling of this sort is valuable to the extent that it provides a framework for research, generates further hypotheses, and encourages complementary statements from related research and related disciplines. The descriptive metalanguage used in this chapter is possibly overpowerful for the data it is called upon to handle, at present. It does have the virtue of demanding a degree of explicitness that a prose statement sometimes fails to compel. At the least, it holds some promise as a possible unifying metalanguage that might encourage the synthesis of some ideas in linguistics, psychology, and neurophysiology.

Notes

1. I am indebted to Professor Robert Hanson, of the University of California at Santa Barbara, for this hypothesis.
2. This idea also emerged from discussion with Robert Hanson.

References

Abercrombie, D. 1967. *Elements of general phonetics*. Edinburgh: Edinburgh Univ. Press.

Boomer, D. S. 1965. Hesitation and grammatical encoding. *Language and Speech, 8,* 148–158.

Boomer, D. S. & Laver, J. D. M. 1968. Slips of the tongue. *British Journal of Disorders of Communication, 3,* 2–12.

Fromkin, V. A. 1971. The non-anomalous nature of anomalous utterances. *Language, 47,* 27–52.

James, W. 1890. *The principles of psychology* (Vol. 1). New York: Holt, Rinehart and Winston.

Laver, J. 1969. The detection and correction of slips of the tongue. *Work in Progress 3,* Department of Phonetics and Linguistics, University of Edinburgh.

Laver, J. 1970. The production of speech. In J. Lyons (Ed.), *New horizons in linguistics.* Harmondsworth: Penguin. Pp. 53-75.

Laver, J. 1977. Neurolinguistic aspects of speech production. In C. Gutknecht (Ed.), *Grundbegriffe und Hauptströmungen der Linguistik.* Hamburg: Hoffmann und Campe. Pp. 142-155.

MacNeilage, P. F. 1970. Motor control of serial ordering of speech. *Psychological Review, 77,* 182-196.

McCulloch, W. S. & Pitts, W. 1943. A logical calculus of the ideas immanent in nervous activity. *Bulletin of Mathematical Biophysics, 5,* 115-133.

Miller, G. A., Galanter, E., & Pribram, K. H. 1960. *Plans and the structure of behavior.* New York: Holt, Rinehart and Winston.

Nooteboom, S. G. 1967. Some regularities in phonemic speech errors. *Annual Progress Report 2.* Eindhoven, The Netherlands: Instituut voor Perceptie Onderzoek.

Chapter 21

ON ELICITING PREDICTABLE SPEECH ERRORS IN THE LABORATORY[1]

Bernard J. Baars

Department of Psychology
State University of New York at Stony Brook
Stony Brook, New York

> *Der Zufall ist beim Versprechen volkommen*
> *ausgeschlossen, das Versprechen ist geregelt.*
>
> Meringer (1908)

1. Introduction

Wilhelm Wundt (1899) wrote that "it is primarily the *sensory* side of psychic life which accords the widest prospect for experimental investigation." Certainly as it applies to psycholinguistics, Wundt accurately predicted the course that experimental work would take over the next hundred years. By far the preponderance of experimentation with higher levels of language processing is concerned with the perception and comprehension, rather than the production, of speech. Experimental control of these higher levels of language generation has been thought to be difficult to achieve; and to see this aspect of the system "laid bare," one must apparently rely on naturalistic collections of spontaneous speech errors (Meringer, 1908; Fromkin, 1973; MacKay, 1970; 1973; Garrett, 1976).

Such naturalistic corpora have distinct advantages and disadvantages for scientific investigation. On the one hand, they clearly portray the nature and variety of a real-world phenomenon that is of great interest in the study of speech. On the other hand, we have no control over the precise preconditions of spontaneous errors so that it is extremely difficult to test causal explanations, or to eliminate alternative explanations for some phenomenon. Freud's work illustrates this difficulty. While his ideas on the origin of verbal slips are consistently brilliant, and, to me, believable, it is extremely difficult to draw testable inferences from the naturalistic corpus that he cites as evidence.

Whenever possible, therefore, the study of spontaneous errors should be supplemented by experimental evidence. Without naturalistic facts, experimental work may become quite narrow and blind; but without experimental research, the naturalistic approach runs the danger of being shallow and uncertain. Both approaches are necessary.

Some progress has been made toward eliciting predictable, high-level errors in the laboratory (MacKay, 1971; Baars and Motley, 1974; Motley and Baars, 1976; Baars and MacKay, 1977). Once they can be reliably induced, these errors can be used to investigate previously untestable hypotheses. For example, evidence has been presented regarding

1. The kinds of conditions that can give rise to speech errors (Baars and MacKay, 1977; Baars, 1977, unpublished)

2. The interactions between sequencing systems in normal speech (Baars and Motley, 1976)

3. The notion of Freudian slips (Motley and Baars, 1976; Motley and Baars, 1979; Motley, Camden, and Baars, 1979; Motley, this volume) and

4. The existence of internal processes that separate "worse" errors from "better" ones in a consistent fashion (Baars, Motley, and Mackay, 1975; Baars, 1977).

These points will be discussed in turn.

2. Methods for Eliciting Predictable Speech Errors

At this point, we have available at least eight different methods for inducing speech errors at differing levels of complexity. In general, these methods can be grouped under the heading "Competing Plans Hypothesis" (Baars, forthcoming), which states two necessary conditions for the experimental induction of speech errors. Subjects can be induced to make predictable, involuntary speech errors if

1. they are given two alternative plans for one production; and if
2. they are denied the time needed to "sort out" these plans.

Following are a number of ways for carrying out this dual approach.

2.1. *Competition by a Violation of Anticipatory Readiness to Respond.*

Children sometimes play games that demonstrate this effect. For example, at the start of a foot race, a child may call out "On your mark—get set—STOP!" Naturally, some of the runners will start anyway. Or one child may ask another to repeat the word *poke* many times, and then ask, "What is the white of an egg called?" The most common answer seems to be "the yolk" (which is wrong). There is considerable psychological and physiological evidence that anticipatory biasing of responses is an inherent part of the organization of action, both in animals and humans, and these demonstrations are not at all trivial in their implications (see, for example, Turvey, 1976; Greene, 1971; Gel'fand *et al.*, 1971).

Using this approach, we can elicit spoonerisms experimentally (see Table 1 for illustration). A memory drum is used to present pairs of words, one pair at a time for about 1 second each. The first column of Table 1 shows such a sequence of word pairs. The reader can personally perform this experiment by cutting a narrow horizontal slit in a card, so that only one word pair is visible at any one time. The

TABLE 1. *Stimuli Used to Elicit Spoonerisms.*

Column 1 Phonological bias technique	Column 2 Word pair reversal technique
Give Book	Dumb Seal
Go Back	Heap Cook
Get Boot	Bail Toss
Bad Goof	
	REVERSE
RESPOND	
	But Goal
Ball Doze	Mad Dash
Bash Door	Dead Level
Bean Deck	
Bell Dark	REVERSE
Darn Bore	Bet Gashed
	Fate Lame
RESPOND	Make Bowl
Ripe Log	Bought Cat
Real Long	
Long Rice	REVERSE
	Fail Sun
RESPOND	
	REVERSE
Big Dutch	
Bang Doll	Sons Toil
Bill Deal	Moon Sore
Bark Dog	
Dart Board	REVERSE
	Maid Pen
RESPOND	Keen Lap
Rack Seal	Deep Cot
Road Sale	
Real Sick	REVERSE
Soul Rock	Down Train
	Waste Term
RESPOND	
	REVERSE

task is simply to move the opening down the list, exposing each word pair for about 1 second. Keep each word pair in mind until the following exposure is presented. If the following exposure shows the cue RESPOND, please say the IMMEDIATELY PRE-CEDING pair of words, out loud, as quickly as possible. One must therefore be prepared to say each word pair out loud during the following exposure, since one cannot predict whether the next exposure will show the cue RESPOND.[2]

It is this readiness to say some particular word pair that is systematically manipu-lated. If one is shown the series *give book, go back, get boot,* one will probably expect the next word pair to have the initial consonants /g/.../b/.... However, the following word pair reverses these initial consonants—it is *bad goof,* and is immedi-ately followed by the cue RESPOND. We find that from 10–30% of responses to the unexpected word pairs will result in spoonerisms, so that people will say "gad boof" instead of "bad goof." This effect works over a variety of phonetic, lexical, or nonsense patterns, and a range of different exposure times from ½ to 3 seconds.

The minimum "phonological bias" for a complete spoonerism is bias toward pre-entry of the later consonant (/g/ in the example). Given a readiness to start with /g/, subjects will tend to say "gad" instead of "bad"; and even without any further phonological bias, this preentry of /g/ appears to "trigger" a postentry of /b/ to produce the complete spoonerism "gad boof" (Baars and Motley, 1976).

2.2. *Competition Due to Reversal of Order*

The Competing Plans Hypothesis generates a number of other methods for in-ducing errors. For example, Column 2 of Table 1 is very much like Column 1: It, too, contains word pairs, but there is no systematic "phonological bias," and instead of the response cue RESPOND, we find a response cue that says REVERSE. Other-wise, the situation is identical. Instructions are to keep each word pair in mind, and whenever one encounters the cue REVERSE, simply reverse the order of the pre-ceding word pair and say this reversed pair as quickly as possible. This method also produces spoonerisms (Baars and Motley, 1976).

The same technique can be used to elicit sentential errors. For example, Table 2 shows a series of sentences that permit the reversal of phrases within each sentence. Thus the sentence "She touched her nose and picked a flower," is followed by "She picked a flower and touched her nose." A series of these phrase reversals is followed by the response cue REVERSE, indicating that the subject should say the preceding sentence in phrase-reversed order, as quickly as possible. This method produces word switches between the two syntactically parallel phrases, much as spoonerisms are produced by word-order reversals. Experimental sentences can be designed that are relatively normal, but that have either abnormal or normal error outcomes, de-pending upon a difference of one word in the sentence (see the following section and Baars, 1977).

TABLE 2. *Stimuli Used to Elicit Word Exchanges.*

She cut a flower and touched her nose.
She touched her nose and cut a flower.
She touched her nose and cut a flower.
She cut a flower and touched her nose.

REVERSE

The boy hurt his elbow and played with the dog.
The boy played with the dog and hurt his elbow.
The boy hurt his elbow and played with the dog.
The boy hurt his elbow and played with the dog.

REVERSE

The lady brushed the dog and called the man.
The lady called the man and brushed the dog.
The lady called the man and brushed the dog.
The lady brushed the dog and called the man.

REVERSE

She picked a flower and touched her nose.
She touched her nose and picked a flower.
She touched her nose and picked a flower.
She picked a flower and touched her nose.

REVERSE

The hunter shot his prey and looked for his partner.
The hunter looked for his partner and shot his prey.
The hunter shot his prey and looked for his partner.

REVERSE

The food smells terrible but the chef looks good.
The chef looks good but the food smells terrible.
The food smells terrible but the chef looks good.
The food smells terrible but the chef looks good.
The chef looks good but the food smells terrible.

REVERSE

2.3. *Competition of Plans for Word Retrieval*

Word blends (MacKay, 1972) can be induced by teaching people to retrieve rapidly one of two possible synonyms on cue. For example, people can be given a list of single words, and instructed to say one synonym when confronted with the alternate one, and vice versa. Whenever "ghastly" appears, for instance, one must say "grizzly," and the reverse. This method produces word blends such as /gɪstli/.

2.4. *Competition by Deliberate Transforms*

When the Competing Plans are systematically related to each other, subjects can be instructed to transform one into another, on cue. For example, subjects are given the sentence "John hit the ball," followed either by the cue ACTIVE or the cue PASSIVE. This method has been shown to elicit errors such as "Ball hit the ball" and "Ball hit the John," MacKay (1976) has also shown that a task requiring past tense transforms for verbs (*taught* from *teach*) results in characteristic errors that support a derivational model of lexical retrieval.

3. Implications of Competing Plans Methods for Normal Speech

While the Competing Plans Framework has been heuristically very useful in suggesting ways in which errors may be induced, it is possible that spontaneous errors have some origin other than competition of this kind. Nevertheless, it is easy to see how some sort of competition could arise in a reasonable model of speech production.

For instance, speech production models must deal with the fact that there is often a one-to-many relationship between a semantic intention and the utterances that can fulfill that intention. That is to say, any one thought can probably be expressed in several different ways. But this fact means that somewhere in the system, one may make a selection among several linguistic plans that can each express the meaning intended. Such a situation can easily give rise to competition, especially if some time pressure exists, forcing a quick choice. If this source of potential error exists in normal speech production, it would obviously be desirable for the system to exercise some form of "quality control" over its plans, prior to output (see Laver, 1973; Section 4 this chapter).

In addition, it is clear from the preceding examples that speech errors that are induced by means of Competing Plans are more than just fusions between those plans. There is no a priori reason why a confusion between the order of two phrases in a sentence should result in a switch of syntactically similar words between the phrases. Therefore it appears that the system operates actively on the plans, even when they arise as anomalous fusions due to higher-level competition.

Experiments with spoonerisms provide perhaps the clearest example to date of this kind of active processing. There are, after all, two methods for inducing them: the "phonological bias" technique and the "word-reversal technique" both described earlier. It may be argued that these methods might work through entirely separate mechanisms, but parsimony suggests that they may represent different ways of inducing the same process to take place.

In this context, it is important to note how regular spoonerisms are. In a sense, they are not "errors" at all. Judged by phonological and articulatory criteria, spoonerisms are perfectly rule-governed utterances. This in turn suggests that some phoneme-sequencing system is performing its normal operations on a lexically anomalous higher-level input, and passing on to articulatory systems a phonotactically and motorically workable plan.

Baars and Motley (1976) proposed that spoonerisms start out in normal speech production as a conflict between the order of two words in a sentence. For example, in the sentence "Today I really made a (bad) goof" the word *bad* is optional, and the sentence is perfectly usable without it. Thus, the adjective may be inserted into the planned sentence some time after the rest of the sentence has been prepared. It may actually be inserted too late, after the command to say the next word *goof* has already been given. At that point, some phoneme-sequencing system may be forced to reconcile the phonemes /#/ /bæd/ /#/ /gʊf/ /#/, but it may be already committed to start with /#/ /g/. As pointed out in the preceding discussion, it can be shown experimentally that the preentry of just this initial /g/ will automatically trigger the postentry of the other initial consonant /b/ into the later position. The result is a complete spoonerism.

Thus, by finding several different methods for eliciting the same kind of error, one can begin to engage in more informed theorizing concerning the nature of normal speech planning and production.

4. Conclusions Based on Manipulations of the Error Rate

One way of using induced errors is by establishing a procedure that results in a known "base error rate," making it possible to study the effects of other factors on this rate. In this way, one can begin to simulate "Freudian slips" by showing an increase in the base error rate in the presence of semantic or situational bias, when the error outcomes express this bias involuntarily (Motley and Baars, 1976; Motley and Baars, 1979; Motley, Camden, and Baars, 1979). These experiments are described by Motley (this volume), and I will focus here on another use of base-rate manipulations: the possibility that certain error outcomes will be suppressed on the basis of contextual expectations. From this kind of change in the base error rate, one can infer the existence of internal feedback processes that control the likelihood of execution of abnormal errors PRIOR TO the act of speaking.

It is easy to see that people do monitor their own speech, because they often correct themselves overtly after making an error (see, for example, Laver, 1973). The problem, however, is to show how such editing processes could occur covertly prior to speaking. In a sense we want to be able to show how people could entertain some unobservable plan for production, and then decide, on the basis of its abnormality, not to articulate it. We are looking, so to speak, for the ghost of an aborted utterance.

Our first approach to this problem was to use the phonological bias technique to elicit spoonerisms at a known rate (Baars, Motley, and MacKay, 1975). For example, errors such as *darn bore* → *barn door* have a lexically real outcome, and this kind of error occurs at an error rate of about 30%. However, it is possible to give people word pairs in this task that look very much like *darn bore,* but that turn into nonsense errors (for example, *dart board* → *bart doard*). This kind of error occurs only about 10% of the time, in spite of its similarity to the first case. Thus, nonsense errors are significantly less likely to occur in this paradigm than lexically real errors.

From this, it is possible to argue that the only way the system can "know" which of these cases will be nonsense and which lexical, is by actually "trying out" the spoonerism by switching the initial consonants. Information concerning the lexical status of the projected utterance is simply not available before the phoneme switch. Therefore, any feedback process that changes the error rate as a function of the error outcomes must work AFTER the consonant switch has occurred.

On the other hand, it is also clear that the lower rate for nonsense spoonerisms must be due to some process that takes place prior to articulation. There is a 20% difference in the error rates of lexical and nonsense outcomes, and we must account for how this 20% "got lost." Now we can bracket the occurrence of this operation on both sides: Any process sensitive to the lexical–nonsense distinction must occur after the consonant switch and before the act of speaking the error. Only then can we account for the difference in error rates.

Of course, suitable control experiments are needed to test alternative explanations.

One such control experiment was as follows. It was found that the difference between the error rates for lexical versus nonsense errors disappeared only if all the displayed word-pairs were nonsense syllables. That is to say, if the comparison was between the word pairs *gad boof* (which turned into the lexical error *bad goof*) and *gaz boov* (which may turn into the nonsense pair *baz goov*), there was no difference in the error rate—both error rates were near 30%. This seemed to be a problem at first, but actually became an opportunity to perform a rather powerful control study.

One possibility, it seemed, why the error rate difference disappeared was that subjects only viewed nonsense syllables on the screen in front of them. Perhaps they were unaware that any of the items could be lexically real, and therefore did not discriminate between lexical and nonsense items. This is often the case in perceptual tasks where subjects are led to believe that they will see only nonsense material. In order to test this possibility, we inserted some lexical word pairs into the identical word list we used before in such a way that the lexical material was totally unconnected to the task. This incidental filler material could give subjects information that the lexical status of their responses might be a relevant dimension in the task. Therefore they might again begin to check their planned responses for lexical appropriateness. And indeed, with this contextual manipulation, the rate for nonsense errors again dropped to about 10%.

This control experiment has several interesting implications. First, it showed that the "editing effect" was not due to our idiosyncratic choice of word pairs. If that had been the case, a contextual change unconnected to the actual word pairs that were compared would not be able to change the error rate.

Second, the control experiment indicated that context can influence which type of error will be edited. This makes a good deal of sense, in view of the fact that we probably edit differently, say, in a locker room than at a formal banquet. Editing SHOULD be context-sensitive.

Third, the control study indicated that the error rate of the nonsense syllables tended to be suppressed, a point that the initial study had left open. In that study (described earlier), a higher error rate was found for lexical errors than for nonsense errors (30% versus 10%). That could be interpreted as showing that lexical errors are boosted in probability, or alternatively that nonsense errors are suppressed. In the three conditions where nonsense errors were irrelevant or where lexical outcomes occurred, the error rate was about 30%; but in the one case where nonsense outcomes were to be avoided (because lexical status was made contextually relevant), the error rate for these nonsense errors dropped to 10%.

More recent work has shown that editing effects can occur with sentential errors as well (see the preceding section and Table 2). For example, the sentence

(1)   She touched her nose and cut a flower.

will produce the error

(1*) She cut a flower and touched her nose.

In the sense that the word order has changed, this is indeed an error. But it is not noticeably abnormal or socially inappropriate. However, the next error is quite peculiar. Starting with the sentence

(2)   She touched her nose and picked a flower.

one can induce the error

(2*) She picked her nose and touched a flower.

One might expect people to avoid (2*) more than (1*), and the error rate for abnormal errors of this kind is indeed about twice the rate of the matched, relatively normal errors.

As before, we can argue that any change in the error rate as a function of the normality or abnormality of the error must occur after the word switch that has rendered the sentence anomalous; and since it was then not spoken, it must also have taken place prior to the act of speaking. The editing process is thus bracketed in from both sides. We cannot avoid the conclusion that in this task, the subjects anticipate the semantically anomalous errors and act in such a way as to avoid overtly making these errors.

5. General Theoretical Implications

These kinds of techniques are reminiscent of experiments in physics, where particle accelerators are used to study the results of collisions between two different kinds of particles. Instead of particle collisions, we are studying the competition between two alternative plans for production in the speech apparatus. But as in the case of particle collisions, we are frequently not sure of what to expect from this competition. The system we are studying is active and highly constrained, and the resultant outcomes of internal competition are not arbitrary, but reflect the regularities inherent in its normal functioning.

Although we have used these methods for less than five years, we can already speculate about the shape of the speech production system as it is reflected in our experimental results. For example, Foss and Fay (1974) have used speech error data to support the "psychological reality" of transformational grammar in speech production. Without going into many of the complexities of this issue, we can still ask whether such a view is consistent with our results so far; in particular, whether our research supports a model of speech production as an essentially derivational system. We have several reasons to believe that such a view must be profoundly modified to encompass our results.

First, a purely derivational model must be modified to account for the effectiveness of Competing Plans in producing speech errors that resemble spontaneous errors. That is to say, if there is any validity to the notion that a semantic intention can be expressed in more than one way, one must deal with the existence of "choice-points" in normal speech production. These choice-points are potential sources of competition, since they represent alternative plans for speaking. It appears difficult to incorporate choice-points into a derivational model, which is deterministic in a top–down fashion.

Second, our two demonstrations of prearticulatory editing indicate that the flow of control in speech production is not just top–down. No doubt there must be some top–down processes, going from a semantic level of representation to word-selection and syntactic levels, and from there to some phonological and articulatory component. However, we have discussed evidence indicating that the rate of a word-ordering error, the word switch in (1) and (2), can be changed by higher levels of control; that is to say, by feedback to a semantic level. Surely the error

(2*) She picked her nose and touched a flower.

is not an error at all by syntactic, lexical, phonological, or motor criteria. It only violates semantic rules, or rules of social appropriateness.

Similarly, the error *dart board* → *bart doard* does not violate criteria at sub-lexical levels, although the error consists of a phoneme switch. In order to change the likelihood of this utterance, one must therefore appeal to criteria at levels higher than the level of the error. Thus the flow of control must be able to cycle upward.

There are powerful theoretical and experimental arguments for preferring "heter-archical" models such as proposed by Gel'fand *et al.* (1971), Greene (1971), and Turvey (1976). Undoubtedly a linguistically adequate grammar must be a necessary part of such a model, but it appears that a purely derivational model cannot have the flexibility needed for the planning and execution of normal speech.

Acknowledgments

I would like to thank Professors Michael T. Motley and Donald G. MacKay for their collaboration in the work reviewed here; I am grateful for their comments and criticisms, as well as those of Professors Victoria A. Fromkin and Peter Ladefoged.

Notes

1. Some of this work was supported by NIMH Grant No. 1, 19964-66, awarded to Donald G. MacKay, and was performed at the Department of Psychology, University of California, Los Angeles.
2. For obvious reasons, the actual experiments contained additional material designed to break up the patterns that are so noticeable in Tables 1 and 2. However, the demonstrations reflect the tasks in their essentials.

References

Baars, B. J. Forthcoming. The competing plans hypothesis: An heuristic approach to the prob-lem of speech errors. In H. W. Dechert and M. Raupach (Eds.), *The temporal variables in speech: Studies in honour of Frieda Goldman Eisler* (Janua Linguarum). Paris: Mouton.

Baars, B. J. 1977. The planning of speech: Is there semantic editing prior to speech articulation? Unpublished Ph.D. dissertation, Univ. of California, Los Angeles.

Baars, B. J. & MacKay, D. G. 1978. Experimentally eliciting phonetic and sentential speech errors: Methods, implications, and work in progress. *Language in Society, 7,* 105–109.

Baars, B. J. & Motley, M. T. 1974. Spoonerisms: Experimental elicitation of human speech errors. Journal Supplement Abstract Service, *Catalog of Selected Documents in Psychology,* Fall 1974.

Baars, B. J. & Motley, M. T. 1976. Spoonerisms as sequencer conflicts: Evidence from artifi-cially elicited errors. *American Journal of Psychology, 83,* 467–484.

Baars, B. J., Motley, M. T., & MacKay, D. G. 1975. Output editing for lexical status in artifi-cially elicited slips of the tongue. *Journal of Verbal Learning and Verbal Behavior, 14,* 382–391.

Foss, D. & Fay, D. 1974. Linguistic theory and performance models. In J. Wirth (Ed.), *Testing linguistic hypotheses.* New York: Hemisphere Press. Pp. 65–91.

Fromkin, V. A. (Ed.). 1973. *Speech errors as linguistic evidence.* The Hague: Mouton.

Garrett, M. F. 1975. The analysis of sentence production. In G. Bower (Ed.), *The psychology of learning and motivation: Advances in research and theory* (Vol. 9). New York: Academic Press. Pp. 133–177.

Gel'fand, I. M., Gurfinkel, V. S., Fomin, S. V., & Tsetlin, M. L. 1971. *Models of the structural-functional organization of certain biological systems.* Cambridge, Massachusetts: MIT Press.

Greene, P. H. 1971. Problems of organization of motor systems. Department of Computer Science, Illinois Institute of Technology.

MacKay, D. G. 1970. Spoonerisms: The structure of errors in the serial order of speech. *Neuropsychologia, 8,* 323–350.

MacKay, D. G. 1971. Stress pre-entry in motor systems. *American Journal of Psychology, 84,* Pp. 35–51.

MacKay, D. G. 1972. The structure of words and syllables: Evidence from errors in speech. *Cognitive Psychology, 3,* 210–227.

MacKay, D. G. 1973. Complexity in output systems: Evidence from behavioral hybrids. *American Journal of Psychology, 86,* 785–806.

MacKay, D. G. 1976. On the retrieval and lexical structure of verbs. *Journal of Verbal Learning and Verbal Behavior, 15,* 169–182.

Meringer, R. 1908. *Aus dem leben der sprache.* Berlin: Behr's.

Motley, M. T. & Baars, B. J. 1976. Semantic bias effects on the outcomes of verbal slips. *Cognition, 4,* 177–187.

Motley, M. T. & Baars, B. J. 1979. Effects of cognitive set upon laboratory-induced verbal (Freudian) slips. *Journal of Speech and Hearing Research 22,* 421–432.

Motley, M. T., Camden, C. T., & Baars, B. J. 1979. Personality and situational influences upon verbal slips. *Human Communication Research, 5,* 195–202.

Turvey, M. T. 1976. Preliminaries to a theory of action with reference to vision. In R. Shaw and J. D. Bransford (Eds.), *Perceiving, acting and knowing: Toward an ecological psychology.* Hillsdale, Maryland: Erlbaum Associates.

Wundt, Wilhelm. 1897. *Grundriss der psychologie.* Leipzig: Engelmann.

Chapter 22

SPEECH ERRORS: RETROSPECT AND PROSPECT[1]

Donald G. MacKay

Department of Psychology
University of California
Los Angeles, California

This paper examines three directions for the course of future research on speech errors: observational refinement (ways of improving how speech errors are collected and analyzed), experimentation (ways of testing hypotheses concerning the nature of speech errors), and theoretical integration (ways of improving and extending our theories). The paper also proposes a general theory of speech production at the semantic level, which summarizes a number of facts concerning errors in lexical retrieval.

The years since Meringer's (1895) groundbreaking work have seen a growing interest in speech errors, beginning first in clinical psychology (see, for example, Freud, 1901), then in linguistics (e.g., Sturtevant, 1947; Wells, 1951; Hockett, 1967; Fromkin, 1971), and spreading now to experimental psychology (e.g., Boomer and Laver, 1968; MacKay, 1971; Motley and Baars, 1976). We all owe Meringer an indirect debt, and many of us (e.g., Freud, 1901; Sturtevant, 1947; MacKay, 1972a; Celce-Murcia, 1973) owe him a direct debt for providing our first source of carefully collected and catalogued data. Vienna seems an especially fitting place to express our gratitude and to assess the accomplishments stemming directly or indirectly from Meringer's work.

We can begin by commending the sheer courage of our enterprise. Following directly in Meringer's footsteps, we have risked the patience and amicability of our friends, families, and colleagues to collect speech errors whenever and wherever they occur in our everyday lives. We have defied the *Zeitgeist* by advocating theories, metatheories, and paradigms that are somewhat ahead of their time. We have dared to advocate radically new methodologies within our respective fields, since speech errors do not fit the traditionally accepted techniques of either psychology or linguistics. We have reached an impressive degree of consensus on goals and methods:

To develop a viable theory of cognitive processes, where errors serve not as a discovery procedure for such a theory, but as data for crediting or discrediting alternative theories. We have come to recognize some of the special advantages and disadvantages of our data and agree on procedural questions to a surprising degree. Gone are the procedures of "proof by imagination," and "counterproof by lack of imagination," "proof by example," and "disproof by counterexample" (cf. MacKay, 1973). The complexity of speech errors shows that a large number of uncontrollable factors can determine any one error, and we now advance hypotheses only when examples greatly outnumber counterexamples. We have convinced ourselves and many others that errors are important and that theories of normal cognitive systems must be capable of breaking down in the same way as the actual system, which is to say that theories unable to explain the errors are necessarily incomplete or incorrect explanations of the actual mechanism. And we have significantly extended our understanding of the planning and execution of articulatory programs.

Yet I cannot escape the impression that we have had less effect on the world than we might have and that the full impact of our work is still to come. The question is what more might be done and where do we go from here. This chapter considers three directions for the course of future research: observational refinement, experimentation, and theoretical integration.

1. Observational Refinement

Our basic observations are collections of naturally occurring speech errors. To refine these observations we must consider ways of improving them, ways of extending them, ways of furthering their description, and ways of refining their analysis.

1.1. *Observational Reliability*

If a corpus of errors is inaccurately recorded, or collected haphazardly on the basis of some theoretical bias (conscious or unconscious), conclusions based on that corpus will be questionable. The situation would be analogous to a badly designed experiment, where no amount of data analysis could overcome the flaws in design. Meringer (1895) realized the importance of observational reliability, and his methods of data collection have much to recommend them, even today. He was clearly not interested in collecting anecdotal data, as once occurred in studies of animal behavior. Lacking the tape recorder, he nevertheless noted the possibility of misrecording an error when hearing conditions were less than optimal. If possible, he interrogated his speakers at the time of error, to verify his records, to exclude nonerrors reflecting, say, intentional humor, and to resolve ambiguities in classification that arise whenever simple records or surface characterizations of errors are considered. To illustrate one such problem in classification, consider a typical example, *The door is not open, I mean, closed.* Although surface appearances suggest a simple substitution of *open* for *closed,* speaker interrogation revealed that in fact the error was a complex blend of synonymic constructions: "The door is open" and "The door is not closed."

Meringer was also sensitive to individual differences and situational effects, and, where atypical, reported the age, sex, educational background, and state of health, intoxication, or fatigue of his speakers. He outlined the context in which each error occurred, recording verbatim what the speakers had just said and what they were about to say, and, when relevant, what they had just heard or seen, whether verbal or nonverbal.

The possibility of selectivity in recording errors cannot be ruled out entirely, but there is every reason to believe that Meringer's corpus was free of major selectional biases since he appeared less interested in confirming any theories of his own than in classifying speech errors, much as a zoologist would classify newly discovered species of animals. He even made special note of errors falling outside prior classifications and was apparently so thorough in his collection of errors and so exhaustive in his interrogation of speakers that he became very unpopular among his acquaintances at the University of Vienna (Sturtevant, 1947).

With the advent of the tape recorder and recent refinements of field procedures (cf. Heynes and Lippitt, 1954; Webb and Campbell, 1966), we are now in a position to improve greatly on Meringer's procedures. Tape recorders overcome the problem, pointed out by Bawden (1900), that speech errors occur so frequently that writing them all down is impossible. Having several trained judges independently transcribe errors from a tape recording also enables estimates of reliability, since even high fidelity recordings do not always guarantee completely reliable representation of speech errors. For example, I found that subjects listening to tapes of Schafer's (1968) *Pardon My Blooper* under optimal hearing conditions often failed to agree with each other or even with themselves on hearing the same error on subsequent occasions.

1.2. *Observational Extension*

Certain theoretically important classes of speech errors occur too infrequently for any one person to collect enough of them, and as Bawden (1900) points out, analysis of speech errors becomes valuable only "when the errors are collected in large numbers and interpreted in the light of inductive generalizations from a wide range of data." Enlarging our collections by at least an order of magnitude seems both desirable and feasible. With the help of trained assistants, it should be possible to extend greatly our collections. Training people to hear, collect, and classify speech errors should not be difficult, especially since speakers often generate surface cues such as "I mean," "excuse me," or "sorry" that indicate the occurrence of an error (see DuBois, 1974). A large-scale program of this kind will require elaborately specified and standardized data collection procedures along with carefully spelled-out ways of protecting the privacy and psychological well-being of our "subjects" or "informants." A campaign to broaden our base of public support may also be necessary since we are not yet completely free from the prejudice that collectors of errors are nuisances and that speech errors are best ignored as weird phenomena that occur once in a while to disturbed individuals under unusual circumstances of interest mainly to psychiatrists. Nonetheless, we have come a long way since the time of Freud (1901). Recent successes in the fields of ethology and social psychology have greatly increased the respect for naturalistic observation, and the time seems ripe for very large-scale data collection using the technological and methodological innovations in field procedures developed within the last few decades.

1.3. *Extension to Other Domains*

The present volume extends our naturalistic observations to slips of the ear, again following directly in Meringer's footsteps. Meringer also developed small but extremely valuable collections of errors in reading and comprehension, in thinking and recall of names and errors in action, for example, looking at a thermometer rather than a clock in order to determine the time of day. Such errors as Meringer collected are important for theories of memory, thinking, reading, hearing, and comprehension, but we need many more observations with less possibility of selectivity and greater attention to the immediate situational context in which the errors occurred.

1.4. *Analytic Refinement*

How can we get the most out of existing observations? Data evaluation procedures, especially statistical procedures, have undergone a major revolution since Meringer's time. Statistical procedures are necessary whenever a large number of uncontrolled factors could influence a phenomenon or its observation, as in the case of speech errors. Given large numbers of speech errors, statistical procedures also enable us to sharpen our hypotheses and to isolate and determine the power of variables in our data. On the debit side, statistical procedures require a lot of hard work; but this is a price that science has always been willing to pay for analytic refinement. It is to our credit that the spirit of the statistical revolution is apparent in every recent study of speech errors, although inexplicitly where it is assumed rather than demonstrated that examples greatly outnumber counterexamples relating to some hypothesis.

1.5. *Descriptive Refinement*

Innovations such as the microscope or computer do not change the basic data, but greatly aid in their description. Since Meringer's time, psychology has developed techniques of data description that are in some ways comparable to the microscope, for example, factor analysis and other scaling techniques. These techniques can greatly aid the description of speech errors. By way of illustration, consider the observation of Meringer (1895) and many others that word substitutions (*table, I mean, chair*) are sometimes semantically similar. This description cries out for refinement. How often and to what extent are substituted words semantically similar? Are there clearly definable subcategories of semantic similarity within the domain of word substitutions? Are word substitutions more often semantically similar than other categories of speech errors? And what is the nature and distribution of the semantic relationships between intended and intruding words: How often is the semantic similarity a matter of logical relations such as inclusion, implication, contradiction, antonymity, subordination, superordination, of part–whole relations, of co-occurrence in usage, of clichés, or of referential similarities? As a first step in answering such questions, we need a way of measuring semantic similarity; and since generally accepted, theoretically based semantic similarity metrics do not yet exist, we must define semantic similarity in some theoretically neutral way.

The following experiment illustrates one well worked-out way. A group of 24 subjects rated the similarity in meaning of over 200 word pairs, using a seven-point scale: 0 representing very different in meaning (e.g., *bird–machine*) and 6 representing very similar in meaning (e.g., *crippled–deformed*). Unbeknown to the subjects, the word pairs were either chosen at random from a dictionary (to serve as anchor points for the "semantically different" end of the scale), or were components of speech errors: word substitution pairs; word reversal pairs; word blend pairs. The ratings were reliable and displayed intuitive or face validity since blend pairs, which often involve synonyms, were rated as highly similar in meaning, whereas random pairs were rated as highly different. Mean similarity ratings were blends, 4.3; word substitutions, 2.8; word reversals, 1.2; random words, .7. Every difference taken in any combination was highly significant (p < .01) except for word reversals versus random words, which were statistically equivalent (p > .10). To determine subcategory effects, word substitutions were further subdivided into "phonologically similar" pairs (operationally defined) versus "others" (about 94% of the data). Mean similarity ratings were .9 for "phonologically similar" pairs and 3.0 for "others." "Other" pairs differed reliably from all remaining categories (p < .01), but phonologically similar pairs were statistically equivalent to reversal pairs and random words (p > .10). These findings suggest that semantic similarity plays a systematic role in blends and word substitutions (and perhaps in paradigmatic errors in general) but not in word reversals (or perhaps any other class of syntagmatic errors). The lower similarity ratings for "phonologically similar" versus "other" substitutions further justifies this subcategorization, and indicates that word substitutions are interpretively heterogeneous, an important finding for the theory of conceptual availability, discussed later in this chapter.

The greater similarity ratings for blends versus substitutions indicates that although substituted words are similar, they are less similar than words that blend, even with phonologically similar pairs excluded. Another remarkable difference between blends and substitutions is that antonyms frequently substitute for one another but never blend. Antonym substitutions, for example, *good,* for *bad* or *open* for *closed* are commonplace, but no one has ever observed blends of antonyms, for example, "clopen" (a combination of *open* and *closed*) or "bood" (a combination of *bad* and *good*). These observations suggest that blends and substitutions reflect different underlying mechanisms. Specifying the details of these mechanisms is impossible at present, but one plausible hypothesis is that word substitutions occur and are corrected when two distinct concepts call upon the intruding and intended forms in succession, whereas blends occur when one and the same concept simultaneously activates two psychologically synonymous forms. For example, a person experiencing something between a draft and a breeze has a concept for which two words are equally appropriate and may come out with "dreeze," the blend of *draft* and *breeze* reported in Fromkin (1973).

2. Experimentation

Analyses of naturally occurring speech errors enjoy face validity (there can be no question of experimental artifact), but are subject to serious interpretive limitations, for example, the fragmentary data problem (see MacKay, 1972a). An additional, as yet undiscussed problem is that studies of speech errors constitute a type of problem-solving discipline involving proof by adduction. We adduce answers to problems such as "Why do word substitutions involve semantically similar words?" The answers provide a satisfactory explanatory fit to the problem they are designed to solve, but since most problems can be solved in many different ways, any one solution may be nonunique. Theories based on adduction must be supplemented by more powerful verification procedures: for example, by experiments based on induction and deduction. Experiments allow the control over observational variables, linguistic variables, and subject variables that is necessary to verify or falsify theoretical claims or hypotheses. Every scientific endeavor recognizes the value of experimentation; the important question is what are the most fruitful experimental strategies, the best ways of maximizing the advantages and minimizing the disadvantages of both experimental and naturalistic observation? I can see four, each with special advantages and limitations discussed in the following section.

2.1. *Simulation Strategy*

Simulation studies try to recreate the determinants of a specific class of speech errors in the laboratory. An example is Brown and McNeill's (1966) tip-of-the-tongue study. What Brown and McNeill did was examine everyday tip-of-the-tongue occurrences, hypothesize their underlying determinants (e.g., fatigue, and relative unfamiliarity with the word for expressing some concept), and then simulate these conditions in the laboratory by reading definitions of obscure words to undergraduates in the late evening. Results of Brown and McNeill's simulation are well known and illustrate the value of this strategy. Other examples are MacKay (1971) and Motley and Baars (1976), who exploited the simulation strategy to study spoonerisms and "Freudian slips." The simulation strategy is especially useful when natural errors are difficult to record, few in number, or otherwise difficult to analyze, but even the most successful simulation provides us with little more than a large, well-analyzed natural corpus. Given such a corpus, the main advantage of laboratory simulation lies in the possibility of exploring the effect of new and more subtle variables and in possible "spin-off" discoveries. As an illustration of spin-off possibilities, consider MacKay and Soderberg's (1971) simulation of linguistic blends in the finger movement system. The finger movement errors they observed, known as "homologous intrusions," demonstrated the role of hitherto unsuspected factors in motoric intrusions, shed new light on the manual motor system, and suggested a general interpretation of motoric blends. As MacKay (1973:802–803) pointed out, "Like synonymic intrusions, homologous intrusions reflect the incursion of one motor program or another, simultaneously activated motor program and in some sense . . . represent the optimal case for a cross-talk model of motor intrusions: The interacting programs for the right and left hand are simultaneously activated at a peripheral level and provide observable rather than inferential evidence for a cross-talk interpretation."

2.2. Hypothesis Testing

We take maximum advantage of both experimental and naturalistic observation by basing our theories first on naturalistic phenomena and only later on experiments. In the case of speech errors the hypothesis testing strategy is as follows: We use detailed analyses of naturally occurring speech errors to develop a model of the speech production system and then subject the assumptions and predictions of the model to laboratory test. Often, however, the hypothesis testing study gives rise to many more errors than the naturalistic corpus on which it was originally based. An example is MacKay (1976) who used Meringer's tiny corpus of tense transformations (e.g., *hat verschrieben aufzuschreiben* instead of *hat verschprochen aufzuzchreiben,* spelling after Meringer) to develop the hypothesis that past tense verbs are stored in the internal lexicon as a base form (e.g., *run*) plus derivational rules that are triggered by an abstract marker, [+past], in producing the surface form *ran.* To test this hypothesis, subjects heard a series of verbs, one at a time, and produced the past tense for each as quickly as possible. The time to produce various past tense forms suggested that the final articulatory program is constructed by means of derivational rules. Even more convincing evidence for these rules was found in the errors that occurred: regularizations (e.g., *digged*); partial alternations (e.g., one person, hearing *catch,* changes the final consonant but not the vowel, producing *cat* instead of *caught*); misalternation (e.g., one person, given *ride,* produced *rid* instead of *rode,* following the pattern of *hide–hid* and *slide–slid*); and misinflections (e.g., *take–taken* instead of *took*). Less frequent occurrences included nontransformations (e.g., *build–build* instead of *built*), backformations, and stutters. In all, there were 367 production errors (more than all existing naturalistic collections combined across languages), collected in less than 20 hours of recording. In addition, there were 106 instances of mishearing, for example, *wade* misperceived as *weighed,* which revealed surprising systematicities of their own.

Another hypothesis-testing study providing large numbers of fascinating errors is

MacKay (1966), where subjects completed sentence fragments, some of which were ambiguous, unbeknown to the subjects. The study was primarily designed to determine the time to complete the fragments, but the completions contained 258 errors that are of interest in their own right. They include systematic misreadings, for example, an ambiguous fragment "Although the idea of Hitler was awful" was misread as *Although that idea of Hitler's was awful;* tangential completions, for example, *Knowing that visiting relatives can be bothersome, I was confused;* spoonerisms, for example, *Having a ball with his case, Merry Pason, I mean Perry Mason... ;* word substitutions, for example, *Before stopping arguing in the court, Wimbleton was perjured, I mean, disqualified;* and ungrammatical completions, for example, *Knowing the minister's hope of marrying Anna was impractical, he disbanded the idea.*

2.3. Direct Induction Strategy

There are many techniques for directly inducing speech errors, and some have been extensively studied, for example, delayed auditory feedback (Fairbanks and Guttman, 1958). When the auditory feedback from the voice is played back to the ears with a fraction of a second delay, speakers reliably generate large numbers of errors. Some are theoretically important, for example, fusions of speech sounds (MacKay, 1973a), and many, but not all, are phonological in nature: transpositions, prolongations, omissions, slurrings, substitutions, and repetitions of phonological components. The full potential of delayed auditory feedback and more recent techniques developed by Baars (1977) and others have yet to be tapped within the direct induction strategy. The goal of this strategy is to determine what theoretically interesting factors increase or decrease the probability of various types of experimentally induced errors. An example of the direct induction strategy appears in MacKay and Bowman (1969), who used errors induced by delayed auditory feedback to demonstrate an effect of practice at the conceptual level of speech production. German-English bilinguals repeated a sentence such as "Then the wanderlust seized him as it once had his grandfather," 12 times, each time at maximal rate. The subjects then put on a pair of earphones and produced another "transfer" sentence as rapidly as possible with delayed auditory feedback. The "transfer" sentence had either identical or completely different meaning from the practice sentence. For example, "Dan packte auch ihn wie einst den Grossvater die Wanderlust" has identical meaning with the preceding sentence although the word order, surface structure, and phonology differ radically.

The results were dramatic: significantly fewer errors for transfer sentences with identical meaning. Moreover, the same transfer effect occurred with monolinguals producing synonymic sentences such as "The woman noticed a famished little infant on the road" and "The lady observed a small hungry child in the street." Such findings illustrate the value of direct induction techniques for theories of the speech production system, such as the theory of conceptual availability discussed in section 3.

2.4. *Subject Selection Strategy*

Meringer viewed subject selection as a convenient means of collecting speech errors. This strategy, combined with experimental techniques, is now commonplace and does not differ from the direct induction strategy except in surface details. See, for example, MacKay (1969), who observed large numbers of errors and the factors that influence them by having a group of stutterers read carefully controlled sentences at maximum rate.

3. Theoretical Integration: The Theory of Conceptual Availability

Our theories can be greatly improved. In some areas we need theoretical diversification: clearly articulated rival hypotheses for stimulating further research. In other areas we need theoretical integration of what is already known. In the area of retrieval processes, for example, we are now in a position to integrate a large number of isolated pockets of fact into a general theory. Retrieval processes determine what, whether, when, and how information in memory becomes available for generating a response, recognizing an input, or solving a problem. Lexical retrieval is an especially interesting example because of the size of the internal lexicon (50,000 items in some cases), its stability (we rarely forget words entirely), its access time (under .5 sec for object names), and its degree of organization (which determines speed of access in all large memories from encyclopedias to computer libraries). The interface between the internal lexicon and the conceptual level is the most important component of lexical retrieval; and the concept of conceptual availability integrates a number of facts concerning this component, some experimental and others naturalistic. The main dimensions of the theory are outlined in the following section.

3.1. *Conceptual Suppression*

Conceptual suppression is a major determinant of conceptual availability, and the role of conceptual suppression in speech errors has been widely discussed. An example from Freud (1901) is the substitution of *battle scared* for *battle scarred* in reference to someone unconsciously considered cowardly.

However, the nature and generality of the phenomenon of conceptual suppression has been more clearly demonstrated in recent experiments on the comprehension of ambiguous sentences. In processing ambiguous sentences, people see either one meaning or the other, but MacKay (1970) has shown that the other "unseen" meaning is usually processed to some extent and becomes suppressed or abnormally unavailable during retrieval of the "seen" meaning.

3.2. *Conceptual Disinhibition*

Concepts that have been suppressed become especially available or hyperactive when released from suppression. Rebound availability of concepts plays a major role in the phenomenon of "semantic blending" as seen in the effects of the "unseen" or

suppressed meanings that frequently crept into the completion of ambiguous fragments in MacKay (1966). Examples are: *After stopping arguing in the court, Wimbleton was perjured, I mean, disqualified* (where the speaker reported awareness of
the meaning *tennis court* and not *court of law*); *Discussing the problems with the
mathematicians in Germany, Oppenheimer grew red in the face* (where the speaker
visualized *mathematical problems* and not *mathematician problems*); *Claiming the
work was done over on the roof, he asked them to do it again* (where the speaker
was only conscious of the meaning "completed over there" and not "redone"). Rebound availability resulting from conceptual disinhibition may also be responsible
for the fact that subjects often become aware of the "unseen" meaning after completing an ambiguous sentence, as well as for the many errors (discussed in the following section) that occur in completing ambiguous sentences.

Conceptual disinhibition may even play a role in "displaced synonymic intrusions" such as *He put the sack in the bag, I mean, car* (from Goldstein, 1968). If
selecting *sack* requires suppressing *bag* at the conceptual level, this intrusion may
reflect rebound availability of the concept for "bag." Freud (1901) was quite correct in stressing the importance of suppressed concepts in speech errors and other
phenomena in our everyday mental lives.

3.3. *Conceptual Salience*

Not all concepts are psychologically equivalent. Freud (1901) documented many
errors suggesting the special availability of concepts important to the personal life
history of a particular speaker. However, some concepts have systematic or universal
salience for everyone. In the visual system, conceptual salience reflects built-in biases
in the way the perceptual system represents colors, shapes, distances, or spatial relations. Consider color for example. Some color concepts such as "red" are more
salient or easier to learn (Rosch, 1973), distinguish (Heider and Oliver, 1972), and
recall (Heider, 1972) than others such as "brown" quite independently of whether
people have names for the colors (cf. Heider, 1972). If, as Berlin and Kay (1969)
argue, color concepts can be arranged in terms of a saliency hierarchy, this hierarchy
should predict the relative availability of color concepts, which in turn should predict the relative probability of speech errors: Words for salient concepts such as
"red" should substitute words for less salient concepts such as "brown" more often
than vice versa, a prediction that should hold for color term substitutions in any
language.

3.4. *Contextual Factors*

Contextual factors play a major role in determining the availability of concepts,
and contextually determined conceptual availability has contributed to the occurrence of many speech errors. Meringer (1908) collected an entire class of such "situ-

ational intrusions," that is, word substitutions attributable to objects just noticed, words just read or heard said, the social relationship between speaker and listener, things recently thought of or weighing on one's mind.

3.5. *Conceptual Practice*

Availability of a concept depends on familiarity and practice in using it. Evidence for effects of practice at the conceptual level are found in MacKay and Bowman (1969), discussed in the preceding section. Perhaps, when producing a sentence, we execute a set of semantic analyses or procedures (see Miller and Johnson-Laird, 1976). Performing these analyses takes time, and like other mental operations, the time they take depends on practice at the conceptual level.

3.6. *Conceptual Complexity*

Conceptual complexity plays the role in speech errors and retrieval time that one would expect under the theory of conceptual availability. Concepts such as "present time" are simpler and more readily available than concepts such as "past time" (MacKay, 1976). Concepts such as "circle" or "square" are simpler and more readily available than concepts such as "oval" or "triangle" (cf. Koffka, 1935). Concepts such as "one" or "singular" are simpler and more readily available than concepts such as "many" or "plural" (Olson, 1974). So are concepts such as "tall" versus "short," and "before" versus "after" (Clark and Clark, 1977).

3.7. *Processing Capacity*

Availability of concepts depends on the attention or processing capacity devoted to them. The effect of attention on conceptual availability is illustrated in the dichotic listening task where people pay attention to concepts arriving in one input channel (say, the left ear) and ignore those on the other channel (the right ear). Dichotic listening experiments show that concepts underlying attended inputs are orders of magnitude more available than concepts underlying unattended inputs and that certain relational concepts may never become available at all without attentional analysis (cf. MacKay, 1973b).

3.8. *Conceptual Coherence*

Some complex concepts are more coherent than others, and coherent concepts are more readily available than incoherent concepts. For example, "table" is a more coherent and readily available concept than "furniture" for referencing an object to which both concepts apply: Sharing more attributes with one another, exemplars of the concept "table" are easier to recognize and conceptualize than pieces of furniture (see Rosch, 1973).

3.9. *Conceptual Connectivity*

No concept is an island unto itself: All are interconnected in many different ways, and the moment to moment fluctuations in conceptual availability that characterize our everyday mental lives is largely attributable to conceptual connectivity. For example, the concept "robin" is connected to the concept "bird" so that increasing the availability of one concept increases the availability of the other. Factors such as typicality (operationally defined by Rosch, 1973) may determine the strength of the connection: Since robins are "more typical" birds than chickens, availability of the concept "robin" increases the availability of the concept "bird" more than does the concept "chicken."

3.10. *Conclusion*

In conclusion, the theory of conceptual availability summarizes a number of facts concerning lexical retrieval, but further work is needed to determine how the dimensions of the theory interact or overlap. Speech errors will undoubtedly continue to play a major role in future elaborations of the theory, whether from natural collections, simulation studies, induction studies, or hypothesis testing studies such as those discussed in the preceding section. The prospects for future studies of speech errors seem good.

Acknowledgment

The author wishes to thank J. Loranger for her help in analyzing the data.

Note

1. The author gratefully acknowledges the support of NIMH Grant No. 1, 19964-06.

References

Baars, B. J. & Motley, M. T. 1976. Spoonerisms as sequencer conflicts: Evidence from artificially elicited spoonerisms. *American Journal of Psychology, 83,* 467–484.
Bawden, H. H. 1900. A study of lapses. *Psychological Monographs, 3,* 1–121.
Berlin, B. & Kay, P. 1969. *Basic color terms: Their universality and evolution.* Los Angeles: Univ. of California Press.
Blumenthal, A. L. & Boakes, R. 1967. Prompted recall of sentences: A further study. *Journal of Verbal Learning and Verbal Behavior, 6,* 674–676.
Boomer, D. S. & Laver, J. D. M. 1968. Slips of the tongue. *British Journal of Disorders of Communication, 3,* 1–12.
Brown, R. & McNeill, D. 1966. The tip of the tongue phenomenon. *Journal of Verbal Learning and Verbal Behavior, 5,* 325–337.
Celce-Murcia, M. 1973. Meringer's corpus revisited. In V. Fromkin (Ed.), *Speech errors as linguistic evidence.* The Hague: Mouton. Pp. 195–204.

Clark, H. H. & Clark, E. V. 1977. *Psychology and language.* New York: Harcourt Brace Jovano-
vich.
DuBois, J. W. 1974. Syntax in mid-sentence. *Berkeley Studies in Syntax and Semantics, 1,*
III-1–III-25.
Fairbanks, G. & Guttman, N. 1958. Effects of delayed auditory feedback upon articulation.
Journal of Speech and Hearing Research, 1, 12–22.
Freud, S. 1901. *Psychopathology of everyday life.* Translated and edited by J. Strachey.
London: Ernest Bern, 1966.
Fromkin, V. A. 1971. The non-anomalous nature of anomalous utterances. *Language, 47,* 27–
52.
Fromkin, V. A. (Ed.). 1973. *Speech errors as linguistic evidence.* The Hague: Mouton.
Goldstein, M. 1968. Some slips of the tongue. *Psychological Reports, 22,* 1009–1013.
Heider, E. R. 1972. Universals in color naming and memory. *Journal of Experimental Psy-
chology, 93,* 10–20.
Heider, E. R. & Oliver, D. 1972. The structure of color space in naming and memory for two
languages. *Cognitive Psychology, 3,* 337–354.
Heynes, R. W. & Lippitt, R. 1954. Systematic observational techniques. In G. Lindzey, *Hand-
book of social psychology.* Reading, Massachusetts: Addison-Wesley. Pp. 370–404.
Hockett, C. F. 1967. Where the tongue slips, there slip I. In V. Fromkin (Ed.), *Speech errors as
linguistic evidence.* The Hague: Mouton, 1973. Pp. 93–119.
Koffka, K. 1935. *Principles of gestalt psychology.* New York: Harcourt Brace Jovanovich.
MacKay, D. G. 1966. To end ambiguous sentences. *Perception and Psychophysics, 1,* 426–436.
MacKay, D. G. 1969. Effects of ambiguity on stuttering: Towards a model of speech produc-
tion at the semantic level. *Kybernetik, 5,* 195–208.
MacKay, D. G. 1970. Mental diplopia: Towards a model of speech perception at the semantic
level. In D'arcais & Levelt (Eds.), *Recent advances in psycholinguistics.* Amsterdam: North-
Holland Publ. Pp. 76–100.
MacKay, D. G. 1971. Stress pre-entry in motor systems. *American Journal of Psychology, 1,*
35–51.
MacKay, D. G. 1972a. The structure of words and syllables: Evidence from errors in speech.
Cognitive Psychology, 3, 210–227.
MacKay, D. G. 1972b. Hierarchic specification of words. Paper delivered to the Conference on
the Problem of Serial Order in Behavior, University of Michigan.
MacKay, D. G. 1973a. Complexity in output systems: Evidence from behavioral hybrids. *Amer-
ican Journal of Psychology, 86,* 785–806.
MacKay, D. G. 1973b. Aspects of the theory of comprehension, memory and attention. *Quar-
terly Journal of Experimental Psychology, 25,* 22–40.
MacKay, D. G. 1976. On the retrieval and lexical structure of verbs. *Journal of Verbal Learning
and Verbal Behavior, 15,* 169–182.
MacKay, D. G. & Bowman, R. 1969. On producing the meaning in sentences. *American Journal
of Psychology, 1,* 23–39.
MacKay, D. G., & Soderberg, G. A. 1971. Homologous intrusions: An analogue of linguistic
blends. *Perceptual and Motor Skills, 32,* 645–646.
Miller, G. A. & Johnson-Laird, P. N. 1976. *Language and perception.* Cambridge, Massachusetts:
Harvard Univ. Press.
Meringer, R. & Mayer, K. 1896. *Versprechen and verlesen.* Stuttgart: Goschensche Verlag.
Motley, M. T. & Baars, B. J. 1976. Semantic bias effects on the outcomes of verbal slips. *Cogni-
tion, 4,* 177–187.
Olson, J. N. 1974. Response latencies and perception times for oppositional adjectives and
singular–plural noun pairs: Implications for hierarchic specifications or words. Unpublished
Ph.D. dissertation, Department of Psychology, University of California, Los Angeles.
Palmer, S. E. 1975. Visual perception and world knowledge: Notes on a model of the sensory-
cognitive interaction. In D. A. Norman and D. E. Rumelhart (Eds.), *Explorations in cognition.* San Francisco: Freeman. Pp. 279–307.

Rosch, E. 1973. On the internal structure of perceptual and semantic categories. In T. E. Moore (Ed.), *Cognitive development and the acquisition of language.* New York: Academic Press. Pp. 111–144.

Schafer, K. 1968. *Pardon my blooper.* Miami: Kermit Schafer Productions (record).

Sturtevant, E. H. 1947. *Linguistic science.* New Haven: Yale Univ. Press.

Webb, E. J. & Campbell, D. 1966. *Unobtrusive measures.* Chicago: Rand McNally.

Wells, R. 1951. Predicting slips of the tongue. *Yale Scientific Magazine, 26,* 3–12.

Index

A

Accommodation, 7, 263–271
Anticipation, *see* Substitution error
Antonymy, 98, 103–104, 107, 323
Aphasia, *see* Pathological speech

B

Blend, 104, 106, 108, 128–129, 194–195, 282, 295, 311, 321, 323–325
Bound morpheme, 7–8, 73, 264–266, 325

C

Competing plans hypothesis, 2, 4–5, 8, 308–316

D

Data collection, difficulties, 82, 126, 196, 209, 214, 232, 320–324
Dysgraphia, *see* Slip of pen

E

Editing, 7, 22, 135–136, 138, 141, 143–145, 157–158, 162, 279–281, 283–285, 287–304, 313–316, *see also* Self-correction

F

Feature system,
  phonological, 3, 47–64
  semantic, 5
  sign language, 183–184
Frequency, target and error word, 99–100, 106
Freudian slip, 2, 29, 37, 84, 101, 123–130, 133–145, 308, 313, 327

G

Grammatical category, 101–104, 107, 267–270

H

Hyponymy, 98, 100–101, 104, 107

I

Impossible sign, 192–193, 196

L

Language change, 208
Lexicon, organization, 71–73, 79, 127–129, 276, 327

M

Malapropism, 71, 73, 236, *see also* Substitution error, lexical

Marked segment, *see* Strong segment
Metathesis,
  lexical, 76, 114, 118, 159, 161, 264–267, 270–271, 310–311, 312, 323
  phonological, 2, 6, 11, 21–22, 51, 83–84, 134–143, 268, 270–271, 309–310, 312–314
  in sign language, 171–176
  and stress, 70, 75–76, 264
Misperception, *see* Slip of ear
Monitoring, *see* Editing, Self-correction
Morphological decomposition, in lexicon, 72, 79, 325

N

Nonword,
  in slip of ear, 214, 238
  in slip of hand, 170–171, 188–192
  in slip of tongue, 6, 29, 91, 134–135, 279, 281, 284, 314–316

P

Pathological speech, 8–9, 81–85
Perseveration, *see* Substitution error

R

Rapid speech, 283–284
Relational network grammar, 5, 274–279, 288

S

Self-correction, 7, 39–40, 74, 87–95, 105, 303–304, 313, *see also* Editing
  aphasic speaker, 85
  covert, 88, 105, 293, 313
Shadowing, 10, 149–155, 157–162
Short-term memory, 105–107, 293, 297–299
Sign language, *see also* Slip of hand
  structural parameter, 166–168, 194
Similarity, 281–282
  morphological, 68–70
  phonological, 3–4, 36–38, 40–45, 48, 53–64, 99, 124–125, 201–203, 208, 241–242, 299, 323
  semantic, 3–5, 97–108, 124–125, 207–208, 322–324
Slip of ear, 10–11, 199–211, 213–230, 231–238, 241–259
  asymmetry, 11, 241–259
  proper noun, 201–202, 204–208
  and stress, 75, 215, 221–223, 237
Slip of hand, 9, 165–196

Slip of pen, 11, 15–17, 22–30, 32, 97, 99
Speech perception, model, 213, 216, 222,
    224–225, 237–238, 258–259
Speech production, *see also* Editing
    model, 70–71, 87, 105, 111, 113, 127, 130,
    135, 149, 154–155, 162, 264–268, 271,
    273–285, 287–304, 312–316f
Spoonerism, *see* Metathesis, phonological
Spreading activation, 5, 277–285
Stress error, 8, 67–79
Strong segment, 9, 36–37, 40–45, *see also* Slip
    of ear, asymmetry
Substitution error, *see also* Metathesis
    anticipatory, 30, 48, 89, 158, 160–161
    lexical, 2, 4–5, 7, 97, 124–127, 323–324

phonological, 3, 35–45, 49–64, 83–85, 127,
    158–162, 268–271
Syllable, omission or addition, 68
Synonymy, 104, 106–107, 128, 323–324

T

Testing, experimental, 5–6, 38–45, 87, 95,
    134–144, 149–154, 157–162, 225, 232,
    274, 284, 307–315, 324–327
Tip of tongue phenomenon, 10–11, 222
Tone error, 8
Transformational hypothesis, 9, 111–121

W

Word association, 103–104, 106